Libby Larsen

MUSIC IN AMERICAN LIFE

A list of books in the series appears at the end of this book.

LIBBY LARSEN

Composing an American Life

Denise Von Glahn

Manufactured in the United States of America
1 2 3 4 5 C P 5 4 3 2 1
∞ This book is printed on acid-free paper.

Library of Congress Cataloging-in-Publication Data
Names: Von Glahn, Denise, 1950–
Title: Libby Larsen : composing an American life / Denise Von Glahn.
Description: Urbana : University of Illinois Press, [2017] | Series: Music in American life | Includes bibliographical references and index. | Identifiers: LCCN 2017019390 (print) | LCCN 2017020909 (ebook) | ISBN 9780252099724 () | ISBN 9780252041150 (hardcover : alk. paper) | ISBN 9780252082696 (pbk. : alk. paper)
Subjects: LCSH: Larsen, Libby. | Composers—United States—Biography.
Classification: LCC ML410.L3206 (ebook) | LCC ML410.L3206 V6 2017 (print) | DDC 780.92 [B]—dc23
LC record available at https://lccn.loc.gov/2017019390

Publication supported by grants from the Dragan Plamenac Endowment of the American Musicological Society, funded in part by the National Endowment for the Humanities and the Andrew W. Mellon Foundation; The Florida State University, Office of Research; The Florida State University, College of Music; and the Henry and Edna Binkele Classical Music Fund.

For Michael,
who has never doubted

Contents

PREFACE: AN INAUSPICIOUS BEGINNING ix

ACKNOWLEDGMENTS xvii

PROLOGUE: A POLYPHONIC LIFE xxi

1 Libby Larsen and the Cultural Moment 1

2 Larsen and Family: Needing to Be Heard 10

3 Larsen and Religion: The Tie That Binds 33

4 Larsen and Nature: Tutoring the Soul 67

5 Larsen and the Academy Years: "My Soul Was Shaking" 99

6 Larsen and Gender: Doing the Impossible 145

7 Larsen and Technology: Challenging the Concert Hall 193

8 Larsen and the Collaborators, Larsen and the Critics 222

CONCLUSIONS: REFLECTIONS ON A LIFE AND THE PROCESS OF TELLING IT 255

NOTES 269

BIBLIOGRAPHY 305

INDEX 317

Preface

An Inauspicious Beginning

I FIRST MET LIBBY LARSEN IN Kansas City, Missouri, in 1998 at the annual conference of the Society for American Music, where she had been named that year's honorary member. By some set of coincidences, I was seated next to her at dinner. She was easy-going, lively, and engaging, interested in everyone and everything. She didn't behave like others of her stature whom I'd met; she didn't wear her celebrity like a badge or a shield. She blended in effortlessly. I was still thinking too much about the new faculty position I'd recently accepted and a paper on Charles Ives that I'd given earlier that day to focus energy on the honored guest to my left, especially one who didn't act like a world-famous composer. She was so normal it was easy to forget who she was.

Eleven years later, in the throes of writing a book about nine American women who responded to the natural world with their music, it was impossible to ignore Larsen or the large number of pieces she had written that referenced nature. And why would I want to? So many of them spoke to me. When another coincidence allowed me to interview her, I leaped at the chance, and this time the meeting was unforgettable. Over two days we discussed the impact of Larsen's Minnesota environs on her thinking, her roller-coaster ride as a contemporary American composer, the inwardness or outwardness of particular pieces she'd written over the years, and motherhood. We both took enormous pleasure in being able to talk about our children and in each other's enthusiasm for the topic. Although I had no immediate plans to write her biography, it was clear that she was someone I wanted to learn more about. When Laurie Matheson invited me to consider writing Larsen's story, I was intrigued. I emailed the composer asking if we could talk about my writing her life. She responded in what I've come to learn is typical Larsen fashion: She characterized the project as "a journey" and pointed the way: "Onward!" It has been a journey unlike any other I have taken. This biography invites readers to come along.

THE BIOGRAPHICAL ENDEAVOR AND LIBBY LARSEN

In a 1985 interview that appeared in the *Paris Review*, biographer Leon Edel (1907–97) summarized what he believed was essential to the genre: "A biography seems irrelevant if it doesn't discover the overlap between what the individual did and the life that made this possible. Without discovering that, you have shapeless happenings and gossip."[1] Edel's charge to "discover the overlap" has guided this project. As all biographers learn, lives do not yield to simple storylines; they don't unfold neatly. Ferreting out, gathering up, reconstructing, and presenting the elusive whole of a person using the discontinuous fragments of a life scattered over decades and miles requires patience and empathy, and even then the best rendering is only partial. A biographer who holds out thinking that in time she will be able to tell the entire, definitive story waits in vain; it will never happen. It hardly matters if the life is concluded and safely framed within birth and death dates, or if the subject is alive and continuing to act and react to her moment in history as is Larsen. There is always another story to be told, another question to ask, from another "angle of vision."[2] Completeness is a canard, as is objectivity, as is the idea that a life has a unified shape beyond that imposed by the biographer. It is the biographer's task to answer to evidence, to write responsibly from a unique position vis-à-vis the subject, and to tell a truthful tale among the many that could be told.

Starting in the latter half of the twentieth century, there has been no shortage of advice for would-be biographers, and it comes from a number of experienced practitioners: Robert Caro, Leon Edel, Robert Gittings, Joan D. Hedrick, Carolyn Heilbrun, Doris Kearns (Goodwin), Hermione Lee, Elaine Showalter, Liz Stanley, and Linda Wagner-Martin, to name just a few whose ideas have impacted this project. Despite their various starting points, they achieve some consensus. Edel's remarks regarding the relevance of biography speak to the basic challenge facing all life-story writers: unearthing the relationships between the life, the time, and the achievements. But there are no simple causes and effects, no one-way, if-then propositions directing human lives. If there were, finding the single, defining moment would be analogous to releasing a parachutist's ripcord: what had been a free fall becomes a controllable, more or less predictable descent to terra firma. It is the biographer's task to unearth the daily struggles, the multiple defining moments, the warring motivations, and the constant choices that are the stuff of life, and then to shape them, to suggest some kind of coherence, all the while admitting, in Liz Stanley's words, that "biographies are ideological accounts of lives."[3]

Libby Larsen has demonstrated an open-minded curiosity about the shape this account will take and has welcomed the idea that she will learn something about herself over the course of the project. She is game.[4] As her biographer I know I will learn something too, and not just about my subject; in previous books I have written, I've learned about myself in the process. In a later statement on the art of biography, Edel insisted that the author's knowledge of a subject be so complete, that having learned the subject's mask, self-image, projected concept, public persona, the biographer can see "the figure under the carpet, the reverse of the tapestry" and bring it to the surface.[5] And that is my intention. Edel's imagery is vivid, and his goal of an integrated life study is a worthy endeavor. What is exciting about this particular project is that my subject is curious about unearthing that figure too.

Prior to the 1970s, biographical theorists didn't discuss the potential differences between life stories of male and female subjects in a systematic way. Perhaps the experts needed Betty Friedan's 1963 exposé, *The Feminine Mystique*, to recognize female lives as separate or at least separable from their male counterparts. Perhaps the change in perspective was inevitable given what else was happening at the time. Whether theorists operated under the tacit assumption that one approach fit all, or that biography-worthy subjects were, by default, male, and white, or whether they were unaware that women were largely absent from serious biographical studies except as helpmates, or that women's lives did not reveal themselves within the confines of traditional heroic plot lines, with rare exceptions, women were not the focus of serious biographies.[6]

Personal experience as a young girl growing up in the fifties and sixties drove home the point for me, and as it turns out it did for Libby Larsen as well. I was hungry for stories about women with whom I could identify. In the juvenile biography section of my local public library I contented myself with children's biographies of Annie Oakley, Clara Barton, and Marie Curie. There were no women musicians or artists of note. Not imagining myself a sharpshooter riding bareback, founding the American Red Cross, or discovering radium or entombed in the Panthéon in Paris was problematic. In a 2012 conversation with me, Libby Larsen expressed a similar experience and frustration: "I looked, and looked, and looked for models, and my school, my little library, didn't have your children's biography series. So we had *Little House on the Prairie* (fictional biography), the *Nancy Drew* books, and the lives of saints, and mythology. It was hard, really hard, even into college, to find biographies. I started finding them by reading about visual artists."[7] That would be the 1970s, and that's when I started discovering women biographical subjects, and mine too were visual artists.

In 1979 Eleanor Munro published *Originals: American Women Artists*. Although it appeared too late to satisfy my childhood yearning for models of women in the arts, I seized upon the book and devoured its biographical portraits. Photographs accompanied each entry; these people looked like me! The next year Laurie Lisle's *Portrait of an Artist: A Biography of Georgia O'Keeffe* appeared. I quietly cheered for the self-directed and determined painter. Today I look at the many bracketed passages, the scribbles in the margins, and the pages of notes I tucked inside the back cover of Lisle's book. I see a bold arrow pointing to O'Keeffe's statement: "You have a chance to get what you want if you go out and work for it. But you must really work, not just talk about it."[8] Although the women in Munro's and Lisle's books were visual artists and I was a musician, I saw that a life as a woman in the arts was *possible*: O'Keeffe said so. It is *impossible* to describe the power of that realization, late as it came to me. I had really needed to read a biography of a Libby Larsen, and as the composer has confided, so did she.[9] Perhaps this book is an attempt to satisfy that need.

With her 1970 biography *Zelda*, Nancy Milford (b. 1938) shined a spotlight on the writer, painter, and dancer Zelda Sayre Fitzgerald (1900–1948). She forced a confrontation between inherited biographical plot lines and women's lives beyond their relational selves: Zelda Fitzgerald was *also* the wife of novelist F. Scott Fitzgerald; she was not merely his foil. Quoting from Zelda's novels and letters, Milford put the so-called muse of the jazz age, "the first flapper," in the center of her own life and of Fitzgerald's; she addressed head-on Scott's appropriation of Zelda's personal experiences and writings for his own novels and the practice of putting his name on her work.[10] Milford's biography catapulted Zelda into feminist iconicity.

In 1973, May Sarton (1912–95) published her autobiographical *Journal of a Solitude* and revealed the complexity and richness of her life as a creative woman who refused to be limited by society's expectations. The durability and resonance of that work and many others she wrote has vindicated Sarton's decision to be open and honest about her beliefs, her achievements, her life choices, her relationships, and her lesbianism. Sarton's forthrightness strengthened the author's power as a model for all women who rejected prescribed roles.[11]

In her 1988 book, *Writing a Woman's Life*, Carolyn Heilbrun (1926–2003) eloquently articulated the need for new scripts for women's lives.[12] A wife, mother, much-lauded academic, ardent feminist, successful mystery-story writer, and eventually celebrated sage, Heilbrun knew whereof she wrote. The appearance of this book and others that insisted upon an enlarged understanding of womanhood and women's places in the world reflected the power and reach of the civil rights movement, second-wave feminism, and environmental consciousness. She observed that traditional narratives denied women ambition, achievement, and accomplishment and demonized those who dared to express anger or seek or enjoy power; Heilbrun insisted that women be the heroines of their own lives, however they chose to construct them. Recognizing that women's lives were often balancing acts of external and internal forces, Heilbrun demanded a woman's right to talk about the personal without being dismissed as sentimental; she championed the "ambiguous woman," the female subject who invented herself.[13] In 1995 Heilbrun took on the challenge of writing about the still-living feminist champion Gloria Steinem in her book *The Education of a Woman: The Life of Gloria Steinem*. Heilbrun's works provide me with wise, encouraging, multifaceted resources for conceptualizing Libby Larsen, a uniquely self-directed composer who continues to be a creative force.

LIBBY LARSEN AS A BIOGRAPHICAL SUBJECT

Like Heilbrun, but a generation later, Larsen chose to design her own life. In addition to being a prodigious and much-lauded composer, she too is a wife and mother, a successful organizer, a tireless advocate for music, and an increasingly celebrated model for women seeking a life of both professional and personal fulfillment. Although she has rejected a career in the academy, a typical home for many twentieth- and twenty-first-century American composers, Larsen regularly appears as guest composer, keynote speaker, and featured resident at colleges and universities across the country.

Libby Larsen (b. 1950) is alive, well, productive, engaged, and impacting American culture, much like Gloria Steinem (b. 1934), even if Larsen's sphere of influence is more focused. Her eclectic music is played and sung around the globe. She has addressed musical societies and professional organizations, occupied a series of prestigious chairs and positions, been commissioned by hundreds of ensembles and solo artists, and won some of the nation's most coveted awards. When, in late 2012, I asked her assistants whether they had noticed any signs of Larsen slowing down, they insisted that the opposite was true: if anything, things were picking up.[14] It appears that Larsen has found her stride, an especially apt metaphor for the composer who in 2013 completed her thirty-third marathon.

Larsen is, in many ways, a biographer's ideal subject. She is a force in her field, but while she is self-aware, reflective, and serious about her work, she hasn't succumbed to taking herself too seriously. She invites questions and responds thoughtfully. If she has not considered something previously, she says so and digs in. Larsen has also maintained a meticulous archive of personal papers, which was originally a repository for important records associated with founding the Minnesota Composers Forum and the result of a desire to document that organization. Over the years Larsen determined that she needed to keep track of her increasingly busy professional life, and today the Larsen archive contains sketches for compositions, personal and business-related correspondence, programs, posters, photos, citations, and all manner of materials related to her career. She and her assistants consider it a point of pride that they can answer any query that comes to them within five minutes. If they can't, they create a new organizational scheme. This biography would not have been possible without Larsen's impeccable and thorough archive.

The composer's inviting availability, welcome and appreciated as it is, however, challenges a biographer to find a position outside of Larsen's personal sphere that allows her to be seen and understood as wholly as possible and from as many different viewpoints as possible. With so much material at one's fingertips, the biographer must remember that there is still more to be unearthed. The biographer needs to write her subject's story from outside as well as inside the subject, knowing full well that whatever story results will be partial, filtered through the sources consulted, and subject to one's "particular angle of vision": a perspective that is "shaped as much by our own biography—our attitudes, perceptions, and feelings toward the subject—as by the raw materials themselves."[15] To that end I have studied Larsen through the observations of dozens of people who have known and worked with her. Many of their insights accompany discussions of particular pieces and so appear within the central chapters of the book; others are collected in the final chapter.

The project is made additionally challenging by the subject and the biographer having much in common: similar ages and placement in family constellations, many shared interests and experiences, and kindred underlying human values. Working with a living subject means that I became a part of the story, a humbling reality. Empathy, while invaluable to any biographer, brings with it its own dilemmas, and separating subject and self requires vigilance and honesty.

Larsen's life and music are as inseparable as they are multifaceted, and she acknowledges this. She comfortably navigates many styles and spheres; their variety reflects the richness of her life. Her birth in 1950 and her home base in Minneapolis put Larsen at the center of the century and the country. This position has provided her with a wide-angled view of the nation's musical cultures and freedom to learn her craft and explore her many voices without crushing pressure to conform to au courant trends or aesthetic "groupthink."[16] Her incorporation of both popular and high-art musical resources reflects a centrist musical aesthetic, one that is comfortable in a concert hall and at an outdoor festival. But her gender, her distance from the nation's most celebrated musical hubs, and her refusal to align herself with any particular group or school have also put her on the margins of inner circles and in-groups of composers. She is not one of them. While doubly inside, she is also doubly outside. But this is her choice. In a conversation early in the project, Larsen talked about her conscious decision to remain on the margins of American musical culture and asked what was for her a rhetorical question: "Do I want to buy into the composer imprimatur system or what?" And then she laughed.[17]

A biography structured along traditional lines, one that takes its shape from the generic arc of a life that is completed or near its end and that has unfolded on center stage, does not serve Libby Larsen. Hers is neither the typical heroic quest story, although there is plenty of victory over adversity and unquestioned success in a sometimes hostile world, nor does it follow the narratives frequently allotted to females of either the exceptional or the unexceptional varieties—empress, muse, helpmate. The story of Libby Larsen, *composer*, does not depend upon familial relationships for its form and structure, although her family is a constant presence in her life and informs all she is and does. Larsen's idiosyncratic life, large parts of which have been acted out in the public arena, demands a study that makes room for and illuminates a successful woman who has defied expected behaviors and rejected categorization. An author writing in 2016 must be cognizant that the resonances of Larsen's music, life, and career are still being created and felt, and their meanings are on the cusp of being understood. Here is where Heilbrun's 1995 study of Steinem provides a particularly useful resource; she left her subject's story open to new experiences and meanings: suggesting no inevitable end, it invites continuation. It is my hope that this biography will occupy a similar position in Larsen literature. Ultimately, a biography of Libby Larsen can succeed only if it goes beyond "shapeless happenings and gossip," as did Heilbrun's of Steinem, and unearths the person behind the persona, the sources of her drive, and the forces that anchor her in place.[18] I hope it invites continued exploration of one American composer's experience.

Libby Larsen: Composing an American Life places Larsen in her geographical, temporal, political, religious, familial, aesthetic, technological, and cultural milieu. It acknowledges the impact of the epochal social upheaval that characterized her youth and young adult life, an era permanently imprinted by car culture, counterculture, the Pill, civil rights, second-wave feminism, Vatican II, Vietnam, political assassinations, the first draft lottery, and the environmental movement. Larsen has mentioned all these events as being powerfully influential in her life.

The book draws upon conversations and interactions with the composer over a period of seven years; interviews with Larsen's collaborators, friends, and family; archival research; musical study and analysis; and the consultation of voluminous documents including the composer's letters, family photographs, scores, and recordings of her music. Organizing themes are those ideas that recurred in our conversations and that the composer eventually identified specifically as being of formative importance: family, religion, nature and place, the academy, gender, and technology. The book discusses select musical works that further reveal and reinforce chapter themes. Music, despite its central importance to Larsen's life, is not all there is to the composer. Going beyond it and basic facts and events of Larsen's life, this study aspires to unearth the person behind the accomplishments.

In a note preceding her song cycle *Songs from Letters*, Larsen wrote that Calamity Jane's "life sheds light on contemporary society."[19] The same can be said of Libby Larsen: her life sheds light on contemporary American society. It also more pointedly illuminates a changing national musical culture, one that despite its growth and globalizing tendencies, is still home to tenacious ideologies, hierarchical thinking, marginalizing practices, and change-resistant power brokers. This book reveals the ways one composer created her own life and her own place in American music.

Acknowledgments

SCHOLARLY ACKNOWLEDGMENTS OFTEN BEGIN with a list of the institutions that provided time or financial assistance for the project. I'll get to them, but I must start by thanking Libby Larsen. She has been a generous and courageous subject, enduring years of questions, requests for information, emails, telephone conversations, and personal interviews. She has shared photographs and sound files, supplied names of possible corroborators, and introduced me to family and friends. She enlisted her assistants, Grace Edgar, Toni Lindgren, and Jason Senchina, in the project and encouraged them to help me. I couldn't have done this project without them. Meeting Larsen's parents and observing their pride and puzzlement over why anyone would want to write a biography of their daughter reminded me of the valuable balancing function that all families provide. Larsen invited me to listen to and watch collaborations in the act as well as join in an evening book group. Thanks to these experiences, I have an enlarged understanding of the ecology of life.

Although I devoted a chapter of a previous book to Larsen and a small group of her nature-inspired works, I would not have considered assuming the daunting task of writing her biography without a suggestion from Laurie Matheson, director of the University of Illinois Press. It was the project I needed at that particular moment, and it has prepared me to take on others in ways I couldn't have imagined. I appreciate the eagle eyes of my copyeditor, Barbara Wojhoski, and my indexer, Kathy Bennett. Any errors or oversights that remain are surely my own.

I'm grateful to Florida State University and Dean Patricia Flowers of the College of Music, who supported a sabbatical application and research-focused semester that allowed me to complete my book. I am fortunate that Pat wants her faculty to do what they do best and provides opportunities for them to do it. The library staff at the Allen Music Library is incomparable when it comes to serving the university's faculty. I regularly benefit from the warm and professional assistance of Laura Gayle Green, Sarah Hess Cohen, Sara Nodine, and Keith Knop. My colleagues in the Musicology Area, Michael Bakan, Charles Brewer, Sarah Eyerly, Frank Gunderson, Margaret Jackson, and Douglass Seaton, have cheered me on for years. Colleagues outside my immediate area have also provided encouragement: Alice Ann Darrow, Larry Gerber, Jim Mathes, Marcia Porter, and Heidi Louise Williams never fail to inquire about my work and offer a perspective unavailable elsewhere. My friend, the artist Irene Trakis, provided stimulating conversations about the intersections of the visual and the sounding arts. Without question, I see more and better because of her.

I have grown because of the opportunity to present my work at national conferences of the Society for American Music and the American Musicological Society, the latter of which has also supported this project with a book subvention award. Numerous speaking engagements at universities across the nation and in Europe have introduced me to new people and ideas that have helped nuance my thinking. I'm especially grateful for the many opportunities to work with Aaron Allen, Mark Pedelty, and Jeff Todd Titon in a series of ecomusicology-related presentations where I've discussed aspects of my work on Libby Larsen. Coediting the Music, Nature, Place book series with Sabine Feisst at Indiana University Press puts me in regular contact with a superb scholar whose comments on my own work have only strengthened it.

My graduate students regularly feed me with their curiosity and energy; they keep me growing. I'm grateful to students in my biography seminars—Sarah Gilbert, Sean Linfors, Lindsey Macchiarella, Haley Nutt, Natalia Perez, Joanna Pepple, Nicole Robinson, Rebekah Taylor, and Dana Terres—for their insights into the biographical endeavor. Interactions with my doctoral students Matt DelCiampo, Amy Dunning, Ashley Geer Hedrick, Megan MacDonald, and Kate Sutton have expanded my horizons in unimaginable ways. Among my students, McKenna Milici has played an especially large role in this project: she has hunted down details, checked facts, read drafts, discussed nuances of the manuscript, copyedited, organized thousands of pages of materials so that whatever I needed was within easy reach, and shared my enthusiasm for all things Larsen. It is no exaggeration to say that without McKenna, this project would not look the way it does. A former student, Matt Woulard, is now a professional music engraver. I am honored to have his elegant musical examples grace this work: he is an artist.

Given the nature of Larsen's compositional process, I was privileged to meet and speak with numerous remarkable composers, conductors, performers, and writers who are her collaborators. I'm grateful for the eloquent insights of Philip Brunelle, the late John Duffy, James Dunham, members of the Fry Street Quartet and Rebecca McFaul in particular, Patricia Hampl, Jeffrey Peterson, Joel Revzen, Vern Sutton, Janika Vandervelde, Rebecca Wascoe, and Eugenia Zukerman. Elizabeth Hinkle-Turner and William "Bill" Brooks provided unique insights into Larsen's residency at the University of Illinois in 1990, and Nolan Valliers, present-day graduate student at Illinois, was invaluable in locating important papers at the university. I appreciate Gayle Sherwood Magee for suggesting his name to me. In an informal dinner with Kelly Harness, I developed a fuller understanding of Larsen's legacy at her alma mater, the University of Minnesota. Graphic designer and communications specialist Jenny Schmitt applied her creative talents to locating an arcane piece of information regarding Larsen's time at the university. Libby Larsen's daughter, Wynne Reece, allowed me to ask her about that most sacred and complex of relationships, that of a mother and daughter. I appreciate her trust.

I have been blessed with friends who've stuck with me for decades. Long before there was such a thing as BFF, they were mine: Tammy Kernodle, Kathy Strickland, and Sherry Williams are present on every page. My family grows dearer with each set of acknowledgments I write. My sons, Haynes and Evan, continue to provide unmatched joy in my life; I love being their mother, and now mother-in-law to Claire and Courtney. Carol and Janet are the best sisters one could ask for; we still dance whenever we get together. My mother, Lorraine Von Glahn, now ninety-four, always wants to know everything I've done in a day and then worries that I do too much. I'm lucky for her continued presence in my life. My husband, musicologist Michael Broyles, has now lived with me through four books. He has welcomed my projects as companions on our morning walks and at our evening meals. Unlike Larsen's parents, who encouraged a young Libby to be quiet at the dinner table, Michael has encouraged me to speak. He has always believed that I had something to say. Over the years I have come to understand what a gift that is. With my gratitude for his patient love, this book is for him.

Prologue

A Polyphonic Life

MUSICIANS USE THE TERM *POLYPHONY* to describe a musical texture containing multiple independent lines of sound occurring simultaneously. A number of scholars have employed the word to suggest the range of considerations they weave together in their arguments. Jan La Rue referred to "the polyphonic thinking" of his analytical approach as "match[ing] the ambiguities of music"; Gustave Reese imagined a "polyphony in prose" to reconcile warring organizational schemes for his study of Renaissance music; and Michael Broyles envisioned "a polyphony of style" to capture what he heard in Beethoven's music.[1] The word works well: individual entities come together to create a new, larger, thoroughly interdependent entity.

The word takes on additional meaning when used in the context of this biography. With its interwoven strands of family involvements and professional activities, spiritual strivings, athletic achievements, feminist and environmental advocacy, academic and administrative accomplishments, and a temperament that compels Larsen to challenge established systems and insist upon being heard, Larsen's life exhibits a dense polyphonic quality. But unlike musical polyphony, which pulls apart relatively easily for study, the multiple strands of Larsen's life resist disentanglement. Charles Ives presented a similar conundrum to his longtime friend and associate Henry Bellamann who "cornered [Ives] on the question of his parallel system of life." In a response that appeared in *Musical Quarterly*, Ives observed: "The fabric of life weaves itself whole. You cannot set an art off in the corner and hope for it to have vitality, reality and substance. There can be nothing 'exclusive' about a substantial art. It comes directly out of the heart of experience of life and thinking about life and living life."[2] And the statement is no less true of Larsen and her music than it was of Ives and his.

Understanding the mechanisms of a piece of polyphonic music requires unraveling and isolating the parts. Looking at individual strands and identifying their function in relation to the whole contribute to a greater knowledge and, one hopes, appreciation of the work; and that is what the following chapters endeavor to do. By separating aspects of Larsen's life, I hope that readers can see important threads pulled away from the larger fabric, although, in reality none of them is free of the others. I have followed my subject's lead and presented the chapters in the order that Larsen listed as the most powerful influences in her life: family, religion, nature, the academy, gender, and technology. Neither she nor I knew at the time that her list would become my organizing scheme. After considering others—a traditional chronological approach; a life-and-works approach; a more ethnographic interview-based approach—a thematic approach emerged as the most natural and effective. Although the specifics of chronology are occasionally sacrificed to get at an overriding idea, the book follows a general chronological arc. Ultimately, readers are reminded that regardless of where I start, my goal is to weave the threads together again, because the whole, in life as in music, is much greater than the sum of its parts. The whole is the thing.

1 Libby Larsen and the Cultural Moment

DURING AN OPEN FORUM AT Florida State University in May 2014, Libby Larsen identified the period from about 1948 to 1962 as "the most radical portion of [the twentieth] century."[1] Her remark puzzled many in the audience, twenties-something graduate students whose births in the late 1980s and early 1990s meant they had little knowledge of what she was referring to beyond secondhand accounts told to them by their parents, many of whom were born in the 1960s. Weren't the sixties supposed to be the decade of radicalism and revolution, and the fifties the decade of stability and prosperity? But those who had experienced the long decade that Larsen referenced understood her characterization. The Cold War, civil rights, television, car culture, and youth culture shaped the second half of the century, and 1962 became a pivotal year on multiple fronts.

The Second Vatican Council, informally known as Vatican II, commenced three years of meetings on October 11 of that year. The changes it instituted rocked the world of the devout twelve-year-old. Looking back on the event, Larsen calls Vatican II "the defining moment in [her] life and consequently in [her] work."[2] A second event overlapped with that defining moment. October 14 to 28 of 1962 were consumed by the Cuban missile crisis, an occasion of political brinksmanship between the USSR and the United States that brought the world to the edge of nuclear holocaust. On October 22, President Kennedy addressed the nation in a somber televised speech to announce the presence of Soviet missiles in Cuba aimed at the United States and his decision to establish a blockade of Soviet ships coming to the island nation. For most of a week Americans wondered whether they should go about their business or stay home and await vaporization. On the fifth day an agreement was reached, and both countries stepped back. The following day the crisis was over.[3] The game of chicken acted out by Kennedy and Khrushchev would remain in the back of Larsen's mind when in 1969 a draft lottery reduced the question of who would become soldiers and likely die in Vietnam to picking balls out of a tumbling barrel.[4] A third event, one that spoke of a different kind of holocaust, had taken place very quietly on September 27 that year. Although unknown to Larsen at the time, Rachel Carson's *Silent Spring* was published that day. The book, a thoroughly researched and informed poetic exposé of the irreversible dangers of certain aerial-sprayed chemical pesticides, would eventually result in a congressional hearing, the selective banning of their use, and wide-scale questioning of our place within a larger ecosystem. In 2014 Larsen was commissioned by the Toronto-based percussion ensemble Nexus to write an environmentally themed work. She composed *DDT*, a piece that uses Morse code rhythmic patterns to embed select words from Carson's book in the music.[5] The composer dates the roots of her general distrust of systems (religious, political, institutional, cultural, and musical) to the cultural turbulence that characterized her first twelve years.

Although the United States debuted as a military power during the Spanish-American War in 1898, and the nation had eventually helped win World War I in 1918, World War II catapulted the country to a preeminent position on an international stage. It was US-led troops that had liberated France, caused the collapse of Germany, and it was the United States that destroyed the Japanese threat by dropping bombs on two of its cities, thus ending the war and ushering in the atomic age. Over 16 million Americans had served in the military. In 1950 it was hard to find an American family that was not still personally affected by the war, and Larsen's was no exception despite the fact that her father had not been among the fighting troops. But the nation was ready to move on. The simultaneously heady and reflective atmosphere of the victorious postwar years resulted in changes that would impact every aspect of the culture.

Industries at home had supported troops overseas, and women had swelled the ranks of factory workers. But women's welcome in factories was rescinded when the war ended and millions of troops returned. With the termination of their jobs, women were assigned a new composite role: wife and mother. They would become full-time homemakers. For large numbers of them, their world stage shrank to the size of a two-bedroom track house. Whole new towns were built to house record numbers of newlyweds and their near-instant families. Levittown, a development of some 17,400 homes housing over 80,000 people about thirty-five miles east of Manhattan, sprang up seemingly overnight. The town became known as "Fertility Valley" and "The Rabbit Hutch."[6] The baby boom was under way, and Libby Larsen was among its results.

A generation of American men whose educations and careers had been postponed or interrupted now filled classrooms as both students and teachers. As Larsen has reflected, World War II military experience and culture were disseminated along with musical training at conservatories and universities across the nation. The impact on postsecondary American music programs would be significant as future "stars" of the musical academy assumed their first teaching positions. In 1946 Edward T. Cone returned from duty in the Office of Strategic Service to an appointment at Princeton; the following year Peter Mennin began a position at Juilliard after having served in the air corps. In 1948 Milton Babbitt returned to Princeton after assisting with secret research for the government, and in that same year, George Rochberg was appointed to the Curtis Institute after serving in the 261st Infantry. Prior to accepting a position at the University of Texas in 1949, Kent Kennan had served in the air corps and been a warrant officer bandleader; also in 1949 George Perle joined the faculty of the University of Louisville following his deployment as a chaplain's assistant in both the European and the Pacific theaters. Perle completed his doctorate using the GI bill's educational benefits. In 1950, after his service in World War II and studies in France, H. Wiley Hitchcock joined the faculty at the University of Michigan. For these and many others, the academy became a comfortable extension of their all-male military experience. With an influx of students and the GI bill footing the bill, new colleges and universities sprang up all over the country. Large numbers of institutions that had been all female became coed to absorb the demand from soldiers eager to get a college degree. With the government guaranteeing tuition dollars through the GI bill, universities weren't taking a risk increasing their numbers, their facilities, or their faculties. Positions were created, and men filled them. Lacking the instant network and benefits provided by the military and its culture, it would take a half century for women to achieve senior positions in any significant numbers at academic institutions. The effects of the war were long and not always obvious or direct, but Larsen became aware of them.[7]

Within months of the start of the 1950s, the United States found itself entangled in another world conflict, this one in Korea. Days after the start of the Korean War, President Truman sent military advisors to South Vietnam to support the anti-Communist government there. Five years later the United States agreed to train South Vietnamese troops. The war that would rip apart the nation's social fabric in the late 1960s had its seeds firmly planted a decade earlier. By the end of 1950, relations with Communist China would be severed, and the Cold War with the Soviet Union was a fact of life. Starting in the 1950s, there would never be a decade that didn't find US troops stationed or fighting in some distant part of the world. The country's participation on the world stage, once initiated, would never end.

For those who were not present at the time it may be difficult to appreciate the ubiquity of the Cold War in every aspect of American life, but Larsen was fully aware. It manifested itself in the Communist-cleansing "Red Scare" pursued by Senator Joseph McCarthy and the House Un-American Activities Committee (HUAC) hearings. Government recommendations that suburbanites build fallout shelters to protect themselves from the effects of radioactivity were mailed to homes; how-to instructions circulated widely in informal civil defense meetings. (It was assumed that urban areas would be the likely targets of nuclear attack and those living there would be annihilated by the explosion.) A majority of Americans believed a nuclear World War III was inevitable. The "Doomsday Clock," a concept born in 1947 among a group calling itself the Chicago Atomic Scientists, made graphic their assessment of "basic changes in the level of continuous danger in which mankind lives in the nuclear age" with a clock image that was referenced and reproduced regularly.[8] The scientists started the symbolic clock's hand at seven minutes to midnight. When the Soviet Union tested its first atomic weapon in 1949, the minute hand moved forward another four minutes. As a result of the US detonation of the first hydrogen bomb in 1952 and competing tests by the Soviets nine months later, in 1953 the hand moved still another minute closer to midnight. Nevil Shute's 1957 postnuclear apocalyptic novel, *On the Beach*, and the Hollywood film that followed in 1959 captured the mood of the time. Although the US government rebutted Shute's scenario and denied that the annihilation of humanity was possible with the arsenal stockpiled by the two nuclear powers, its clinical reassurances offered little comfort to a school-age population practicing civil defense "duck-and-cover" drills and regularly hearing talk of radiation poisoning. Larsen recalls being assured that "the Russians wouldn't bomb the middle of the country," but that was small comfort, and she's not forgiven the government for "terrorizing a whole generation of children": her generation. The scar is deep and not completely healed. Fifty years later she acknowledged, "I've thought that on and off for years, and I know it's silly."[9] But it's hardly silly to fear that the whole world could be disintegrated with the push of a single button when that was Larsen's reality.

It wasn't until 1960 that the Doomsday Clock returned to the seven-minute mark and then stayed there or even further back for the next twenty years, but even that period was not without its extraordinarily tense moments as the Cuban missile crisis made clear.[10] The Soviets launched the satellite Sputnik in October 1957. The possibility of constant surveillance, no longer merely the result of a renegade senator or one's business associates snitching and turning former friends into HUAC, but of a hostile nation tracking Americans' movements, contributed to a more or less constant, low-level national paranoia.[11] The American response with its own satellite, Explorer I, in January 1958 crystallized the space race. In October 1958 the government founded the National Aeronautics and Space Administration (NASA), and eighteen months later NASA chose its first seven astronauts.

But Larsen's first decade was also an era of unprecedented prosperity; there was some substance beneath the veneer of stability. Beyond the pall cast by politically motivated witch hunts and technology that frightened even its inventors with the enormity of its destructive power, a range of social movements and changes exerted their own influence upon a population desperate to achieve a degree of equilibrium and possessing the financial resources to do it. "Rock-and-roll," a phrase popularized by the Cleveland disc jockey Alan Freed, recognized the distinctive music of a newly empowered group of young people.[12] Discretionary income meant young people had economic clout, and they could buy their music. The newly introduced, inexpensive "45," a seven-inch record containing a single song on each of its A and B sides, fit the financial and musical needs of the teenage buyer. Special turntables and record boxes played and stored one's growing collection. The 45 enjoyed its golden age in the 1950s, and youth bought and swapped them regularly.[13]

A burgeoning car culture, one embraced by the entire Larsen family, worked hand in glove with the new teenage music scene. White, middle-class parents might have dreamed of two cars parked safely in every garage, but their children actively embraced a different aspect of car culture: "pedal to the metal." Government-built highways provided thousands of miles for teenagers to "cruise" listening to their music free from watchful eyes and disdainful ears. Dozens of rock 'n' roll hits referenced cars and teenage culture. Forget that the roads had originally been constructed as part of President Eisenhower's plan to facilitate the easy transport of munitions across the country if that became necessary. As the former supreme commander of Allied Forces in World War II, Eisenhower brought a military mentality to the oval office. It was hard to avoid the war's long shadow. Like trains of earlier times, cars became the symbol of freedom. Rock 'n' roll and car culture united youth and alienated parents and fed a "generation gap" that only grew in the sixties. In 1965 Jack Weinberg (b. 1940) would capture the mood of his generation with the words "don't trust anyone over 30."[14]

Images of "perfect" families—upper middle class, white, Christian, and heterosexual, with a working dad, a stay-at-home mom, and two or three children—filled living rooms weekly thanks to television shows such as *The*

Adventures of Ozzie and Harriet (1952–66), *Father Knows Best* (1954–60), *Leave It to Beaver* (1957–63), and *The Donna Reed Show* (1958–66). Fathers were clean-shaven, good-humored, and wise, mothers were beautifully coiffed, patient, and subservient, and children were amusing, grateful, and respectful of elders; they capitulated to parental logic with only minimal resistance. The power of television series to shape and disseminate persuasive cultural models was just being recognized, but the distance between reality and the impossibility of such family romances weren't acknowledged or challenged until later.[15] In many ways, Larsen's family appeared to model this ideal. Television programs of the 1950s reassured large numbers of white Americans that they were safe and all was fine.

The civil rights movement, however, was second only to the Cold War as a marker of the decade. Although it would become synonymous with the sixties, its roots were already deep in the 1950s. The overwhelmingly white population of Minneapolis meant that Larsen wasn't an eyewitness to racial unrest, but as with so many aspects of American culture in the postwar period, it was there to be followed on nightly news reports.[16] You didn't have to be there to know that something big was happening.

For close to a half century the National Association for the Advancement of Colored People (NAACP) had fought to integrate housing and fight public school segregation. On May 17, 1954, in one of the most celebrated cases in the nation's history, *Brown v. Board of Education*, racial segregation in public schools was declared unconstitutional.

Throughout the early fifties, numbers of African Americans had challenged Jim Crow laws, but it was the December 1, 1955, refusal by Rosa Parks, an African American seamstress, to concede her seat on a bus to a white man, that prompted the Montgomery, Alabama, bus boycott. Close to a year later, on November 13, 1956, bus segregation in Alabama was declared illegal. Changes in the quotidian social order, in the South especially, were not welcomed by large numbers of the white citizenry. Nineteen senators and eighty-one representatives from across the region signed a manifesto, which accused the Supreme Court of a "clear abuse of judicial power." The signatories closed their statement "with the gravest concern for the explosive and dangerous condition created by this decision and inflamed by outside meddlers."[17] Putting aside questions of the purity of their motives, the signatories' concerns about violence were spot on and would become realities over the next fifteen years as racial confrontations increased and violence erupted across the nation, incidents that for the most part were caught by television cameras. It is an uncomfortable truth that many of the acts of violence were ignited by the very people who claimed to fear their explosion. Violence would be the price of abolishing Jim Crow laws and institutionalized racism.[18]

In April 1957 the United States Congress approved the first civil rights bill since the Reconstruction era, but it only stoked more challenges to forced integration. At the beginning of the September 1957 school year, Arkansas governor Orval Faubus used his state's National Guard to bar nine African American students from entering Central High School in Little Rock, and President Eisenhower responded by federalizing the same guard to enforce the new law. Faubus eventually backed down. The "Little Rock Nine" endured verbal and physical abuse of a most heinous kind, but five of them graduated. Within the first three years of the 1960s, other acts of nonviolent protest, including sit-ins, challenged a variety of discriminatory practices. The lawfulness of whites-only lunch counters was tested; Freedom Riders pushed southern states to acknowledge the right of all law-abiding citizens to ride buses from one state to another; and public universities were made to admit all qualified students regardless of race.[19]

Even with the ever-present shadow of nuclear confrontation looming and civil unrest growing in the decades of the fifties and the early sixties, the United States enjoyed a number of notable achievements in science, technology, and the arts. Larsen's first ten years were shaped by these events as well. A steady stream of defectors from Eastern Bloc nations sought sanctuary in the West and brought their skills and talents with them. Musicians, dancers, athletes, writers, and scientists took flight starting in the 1940s and continued through December 1991 and the dissolution of the USSR.[20] They embarrassed the Soviet Union as they enriched the United States. The decade saw the inauguration of transcontinental television, Buckminster Fuller patenting his geodesic dome, the first successful triple jump (loop) landed by an ice-skater (Dick Button) in a Winter Olympics, the first commercial sale of color televisions, the description of the double helix DNA molecule, the first use of Jonas Salk's injected polio vaccine followed by Albert Sabin's perfection of an oral preventative, the first practical transistor radio to be sold, the first operational transatlantic telephone cable, the beginning of jet airline passenger service, and the Texas pianist Van Cliburn's win at the First International Tchaikovsky Competition in Moscow, which became as much a political victory as a musical accomplishment in the Cold War era. The ticker tape parade down Broadway that greeted the twenty-three-year-old Cliburn upon his return to the United States made him an unlikely national hero and the only classical musician ever to be so honored. It is one of the many ironies of the era that music of one kind should be the cause of familial anxiety and blamed for the moral decay of a generation, and music of another kind credited with being the source of a singular, unifying moment of national pride.

The 1950s saw other musical firsts that Larsen only became aware of later: the premiere performance of *4′33″*, John Cage's "silent" piece; the emergence of Leonard Bernstein as an American musician to be reckoned with; the first performance of Edgard Varèse's *Poème électronique*, a work of recorded and created sounds played at the Brussels World Fair; the publication of Marion Anderson's *My Lord, What a Morning* detailing her experience as an unlikely civil rights activist starting with her 1939 Easter concert at the Lincoln Memorial; Elvis Presley's performances on *The Steve Allen Show* and *The Ed Sullivan Show*; the first national *American Bandstand* telecast with Dick Clark as its host; and the founding of the Columbia-Princeton Electronic Music Center, which would provide one of the most lauded American homes for electronic music creation for decades to come. The decade also saw the publication of E. B. White's children's classic, *Charlotte's Web*, the book that inspired one of Larsen's early operatic endeavors, *Some Pig*.

It has been argued that children are at their most absorptive and open to external influences in their first seven years. They uncritically mimic "not only the sounds of speech, the gestures of people, but also the attitudes and values of parents and peers," who are themselves affected by the larger cultural zeitgeist.[21] It is not hard to understand Larsen's characterization of the period 1948–62 as the most radical. Even a cocoon-like home environment deep in the center of the country could protect a child only so much; ultimately the cocoon would be shaped by the atmosphere around it.

Within a few years of entering her adolescence, Libby Larsen witnessed epochal changes in her church, the emergence of second-wave feminism, the first murmurs of the mid-twentieth-century environmental movement, the "invasion" of the British rock group the Beatles, challenges to the meaning of patriotism and good citizenship as a result of the nation's increasing involvement in Vietnam, the widespread use of drugs as recreational rather than purely medicinal, and the nation's reputation as the unquestioned authority on the world stage battered and held up to ridicule. Before she was twenty, Larsen would watch political assassinations become recurring news stories. In a period of five years, June 1963 to June 1968, five public figures would be gunned down: Medgar Evers, John F. Kennedy, Malcolm X, Martin Luther King Jr., and Robert F. Kennedy.[22] As with popular thirty-minute family shows, you could watch it all on television. Like many children of the time, Libby remembers exactly where she was sitting in her classroom when news of President Kennedy's assassination was announced.[23] And it was replayed on television too, along with the murder of Kennedy's alleged assassin, Lee Harvey Oswald. If the 1950s had suggested one was likely to die as the result of an obliterating but dispassionate nuclear attack, the 1960s personalized the violence with the weapon of choice being guns. By the end of that decade the nation seemed to have lost its moorings. Libby Larsen headed off to college.

2 Larsen and Family

Needing to Be Heard

AMONG THE MILLIONS OF TRANSACTIONS THAT occur within families, a small handful might stand out and become vivid memories: moments of extraordinary joy or sadness, or sudden enlightenment, or a particular encounter, or a heated exchange. At the time, these moments carry greater or lesser weight for the individuals involved; considered from a distance, however, they can provide insights into family dynamics beyond their immediate consequence. In the case of Libby Larsen an incident when she was a very young child was one such moment; it left a permanent mark; it has shaped her. It tells lots about her family and the young composer's perception of her place within its constellation. It also reveals one of the recurring themes in Larsen's life: a need to be heard, a compulsion to communicate.

Among Larsen's earliest memories was when her parents tried to bribe their "chatterbox" child with the promise of a "Ginny" doll if she would remain silent during dinner for two full weeks.[1] Ginny dolls were eight-inch childlike, dress-up dolls that were widely popular among girls in the 1950s. Introduced in 1951, they reached the height of their popularity in the 1950s before losing out to other dolls and figures. They were the coveted thing, the equivalent of "Barbie" dolls starting in the 1960s and "My Little Pony" in the 1980s; and Larsen's older sister had one. The composer has vivid memories of family dinners; listening to her describe the scene puts us at the table with the enthusiastic child.

> In our family we always ate dinner at 6:15, and we always set a big dining-room table. Full set. Full china, full . . . and then my father would come down and would sit at the head of the table. And we were not supposed to talk. My dad could talk. And he would talk about some scientific thing, and he still does this, and so he would ask us how our days went. And all he really wanted were two or three words; he didn't actually want to know how they went. Or maybe he did, but he had no skills in listening. . . . And so we would begin our dinner ritual, and my dad would say to one sister,

so how was the day going? And she would begin talking and I would interrupt . . . "Hey, I did yah di da, yah di da" . . . because I was young. And my parents didn't like this; they wanted me to be quiet.[2]

Larsen's all-consuming need to communicate exhausted her parents, especially by the end of the day. Her exuberant interruptions disturbed the established order of the formal meal, which included her father presiding over the dinner-table stage. A similar scene was repeated at her grandparents' house, where the Larsen family went each Sunday for dinner. Larsen recalls her maternal grandfather holding forth while the children sat quietly. She wonders if her mother brought the dinnertime ritual with her from childhood experiences in her strict German-Irish family. With an older sister having a doll, and with the seemingly indefatigable Libby on record as loving it and wanting one, her parents likely thought it a reasonable strategy to achieve their goal of order and quiet at their table by offering a bribe.

For the energetic, physical, and vocal child, a born communicator who learned to speak in full sentences unusually early, the impossibility of being silent was obvious, as her recollections make clear.

And I tried so hard, probably only for two days, but it felt like the rest of my life, and finally I just burst out and said "I can't do it," and they didn't give me the doll. And I realized then that they didn't actually want to communicate. They actually didn't *want* to communicate with *me*. I don't know about my other sisters; maybe it's different. I just thought at that point, well screw it. I'll go find my own system to communicate. They haven't changed at all. And that was really mean; that was really mean . . . it was like asking an elephant to stand on toe.[3]

With the benefit of time, Larsen's action looks almost pragmatic and businesslike. As she explained, she knew there was already a doll in the house, and she could probably play with it when it wasn't being used by her sister; a doll of her own simply wasn't worth the price she was being asked to pay. Whether such thoughts actually guided her behavior at the time is impossible to know. In the end, the short-lived peace was broken, and the child Libby resumed her full, if unwelcomed, participation in evening meals. The episode convinced Libby that her parents weren't interested in what she had to say; they didn't want to communicate with her. They wanted her quiet. That this same child would emerge three decades later as one of the most prolific composers of the latter twentieth and early twenty-first centuries, and beloved especially for her *vocal* works, casts the parental bribe in a particularly unfortunate light. But the incident also suggests something about Larsen: she knows what she can and can't do; she knows what she will and won't do; and she knows there will be a price. Even at a young age, Larsen exhibited a kind of emotional courage. On multiple occasions she has speculated that if she were that same child today, she would likely be diagnosed as hyperactive and medicated to control her behavior. She sighs in relief that she was not and frets about those children who are. Larsen explained: "I'm a total warrior to not drug kids. Just don't do it."[4]

Larsen recalled other family dinnertime encounters in a 1998 interview with Vivian Perlis. She reviewed the "formula" by which her father "would talk about whatever he was working on . . . and [her] mother would always talk about what book she was reading." This created an atmosphere where "the talking about and considering of ideas was highly valued. And also the ability to fail was highly valued, which was interesting." And then she discussed a particular dinnertime ritual coinciding with "report card time":

> We would all deliver our report cards and my father would read each grade and comment on each grade. And then sign the back so that we could go on. But if the grade had gone down for some reason or up for some reason, he always wanted us to tell him about it. "Tell me why. Tell me what this is about. Tell me what is happening." And if we got A's in conduct, which was how we conducted ourselves, he would feign, but really mean, that he didn't like that. Isn't that interesting? . . . We weren't rewarded for A's in conduct. We were encouraged to question. If we disagreed with something, to speak up. And rewarded by my parents in the report card ritual for being a little feisty—not too feisty, but a little feisty. And that's something I'm grateful for.[5]

Encouraging daughters to be "feisty" at school seems contradictory to earlier directives to be silent and well behaved at the dinner table. Perhaps there were places for questioning authority, even if the home was not one of them. Learning to talk about ideas and to value failure were the more positive life lessons Larsen took away from mealtimes. Such are the mixed messages parents send their children without always recognizing the confusion they sow. From a distance of almost sixty years, the dining-room table can be an uncomfortable place for meals for Larsen. It might explain why until recently she and her husband didn't own a formal table, and even now they don't eat dinner there.[6]

Although Larsen's dinnertime encounters occurred in the 1950s, the idea that "a child should be seen and not heard" dates back centuries and can be found in a collection of homilies from the late 1300s titled *John Mirk's Festial*. Mirk was an Augustinian canon at Lilleshall Abbey in Shropshire, England. The *Festial* collection "was designed to be accessible and entertaining, as well as orthodox . . . and taught both the priests who used the sermons, as well as their audiences, the fundamentals of the Christian faith and doctrine, illustrated by many stories."[7] In a churchgoing family, the Larsen parents' practice of quieting their children was sanctioned by religion, which for the child Libby might have given it extra authority, at least in her early years. In its original iteration, "a mayde schuld be seen, but not herd," the proverb was directed more generally at all very young children, but over time its message was aimed more pointedly at any unmarried woman. Two messages emerged: women are interchangeable with children, and both are expected to keep quiet.[8]

Mirk's maxim would have been reinvigorated in a post–World War II culture that removed women from the public positions they had occupied during the war years to make room for men and characterized their new roles as subservient to their heroic fathers, husbands, and brothers. Although Larsen's father did not serve in the military during World War II, his work as a food chemist impacted the rations soldiers ate, so he contributed to the war effort indirectly. Larsen believes her father regretted not serving; he "miss[ed] out on his own generation's talisman, their touchstone." It is impossible to know whether his absence from military service during World War II affected the way he was treated by returning veterans who had formed very close bonds with one another during their wartime service. To have "not served" required an explanation, and perhaps one that went beyond his 4-F classification because of "flat feet." It is not hard to imagine him feeling left out of a formative experience shared by the majority of his contemporaries. The patriarchal social structure ensconced in postwar American society and reinforced with fantasy families in television series was mirrored in Larsen's home and enacted at the dinner table. Larsen's story, while singular and unique in its details, is also paradigmatic.

Until the latter years of the twentieth century, large segments of society customarily silenced both children and women either by selectively ignoring or disregarding them or by more aggressively limiting their experiences and squelching their utterances. The Larsen family's practice, quaint as it may seem to most twenty-first-century readers accustomed to empowered children and women, was not unique or even uncommon at the time. Many children (and women) were consigned to roles as quiet observers or only very limited participants in a range of rituals. What was unique in the Larsen household was the particular child being silenced, the particular child being bribed to *silence herself*. And what that child knew early on was that she just couldn't do it. She would find another way.

Larsen's parents had met at the University of Minnesota while Robert Larsen was finishing a PhD in food chemistry and Alice Brown Larsen was completing her bachelor's degree in English. They moved to Wilmington soon after their graduations so that the newly minted "Dr. Bob" could begin a job with DuPont.[9] A month after receiving her degree, Alice gave birth to LuAnne. Two and a half years later Molly was born, and then Libby. While there the young family lived in a carriage house on the Willcox Estate in Wawa, Pennsylvania, about twelve miles from Wilmington. Despite having returned to the area as an adult to see her natal place years later, the composer has only one real memory of her earliest years: she remembers "the sound of horses' hooves," the Doppler effect that resulted as horses chased foxes close by the house during the hunts that took place on the estate.[10] Larsen was a keen listener even as a toddler, so not surprisingly sound provided her single memory of Wilmington. While there, Robert was approached by the military to move to Chicago. He was drafted into the Quartermaster Corps to undertake food research that would benefit soldiers on the ground in Korea, and he worked at the Food and Container Institute, where he was made director of the cereal unit. From there he was hired by the Pillsbury Company as director of research, and the Larsens returned to Minneapolis. Dr. Robert Larsen quickly became the "golden boy" among researchers.[11]

By the time the composer was four, she had lived in Delaware, moved to Chicago briefly, and was headed to Minneapolis, all as a result of her father's employment. And this too was typical of 1950s families. The father's career determined where families lived and when they moved, and his schedule often determined a family's daily routines. After a peripatetic first few years of marriage, her parents gratefully returned to their home state. Libby Larsen remains there to this day, and after sixty years it has become her home state as well.

The family's brief sojourn in Chicago left Libby with little more than a hazy sense that it was "not a happy time. Not happy." She recalls, "My mother, I think, was probably pretty depressed. She probably had post-partum. I don't know what it was, but she was pretty depressed . . . and I was supposed to be too little to remember any of this." Larsen remembers spending "hours and hours in [her] crib. And sometimes [her mother would] tie [her] into it with towels." Knowing Larsen's kinetic being, it is hard to imagine her being physically constrained. But with the distance of decades and experiences to provide perspective, Larsen empathizes with her mother: "She had a four-year-old, and a two-year-old, and a baby. I know what that means, what kind of energy it takes to keep that going, and my dad working for the government at the time. I think they were happy to leave." The drive from Chicago to the Twin Cities is a more vivid memory. Larsen states, "I remember it really well, and I was too little to know that." It's tempting to think that her earliest experience with constraints made the 350+ mile car trip especially thrilling. In days before seatbelts, passengers moved freely inside cars; young children regularly climbed onto and over seats. They bumped up and down along with the roads. There was lots of motion inside the moving car. Larsen would have seen trees and billboards whisking past her as well as felt the motion of the car as it headed north and west to the Twin Cities. Perhaps her fascination with long-distance transportation, with trains, and cars, and buses, and planes, has roots in this early liberating experience. Perhaps the young Libby could sense her mother's relief as she headed back home, where Alice Larsen would have family and friends close by.

Soon after returning to Minneapolis, Alice Larsen gave birth to her fourth daughter. Within the family, older sisters LuAnne and Molly would be referred to as the "big girls," and Libby, Duffy, and Maggie, who was born five years after Duffy, became the "little girls." As the composer reflects, this was a curious division as she was just eighteen months younger than her sister Molly, but she was four years older than Duffy and nine years older than Maggie. Despite the parents' grouping, in practice Libby wasn't part of either pair. As Larsen recalls, "They made a conscious split between us," and the divide was palpable to her. Her two older sisters "had their own language; they had their own bonding," and she was not a part of it. She floated in the middle. Larsen did form a close bond with Duffy and remembers taking care of her, "bringing a very young Duffy food, climbing into her crib, and playing with her, a lot." They slept in the same bedroom, and "every night [Libby] would hold her hand until she fell asleep." Of Larsen's three surviving siblings, Duffy is the one to whom she remains closest.

School was another environment that shaped her; it was clearly important to the budding musician and composer. Over years of conversations, Larsen talked about her early school memories. She recalls:

> Until I learned to be still, not quiet, I was always getting into trouble for being kinetic. So I always had the seat in front of the teacher's desk or in the back by the closets where I could look out the windows, so I wouldn't be disturbing. . . . I'm thinking about what it was like to sit at Christ the

Figure 2.1. The Larsen family, December 1963. Libby Larsen is at the far left. Reproduced with the kind permission of the composer.

> King School, with the old fashioned desks that were nailed down in rows. *Eight years of that!* Having to sit down and fold your hands and for me to sit in a nailed-down chair and be quiet . . . I can remember sitting with my hands folded so that I didn't get in trouble, and looking out the window . . . which I still do when I'm thinking . . . so I could notice all the modes of oscillation that are going on. . . . So I learned to go inside in that way . . . so that my brain was [in motion], but my body was acceptably quiet.[12]

Although it was not without its frustrations, formal education ultimately provided Larsen with the skills and opportunities she needed to communicate, and there were moments of pure joy along the way. Thinking back to an early experience at Robert Fulton Elementary School, Larsen recalls a young Hawaiian teacher, Miss Yamamoto, who taught her eighteen kindergarteners how to hula and had them dance each day before nap time. Larsen remembers the beautiful hand movements that went with the dance that her teacher taught to boys and girls alike: "She taught us the spirituality of hula. It wasn't Hollywood hula, it was real hula . . . which is as sacred as chant is to the Catholic Church."[13] Respecting the energy typical of normal, healthy five-year-olds, Miss Yamamoto allowed the children to whisper during their "naps." Movement and chatter were part of her classroom; the lively Libby was confirmed. It was a radically different environment than the one she had sensed at home.[14]

Larsen also vividly recalls teachers at Christ the King School, which she attended starting in first grade—and not just their names but their looks, their manner, the way they interacted with the children. Walking to her school dressed in her conspicuous Catholic school uniform, Larsen stood out as she crossed the public school playground, the best shortcut to Christ the King. She remembers running as fast as she could to avoid the small rocks and stones thrown at her by the public school children. Perhaps that's where she learned to love running. Regardless, risking the early-morning gauntlet rather than take the longer route provided a test of her courage; the composer recalls that she chose to take the chance and survived unscathed. Her time at Christ the King, 1955–64, was rewarded; the dedicated nuns of the Sisterhood of Saint Joseph of Carondelet loved their student Libby into being. Her gratitude is audible even from the distance of five decades: "I think the great luck in my life was that I learned to write music in first grade. That was the luck; that was the luck. Because I could speak! So once I learned how to write music, and there wasn't the idea that only composers do this, this is a way of expressing yourself, it was brilliant. Those nuns knew! Language, math, and music . . . so gradation, symbol, and group and regroup at ever more sophisticated levels."[15]

The Sisters of Saint Joseph of Carondelet were the American followers of a half dozen French women who had come together in 1650 in Le Puy-en-Velay, France, to tend the impoverished of their community. Their good works were noticed, and the sisterhood grew. When a group sailed to the United States in the 1830s, they established an order in Carondelet, Missouri, thus giving the sisters their American name.[16] Larsen observes that the kind of caring attention she received at Christ the King, while not regularly associated with Catholic nuns more generally, was typical at her school: "They did it with every student. I think they were there for their individual students. Maybe that was their calling." Although she grew up in an overwhelmingly female household, this would be Larsen's introduction to an environment shaped at least in part by women. This community of strong, intelligent, humane women, who empowered and confirmed her, left an indelible mark. Larsen recalls individual teachers:

> My first-grade teacher was Sister Helen Marie. She probably was near retirement, so she had fifty or sixty years of history, and she's the one who taught us everything, and it was all so easy, we all just learned how to write music; she passed it on. . . . My second-grade teacher was Sister Leo Irene. And she was a brand-new nun, and she was so young. I know she knew what was happening [regarding impending changes to the Catholic Church that would manifest themselves in Vatican II], and she continued [what Sister Helen Marie had begun.] And she was so vivacious and full of life. I thought I wanted to be a nun. But what it was [was] her energy. So we had Sister Helen Marie, who was all calmness, and Sister Leo Irene who was all "let's ford the stream and climb the mountain!" Mrs. Grahams was my third-grade teacher. Also lucky! She loved music, really loved it, and really knew it. Her son played organ in the church, Louis Grahams. And he was a great, great, great musician. So we did music every day. We sang, we got up and moved, so we continued music. And then my fourth-grade teacher was also near retirement, Sister Naomi. Brilliant, she knew how to handle all kinds of children, and fifth grade was Miss Lane, who was just a lovely young woman who I ate alive.[17]

When I asked the composer why Miss Lane drew that reaction, she paused, clearly never having thought about it. And then as if a light went on, she responded: "Ahhhhh . . . cause Miss Lane didn't know music! She didn't continue it at all. She didn't know how to. That's it! That's it! By then I was writing. I was writing what I heard in my head."[18]

Given that Larsen's primary mode of expression was music, and that she thrived in classrooms where music was a way of thinking, discovering that her teacher was unschooled in its operations and deaf to its effects was disorienting. How would the child Libby communicate? Who would listen to what she had to say? It's easy to understand her unfriendly reaction despite Miss Lane's "loveliness." Thankfully Larsen still regularly sang Gregorian chant during church services. She had that outlet in fifth grade and at least for one more year. As she has explained, "Everyone learned to read and sing Gregorian chant, and learned to sight read using movable 'do.' We started in the first grade and sang and read through sixth grade, until the ecumenical council happened, and Gregorian chant was eliminated from the music program."[19] Larsen's despair at the removal of this mystical, transporting music from her daily experience was profound. With chant, Larsen explains, "I always knew I was being touched by something otherworldly."[20] Now she sensed that the world she knew and treasured was being dismantled, and it was. If the young Libby could not abide the patriarchal system at work in her family, the changes wrought by Vatican II set the seeds of her suspicion of all systems. Her sense of betrayal by the church colored the rest of her life. She would leave organized religion and find spiritual nourishment elsewhere.

Although the family rule was that children could not begin piano lessons until they were seven, Larsen explained that her mom "let [her] diddle on the piano while she was making dinner. [Her] dad wasn't home yet."[21] On her Web site, Larsen recalls her first musical experience as watching her sister LuAnne practicing.

> I was about three years old, and standing at the piano, which my sister was playing, and my eyes were at the keyboard level. I was holding onto the piano and I think even gnawing on it a little. I remember feeling the whole piano vibrating and moving, and I knew that somehow her fingers were making that sound and vibration. I couldn't wait for my turn. As soon as my sister was finished practicing, I got up onto the piano stool and "wrote" a piece. It was just a series of clusters that I came up with, ordered and restructured, but when I had played my piece through I climbed down and found my mother in the kitchen and asked her what she thought of my piece.[22]

Larsen describes her mom as "receptive, tolerant, benign, which has its purpose, but then she didn't know anything about composing," acknowledging, "So I don't know that she knew it was anything but just goofing around."[23]

As promised, when Larsen turned seven, she began lessons at Christ the King with her first teacher, Sister Colette, whom she describes in glowing terms. "She was a French Canadian, and a ball of fire. She was a great teacher. Yeah! She was great!"

> She was extraordinary in the kinds of repertoire she gave me. I played very unusual repertoire—Mozart, Bartók, Stravinsky, Japanese music, and boogie right away. That variety was very important in introducing so many different musical sounds and colors to me. We'd do Two-Part Inventions, and Bartók. She had an eclectic ear, and maybe she recognized my eclectic ear. I don't know if this was the case for other of her students. But it made sense to me because we learned the church modes and then you have

Figure 2.2. State piano contest winner 1963. Libby Larsen is second from right. Reproduced with the kind permission of the composer.

Bartók and you just flow right into that more than Bach actually. The flow of Bartók is much more akin to chant. She was a great teacher, and she set the bar for her students at state: "You're going to win state." But not by competing! "You're just going to be so good that you'll win state."

And Larsen did as Sister Colette predicted and eventually won the state piano competition; teacher and student were well matched. It was no stretch for the young, open-eared child to embrace a variety of musical languages.[24] Regularly singing Gregorian chant had prepared her for the modal sounds and flexible, un-square rhythms of Bartók's *Mikrokosmos* and non-Western musics. Listeners can hear Sister Colette's lessons in Larsen's music today. The encyclopedic embrace of styles, the unencumbered pulses, the unbound musical line are all a part of her bequest to the mature composer. Sister Colette's dedication to doing one's best is also observable in the adult Libby Larsen, who accepts no other standard. But it was not all easy sailing for the young student, who was by her own admission "a handful." Larsen recalls: "Sister Collette and I fought like cats and dogs, because I wouldn't do my Czerny exercises, and then we had to do scales, and then we'd do I, IV, I, V7, I. And

I wasn't strengthening my hands, I just wasn't, and it really frustrated her. She'd fly off the handle, and I'd fly off the handle and I'd run out and slam the door! And she'd come out and get me and slap me on the back and say, 'Y mais jamais vous!' It was great!"[25] With a twelve-year-old Libby just beginning to comprehend the breadth and depth of changes instituted by Vatican II, she suffered another setback in her musical world when Sister Colette was transferred to a different parish. For her last year at Christ the King, Larsen took lessons with her replacement, Sister Rosanne, who was "a *good* teacher." But like Miss Lane, Sister Rosanne didn't stand much of a chance. Rather wistfully Larsen conceded: "I guess I was in love with Sister Colette."[26]

Upon leaving the care of the sisterhood of nuns who had taught her so much, Larsen attended and graduated from Southwest High School, where music was little more than rote singing. Attempts to interest her high school music teacher in her youthful compositions failed. The teenaged Libby took piano lessons with Irene Anderson, a teacher who lived within walking distance of her family's home. Mrs. Anderson was in her mid-fifties and so an experienced teacher like many of the nuns Libby had loved so much. Recognizing the talent and spirit of her new student, Anderson encouraged Libby to do whatever she wanted to do and offered to help. Larsen recalls her new teacher's gift to her.

> And the gift was, there was some kind of contest; I don't know what it was. I had to learn a number of pieces and play them for an adjudicator who would take time and give you constructive criticism. So the adjudicator that year was Louis Lane, a great educator, and I think a conductor. And so I wanted to learn twenty pieces! And Mrs. Anderson said, OK, and so I learned the twenty pieces, and of course, maybe only one or two of them were to the point that they could be adjudicated, but she let me do it. So I went to Louis Lane and played the pieces, and he took two or three hours to help me understand that you do one thing as deeply as possible and then you might begin to understand a piece of music. I might not have learned to "grieve for lost opportunities" without that experience.[27]

She learned that one couldn't do everything thoroughly and well; choices had to be made about where to focus energy. Whether the decision involved which pieces to concentrate on, or later, whether to become a skier or a sailor or an economist or a musician, Larsen discovered that she needed to let some things go: "Actually let it go and grieve for it." As she looks back on the experience, Larsen acknowledges that she was fortunate to have learned that lesson in her teens.[28]

Both of Larsen's parents "loved music." According to the composer, they provided "a real healthy amateurism in [her] background."[29] The family owned a large LP collection that was regularly playing—not classical works but popular music of all kinds. Robert Larsen was a passionate amateur clarinetist and loved Dixieland, and as a result the family heard a lot of Dixieland. Larsen also recalled a family myth about her mother having been a concert pianist as a young woman.

> We always had her grand piano in the house, but she never played it. So there was this mythology that my mother was this great pianist, gave this major recital when she was seventeen, and we had this gown . . . and then she never played again. I never heard her play, not once in my life. I don't even know if that gown [was the recital gown]. . . . So there was this idea that there was this piano, and all this great music had been made on it, and she loved music. In the kitchen we had a record player, and she loved big band, she loved stride boogie piano, she loved Broadway, a lot of Broadway, and that was about it for her. But there was always music on in the house. Always. None of it classical.[30]

As little girls often do with their mother's bridal gowns and fancy dresses, Larsen and her sisters used their mother's formal "recital gown" for their own dress-up games; it's easy to imagine a romantic story growing up around the posh frock. Given the value of music in the household, and the child Libby's undeniable talents as a pianist, vocalist, and composer, it is possible that Alice Larsen had been a talented musician herself and given classical recitals as a young girl. But we can document her activities from the time she was twenty-two, when she had just graduated from college, married, and become a mother, and it is clear that she had no sustained musical career. Nevertheless, Larsen vividly remembers her mother singing and dancing to the record player while preparing dinner; music provided a continuous soundtrack in the household. Gregorian chant at school and Bartók and Japanese music with Sister Colette, and then Chuck Berry, Petula Clark, and Joni Mitchell as well as Dixieland and Broadway musical soundtracks at home provided an unusually eclectic musical world for the time. It follows that Larsen's music effortlessly sings, swings, stomps, and dances. Her composer's palette contains her rich American musical heritage growing up.

If Larsen's parents had been frustrated by their middle daughter's insatiable desire for verbal communication and were incapable of providing the interactions she wanted, they easily understood her need for physical engagement and found multiple outlets. Perhaps her father, in particular, was more willing to pursue outdoor activities with his daughters because such things interested him as well. Larsen has credited him with encouraging his daughters to pursue individual sports. From a young age, Larsen came to life in the outdoors; she ran, danced, biked, swam, played tennis, and skied. She explained: "I'm a very physical person. If I could live in a tree, I would."[31] When Larsen was about seven, her father bought a small sailboat and taught his daughters how to race on the water. Lake Harriet became the locus of multiple events. During the summer months the band shell, which was situated on the water's edge, was the site of regular evening concerts. The music could be heard across the lake and throughout the neighborhood. Physical activity, fellowship, and music all came together out-of-doors. Larsen recalls "hanging around down at the docks with a lot of sailors on Lake Harriet. There would always be multi-generations there, parents and kids."[32]

Lake Harriet was the place where neighbors came together and where Larsen learned to swim. Like discovering her fundamental need to communicate through dinner-table encounters, sailing competitively on the nearby

Figure 2.3. Libby Larsen at the newly rebuilt Lake Harriet Concert Shell, 2012. Photograph taken by the author.

lake galvanized another essential aspect of her makeup: a courageous spirit. Larsen has talked about her early racing days and their role in strengthening her fortitude.

> With sailing you're out on a boat, and it's really windy and you weigh about forty pounds and you're trying to hold that boat down at age eight or nine, and there are other boats coming at you, and you're trying to go around a buoy, and it is really scary. You just kind of think, "I could die." Even though it's from a child's perspective, you know you've got a choice for courage there. You either just go into the fray and pick your course and make it around the buoy, or you go outside and you just don't even deal with it. You know you'll get around the buoy; it will be fine, but you will not get around it well. And you will not have faced the wind. . . . I know it's true that somehow that experience of sailing, of just every time you have a decision for courage, you "man the tuits" and go.[33] Many times in my life, almost once a week, I see a situation that looks dangerous, maybe it's a panel of my peers and I just say, "Man the tuits" and we just go. Pull

Figure 2.4. Libby Larsen and her sister Molly George in 1968 racing their sailboat on Lake Harriet, Minneapolis. Photograph by Dee O'Neal. Reproduced with the kind permission of the composer.

the sheet; make the sail take the wind; get ahold of the rudder, and be completely vigilant so that you don't hit anyone, or be hit, or hit the buoy. You have big boats coming for that spot, and you're a little boat, and everybody's yelling, "Right of way," and a lot of them are men and they're bellowing, and you just think, "Man the tuits." I think that's it. . . . And I thank my father for that.[34]

Beyond learning how to face challenging situations, Larsen also developed an appreciation for self-discipline and understanding rules. She explains,

> And here's something else that was so great about rounding the buoy: there are all kinds of nautical laws at work. You have to give right-of-way under many different circumstances. If you deliberately hit a boat, then you might be thrown out of the race, just all kinds of things, and you know that every skipper who's trying to get around that buoy knows that if anybody violates a law then you're going to go into a protest situation, a court situation, where the judges are there and you both present your cases using little boats. So you had to know all the rules of buoy rounding. So if I was wrong and seven years old and I violated the rights of Dr. Stephens, who was forty years old, then he's going to throw me out of the race. And vice versa. An even playing field. No gender, no age, no nothing, just the buoy, the boat, you, and the rule book.

In 1845 Margaret Fuller had argued that no occupation should be off-limits to women. "Let them be sea captains if you will" became one of her most oft-quoted remarks. The nineteenth-century writer would, no doubt, have approved of Larsen's sailing skills and determination.[35] Rather than be cowed by the possibility of a protest, Larsen welcomed the opportunity to defend her position, which she admits she had to do many times: "There are very strict rules of what you can do and how you can do it, and under what circumstances you can steal somebody's wind; under what circumstances you can send someone off course. It's very complicated . . . a really elegant set of nautical rules for sailboat racing, and so you know everybody understood that protesting was all part of the yacht club ecology. We understood that once a protest was resolved, we would resume good fellowship."[36] Water activities on Lake Harriet involved all the Larsens in one way or other. Although her mother didn't sail, her father did, and more than that he judged. As Larsen explains: "I knew the rules very well, and he knew the rules very well. He likes to get better at things too, and so he just started judging on Lake Harriet, but he worked his way up in judging, so that he judged the Pan-Am Games for one of the Olympics. And he really worked his way up. But it wasn't out of ambition; it was out of getting better. And actually that is true. I maybe inherited that from watching him: You like something; you get better."[37]

Alice Larsen took charge of teaching her daughters to swim, which she did by taking them to the small beach on the edge of Lake Harriet. Before trusting that they were safe in the water, Alice insisted that when they thought they were ready, the children jump off the dock fully clothed and demonstrate that they could keep themselves afloat. She told them, "Take off your shoes, and tread water. Shed any other clothing you can, but keep treading." As Larsen's mother has explained, "I figured that was the best way to keep those kids safe. You could drown from shock from just the way your clothes dragged you down, but if you've been through it once you will think well this is [what I have to do]. We lived near the lake, and it was just part of your growing up."[38]

Alice Larsen also became active in the Girl Scouts, where she took on a leadership role, was elected to the organization's national council, and accompanied Libby and her troop on camping trips. Among the memorable Girl Scout activities that the composer recalls was a reforestation project in northern Minnesota, where she and her fellow scouts spent a day planting "hundreds and hundreds of tiny pine trees."[39] In a "tent conversation" later that night, Libby and her friends wondered, "Are we now, or are we then?" She explained that the girls had identified completely with the trees, they had become the trees, and they pondered whether they, like the seedlings, contained their futures. Were they their future at that very moment? Was there such a thing as a future, or was it all present.[40] Larsen's love of sports and the outdoors was an essential aspect of her makeup, and it was encouraged and shared by her family.

Never one to accept conditions she believed were unfair or to make do with the status quo when she needed something different, Larsen, while she was still a teen, began her practice of creating opportunities where none existed. Today she speaks of the joy she experienced running and skiing and warmly recalls her sailing days; and while athletic experiences might not appear to be obvious influences in her music, her empathy with the natural world and its motions, rhythms, processes, and cycles is a direct result of her time spent on water, in mountains, running long distances over the northern woodland terrain that is her Minneapolis home, and generally feeling the pure joy of being in harmony with her body in the out of doors. Rhythms, processes, cycles, and all manner of momentum are audible in her compositions.

Beyond outdoor activities, the "rawboned" Larsen family shared one other passion: cars.[41] 1950s car culture thrived in Minneapolis, and the extended family was in the middle of it.[42] As I learned in a 2012 interview with Larsen's parents, even from a distance of over fifty years, their passion hadn't diminished. Listening to the family speak about a prized 1957 Thunderbird (yellow with white leather interior and a "really space-age scanner radio") brought their mutual love affair to life. Although Larsen learned to drive on "a big old station wagon," which her father agreed was "a terrible car," after getting rid of it, Robert Larsen took to feeding his love for beautiful cars, and mother and daughter shared his bliss. The Thunderbird was followed by a '65 Mustang and then a Camaro, but the '57 T-Bird took pride of place in his heart and theirs. Robert loved its beauty and its design, so perfect for speed. He admiringly recalled its style. Alice Larsen shared a story of secretly taking the car out on a not-yet-finished piece of highway, moving the barrier cones, and racing it up and down the road one beautiful spring day, and Libby remembered getting the keys from her dad to run a quick errand to buy a loaf of bread from the store just two blocks away and then driving for a couple of hours. He never questioned the length of her absence when she returned: a love of cars was something he understood. Where cars were concerned, rules were bent. A prized photo shows a radiant teenaged Larsen sitting in the driver's seat: a woman and her car. When I visited the senior Larsens in 2012, they showed

Figure 2.5. Libby Larsen behind the wheel of the family's '57 Thunderbird in October 1969. Reproduced with the kind permission of the composer.

me a small model of a pale yellow T-Bird, a gift from a car dealer who knew how they felt about the vehicle; it was clearly among their prized possessions.

As with much of what is most meaningful to Larsen, the car found its way into her music. It became, in fact, the inspiration for one of her most exhilarating pieces, a quartet for violin, cello, contrabass, and piano that she wrote in 1983 called *Four on the Floor*. It's little wonder that the piece is among her parents' favorites; it explodes with power riding on a boogie-woogie beat; in so many ways, it's her family's piece.[43] Exploring *Four on the Floor* allows readers to step into the car with the composer, put the top down, vibrate with the purr of its engine, rip through the countryside, and revel in the intense beauty of a perfectly designed machine. Listeners experience Larsen's love of motion on wheels three years before John Adams took his own short ride in a fast machine in 1986.[44]

Larsen's five-minute joy ride was premiered and recorded by the Minnesota Arts Ensemble, a group of young, professional musicians closely associated with the Minnesota Composers Forum in the 1980s.[45] Even in this regard, the piece is a product of family, albeit an enlarged professional one: one that Larsen was instrumental in creating. A note to the score acknowledges her debt to American culture and pays homage to her mother's musical preferences: "Inspired by boogie-woogie, *Four on the Floor* is a celebration of American music and American musicians. The metronome indication is 138–144 to the quarter note, a speed verging on breakneck—and breakneck is the theme of the piece: an America that is speeding up faster and faster, jazzing into eternity.[46]

Larsen wastes no time. The pianist lunges and grabs a triple *forte* chord, and the strings jump in with equally loud snap pizzicatos; listeners are thrown back in their seats as the musical machine takes off. Tritones color every beat of the first five measures, bringing with them centuries of associations with tension and danger; their sounds characterize the piece. Musicians and gears engage as Larsen reaches her cruising speed at measure 6: the boogie bass kicks in (ex. 2.1). The signature 4/4 pattern sets the pace, and thereafter, with the exception of a single lengthy downshift beginning at measure 48 (ex. 2.2), listeners and music zip along.

The more relaxed mood is signaled by one of only five measures that deviate from the 4/4 meter. Carefully placed measures of 6/4 momentarily expand the time between downbeats; listeners hear Larsen applying the brake, or maybe it's the clutch. She shifts gears. Blues, fiddling, and barn dances mingle in a boozy "poco meno mosso" middle section. Piano and strings trade "swinging triplets."

Example 2.1. *Four on the Floor*, mm. 6–9

The strings' "slow glissando" in measure 57 makes them sound drunk. It's tempting to think the driver is intoxicated by the sheer exhilaration of handling this beautiful machine. But not for long; the composer speeds up, switches gears, and takes off again at measure 85. Tremolos shiver, pizzicatos crack in the air, and undulating quintuplets capture the swerving movements of the car as it takes the corners and rides "lightly," as if it's floating above the surface of the road. Even as the pistons pulse their regular rhythm, Larsen's score is filled with unexpected accents, scoops, swoops, slides, and runs. Repeated, pounded octaves by the pianist pay homage to Jerry Lee Lewis, and Larsen makes a note in the score to that effect just in case listeners don't get her reference to the "the Killer," one of the family's favorite performers.[47] The passage finishes with a signature Lewis glissando that unleashes a series of ad lib *fortissimo* motions in the strings. The players fly freely along their fingerboards catching an occasional notated pitch, while the pianist gathers up notes from the lowest end of the keyboard in its series of ascending octave eighths that meet head-on with a descending right-hand passage. The syncopating three-pulse groupings in the right hand provide additional tension and excitement when heard against the coursing duple left-hand accompaniment. At beat one of measure 162, the composer instructs her string players to "Play any note you land on. Use marcato at the very least" (ex. 2.3).[48]

Example 2.2. *Four on the Floor*, mm. 47–51

What might seem like unchecked recklessness, the composer metaphorically taking her hands off the wheel for a moment, is in reality a meticulously crafted spinning out of a small number of musical ideas. The beauty of the Thunderbird and its musical progeny is the elegance of the design. As with so many of her pieces, Larsen uses only what she needs: a minimum of rhythmic, harmonic, and melodic motives. She recycles these in different combinations

Example 2.3. *Four on the Floor*, mm. 156–62

and creates new effects. There are no spare parts. She also knows what her instruments and instrumentalists can do. Her years of piano lessons show in the thoroughly pianistic quality of her writing for the instrument; everything fits in the hand as if custom made. The joy Larsen took in cruising in the family's prize car is audible in the lighthearted exuberance of the music, but that spirit hides the technical difficulties of the piece. Playing up to tempo requires significant chops. One is reminded of television commercials showing sleek sports cars rounding mountain passes at blinding speeds and the disclaimer that appears in small print at the bottom of the screen warning viewers: "These are professional drivers on a closed course."

Four on the Floor is the first of a number of pieces in which Larsen welcomes her performers and listeners to *become* other than they are. Here she invites everyone to "become the gearbox"—or maybe the driver, or maybe both. In later works she will encourage people to become wheat (*Deep Summer Music*) and fragrance (*Downwind of Roses in Maine*). Summoning musicians and audiences to become the sounds, to enter into the "it of it," promises a deeper experience and understanding of the phenomenon she is musicalizing. Sinking down into the sounds, becoming the momentum of the T-Bird as it purrs along the highway allows the composer to share a personal youthful experience, one that has stayed with her and her family all these years.

3 Larsen and Religion

The Tie That Binds

WHEN I ASKED THE COMPOSER TO IDENTIFY the most powerful influences in her life, Larsen unhesitatingly named "religion" and, more specifically, "growing up Catholic" among the first. But many conversations later, it was clear that the word *religion* did not capture all she was thinking of; *Spirituality*, the composer suggested, might come closer.[1] Religion for Larsen is larger than any single organized system of beliefs shared by a community of believers and practiced in a social setting. Better terms than *religion* or *spirituality* might be *faith practices* or *belief system*, but I'll stick with the word *religion* simply because of its economy, and it was the one Larsen used first.

Religion in Larsen's world is inextricably tied with nature, with gender and feminism, with a range of institutions, and back to her family. There is no corner of her life untouched by religion, or more broadly, by her unique spirituality. Seismic changes in the Roman Catholic Church when Larsen was a young teen, a time that she has described as "our wonder years," presented the always ruminative child with her first opportunity to reconsider, question, challenge, and eventually reject the most influential system she knew outside her family: the church. Systems become a recurring theme in what follows.

Larsen admitted to questioning the Ten Commandments one by one as a fourth grader, especially number 4, "Honor thy Father and thy Mother," and pressing for answers to the contradiction she perceived in the church's assurance of a god that was all-merciful and its insistence upon the existence of hell. In retrospect she feels for "poor Sister Naomi, bless her heart," but "the incongruities of systematized religion, full of the barnacles of a culture" troubled the ten-year-old.[2] As Larsen explains, "The mystical part of spirituality was pretty much put in a box on a shelf in sixth grade. Vatican II is the defining moment in my life and consequently in my work."[3] Larsen's reaction to Vatican II reforms, the changes prescribed in *Sancrosanctum Conciliium*, was not singular or unusual, although its lingering impact may be more obvious (and audible) given the broad dissemination of her ideas through her music. Similar feelings were shared by many Catholics for whom the mysterious, sensory, transporting aspects of the traditional ritual had been what they sought in religion. Rituals, more generally, were among the most palpable manifestations of religion for the school-age Larsen.

> First through eighth grade, the rituals for how one walks in the halls, how we walked to the church, which was just across the parking lot from the school, how we filed into pews, the physical manifestations of genuflecting, or bowing of the head, in other words, it's what I've come to think of as medieval rituals of silence . . . they were the first and foremost and most consistent of the active ways in which religion really made itself known to all of us. That

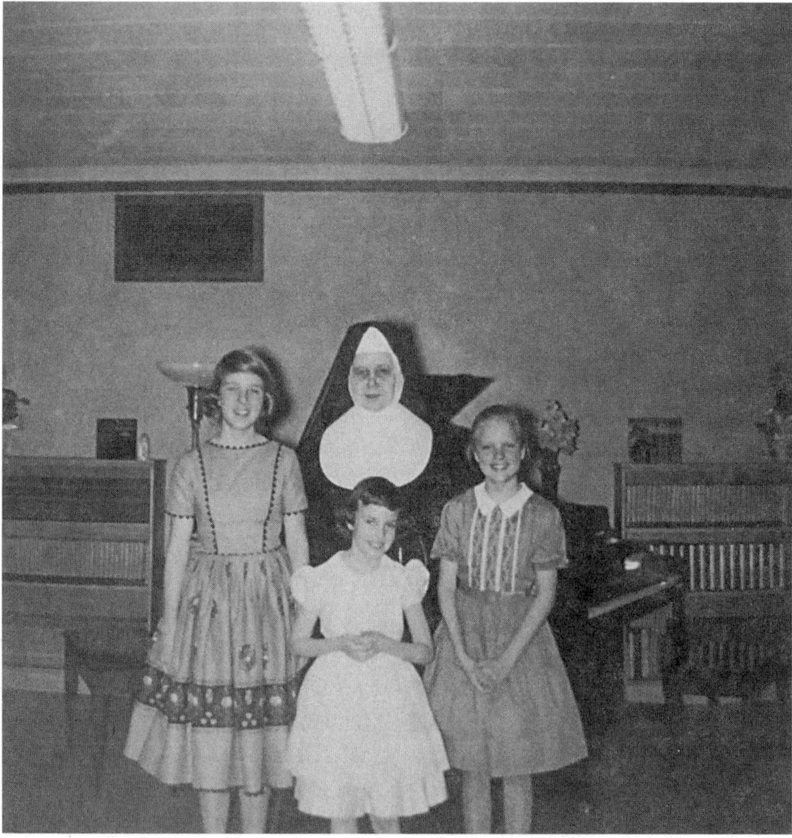

Figure 3.1. Libby Larsen with her sisters Luanne and Molly and Sister Colette at her first communion, April 1960. Reproduced with the kind permission of the composer.

we as a group [were] not to be individuals, but rather to be part of an ancient ritual. At least three or four times a week we would practice these things.[4]

For unbelievers in an increasingly secular society, it may be hard to fathom the sense of confusion and betrayal that visited so many Catholics worldwide upon the sudden disappearance of medieval practices that accompanied the conciliar reforms, but that makes the feelings no less real, or their loss no less traumatic for the faithful. In the intervening decades, post-conciliar scholarship has become a specialty all its own with practitioners from an array of disciplines including religious studies, cultural history, sociology, and institutional psychology exploring the effects of the 1960's council. Among the most recent studies in the field is one written by a musicologist. In Vincent E. Rone's 2014 dissertation on the response of the French Organ School to the radical changes implemented by Vatican II, he references theologian David Torevell's observations that "church leaders after the Council largely ignored the transcendent dimensions of the liturgy, which led to the loss of features like reverence, mystery, and awe."[5]

Rone observes that chant had been woven into the fabric of church ritual over millennia; it resisted identification with a particular place; it suggested timelessness. He quotes sacred-music scholar David Crouan, who argued that "[Gregorian chant] becomes an invaluable aid to fathoming and penetrating the meaning and import of the mystery being celebrated."[6] And Larsen was aware of the connection between music and chant and mystery: "I knew that it was associated with many rituals of the church, but I don't think I knew that it was religious though it did feel otherworldly. I felt that no matter what service we were singing in Gregorian chant, I was being touched by and also touching something much greater than the common daily rituals that we were performing."[7]

In effect, the *sound* of the church was one with its mystery, message, and identity. It was an aural marker of religion. The directives in *Sancrosanctum Conciliium* to modernize the liturgy, to make it more welcoming, friendly, and familiar to the congregants, in many ways to bring it down to earth, altered the fundamental sound of worship, an aspect of religious practice to which Larsen had been especially sensitive and attuned. She explains, "I realize in retrospect that I was really, really hurt musically, in every part of my body. The music that replaced it was bad, and I didn't have the capacity to understand what the church was trying to do."[8] At the same time that guitars replaced the organ and "contemporary" urban folk-style songs drowned out chant, the church lost its mystery, and it lost the adolescent Libby.

Larsen's crisis of faith occurred too early to interrupt a career, but it caused her to lose her belief in the religious institution itself, and that would affect her life's work. As she moved to the periphery of an ancient institution and system, she developed a basic suspicion of all systems. Along with many disillusioned Catholics, however, she remained deeply spiritual; she created her own "religion" rooted in her deep love of nature. In a July 2000 article "New Music for Organ at the End of the Twentieth Century," author Marilyn Perkins Biery illuminates Larsen's continuing religiosity when she describes the composer's creative ritual as beginning "by singing (to herself) the ancient hymn, *Veni Creator Spiritus*, in order to call forth creative inspiration from her muse."[9] Larsen has acknowledged that she continues to prepare the same way, although more often than not now she sings in her head rather than out loud.

Beyond the removal of ancient musical genres and sounds from congregational services, another change wrought by Vatican II had to do with the diminishment of the worship of the Blessed Virgin Mary; and this too struck Larsen personally.

> My understanding of Mary in the contemporary Catholic Church is that her job was to be an intercessor, . . . and I never really heard of her, or thought about her, or was directed to think about her in any other way. My relationship with her, especially as a young, pre-adolescent was complete devotion to that idea. That I could pray to her using my own prayers, and I could speak with her and she would be the intercessor to God, the patriarchal trio. I would envision this lovely woman gliding into a great hall, and there would be the trio, the Father, the Son, and the hovering Holy Spirit and they would never refuse her. She could glide right up to them.[10]

Although the sisters at Christ the King were ever present in Larsen's education, the women of the order of Saint Joseph wielded no significant power within the larger church institution. Within the school walls, posters of Jesus, Mary, and Joseph, and some of the saints hung in classrooms, and four-feet-tall plaster statues stood guard on every floor in the nooks and crannies of hallways. Larsen remembers their presence: "Always benignly watching us, always there, benevolent, but watching."[11] With the uppermost echelons of the Catholic Church hierarchy completely dominated by male figures—from priests to bishops to cardinals to pope, all the way up to Larsen's patriarchal trio—the Virgin Mary had occupied a unique and remarkable position. While not worshipped per se, the "Mother of God," the "Queen of Heaven," possessed rare powers as an intercessor. She was prayed to as a portal to God. She was a cherished icon in paintings and statuary, often portrayed cradling or alongside her son, Jesus, and this practice continues today. She was enshrined in sacred gardens, "Mary gardens," a reminder of medieval associations of Mary with flowers and herbs. She was celebrated in monthlong devotions in May and with outdoor festivals, which Larsen enjoyed as a young child in Minneapolis. The Magnificat and a whole genre of Marian antiphons were evidence of Mary's unique musical status within Catholicism.[12] Music and Mary were closely associated in church practice through chant, and both were profoundly meaningful to Larsen.

If Mary was not wholly removed by Vatican II reforms, she was effectively reassigned, some might say demoted. Simultaneously with budding second-wave feminism and the emergence of civil rights movements across the globe, which both threatened established power relationships within and outside the church, the church fathers reimagined Mary's role as smaller and less significant. Removing chanted Latin hymns removed Mary. Insisting upon a more direct and immediate, "immanent," relationship to God diminished the need for her intercessory powers. May devotions to the Blessed Virgin Mary fell out of practice during the 1970s and 1980s, and they have only recently begun to make a comeback. When believers objected to Mary's seeming disappearance, the church denied it was true or that they had any such intentions, but in 1965 Pope Paul VI asked that May devotions focus upon "special prayers for peace." Given the escalation of violent conflicts across the globe at the time, this was not an unwise use of the power of prayer, but it was not a substitute for setting aside and recognizing this single beloved female figure with a month devoted especially to her. The system that had taken away chant and ritual also seemingly took away Mary, and the teen-aged Libby, who had never formally studied Marianism, or icons, or why any of it was created, became increasingly distanced. She began to wonder, "Why do we need a Mary, or a Jesus? That," she has concluded, "was left to me to study for the rest of my life . . . and I study her to this day. I actually have quite an intimate relationship with Mary."[13] In 2010 Larsen would use a melody from a medieval mass, *In Festis Beatae Mariae Virginis* (Festival of the Blessed Virgin Mary), as the unifying idea of a quartet *Rodeo Queen of Heaven*, her own homage to a still-present and powerful Mary.

An awareness of systems—natural, religious, ideological, mechanical, economic, military, industrial, educational, philosophical, and social—became lodged in Larsen's consciousness early on and inheres in and inspires her thinking and music still. In July 2014, the composer herself reflected: "I've been thinking about my creative output and my lifelong interest in systems: natural (nature), transportation (of ideas, people, goods), religious, musical, mathematical, linguistic. I seem to have a deep seated desire to understand how systems interact with life and how life seems reliant on systems for its perception of being. And for some reason, I want to compose music about this."[14]

Larsen needs to understand her relationship within and to systems. As the previous chapter made clear, the Sisters of Saint Joseph of Carondolet at Christ the King School exerted enormous influence on the young child. For Larsen, the educational system there worked. The nuns gave Larsen the tools to think in music, and so to communicate; she learned the flexibility of "moveable do"; she embraced the measureless, undulating freedom of Gregorian chant, which opened her to the rhythmic and harmonic liberties of Bela Bartók and Japanese musics. But beyond quantifiable musical skills and eclectic tastes that Larsen would take with her into her composing career, the sisters of Christ the King gave her something more profound. In Larsen's words, "Their sense of loving, giving, openness, generosity, you know, this is what human beings do . . . I must have gotten it there. I think I owe them my life, actually."[15] And this was the nuns' mission; this was their religious calling: to model a practice of human interaction. They appear to have modeled Larsen's well-known generosity and openness, which she shares with something resembling religious zeal. She took that part of the church with her.

How has religion impacted Larsen's music? How does her music reveal the impact of religion in her life? Even the most cursory survey of forty years of compositions reveals broadly religious works present in every decade of her career. Their quantity and variety—over four dozen works across genres—support Larsen's observation that religion has been the most important theme in her life. Choral pieces, chamber pieces, vocal sets, works for organ, and special fanfares and anthems for Christian holy days and seasons express the majority of her religious musical thought most directly. But less specifically religious works are also inspired by a sense of spirituality that goes beyond Christianity or any single religious practice. Many of those pieces leave no clues to their religious or spiritual connections in their titles and focus more fully on nature. Perhaps her habit of beginning each new work by singing *Veni, Creator Spiritus* is most telling; perhaps all of Larsen's works have some roots in religion.

Not all of Larsen's religious pieces are *serious* testaments to faith; an irrepressible sense of humor emerges from time to time even in this category of works. A relatively early set of songs, *Saints without Tears*, composed in

1976, shows Larsen's willingness to stand back, assess, and gently needle the church; she has fun. But in 1975, just a year earlier, a number of local priests had refused to marry Larsen and her Catholic fiancé, James Reece, in the rose garden of the nearby park. They pointed out that it was not a sanctified space, and all attempts to change their minds failed. Various family members were traumatized by the idea of a nonchurch wedding, her mother especially.

Alice Brown Larsen's uncle, the Most Reverend James Duffy (1873–1968), had been born and reared in Saint Paul and served as a priest in various parishes in Minnesota before becoming rector at the cathedral parish in Cheyenne, Wyoming. In 1913 he was made bishop of the Diocese of Kearney (later the Diocese of Grand Island) in Nebraska and served in that position until 1931. Upon retiring, he assumed a titular bishopric and maintained that position until his death in 1968, which made him the senior bishop in the United States in age (he was ninety-four years old) and years of consecration (fifty-five years).[16] According to the composer, he was always spoken of with reverence. A hand-carved rosary that had belonged to him hung in the upstairs hallway of the Larsen's house, making the composer feel "as if [she] could never be [herself] upstairs; it too was always watching."[17] The church hierarchy was inescapable. Marrying somewhere other than in a sanctuary must have been inconceivable. The couple refused to be cowed by the church, however; the ceremony went ahead in the rose garden, and Jim and Libby were married by Unity ministers. The event would nonetheless be recalled by the composer as just another instance of the church imposing what seemed like senseless rules, of the church missing the point of what was most important. If one knows the personal context of the creation of *Saints without Tears*, it is easy to imagine that the cheeky attitude on display in the piece came naturally to Larsen at the time.[18]

Setting poems by the Pulitzer Prize–winning author Phyllis McGinley (1905–78) to music, Larsen focuses on the more human sides of five saints: Saint Anthony, who took on the devil and then headed to town to do the same with more-human types only to decide that he preferred wrestling with the former foe; the problematic Saint Bridget, whose pathological generosity "drove her family mad"; the "scandalous" Saint Francis of Assisi, who, much to Elias's chagrin, insisted upon the presence of singing at his deathbed; the all too familiar and cozy Saint Teresa, who was frustrated by God's lack of response; and the "holy man, hero, hermit, martyr, mystic, missioner, sage, and wit" Saint Thomas More, who managed to love God and his family equally despite his disagreement with Henry VIII and the church, which cost him his head. Saints Bridget and Thomas must have spoken directly to Larsen with their ever-present families watching and enduring the results of their loved ones' actions.

Pulling music out of text and matching mood to message, Larsen uses a decidedly untranscendent style for *Saints without Tears*. The ecumenism of her sources places Larsen in an American composers' tradition that includes Charles Ives and George Crumb, two composers who looked beyond expected repertoires and sounds for their basic materials. It is also at home with the "polystylism" of Alfred Schnittke, the Russian composer who popularized the term early in the 1970s.[19] Her innate lyricism and sensitivity to American English, qualities for which Larsen would be increasingly lauded as her career unfolded, are on display in every measure. A more detailed discussion of the set reveals the range of Larsen's imagination, the breadth of her frame of reference, and the sureness of her developing craft in 1976.

The work was originally written for soprano, flute, and bassoon, and the presence of the bassoon immediately signals the potential for humor. The instrument's long association with buffoonish characters prepares us to expect a laugh, and Larsen does not disappoint.[20] In the first song, "The Temptations of Saint Anthony," after an initial confidently sung high D-flat, the bassoon "wavers" and then tiptoes through a series of staccato eighths while the soprano sings "Off in the wilderness bare and level, Saint Anthony wrestled with the Devil." Listeners track the saint's escapades in a song where accents land like individual steps on each syllable of the opening lines. Alternations of calm and quivering passages in the bassoon and trilling flute convey nervousness. Perhaps the initial bravura masks an insecure saint; we can empathize with him (ex. 3.1).

The musical texture is open and transparent, reflecting Anthony's exposure to the elements. Larsen is sensitive to instrumental colors and gives them space to be heard. With the exception of a few passing moments of consonance, the song (like Anthony) lives in a dissonant world. The devil is present in plentiful melodic tritones in the vocalist's line and in clashing semitones when the three parts come together. The elastic rhythms of this song have nothing to do with the timeless transcendence of chant, even if Larsen learned them there. Instead she needs the freedom they provide to follow the tough-guy saint from wilderness to town and to suggest, perhaps, the absence of order in the devil's realm. Discarding traditional servitude to a single, all-powerful time signature allows Larsen to follow the words and have them create their own meter.[21] The lyricism of Larsen's vocal lines results from her honoring the unique lyricism of the language. She hears the music in language. With the first song clocking in at just under a minute, Larsen sets

Example 3.1. *Saints without Tears*, "The Temptations of Saint Anthony," mm. 1–10

the stage for a fast-paced, lively encounter with five saints and demonstrates her aptitude for the task.

In the second song, "The Giveaway," listeners hear the barely contained frustration of Saint Bridget's "near and dear" as they watch their generous child give away everything they own. Dry, staccato passages flying by at a vivace tempo sound like a ticking time bomb. The singer catalogs Bridget's gifts in an incessant recurring dotted pattern. Family jewels and food, and shoes and mattresses disappear to the accompaniment of flute flutters. It is easy to imagine Larsen tipping her composer's hat to eighteenth-century comic opera conventions; here is a new take on the famous catalog aria in Mozart's *Don Giovanni*, except in that case the list being enumerated was of sexual conquests and not of material goods. The bassoon alternates between a walking bass line and syncopated punctuations. There is a compulsive quality to the music. When Larsen moves from enumerating bestowed items to assessing Bridget's generosity and suggesting moral lessons, the music broadens and slows down; long legato lines supplant staccatos for the singer and instrumentalists alike, but this does not last. As the song nears its end, the singer asks who deserves our sympathy more, the generous saint or her long-suffering and materially bereft family; and the music returns to its opening nervous patter. It is a toss up, and Larsen will not decide for us.

With two fast songs completed, the conventions of musical structure require a temporal contrast. "Sonnet from Assisi," the third song (ex. 3.2), slows down the action, which suits a description of Saint Francis's death scene. Larsen engages more directly in word painting in this song than in the previous two. When we learn that the saint "had a heart for tune," the flute obliges with a brief, tripping melodic fragment; the line "with what remained of breath" is followed by the same instrument panting a brief series of repeated staccato notes, and then softly doubling the vocalist's downward exhalation.

The announcement of "scowling" Brother Elias's entrance signals an occasion for humor. Elias, also known as Elijah, "the loftiest and most wonderful prophet of the Old Testament" and a figure known for "his zeal for the law," comes across as a tedious martinet thanks to Larsen's musical personification.[22] An ostinato-like figure in the bassoon suggests his rigidity, perhaps Larsen's comment on the church. Once again, the bassoon does its job of characterization. By the end of the song, the instrument is reduced to a sustained (perhaps defeated?) low note as the flute recalls its original playful melodic fragment. Listeners hear Larsen's enjoyment of Elias's comeuppance as she sets McGinley's lines: "Elias gave him sermons and advice instead of song, which simply proves what things are sure this side of Paradise. Death, taxes, and the counsel of a bore. Though we out-wit the tithe, though we make death our friend, bores we have with us to the end." Elias, as the bassoon part, sticks to his note and fades away to the end, while Saint Francis, as the flute, sings and transcends his earthly life.

In the fourth song, "Conversation in Avila," Larsen paints Saint Teresa as a person decidedly of this earth. McGinley's text wastes no time explaining the

Example 3.2. *Saints without Tears*, "Sonnet from Assisi," mm. 101–10

saint's unique relationship with God: "Teresa was God's familiar / She often spoke to him informally / as if together they shared a heavenly joke." A lover of literature as well as of God and aware of her own physical attractiveness, the Spanish saint has been described as "beautiful, talented, outgoing, adaptable, affectionate, courageous, enthusiastic, she was totally human." Sounding more like a modern-day high school cheerleader than a sixteenth-century mystic, she nonetheless dared to insist upon the right to do her work "even in the man's world of her time." Because of that she "was misunderstood, misjudged, [and] opposed in her efforts at reform."[23] Larsen captures Teresa's achievements and attitude more than her struggles and serves up a quasi-sultry saint. This is clearly no Marian-inspired hymn. A "detached, walking bass" line for bassoon struts through the song.[24] The music sounds popular, not holy. We can hear Teresa's physicality as triplets push and pull apart beats and notes slide into place. Larsen instructs the singer to adopt a "blues-like" delivery and the instrumentalists to play their parts like a "dirty boogie." Over the wind instruments' final tremolos, Larsen writes "raspberries," and listeners hear the ultimate sonic snub. In the middle of this set of five songs, "Conversation in Avila" foregrounds popular-style musics, which along with ancient church music and eighteenth-century opera is another repertoire that Larsen knows intimately. And this one ties back to her family: Alice Larsen's favorite records inspired the soundtrack for this saint.[25]

The set ends with "Paterfamilias" (ex. 3.3), an homage to the beloved family man Sir and Saint Thomas More. McGinley enumerates Saint Thomas's sterling qualities, and Larsen provides a dependable rocking accompaniment underneath. The moderate 6/8 meter recalls the soothing rhythms of a barcarolle. In a "poco agitato" section toward the middle of the song, however, Larsen ribs those saints who are "alien and hard to love, wild as an eagle, strange as a dove, too near to heaven for the mind to scan" with loud music that shakes and fusses and chases itself in circles: the flute tremolos, and the bassoon gets caught in a scalar loop that the flute picks up.

Descriptions of Thomas, by contrast, are set to quiet, "tranquil," solid music, and in this setting the bassoon provides the foundation for his soothing sounds. Even Thomas, however, is not immune to Larsen's wit. When his abilities to pun in Latin are extolled, Larsen has flute and bassoon sing the "Dies Irae"; the "Day of Wrath" dances in flute and bassoon unisons. It will be the church that brings about Thomas's demise.

If the church was a volatile institution, capricious in its application of rules, Thomas More, "this family man," found peace in the comforting sounds of his children's names. Four references to Margaret, Elizabeth, Cecily, and John return unaltered each time. They are a source of stability. One wonders whether Larsen (whose given name is Elizabeth) heard herself being referenced. As one of five children who had always lived close by multiple generations of relatives, and who had just married the year before thus creating her own family, Larsen likely appreciated the rich personal associations a contemplation of Sir Thomas More as family man conjured.

Saints without Tears offers a glimpse into Larsen's musical thinking early in her composing career; she is still a graduate student honing her craft. It also

Example 3.3. *Saints without Tears*, "Paterfamilias," mm. 197–204

provides a perspective on her stance vis-à-vis religion. Religious personnel provide the subject matter of Larsen's music, yet despite her Catholic-school upbringing, she is comfortable employing McGinley's humorously irreverent characterizations of the saints and matching them with equally irreverent music. She is not daunted or constrained by their lofty positions in the church hierarchy, and we hear that in rhythms that are free and elastic and a harmonic language that embraces tonality, chromaticism, and high degrees of dissonance. Having a bishop in the family might actually have given Larsen a more eye-level perspective on the saints.

Her sympathy for American English is palpable and as evident as her joy in the nation's vernacular musics; she understands both languages. Popular musics—the blues and boogie-woogie in particular—are an important source of reference in this set as they would be in *Four on the Floor* (1983) and a variety of later works. Awareness of Western musical traditions, whether of instrument associations or signature motives, such as the "Dies Irae," deepens the meaning of the set for those in her audience who recognize the references. The ancient sequence from the requiem mass has been quoted over the centuries by composers as varied as Haydn and Liszt, Crumb and Rachmaninoff, Sondheim and Shostakovich, and dozens of others, but perhaps among the most famous uses is in Berlioz's *Symphony Fantastique*; and in places he too sets it quasi-humorously. By employing "Dies Irae" in her song, Larsen stakes a claim for herself in a long tradition of art music composers.

Having had the mystery stripped from the liturgy when she was still young, Larsen goes one better and exposes the mundane qualities of the saints' lives. As she will do many times throughout her career, Larsen goes to a female writer for her text. Speaking from a woman's perspective and listening to a female voice are important to Larsen. But women saints receive no special treatment in this set; they are subject to equal amounts of affectionate ribbing. As happens often in her works, Larsen's humor accompanies a more serious idea. While she emphasizes the humanness of these holy people, she simultaneously suggests the holiness of mere mortals. Bringing saints (down) to our level, she opens up the possibility of our own transcendence.

Over her career Larsen has set both Catholic and Lutheran editions of a *Celebration Mass*, created multiple choral arrangements and adaptations of psalm settings, and written religious-themed music using Gospel verses and a variety of nonbiblical texts. But she has not confined her religious works to those containing a texted message. Excited by a uniquely American rhetorical form, in 1997 she captured the cadences of a revival preacher in *Holy Roller*, a sermon in sound for solo alto saxophone and piano.[26] Larsen explains: "*Holy*

Roller is inspired by classic revival preaching. To me, revival sermons are stunning musical masterpieces of rhythm, tempo, and extraordinary tension and release. The music flows directly from the language, cajoling, incanting and repeating, at the same time magnetizing and mesmerizing the listener with its irresistible invocations. The music is the language, the language is the music and the result moves the spirit to other states of being."[27]

With its first sounds, the solo sax announces something secular, and the blue notes that inflect the opening ten seconds reinforce that reading. Over the course of the homily, however, Larsen weaves both secular and sacred melodic threads. A fragment of "When the Saints" sounds briefly before it cedes to the first phrase of Robert Lowry's hymn tune "Shall We Gather at the River." Three minutes later Larsen introduces "God, Be with You 'til We Meet Again." Listeners eventually get to hear this entire hymn. The gradual construction of the whole tune recalls Ives's practice of cumulative forms.[28] She creates a millennial Ivesian tapestry.[29] Within seconds the two sacred tunes trade off phrases and egg each other on. We can almost hear the back-and-forth swoons and "Amens" of the assembled. Fire and brimstone boil over in a musical oration that is dissonant and intense. A boogie beat dials up the excitement. As the piece nears its end, "Saints" returns, and the three tunes spin; the "preacher" rises to a fever pitch of religious ecstasy, and all those gathered are lifted off their feet.

Here is religious transcendence, compliments of a different kind of music: no Latin, no voices, no chanting, no organ, just pure sound, but transporting nonetheless. The heightened state induced by *Holy Roller* demonstrates that the rapturous condition Larsen had identified initially with chant can be conjured in other musics as well, and she does not hesitate to show how.

In 1982 Larsen collaborated with fellow Minnesotan, writer Patricia Hampl, to create a work titled *In a Winter Garden*. The forty-minute quasi oratorio, subtitled *Advent Meditations and Carols*, was written for a mezzo-soprano who sings the role of "Sister" (abbess of a convent), a tenor who sings the role of "Thomas" (longtime gardener at the convent), a soprano soloist and SATB chorus who together sing the role of "The Garden," and a chamber orchestra that includes percussion instruments especially suited to creating otherworldly effects: orchestra bells to be struck with a variety of mallets, tom-toms, a triangle, a small bell of indefinite pitch, glass wind chimes, clusters of small bells, claves, and "a sustaining shimmering instrument of varying, indefinite pitches."[30] Where the bassoon led listeners to expect something humorous in *Saints without Tears*, and the saxophone projected the careening speech melodies of a revivalist preacher in *Holy Roller*, high-pitched and tinkling sounds in *Winter Garden* suggest the crystalline quality of snow and the magical atmosphere of an icy white, blanketed world. The piece gave Larsen and Hampl, both products of Catholic religious upbringings and Twin Cities' weather, the opportunity to explore a number of ideas that were important to them: the struggles associated with faith; the impact of long, deep, snowy winters; the idea of endings; the significance of gardens; and the meaning of memory and wonder. Larsen brought her personal observations of the sisters at Christ the King struggling with their faith to the piece.[31] And Hampl brought her own upbringing as a Catholic girl. She explains: "It was natural for me to set that text in Catholic terms. For me, being born Catholic was as decisive as being born American."[32] Neither was a stretch. Larsen has elaborated how the collaborators chose their topic: "Shortly, our discussion led to Advent and the medieval practice of Advent as the season in which to contemplate the end of the world. We agreed that the subject was both timely and elegant. More importantly, it suggested words and music to our collective creative sense. Our work together had produced a surprising new third voice—one which neither Patricia nor I could claim singly."[33]

Larsen's reference to the timeliness of the subject speaks to her awareness of the threat of nuclear holocaust that had increased again in the early eighties after having lessened during the previous decade. George Orwell's dystopian novel *Nineteen Eighty-Four*, written in 1949, was in the backs of many people's minds at the time, and not just because of its title. In a statement that appeared in the *Bulletin of the Atomic Scientists*, the tenuousness of the world situation was laid out: "Three minutes to midnight: In January 1984, the Doomsday Clock's hand creeps close to midnight as the two superpowers stop talking. After a decade of relative arms stability, the Cold War reached new heights between 1980 and 1983 as the Soviet Union invaded Afghanistan, the United States pulled out of the Moscow Olympics and communication between the two superpowers all but ceased. *The Bulletin* took these as ominous signs and advanced the Doomsday Clock hand as close to midnight as it had stood since the arms race began in 1949."[34]

A set of Advent mediations and carols "to contemplate the end of the world" was no hysterical reaction on the part of a pair of imaginative women in the Midwest, not when the possibility was palpable. Hampl would be impressed by Larsen's pragmatism when it came to writing a work whose message was timeless rather than dated, even if it was inspired by real, current events. But Hampl acknowledges her awareness of the historical moment in her own notes to the piece.

> The story—or circumstances—of the piece is simply told: A contemplative nun who is troubled and unable to pray seeks to resolve her spiritual dilemma as Christmas approaches. She is unable to concentrate because of her terror over "the end of the world." It is an ancient terror . . . but it carries a contemporary alarm. Like many of us, Sister is unhinged by the threat of nuclear war ("Don't we all think of it lately?" she says). Thomas, the convent gardener, goes about his work—the tasks of decoration and celebration—and provides her, as the season itself finally does, with the courage she needs to be joyous even in the midst of her recognition of peril.[35]

Hampl's father was a florist, so she understood flowers and gardens and their power to heal; growing up in a part of the country where very little blooms for much of the year, she also appreciated their real and symbolic value. In an interview with Diane Rehm, Hampl confessed that having all the flowers around "was magical especially in Minnesota."[36] Hampl's memory of flowers excited her imagination. Working with the composer, Hampl explains, "I found myself subtly but definitely nudged and propelled into language and rhythms I might not have found on my own."[37] *In a Winter Garden* is the product of a collaboration of sensitive artists, sympathetic souls, and shared experiences. Beyond the partnership with Hampl, the work grows out of Larsen's schooling by the Sisters at Christ the King, her fractured relationship with the church, the challenging natural environment where she lives, her regard and appreciation for gardens, and ultimately her inextinguishable hopefulness.

The piece comprises a series of four alternating meditations and carols: soloists reflect and the chorus comments. Larsen lays out Sister's world in the opening moments of the first meditation, "The Evergreens" (ex. 3.4). Listeners hear the snow-shrouded garden in a soft, still soundscape. The music seems stuck in place, or perhaps it is momentarily frozen under the snowpack. Larsen provides time and space to listen to and around the sounds and luxuriate in their timbres; this is a moment for going deep. There is also time and space to think about everything listeners are hearing. The essential intervals, motives, and gestures that hold the work together are all present in the first seconds of the piece. Although listeners may be unaware, the sparse musical atmosphere is a metaphor for what the abbess needs to learn to recover her faith: although easily overlooked, everything is there in front of her.

Over the course of the work, Abbess and listeners become increasingly aware of the importance of details. Impending apocalypse heightens the value of even the simplest things. Immediately following Sister's initial, unaccompanied, "pensive" observation that the snow seems never to stop, a repeating

Example 3.4. *In a Winter Garden*, "The Evergreens," mm. 1–12

Example 3.4. *(continued)*

major-second dyad sounds; the tense interval returns throughout the piece and keeps the emotional strain of the particular times present in listeners' ears and minds. It opens and closes the first meditation, recurs throughout the intervening movements, and returns a final time to introduce the last mediation, "Christmas Rose."

A second detail of the opening meditation is the five-note flash of sound in measure 4. Like sunlight glinting off an ice crystal, there is something dazzling about the ascending gesture. The figure sounds three times before Sister makes it her own in a "dramatically" augmented iteration where she confesses, "I miss the flowers."[38] Like the recurring dyad, this motive returns throughout the work, sometimes literally, sometimes transposed, other times expanded to form part of a larger statement as is the case in the opening of the final carol, the "Christmas Rose Carol" (ex. 3.5). The chamber orchestra plays the ascending flashing figure, while the dyad is grounded in the Garden Chorus.

What had been a mere streak of sound at the beginning and a recurring motive throughout the oratorio becomes the essential melodic material for the final carol. It accompanies Hampl's lines "Here is the rose of the season" and "Now is the time we blossom with faith." The omnipresent snow that had silenced the "gorgeous, loud colors" of the flowers and caused Sister to "drift" from faith "like snow" now produces the "Christmas Rose."[39] All the evergreens and bright flowers that Thomas had brought to her attention couldn't accomplish what this small, single blossom achieves. Its whiteness allows Sister to see the snow differently and to find her faith still alive in her "frozen," "mute" world. In the flower's simplicity she feels "touched with peace and grace."[40] While the threat of nuclear holocaust had not lessened when *In a Winter Garden* premiered in 1982, Larsen's music and Hampl's text insist that attending to the smallest details of life is one path out of despair, and possibly even a step toward hope.

In a Winter Garden exemplifies the dilemma inherent in thinking about Libby Larsen's life as amenable to thematic boundaries, useful as they are to organizing a biography. Although I consider this piece in a chapter on religion, it provides insights into Larsen's ideas about nature, place, gender, and musical aesthetics as well. Larsen's works seamlessly interweave a lifetime of influences and interests; every composition has multiple resonances. In this way her music and her life are one: just as her life resists compartmentalization, so too does her music.

A majority of Larsen's pieces could be studied for what they say about an array of musical styles. Here, too, boundaries serve little purpose, except, per-

Example 3.5. *In a Winter Garden*, "Christmas Rose Carol," mm. 585–98.

haps, to show their easy breach. *In a Winter Garden* owes equal debts to early Baroque opera and Broadway. Supple, through-composed vocal lines, sensitive to the rhythms and melodies of the words themselves, recall Monteverdi's *L'incoronazione di Poppea*, while Thomas's delivery style in the "Frozen Fountain Meditation" and the modified strophic form of "Hot House Carol" sound like

Example 3.5. *(continued)*

Sondheim has sneaked on stage. Debussy makes a cameo appearance in the "Frozen Fountain Carol" when Larsen transposes and modifies the opening gesture of his piano prelude "La fille aux cheveux de lin." Faint pre-echoes of her own *Symphony: Water Music*, published in 1984, appear in the third meditation, "Hot House: Meditation." The symphonic homage to Handel and Lake Harriet will become Larsen's "coming out" symphony and show her at home

Example 3.5. *(continued)*

in the preeminent instrumental genre. Where purists might be confused or disdainful of her stylistic polyglotism, her aesthetic is thoroughly American and an honest manifestation of her musical appetites and facility. Just as Larsen would not allow herself to be limited by the church's notion of what is acceptable liturgical practice or sanctified space, she won't be restricted to speaking a single tongue, not when she is fluent in many and enjoys them all.

Missa Gaia: Mass for the Earth (1991–92) is another example of a piece that refuses confinement by category or musical style. Texts from Wendell Berry, M. K. Dean, Gerard Manley Hopkins, Maurice Kenny, Meister Eckhart, the Bible, the Chinook Psalter, and Joy Harjo guarantee its cross-cultural approach. Its performing forces include SATB chorus, string quartet, solo oboe, four-hand piano, and, once again, a large and eclectic percussion section: bass drums, maracas, marimba, orchestra bells, suspended cymbal, temple blocks, triangle, tubular bells, vibraphone, and woodblock.

In this case, the array of percussion instruments allows Larsen to evoke the variety of cultures from which her authors come. I discussed this work at length in a previous study that focused on Larsen's nature-related works,[41] and it is comfortably at home in that framework. But given Larsen's intention that it be "a *mass* for our times," a modern treatment of the "source and summit of the Christian life," "the sum and summary of [the] faith," *Missa Gaia* merits a second look in a chapter devoted to religion, and especially at a moment when the connections between religion and the natural world have recently been reinforced by none other than the head of the Catholic Church, Pope Francis.[42]

In August 2014, the pope, who took his name from Saint Francis of Assisi, patron saint of animals and the environment, prepared an encyclical addressing what he called "environmental exploitation, the sin of our time." Theologian and ethicist Christiana Peppard explains the resonances of Francis's undertaking:

> For a Pope to say that deforestation and ecological destruction are the sins of our times is really throwing down a gauntlet. It prompts Christians, especially in the U.S., to think about how we understand sin and how we understand responsibility. So much of Western moral tradition, whether theological or philosophical, has really been based upon a very individualistic paradigm wherein I commit some kind of action, usually intentionally, and it's seen as wrong or sinful. . . . What's really interesting about applying the language of sin to environmental destruction is that there is not necessarily one person who is the sole cause of things. Causality is much more complex. It has to do with patterns of global economy, of governance, of incentive, of poverty, of the need for arable land and subsistence. And how we think about sin in that context is complicated, and I appreciate that he's trying to complicate the picture.[43]

As Larsen had brought her deep knowledge of upper Midwest winters to *In a Winter Garden*, the leader of 1.2 billion Roman Catholics brought his personal experiences with deforestation in his native Argentina to bear on his papal priorities. Watching the results of irresponsible mining or lumbering practices that rendered local communities impoverished and without access to basic resources, most especially fresh water, energized the pope's passion for this environmental and moral issue. By portraying the earth as God's creation, one that is, as Peppard characterizes the pope's statement, "good in and of itself [and] not here merely for human use or for economic gain," Pope Francis casts degradation of the earth as "not just a sin against fellow humans, but also perhaps a sin against God, and the integrity of the created order."[44] Given the impact Christianity had on scientific thought and its articulation throughout the eighteenth century, and the role Christian doctrine had in establishing a context for the belief that humanity had dominion over the earth and hence carte blanche to use it for its purposes, Pope Francis's encyclical represents a startling rereading of long-held beliefs and behaviors.[45]

Behind the pope's 2014 encyclical is his belief in the moral and spiritual bond that we have with the earth and one another. The same belief inspired Larsen's *Missa Gaia* in 1991. The idea of connection to each and all is basic to the structure of the piece where it comes to life in musical and poetic circles. Larsen discusses the importance of that image in her program notes to the score: "The theme of circles permeates the entire work from the texts to the music, which uses the circle of fifths both as a melodic theme and as an instrumental motive. Although I have not asked the oboe to do so in this work, the oboist is one of the few instrumentalists who can breathe circularly. The string quartet traditionally sits in a semi-circle."[46]

The basis of Larsen's musical system and structure in *Missa Gaia* is the *natural* overtone series; it embodies the larger philosophical system at work in the piece, one that honors nature's cycles.[47] The circles of individual movements occur within the circle of the larger piece. The circle of fifths, source for the melodic material that opens Berry's Introit, and present throughout the entire *Mass*, also closes Harjo's Benediction. Berry's poem "Within the Circles of Our Lives" lays out the concentricity of our existence: our lives take place within years, within seasons, within lunar cycles, until we return to the earth. Everything comes from and returns to the earth. Circles also symbolize Larsen's understanding of the symbiotic relationships of the spiritual and the natural, of which humanity is a part. Her embrace of diverse poetic sources reflects Berry's idea of humanity "joining each to all again."[48] But despite these references to harmonious affinities, Larsen's *Mass* depends upon the coexistence of differences to make and support its point. She explains:

> The *Missa Gaia: Mass for the Earth* is a mass for our times which adopts the form and spirit of the traditional Mass and replaces the texts with words addressing human beings' relationship to the Earth. *Missa Gaia* is a celebration of those of us who live on this land, a land which can be terribly beautiful and gentle, a land which can be harsh—but which is always giving and always renewing. The texts are drawn from the Bible, from Native American poets, Joy Harjo and Maurice Kenny, from medieval mystic Meister Eckhart, from the Chinook Psalter and from poets Wendell Berry and Gerard Manley Hopkins.[49]

Larsen's *Mass* divides itself according to the traditional parts of the form: Introit, Kyrie, Gloria, Credo, Agnus Dei/Sanctus, Benediction, but the similarity of her mass and more traditional ones stops there. Within the architecture of the mass, no single religious practice is privileged, even though a mass is a Christian ritual. Texts come from Christians—a Baptist Sunday School teacher and an Anglican convert—as well as a medieval German mystic and Native American animists, and all express their belief in interrelatedness, wholeness, and a unifying power. There is no religious hierarchy inherent in the work. Larsen shed any allegiance to them when she left Christ the King. The many unison passages demonstrate her belief in a shared endeavor, the unity in our diversities. Throughout the work, texts are free from dense contrapuntal textures that hide or confuse their message. The range of vocal writing keeps the piece accessible and available to more different types of performers than virtuosically demanding works. The most difficult challenge is singing the widely disjunct melodic lines produced by the circle of fifths. *Missa Gaia* argues for the presence of a divine force across time, place, tradition, gender, and culture. No one enjoys a privileged position. *Missa Gaia* also reflects essential tenets of Larsen's spiritual beliefs: humankind and the natural world are one and the same; we are directly connected to each other; and the divine, however imagined, is omnipresent and available to all.

Having left the church more than fifty years earlier, Larsen is as intensely engaged with spiritual questions as ever: She continues to explore the roles that religion has played over time and in contemporary society. And like her first religious works, these newest ones resist simple categorization; their multivalence argues for the continuing integration of all aspects of her life. Larsen ponders what purpose religion served in the past: "why did we need it?"[50]

This chapter closes with a discussion of a piece that focuses on the *first* Mary, the object of Libby's devotion as a child: the Virgin Mary; Mary, the mother of God; Mary, the Queen of Heaven: in this case she is the *Rodeo Queen of Heaven*. The unusually named piece is actually taken from an artwork, a santo, that Larsen saw in a museum.[51] She describes the encounter in the program notes to the score:

> Wandering through the Denver Art Museum . . . I happened upon an exhibit of contemporary Western Art. Amidst paintings of vast June skies, western grass pastures, ranches dwarfed in their landscapes, cowboys and any number of familiar icons of the American West was a glass vitrine which housed a hand-carved wooden, hand-painted Santo, 26½ by 9½ by 8½ inches. The image was a Madonna and Child dressed in Rodeo garb. I walked by at first. Then I walked by again. After my fifth pass I stopped, utterly arrested by the work Rodeo Reina del Cielo "Rodeo Queen of Heaven," by Arthur Lopez.[52]

In an interview Larsen expanded on that moment and its greater resonance:

> There she was, sort of off in a corner by herself, tucked in a little corner, beautifully lit, but not brazenly lit, and I just kept going back, and back, and just studying, studying her, but not thinking about it, studying her *emotionally*. I kept *feeling* as I stood there, and still and all, at that point in time, I was not thinking about making music. I was just doing what I do in art museums, which is just to study the objects. But very quickly [when it came time to writing a commission for the group enhakē] I thought this is what I have to write. There seemed to be a truth there that is *real* and *sacred* at the same time, which sounds like a dichotomy, but I don't think it is. We perceive that being real doesn't mean being sacred in our culture. To bring the mystical and the holy to the daily life, perhaps that's the influence of the nuns who do it, the nuns who struggle and strive to live and lead a sacred, domestic life.[53]

It is easy to imagine the appeal of this particular santo to Libby Larsen. The art form would have been familiar, given her having been surrounded by iconic saintly statues at Christ the King. But this Mary would never have appeared in Larsen's Minneapolis school hallway. This Mary was from another place and culture. Hardly timeless like the chant that Rone argues defied a point of origin, this Queen was obviously the product of contemporary American culture and the American Southwest more specifically; and she broke other rules as well. Lopez's Queen of Heaven is dressed in a matching embroidered vest and skirt; she has a holster slung sideways, low on her hips. The pearl handle of her revolver is visible. With a tiny waist and a clear bustline, Mary's clothes don't hide her female form; no neutering robes for this Queen. A leather-gloved hand supports a miniaturized mature Jesus in the crook of Mary's arm, and he's dressed like a junior rodeo star with chaps and the obligatory cowboy hat. Both mother and son have lariat halos, and each holds a scepter with cross. As Larsen explains: "There's no gliding about for this Mary."[54] Indeed Mary's feet are firmly planted in her needle-worked, Marian-blue cow*girl* boots in the wooden base. The santo is simultaneously outrageous and reverent and would catch the eye of any visitor, not least of all a woman who had been devoted to the statue's namesake. There's a jarring visual counterpoint between the serenity apparent in Mary's eyes, and the Jane Russell–like soft brunette curls that touch her shoulders, and the getup she wears. Whose Mary is this? Larsen makes Lopez's cowgirl queen her own.

Among the chants Libby recalls singing many times during her elementary school years were those from the *Mass of the Blessed Virgin Mary* (*In Festis Beatae Mariae Virginis*). Like the hymn tunes that were lodged in Ives's aural memory, and which he mined throughout his career to ground and structure his pieces, chant melodies are a similarly familiar repertoire for Larsen. Like the "Dies Irae" that she used in "Paterfamilias" from *Saints without Tears*, they bring with them personal, religious, and cultural significance.

When Larsen accepted a commission to write a work for enhakē,[55] a young, technically fearless, multiethnic quartet making its Carnegie Hall debut in 2010, the image of Lopez's santo and the echo of sacred chants from *Beatae Mariae Virginis* came together and inspired her own *Rodeo Queen of Heaven*. Larsen captured the seemingly incongruous visual counterpoint of Lopez's artwork in a musical mash-up that weaves chant with fiddling, jazz, and, of course, boogie. As in *Saints without Tears*, or *Holy Roller*, or in the various poetic sources of *Missa Gaia*, there is no contradiction in the pairing of the sacred and the profane: the mystical and the mundane share equal parts holiness. References to a few specific moments in the *Rodeo Queen of Heaven* point to the continuing impact of religion on Larsen's music and life.

Like a rodeo bull rider sprung from his holding pen for a seconds-long ride, Larsen's players "Explode!" into our presence (ex. 3.6); this is intensely physical music. At measure 5, strings join in the piano's gallop, and at measure 6, a scooping jazzy figure in the violin evokes the sounds of a whinnying horse. Larsen's call for "intense fiddle, non vibrato" sets the scene. We're not in a typical "sanctified space," and Mary is definitely not gliding.

Yet in the very next measure the clarinet introduces the first fragment of a chant melody. Larsen draws upon music from her childhood and weaves

Example 3.6. *Rodeo Queen of Heaven*, mm. 1–8

Example 3.6. *(continued)*

bits of a twelfth-century Gregorian mass, the *Mass of the Blessed Virgin Mary*, into her religious chamber work. As she explains: "I set about to create a raucous, fluid musical Santo—a partner to Arthur Lopez's work."[56] The strings follow and offer their own fragmented statements of the plainsong, but the piano continues its galloping pace. If, in the past, the church had determined what was sacred and what was secular, what was a sanctified space and what wasn't, Larsen's music, like Lopez's santo, challenges its authority and blurs that boundary. There is no hierarchy of musics in Larsen's spiritual world. Rather than insist upon an exclusive domain for the church's message, Mary comes to the rodeo, and chant joins other musics where they are. Always the intercessor, Mary invites viewers and listeners to find their way to God by bringing God to them. Lopez and Larsen do similar things with their artworks.

Over the course of the ten-minute piece, Larsen returns to chant multiple times, just as she returned to the santo during her museum visit. She indicates which sections of the mass she draws from with bracketed references to the Gloria, the Sanctus, and the Agnus Dei. There is a single extended contemplative moment about two minutes into the work where chant is foregrounded. It is a welcome break in a piece that is more about motion and activity than about stillness. Larsen describes the B section as "Slowly, suspended." This is a "free chant," and everyone is instructed to "push and pull each phrase" (ex. 3.7).[57] Although the composer provides meters and bar lines, the ten-measure interlude between faster and louder passages, which includes no fewer than nine meter changes, is not bound by temporal rules other than the rhythms of the flowing chant melody.

Listeners hear chant from different perspectives as it is delivered with Baroque bowing and then pushed by "power drone" perfect fifths; it sings accompanied by jazzy pizzicatos, evokes the blues or fiddling, and struts with walking and boogie bass lines. As Larsen has proven on multiple occasions, she is at home with all these styles; she understands their distinctive characteristics so well that the briefest gesture conveys their sound and significance (ex. 3.8).

In *Missa Gaia* unison choral passages had conveyed Larsen's belief in the communal bonds that tie all humanity and earth in a seamless circle. In *Rodeo Queen of Heaven*, unison chant passages recall the rituals that Libby remembers being taught where the goal of practicing how to sit, walk, enter a church pew, and genuflect was to make one an indistinguishable part of a community, to lose oneself among the company of believers participating in a timeless tradition. Chant in *Rodeo Queen of Heaven* offers flashes

Example 3.7. *Rodeo Queen of Heaven*, mm. 47–56

Example 3.7. *(continued)*

Example 3.8. *Rodeo Queen of Heaven*, mm. 60–63

Example 3.8. *(continued)*

of transcendent possibilities, as well as opportunities to lose the self in a community of believers.

But Larsen does not forget the site of this particular Marian tribute. As the piece originally exploded into our consciousness, it leaves the same way. We are at a rodeo, after all. With instructions to "Go! Go!" and to play "raucous to the end" Larsen's players gallop out of our hearing, and one can almost imagine Mary in the stands whooping and hollering them on.[58]

4 Larsen and Nature

Tutoring the Soul

I FIRST CAME TO LIBBY LARSEN'S MUSIC through her nature-related compositions. I was struck by the number of works whose titles claimed a connection to water in all its forms, the seasons, the earth, the atmosphere, gardens, animals, light, the upper Midwest and its particular cold climes, or that revealed a broad awareness of her place within a larger ecological endeavor. She was a perfect subject for a book that explored women's responses to "nature" in musical composition. For that earlier project I wrote on her *Symphony: Water Music*, *Missa Gaia*, and *Downwind of Roses in Maine*. Over the years I uncovered still more pieces whose references to nature were not obvious in their titles but whose affinities were no less real. Nature-inspired pieces, like religious ones, are present in every decade of Larsen's composing career, and I discovered that it is often impossible to separate the two.

Larsen's engagement with nature was and is wide ranging and deeply personal. Conversations with the composer over a seven-year period have reinforced that reading: Larsen has always been aware of the natural world and valued it above everything else. It speaks to her senses and her soul. It allows for infinite possibilities of thought and structure. It has no boundaries. Nature invites and reinforces Larsen's all-encompassing approach to life.

The composer has reflected on the connections she understands to exist between her music, nature, and religion:

> You could say that nature equals religion. If the grace of religion is to inspire reflection on being, then that's music. Music is reflection on being, which is in all of my pieces, whatever the piece is. Why else do we need to contemplate ourselves in a system of worship? There are a lot of reasons, but isn't the greatest reason of all to understand and become comfortable with the fact that we are. I would say that nature is religion, which means that all music is sacred; at least I approach all music as being sacred. . . . [Hence], *Veni Creator Spiritus.*[1]

Larsen's attunement to nature became obvious when she was young. The distant thud of horses' hooves and their movement through space are among her earliest memories. This makes Larsen's awareness of her environment as old as her conscious being, and like her cherished memories of religious practices, it is closely aligned with sound. Her sensitivity to sound valorized both nature and religion. She heard her world. The young child's need to be listened to within her family becomes more understandable: being heard conferred meaning. Larsen explains her simple desire for consanguinity with nature: "I don't want to look at it, or comment on it, I want to *be* it. Yes, I want to *be* it. I want to *be* the wind, *be* the heat, *be* the fragrance, *be* the wheat, *be* the snow, . . . which is impossible, it's all impossible, physically."[2]

When I asked the composer how she might visualize her ideal relationship to nature, she recalled a line drawing that she'd bought years ago from a young Chinese artist who had recently immigrated to the United States. As Larsen described it: there was a large chasm with a river at its base, "and she drew herself into the rocks. She's *in* there, and it's just beautiful. And that's what I want to be. I want to be it."[3]

It is no coincidence that Larsen named "nature" second only to religion among the most important forces in her life; not only was it imprinted in her aural memory, but it was also, quite literally, to nature that Libby repaired when she left the church. Nature and religion are inseparable in her thinking. Scalded by Vatican II reforms and unwilling to endure the removal of all divine mystery, Larsen began a new Sunday-morning ritual around age twelve. She would ride her bike to the nearby park, climb a favorite gingko tree, and sit in one of its crooks to reflect and commune; there she found the transcendence she craved.[4] Rejecting the institution that Libby felt had rejected her and impatient with limited opportunities for women within the church's fold, she escaped to what she saw as an ungendered, unhierarchical place: nature.[5] Male, female, young, old, nonhuman others, and inanimate objects are coequals and mutually dependent inside nature. If the church had no roles for women as musicians, leaders, or partners in its archaic and calcified systems and practices, nature, always refreshing itself in cycles of birth and death, did. High inside the gingko tree, Libby had an aerial view of an always-renewed world. She was part of a more important endeavor than anything imagined by an institution, and one that was not of human design. Nature became her church and her sanctuary. It is no surprise that years later she would want to be married in this sanctified space.

Like Christ the King, nature provided Libby with a variety of classrooms and teachers, but none of them demanded that she be quiet or still. Nature didn't insist on silence or invisibility. In nature Larsen could move about freely, make noise, join in the constant chorus, interact as she needed, and expand and refine her composer's skills, listening chief among them. Here sounds were even more flexible and free than chant: untuned, untempered, unbeholden to aesthetic rules and taste preferences. Here was a counterpoint that was unfettered by sixteenth-century Council of Trent guidelines to keep intervals perfect or texts uncomplicated. And while the architecture of a cathedral could create magnificent sonic effects, so too could open spaces where nature's musics wafted and comingled in the atmosphere with sights and smells. Larsen's contagious energy joined the energies around her in the outdoors. She could be with the wind, rain, and snow and become one with their rhythms and silences. Without plan or intention, the sensations, sounds, and systems that Larsen absorbed outdoors provided a library of materials and ideas from which she would draw for the rest of her life. Nature's democratic soundscape became a model for Larsen's own unhierarchical music. That so many of her nature-related pieces reference the upper Midwest and its particular environment demonstrates the power of her experiences within that place. Her nature pieces are personal. The nature of the upper Midwest anchors Larsen as much as her midcentury birth. She is centered by place and time.

From a young age Larsen enjoyed running and riding her bike, and the many parks in Minneapolis provided miles of winding pathways to do both. She swam in the lakes near her home, and she sailed and skied. Water in all its forms was a constant in her life and her thinking, and it inspired some of her earliest nature-related works. It became the focus of her first symphony, a commission from the Minnesota Symphony Orchestra when she was composer in residence there. The four movements of *Symphony: Water Music*, "Fresh Breeze," "Hot, Still," "Wafting," and "Gale," gave musical expression to her thorough knowledge of lake environments.[6] "Fresh Breeze" musicalized her desire to "refresh the symphony form."[7] The composer has explained her affinity for water, which unsurprisingly focuses on its sounds: "I often keep myself company with the sounds of water—the deep boom of ice as you walk across a frozen lake, the lapping of water on shore in both cold and warm water (they are different), the crunch of snow, the whoosh of a wave when it hits the side of the sailboat, the drip of an icicle melting, all these things. I'm interested in the energy of water in both its inert and active states. And how water and light interact; and water's viscosity."[8]

She was also aware of the "slow" sunrises and the interminable winters that characterize the upper Midwest. Nature's rhythms provided a different kind of time, more seamless and less obviously marked than Western music's brief recurring patterns, and they would inform her thinking as well. She learned to appreciate the lengthy seasonal vigil that preceded the arrival of the first crocus in spring when it finally pushed its way through a barely thawing, still-snow-covered earth to meet the sun's gaze head on. The long-sought color of a first flower and its subtle fragrance were not lost on a Minnesotan who had stared out her kitchen window at a white landscape for months anticipating just such a sign of renewal. According to Larsen, much as she was aware of the natural world all her life and felt a deep peace when outdoors, it was not until she wrote *Ulloa's Ring* in 1980 that she realized she needed to be *in* nature. She explains:

> Ulloa's ring is a conical rainbow that's created by a certain kind of light up above the clouds. It's also called the "Ring of Glory." Pilots were the first people to start reporting these. You can see them from airplanes from time to time. And I've seen maybe a handful of them as I've been flying, and plastered myself against the window. They bounce and reshape themselves as the clouds are shaped. And you don't feel any weight. What you feel is coloration of energy in the cloud; and that particular piece was the first time I was conscious of the fact that I was *trying to be inside it*. . . . And then after that I did *The Atmosphere as a Fluid System*, and *Aubade*, which is about light and all those things, but not consciously. But *Ulloa's Ring*, it unlocked something, and then *Water Music*, and then it just unlocked.[9]

On another occasion she named *Up, Where the Air Gets Thin*; *Downwind of Roses in Maine*; *Concerto: Cold, Silent Snow*; and *Slow Structures*. This chapter considers nature pieces Larsen has identified that I've not discussed elsewhere: *Ulloa's Ring* (1980), *Aubade* (1982), *Cold, Silent Snow* (1988), and *Slow Structures* (2005). I'll also touch upon pieces that she's worked on more recently that have clear connections to nature and the environment and reflect a more foregrounded and conscious environmental message.

Among Larsen's nature pieces, the flute is a favored instrument, and each one of these pieces features the instrument either in a solo or among a small ensemble. In this regard she joins a musical tradition that associates the flute with naturalness. Larsen believes that "it is the closest instrument to being air itself (except for voice, for which [she] regularly compose[s])."[10] Ancient flutes made from hollow bird-wing bones or carved from mammoth tusks "wear" their connection to nature. The instrument was once a part of a living being, a direct product of the natural world. But Larsen preferred the instrument for reasons that went beyond historical accuracy or a desire for an authentic sound; she acknowledged that her attraction to writing for flute was partly due to a longtime friendship and collaboration with the flute virtuoso Eugenia (Genie) Zukerman.[11] As in *In a Winter Garden* and her collaboration with Patricia Hampl, Larsen's close relationships with accomplished, creative women across a range of fields have inspired and nurtured her. Although Larsen had been born into a family of girls, the Sisters of Saint Joseph of Carondolet formed her first community of female supporters; today a network of exceptional women colleagues and collaborators helps Larsen speak and be heard. Nature connects to gender like religion connected to nature: seamlessly, effortlessly, and thoroughly.

Larsen wrote *Ulloa's Ring* for Zukerman on a commission from the Schubert Club of Saint Paul.[12] Her string of verbs finds musical analogues in the piece.

> Ulloa's Ring is a conical rainbow; a complete set of circles of spectral color. A Ulloa's Ring is formed at the edge of a cloud where, like an elusive target, it *spins, weaves, bends* and *waves*, always just ahead of [the] eye, always on the cloud side opposite the sunlight. The size, depth, and color intensity of a Ulloa's Ring is determined by the density and shape of the cloud. Standing solidly on Earth, one cannot see a Ulloa's Ring. It can be seen only from an airplane, in the mountains; any place one might find oneself in the midst of clouds.[13]

THE CIRCLE OF ULLOA. p. 178.

Figure 4.1. Ulloa's Ring as it appears in *Meteors, Aërolites, Storms, and Atmospheric Phenomena* by William Lackland (1871; New York: Scribner, Armstrong, 1876), 178.

A fleeting alignment of light rays and water droplets sounds in the chimerical character of Larsen's *Ulloa's Ring*. But the piece does not float unchecked. At the macro level, the basic arch-like shape of the rings finds a musical correlate in the vaguely arch-like dynamic trajectory of the work: Larsen starts and ends softly. At the micro level, recurring motives weave a cohesive fabric. Sounds are simultaneously evanescent and substantive; as they swirl and spin, they wreathe musicians and listeners in a "Circle of Glory" analogous to the one that surrounds and embraces a mountain-top viewer or an airplane passenger. Composer, performers, and listeners are simultaneously within and without the ring of light and sound; the intimate flute pulls everyone inside the ring like the Chinese artist who drew herself into the mountain, and the responding, commenting piano moves outside the circle casting the shadow that appears at the center of the rainbow. It is easy to understand how *Ulloa's Ring* "unlocked" a way of thinking about nature *and* music for Larsen. Inside the airplane, inside the clouds, inside the rainbow, she notes, "I could see right down the center of the cone."[14] *Ulloa's Ring* was the first time Larsen became nature *in* music.

The performance key shows the range of sounds she requires for the piece and the symbols devised for their indication. Zukerman's sparkling and virtuosic realization conveys the rare brilliance of the phenomenon and the flutist's own deep engagement with the generating idea.

Ulloa's Ring Performance Key

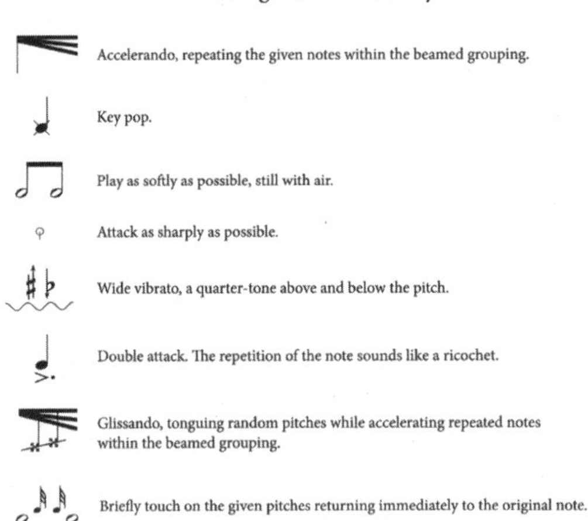

Figure 4.2. *Ulloa's Ring* performance key.

Zukerman and Larsen enjoyed a mutual interest in the natural world that went beyond nodding to environmental causes; each saw herself as part of a larger system of being, something bigger than human-engineered institutions. Zukerman even wondered about the possibility of a connection between Larsen's running and her need to be one with nature. She recalls:

> We very much had a passion for the natural in every form. I even remember a conversation we had about the Gaia theory—that organisms somehow interact to form a complex self-regulating system that maintains conditions for life on the planet. Just thinking about it now, maybe we were both drawn to this theory because each of us had much chaos in our lives, and a self-governing benign force appealed to us. [It] still appeals to me, even though chaos now seems to govern everything in this troubled world. I think the natural world appeals to all artists because of its seeming simplicity, beauty, nobility and mystery—all elements which I "hear" in Libby's music. And it makes me wonder if running for her is a way to connect with the air, wind, the sky, the sun, the rain—the natural world.[15]

Zukerman's observation seems spot on. Although Larsen is a dedicated marathoner, she doesn't run for speed or competitive edge or even to stay in shape; as she put it, "I run for joy, just joy."[16] While outdoors, as Libby inhales lungs-full of fresh air, a transfer of energies takes place. She fills herself with the natural world and exhales herself into it; she is in it, and it is in her, and she is one with it. She *is* it. Understanding how the materials of *Ulloa's Ring* interact, connect, and cohere suggests how water, light, and energy compel Larsen's nature music.

The first two minutes belong to the flute alone, and Larsen uses them to evoke the atmosphere she'll explore for the remainder of the piece. Ulloa's rings first appear and coalesce in stuttering, telegraphed sounds that tap and rap their ghostlike presence; almost immediately they evaporate into the ether in smokelike wisps that curl and spin around themselves as they disappear. Larsen identifies the importance of this swirling figure by placing a box around it each time it sounds. Pulsed notes and swirling gestures return throughout the fourteen-minute work creating distinctive soundmarks for an otherwise "elusive" (musical) atmosphere.[17] The repeated notes become as light waves and the flowing figures like water (ex. 4.1).

Sounds softly flicker and disappear; they come from all directions, close by and far away, "as an echo." Small, explosive pops release pent-up energy in the highly charged atmosphere. Notes waver in wide vibratos and flutter-tongued passages. There's a shimmer to the sound, in part a result of the timbre of the

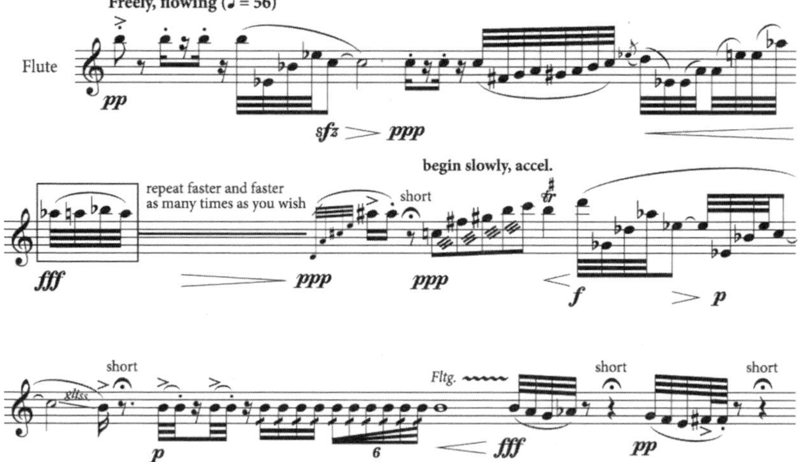

Example 4.1. *Ulloa's Ring*, page 1, lines 1–3 of manuscript

silvery instrument, but no less so because it is written into melodic figures that bounce off or bend around one another. Listeners can hear the light waves. Metallic-sounding threads weave and knot together in the air. Between the sounds, Larsen composes the infinite space of the atmosphere in short silences that unexpectedly poke through, but there are few moments of sustained stillness or quiet; there's too much going on.[18] Ulloa's rings are dependent upon an unbroken interaction of light and water, and stillness would signal their disappearance. The constantly changing light show is sonified in a sound world that kaleidoscopically remakes itself in continuously varying pitches, rhythms, gestures, and moods. Larsen has her flutist sound "sweetly," then "suddenly energetic," and "as if covered," and all within the first two minutes of the piece. Later on the flutist will play "warmly" and then "molto secco" (very dryly). There are no key or meter signatures to ground the piece in predictability, but why would there be in a composition that is about a weightless and suspended entity that only briefly materializes in the air? No human systems control Ulloa's rings. They can be suggested but never contained.

Larsen's slow tempo marking (quarter note = 56) is conducive to the feeling of suspension or hovering that prevails in many instances, but it also seems at odds with the nearly incessant surface activity that fills the opening section of the piece. In truth, there's nothing slow about any aspect of this piece; energy is always cracking and sizzling. Numerous accelerandos push the ceaselessly vibrating music forward. Despite more than a half dozen rests (with fermatas), they are simply moments to catch a breath; they don't augur a break in the action. In fact, the flute's opening recitative sounds as if it is one continuous extended movement through the rings that comes to a close only at the two-minute mark with Larsen's instruction to the flutist to play triple *piano* and very legato before fading away to nothing (*niente*).[19]

Larsen's nothingness is merely an invisible seam in the fabric of the rings; she then turns her attention to another aspect of the rainbow. The piano brings a new set of colors and expressive possibilities; sounds plucked from the highest and lowest ends of the keyboard expand the sonic range. The piano also introduces another soundmark gesture, one that reinforces harmonic ambiguity. Within the first seconds of entering, the pianist lightly plays a quick series of dyads that, while consisting of fifths, fourths, and thirds, avoids any sense of being in or suggesting a key. Nothing implies tonality or groundedness. Neither the rings nor the observer is earthbound. The importance of this new soundmark is evident in its frequent appearance throughout the piece and also in Larsen's having drawn a box around its final occurrence at the end of the piece (ex. 4.2).[20] After entering with its own signature figure, the piano immediately picks up the flute's swirling motion. The piano's dyad figure will be heard over a dozen times before the piece is over, but perhaps most memorably in the last moments of *Ulloa's Ring*, when it sounds and fades out just after the flute plays a final swirling gesture.

With the sustaining pedal depressed, the piano initially blurs and blends with the flute, but the instrumental relationship is not one of mystical union. Except for the opening flute recitative and a "freely, lyrically expressive" piano solo that lasts about ninety seconds, four and a half minutes into the piece, the two instruments engage in a spirited banter, oftentimes producing a mu-

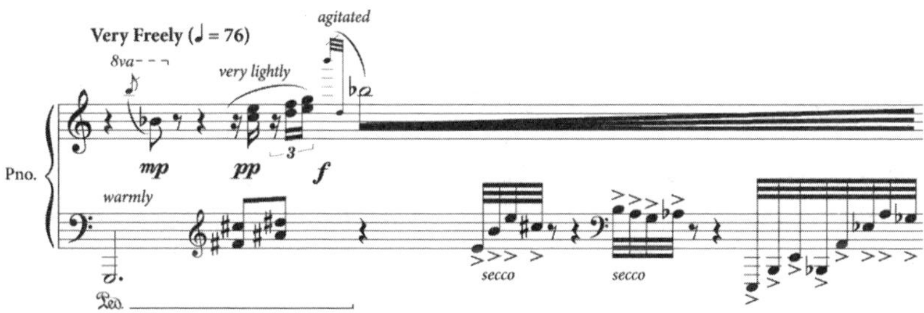

Example 4.2. *Ulloa's Ring*, page 2, first staff

sical frisson. There is a palpable kinetic charge between them. The piano solo interrupts that exchange. Perhaps Larsen wanted an opportunity for the flutist to catch her breath, or she felt the need for a contrasting "B" or even "C" section. Is this where the music moves from *being* the phenomenon to a position outside contemplating it? If so, this is no typical lyrical contemplation. Although soft and gentle, with multiple instructions to play passages molto legato, continuous dissonant chords suggest a larger notion of expressive beauty than tradition has favored. This is another aspect of *Ulloa's Ring*. Although Larsen was clearly dazzled by what she saw from her airplane window, her state of wonder did not translate into a conventionally beautiful sound world, not even in this single extended, expressive passage. There are no soaring melodies or rich, chromatic harmonies to transport a listener into a state of bliss, although brief melodic fragments flit through the soundscape on multiple occasions during the work. This is not about transcending the phenomenon and achieving a state of nirvana; it is about getting into the phenomenon and living in its energy. There is something of a scientist's more than a romantic's appreciation and wonder at the rings. The piece is about atomistic energy, "life force," and it is unrelentingly excited and dissonant; tritones, major sevenths, and minor ninths, all favorite sounds of the composer's, sonify Larsen's intense "lyrical" moment (ex. 4.3).

The ring is dynamic and charged even while the governing pulse remains within a moderate tempo. It doesn't get faster than a quarter note = 76 until close to the end, but even there, the controlling pulse only reaches a quarter note = 84. By the final seconds of the work, the players have slowed to reclaim a pulse close to the one that began the piece. But at any point in the work individual passages speed up and slow down; they often gain momentum as they move through a gesture where Larsen instructs her players to "push ahead" or to "build intensity." Over and over Larsen encourages the instrumentalists to play "freely," "very freely." Ultimately, *Ulloa's Ring* is not about tempo or beat, as traditionally understood. It is not about melody or harmony or consonance or dissonance either. It does not conform to a conventional form or an identifiable style, a situation that will confound more than one critic talking about a variety of Larsen's pieces over the years.[21] And while it is about energy, it is not about alternating or direct current. It is about the energy of light and water and being in their field as they cohere; Larsen colors that energy in music that sparks and snaps and undulates and wavers. Larsen wants us to join her inside the ring and the sounds and become that energy. If it works, listeners hear with new ears, just like a person experiencing Ulloa's ring looks at the sky with new eyes. It seems logical that a composer famous for her energy would respond

Example 4.3. *Ulloa's Ring*, piano solo, page 5

to a phenomenon that discharged an equally intense force field. Having such vitality reflected back may have been why *Ulloa's Ring* unlocked something in Libby Larsen. She understood what it was like to be inside that energy, and in composing *Ulloa's Ring* she wrote what she knew.

Larsen took advantage of the opportunity to explore a different kind of natural energy in 1982, when she accepted a commission from the Composers Commissioning Program of the Minnesota Composers Forum to write another flute piece for Genie Zuckerman; this one allowed both Zuckerman and Larsen to explore the cantabile qualities of their musical beings in a fully solo medium. In *Aubade* Larsen composed a more familiar phenomenon and simultaneously revealed her upper Midwest point of view. Here is an example of place directly animating Larsen's nature music.[22] In a spoken program note to a 1988 performance, Larsen explains her perspective: "My *Aubade* is a piece to welcome the rising of the sun, but particularly the kind of sunrise we get in the Midwest, which takes a very long time. Dawn sometimes takes an hour or so to happen. It's not particularly glorious, but it's very peaceful, very calm, a very unfolding way to begin the day. I tried to capture that kind of energy in this piece."[23]

Larsen is aware of the geographic, historical, and dramatic function of her dawn greeting within a tradition that spans time and cultures, as she demonstrates in a composer's note:

> *Aubade* is a word drawn from several sources: Auba (dawn), Alborada (Spanish), Albus (white). . . . It is a song, or poem to greet the dawn and usually denotes music of a quiet, idyllic nature. It is also seen as a morning love song, or a song or poem of parting lovers at dawn.
>
> In the 17th century, noblemen held gatherings, feasts in the morning for which Aubades were composed. They were played in the open air just as the sun began to break the horizon.[24]

Like many such pieces, Larsen's *Aubade* is slow (quarter note = 40) and relatively short, under five minutes. With the exception of a single passage toward the middle of the piece that is faster and louder, *Aubade* resides in a deliberate and soft temporal and dynamic space. Although no meter or key signatures confine this piece, recurring pitches and gestures provide a cohesiveness that is more audible than in *Ulloa's Ring*. This may be the result of the brevity of the work, the singularity of the timbre, and the strategic recurrence of unifying motives. Perhaps it is just easier to anticipate the predictable process of dawn than the wholly unexpected materialization of the rare and evanescent "ring of glory." There's something comfortable and known about dawn.

In contrast to the ambiguous tonal world that Larsen created for Ulloa's heavenly habitation, she musicalizes her earthbound experience of dawn in the large, structural pitch-centeredness of *Aubade*. The exact sounds and figurations of the whispery, deliberate opening return two minutes into the work and then again at the end of the piece. We hear the tension of the slow rising sun as it pulls itself into the morning sky. The pitch D forms a horizon line at the beginning and again at the end of the piece, although there is no sense of being in a key, despite the early importance of the dominant pitch A. The mixed whole-tone/D major hybrid scale that closes the first line creates a fuzzy harmonic world. Perhaps this is an apt sonification of the dim and indistinct early-morning light that cautiously overcomes the fixed horizon line (ex. 4.4).

Free from any temptation to write glorious fanfaric music more appropriate to popular stock images of dramatic sunrises—those photos showing the sun piercing the horizon and exploding into brightness—Larsen sticks with her experience and composes the measured start to an upper midwestern day. The deliberateness of the act infuses and shapes the energy and motion of the work. Thirty-two years after premiering the work, Eugenia Zukerman recalled the experience of playing Larsen's dawn song: "It's a wonderful piece; I just love it. I still play it. What's terrific about it is that it's a piece that just sort of unfolds. It keeps unfolding, it's very dreamlike, and it's a real reverie that allows the flutist to be incredibly expressive. It's a short piece, but it works wonderfully, and you never play it the same. It's just one of those pieces that allows you to sort of wander, and it's very special to me."[25]

In a soundscape dotted with twittering birdlike sounds, a trio of ascending fragmentary figures coaxes a reluctant sunrise: the first is a series of anywhere between three and seven climbing pitches that varies in number and value; the second is a string of triplet figures that starts at the highest pitch, dives downward, and then springs back up; and the third is a repeating combination figure of four notes, the first three of which ascend only to ultimately fall back to the place of the second note (ex. 4.5).

All three of the figures appear, disappear, and reappear with few literal repeats, but their near-constant presence is enough to create a sense of coherence; their most important commonality is a stolid but irresistible urge to rise. It is a testament to the cumulative power of these small ascending figures that the piece feels as if it has quietly risen like the sun despite the final sounds literally replicating the opening ones. Echo-like dynamic contrasts halfway through the piece suggest many early-morning soundscapes

Example 4.4. *Aubade*, first line of music

Example 4.5. *Aubade*, line 6 of score

when birds call and sing to one another from all directions and pitch levels. Flutter-tongued notes, which first appear just after the two-minute mark, and then wide, wobbling vibratos that introduce the last minute of the piece and comprise its final sounds blur time and pitch; their slow oscillations embody the languid scene. Larsen's world wakes up gradually without fanfare or glitz. The solitary flute provides an intimate experience of sunrise. The sun has "wandered" into position. The sound of Larsen's upper-Midwest morning seems to repeat stereotypical notions of a midwesterner's temperament: grounded, soft spoken, polite, and thoughtful with no need to call attention to itself. The sun has risen, and we are still in place (ex. 4.6).

Larsen is intrigued by rare events and quotidian occurrences alike: she responds to them with equal wonder. And the same holds for the specific environment she calls home in the upper Midwest even after having lived there for more than sixty years. Snow and cold are synonymous with Minneapolis; six-month snowy seasons are not unusual. Although summers bring warmer weather and patches of annuals that spring up overnight, planted by color-deprived Minnesotans, and swimming and sailing activities entice large groups of neighbors to gather and socialize at the many lakes for picnics and evening concerts, each year the people of the upper Midwest test their collective mettle with stoic endurance of months of tireless winds, white-covered ground, and subfreezing temperatures. Chains accessorize cars the way heavy coats, boots, ear muffs, scarves, and mittens constitute standard fashion items for any northern citizen. Bicyclists assume that snow tires are

Example 4.6. *Aubade*, last line of score

ordinary gear; feet of snow do not discourage those determined to minimize their carbon footprint. Even downtown structures are dressed for the cold. Garlands of sky bridges hang between buildings and fill with pedestrians who prefer to walk high above the street within the glass enclosures rather than risk frostbite, windburn, and invisibility navigating the snow-shrouded streets below. Given the realities of her natural environment, it follows that many of Larsen's nature pieces focus on the look, feel, and sound of cold and snow. She knows them well. She has endured the blinding frontal attack of driving snow in high winds and been dusted by the effortless fall of snowflakes in moments of stillness. She has skittered through snow tunnels and slogged across unshoveled sidewalks. She has lain down in snowy fields and left Larsen-sized snow angels. The frozen medium provides her with limitless opportunities to explore her world and to think about the interactions of light and liquidity, energy and inertia, sound and stillness.

A cold, colorless, snowy backdrop provided the setting for Larsen and Hampl's *In a Winter Garden*, a piece that comments as much upon nature and place as it does upon religion and faith. When I asked Hampl about the importance of the collaborators' shared knowledge of Midwest winters, she was clear: "Winter of course is at the heart of the piece, its conception. In a sense its entire vocabulary." And then she pointed to a particular moment in Larsen's "Fountain Carol": "I can still hear the icicle sound of the fountain carol. She aced that."[26] It is intriguing to think of a "vocabulary of winter" and what the musical equivalent of words or syntax might be. What does winter sound like? How do we hear winter? The poet Wallace Stevens (1879–1955) considered such questions in his poem "The Snow Man," whose first line lays down the minimum requirements: "One must have a mind of winter." The poet-listener heard "misery" in the wind, and the "sound of a few leaves / which is the sound of the land." He understood "the listener, who listens in the snow," and hearing "nothing" hears all there is.[27] Larsen has the requisite "mind of winter" and brings it to her music. What does her winter sound like? And what about an icicle? Two of her nature pieces provide potential answers: *Concerto: Cold, Silent Snow* (1988), a large, public, "display" piece, and *Slow Structures* (2005), a more "inward" and personal expression of the winter season.[28]

Both pieces focus on snow. Both pieces are inspired by poetry. Each also uses a nontraditional, multimovement structure with individual parts that suggest musical analogues to poems, and each seeks to move from the contemplation of the immediate and particular to the consideration of something larger and more universal. The transcendence Larsen found in pre–Vatican II religious practices and experienced in singing chant is also available to her in wintery nature.

Larsen explains that in *Concerto: Cold, Silent Snow* she is "attempting to immerse the listener in the act of snowfall. . . . The point of view lies in the midst of snowfall."[29] Eight years after the "unlocking," epiphanic *Ulloa's Ring*, the composer wishes her listeners to be the snow, much as she would twelve years after the *Concerto*, wish her listeners to "be the fragrance" in *Downwind of Roses in Maine*.[30] As early as 1980, Larsen was clear about her desire for oneness with nature, and she reaffirms this in 1988 with her composer's note to the *Concerto*: "Most of my instrumental compositions work to reintegrate our post-industrial revolution human personality with the human psyche and nature." And then she names "the poets Goethe, Rilke, Blake, de Nerval and Robert Bly" as "working in the same areas. . . . We are all working towards what Robert Bly calls 'News of the Universe.'"[31]

Larsen's empathy with fellow Minnesotan Robert Bly (b. 1926) provides another opportunity to observe her refusal of categories or marginalization. Although a frequent collaborator with women writers and performers, Larsen does not limit her sources of inspiration or insight by gender. She is part of a larger, centuries-long endeavor of those doing a similar kind of work and is unafraid to put herself in their company. *News of the Universe: Poems of Twofold Consciousness* is Bly's collection of 150 poems by dozens of poets published in 1980. "Twofold consciousness" is his phrase for what humanity needs to develop in order to move beyond the human-centered worldview propagated by Descartes and rationalist philosophy in the seventeenth century.[32] Through thoughtful pairings of poetry and commentary, Bly asserts that it is only by reconciling our anthropocentric *inner* consciousness with the *outer* consciousness of both sensate and mute others in the universe that we can honor "the spiritual intellect and the soul of the world."[33] He insists that the "news" to which his title refers is not new but rather a contemporary reevaluation of earlier thought wherein "the ancient union of the day intelligence of the human being and the night intelligence of nature become *audible*, palpable again."[34] The "audible" quality of this ancient union is Larsen's invitation to make her project musical. Bly's collection becomes an alternative sacred book to the mid-twentieth century *Good News Bible* and takes as its authority not man, or even humanity, but the entire natural world.[35] Larsen's determination to be fully immersed in nature and her efforts to compose that nested position in her music locate her within a larger late-twentieth-century ecological consciousness: as she is one with nature, she is one with her time. This perspective is even more apparent in *Slow Structures*.

Myriad aspects of time and place inspire Larsen's nature pieces. In remarks about *Slow Structures*, a work for flute, cello, and piano, Larsen reminds listeners of the importance she attaches to her particular place: to both its weather and its artistic community. Her membership in the hearty clan of northerners means that she is especially attuned to the beauty that attends her frozen climes. And she is on a personal mission to share what she understands. She explains: "I have lived much of my life in Minneapolis, Minnesota, near the Canadian border in the United States, where a kind of frozen, austere beauty inspires the hundreds of writers, painters, dancers, and composers who live here. Here, we know the rhythm and flow of water in all its guises in ways that are known only to people who live in cold, northern climates. Living with snow tutors the soul in mystical understanding of how time operates on us as human beings."[36]

Identifying her location in the composer's note may have been a response to the site of the premiere of the piece, Potsdam, Germany, and an audience that was likely unfamiliar with the specific geography of the United States. But the composer goes beyond merely identifying her state's proximity to its Canadian neighbor.[37] According to Larsen, her northern Midwest locus endows her and her fellow citizens of the cold with special insights into a more universally experienced phenomenon: time. Only northerners, she claims, understand "the rhythm and flow of water" in all its moods and ways, moving and motionless. The frozen environment yields insights into time and "tutors the soul in mystical understanding."[38] Given one's perception of time in a still environment, it is no wonder that Larsen has mastered the art of "going deep"; when motion is thwarted moments seem to dilate; time appears vertical. That Potsdam, Germany is almost eight degrees farther north than Minneapolis meant Larsen's audience might welcome her claim of specialness on their behalf and empathize with this reading. Larsen takes her outliers' location and connects its remote, cold, quiet, slowness with access to greater wisdom. She invited her audience of northern Germans to do the same. In a piece that is inspired by winter snow, "its tempi, its beautiful, translucent light, [and] its mystic, infinitely shifting suggestive shapes," Larsen reverses the idea of what is central and what is marginal to the contemporary composer.[39] She privileges remote stillness over constant activity, and quietness over the din.

How does Larsen *speak* cold or stillness in music? Does the vocabulary of winter consist of particular sounds, gestures, rhythms, timbres, or articulations? How dependent is a listener upon a title to translate what is being said? It is easy to imagine sharp, crisp staccato articulations as the brittleness of icy, cold air, and the high, metallic timbres of the flute sounding the brilliant glint of a winter sun ricocheting off snow crystals. Many such figurations occur in both *Cold, Silent Snow* and *Slow Structures*, but they also appear in *Aubade* and *Ulloa's Ring* and other pieces as well. They are not the exclusive property of wintery music. Perhaps all the pieces are related by the presence of water or light, so they share a common gestural vocabulary.

The relative speed and ferocity of wind are served well by music's temporal unfolding and can be conjured by adjusting the surface rhythms and dynamic levels of any number of tightly coiled or loose swirling figures. Again, all four pieces contain this kind of figure, but it also appears in other works having nothing to do with reflections on winter or nature. Beyond musicalizing aspects of the inanimate world, tremolo and flutter-tongued passages might actually capture the vibrations of a shivering body, but they too could suggest other associations and be similarly convincing.

Ultimately understanding Larsen's "vocabulary of winter" does not require finding actual cold or stillness in the music (an impossible task unless one is looking at growth rings in the trees used to make wooden instruments; such rings actually leave traces of weather events including especially harsh seasons) or assigning lexical equivalents to audible shapes. Larsen's titles are integral parts of her works; she presents them to listeners along with the sounds, and they can provide entry points into her thinking. Allowing oneself to be bathed in sounds that are conducive to imagining the conditions and states she references in her titles is all that is needed. Although the internal logic of Larsen's music doesn't depend upon an accompanying narrative or a provocative image to make musical sense, if listeners aspire to move beyond tracking sounding forms in space or need a prompt to engage more deeply with what they are hearing, then Larsen's titles offer that assist.

It may be that the greater challenge to *speaking winter* in music lies not in expressing the sounds and movements associated with the season but in finding a vocabulary to convey the depth and distinctiveness of its silence and stillness. A temporal sound art seems to defy their rendering. But that does not keep Larsen from using her medium to contemplate these two integral aspects of Minnesota's snowy winters or from examining "the slow formation of frozen form."[40]

Larsen notes that she composed *Slow Structures* "in the manner of an object poem, which takes its inspiration from winter snow."[41] Here is another instance of Larsen's music being inspired and informed by her broad knowledge of other expressive modes, in this case poetry. As in traditionally fashioned object poems that employ words, Larsen focuses on the "physical form, functions, and potential" of her subject: snow.[42] She leads her listeners to a "fresh perception of the subject," but in her case, without verbal mediation beyond suggestive titles.[43] Through her musicalization, listeners are invited to experience snow in what she calls "its mystic, infinitely shifting suggestive shapes."[44] Like the best object poems, the greater significance of *Slow Structures* lies not in its literal description of the object but in its metaphorical power and intimation of a greater "spiritual truth."[45] Larsen explains the snow-inspired form of her piece:

> The music begins with the force of a blizzard, slightly fierce, virtuosic in its gestures, and given form by the impetus of the force of nature. Then, the musical motives begin to settle in relationship to each other, slowly creating a structure which is both recognizable and unrecognizable. Within the structure, the musical gestures of the opening express themselves in new ways in which we recognize them only by what we can no longer audibly perceive. Finally, the slow structures in which the musical elements have been operating begin to loosen, melt as it were, creating a hypnotic atmosphere—much like the hypnotic effect of the drip of a melting icicle.[46]

The eighteen-minute work has four movements, each of which takes its title from the briefest fragments of winter-focused poems. The titles of the first two movements, "The Mad Wind's Night Work" and "Slow Structures," are lifted from the last three lines of Ralph Waldo Emerson's "The Snow-Storm." "Silent Syllables," the name of the third movement, comes from the final stanza of Henry Wadsworth Longfellow's poem "Snow-Flakes"; and the title of the final movement, "Snow-Melting Time," comes from Robert Bly's translation of Tomas Tranströmer's poem titled "Snow-Melting Time, '66."[47] The last movement provides listeners with another chance to experience "the icicle sound" that Patricia Hampl noticed years earlier in "The Fountain Carol" of *In a Winter Garden*, but here it is no benign crystalline shape. Water is a fixture of Larsen's physical world as well as her consciousness and music. Gaseous, liquid, and frozen, water permeates her sense of movement and time and sound and silence.

The "mad wind" blows musical materials into the soundscape. Flute, cello, and piano attack "ferociously" with loud, stinging, pizzicato figures.[48] Larsen fills the air with sounding ice crystals. Listeners are pounded by squalls of piercing dissonances that swirl everywhere; there is nothing here to recall the contemplation-inducing snowfall of Sister's world in the earlier piece. At measure four, a churning ostinato in the piano left hand channels the frenzied gusts into steadier winds; it drives the piece forward and persists for the majority of the movement. Basic ingredients for Larsen's *Slow Structures* arrive on a violent "virtuosic" wind that needs to calm before "the frolic architecture of the snow" can assume any lingering shape (ex. 4.7).[49] Harmonic and melodic tritones and major sevenths, as well as a three-note keening melodic fragment, first heard in the piano right hand with the entrance of the ostinato, emerge from the maelstrom of the first movement to become

Example 4.7. *Slow Structures*, movement 1, "The Mad Wind's Night Work," mm. 1–10

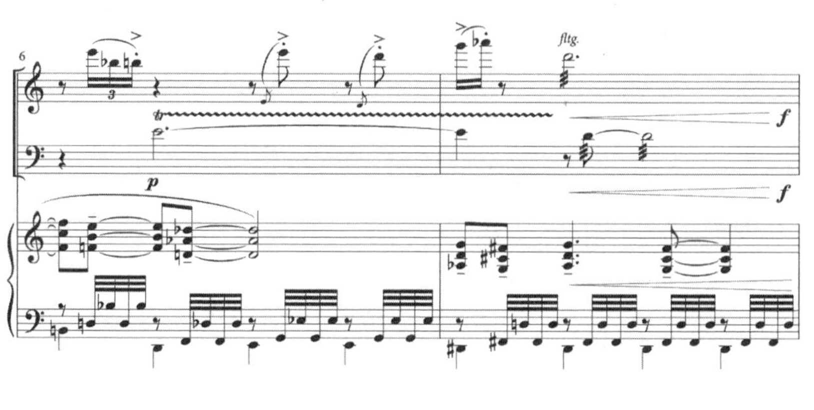

Example 4.7. *(continued)*

basic structural elements for the entire piece. Despite their transformations they hold the work together until the melting edifice disappears *pppp*.

Slow Structures explores forming and form and process and time, using snow as the object of study. Larsen honors the evanescence of her medium with a piece whose precise sounds suggest the unique individuality of snow crystals but whose large architecture reflects their interaction and change over time. Larsen has the structure grow out of and disappear with the object. The result is a piece that does not adhere to eighteenth- and nineteenth-century notions of formal unity despite the tight motivic relationships that inhere throughout the work. Listeners hoping for clear harmonic signposts or predictable appearances of contrasts and continuities common to centuries of pieces will not find them in the sonic architecture of this work. And that has implications for all aspects of the piece. Although the first movement grabs listeners with its rousing start, which respects classical conventions regarding the assigned role of an introductory movement, the steady state dissonances; wind-blown, seemingly undirected musical ideas; and continuous unfolding material reminiscent of through-composed works challenge listeners to locate or identify discrete functioning parts. Only by recognizing what emerges in the second and third movements can listeners discover what was most important from the start. In a sense, the beauty of snow reveals itself once the blizzard has ceased.

Movement 2, "Slow Structures," is significantly quieter, slower, and more transparent than "The Mad Wind's Night Work." The disorienting activity of the first movement is replaced by a feeling of stunned suspension, much like the eerie stillness that often follows a beating storm. A "distant," oscillating, "bell-like" drone sounding a major seventh high in the upper reaches of the piano right hand suggests the presence of perspective, perhaps of time, but there is nothing to compel our passage through it (ex. 4.8).[50] Larsen composes a different kind of time; one that marks its existence not in seconds, minutes, or hours, but in longer intervals apprehensible only to those who sink deeply into the present moment. The architecture of snow emerges at this pace.

Omnipresent major sevenths relate the harmonic worlds of the first two movements. A descending melodic figure, first introduced in "Mad Wind" at measure 4, and present in a new guise at measure 6 in "Slow Structures," gives the movements similar shapes. Larsen's slow snow structures crystallize where they fell, and as they do their outlines are forged and tempered by the elements, meteorological and musical. Here are Larsen's motives "both recognizable and unrecognizable."[51]

It takes nearly four minutes for the occasional flourishes that interrupt the drone to gather enough momentum to hint that this is a morphing form.

Example 4.8. *Slow Structures*, movement 2, "Slow Structures," mm. 1–11

And during this time there is little to distract a listener from the contemplation of individual sounds. Time has slowed down, and listeners can focus on what would normally go unnoticed. Cello harmonics and whispering flute whistles that float above impressionistic piano chords freeze the piece in time. At measure 27, however, halfway through the movement, a poco animato speeds up the glacial pace of change; it signals the start of increased activity. Although the drone continues, alternately tucked inside the cello line or dropped into the lowest reaches of the piano left hand, quickening surface rhythms affect the perceived rate of change. Flutter-tongued pitches, wide-wobbling vibratos, jeté cello descents, and looping groups of four notes presage transformations occurring within the structure even if they are unmeasurable; "Slow Structures" becomes a barely moving moment in time. Its length, longer by two minutes than any of the other movements, means that the music is fixed in place for more time than it is not, much like the upper Midwest is frozen in place more months than it is not. Sound becomes the object of contemplation, and listeners develop a fresh perspective on snow and time.

By contrast, the third movement is the shortest of the four, just two and a half minutes. Its rocking, uninterrupted repeated patterns mark and regularize time's passage in a way that is unprecedented in the piece. Even the larger phrase structure is parsed in more traditional eight-measure groupings.[52] Yet the constancy of the temporal world in "Silent Syllables" doesn't push listeners toward a goal; instead it creates a timeless, hypnotic space. Larsen removes even the smallest suggestion of motion when, with a single exception, she confines the cellist to its open strings and denies the possibility of vibrato. On two occasions she asks the cellist to play "whitely" on its lowest note, C. In fact, the few, widely spaced notes and numerous measures of rest that comprise Larsen's third movement score create their own white field of contemplation. The page is mostly empty (ex. 4.9).

We *see* individual "syllables" as we *hear* the voluptuous silence of the soundscape. Larsen instructs the pianist to play "frozen" chords within a "suspended" timelessness, and evokes the silent white world in a dynamic compass that ranges only once beyond *ppp* to *mp*. And yet the relationship of this virtually mute cosmos to the blustery one that began the piece is audible in the major seventh and minor third intervals that open the movement, and the strategic, structural tritone that jars a listener out of complacency at measure 15. As the volume reaches its peak, the cello plays a ringing G-sharp; the note pops out within the series of repeated Ds that surround it. The tritone sparkles as well against the flute's "shimmering" high D that accompanies

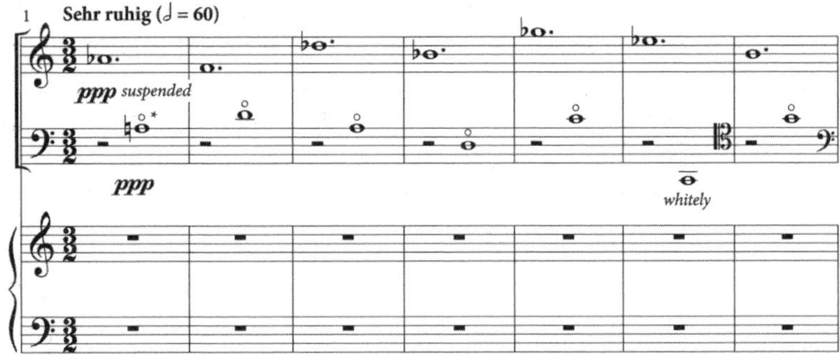

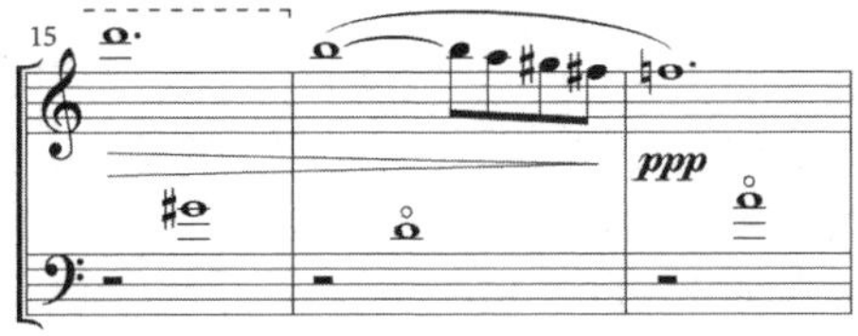

*Harmonics written where sounding
**Chords should be equally balanced
***Open D drone with D harmonic double stop

Example 4.9. *Slow Structures*, movement 3, "Silent Syllables," mm. 1–17

it.[53] Here is the one instance of a stopped string, and the moment is clearly dramatic, but it gets no more time than any of the other pitches. It focuses our attention but is all part of a continuous whole.

No figures or motives presented in the two previous movements return literally in the third movement, and even repeated pitch and interval combinations within the third movement appear slightly changed each time they occur. Despite the constant variations, however, there is enough essential cohesion to unify the parts and the whole; it is all snow. Larsen's sound world has more in common with the shifting creations that blossom inside a kaleidoscope than with the expected behaviors of musical materials in common-practice structures. Longfellow's silent snowflake syllables become Larsen's soft, sovereign sounds. The autonomy of each note played by the flute and cello means that they remain syllable-like. Syntax comes later, and meaning after that. Listeners will discover the significance of snowflake relationships in time. Larsen's assignment of the least "activity" to this third-movement emphasizes the dramatically different concepts of motion, time, and drama that she is exploring. Quiet suspension fills the position normally accorded a minuet and trio or a scherzo in traditional multimovement works. Where once there had been a rousing dance, now there is frozen silence. What the composer is noticing is nearly invisible and inaudible. To appreciate her evocation, listeners must sink into a world of vertical time and be still with her. Larsen composes Thomas Merton's *temps vierge*, "not a blank to be filled or an untouched space to be conquered and violated, but a space which can enjoy its own potentialities and hopes—and its own presence to itself."[54]

Were the piece to end with the close of the third movement, listeners would remain within a timeless contemplative space. But Larsen is not done exploring her object. At the premiere of the piece, Larsen read aloud Robert Bly's translation of Tomas Tranströmer's poem "Snow-Melting Time, '66" prior to the fourth movement. She prepared the audience for the rushing snowmelt that would end the piece.

> Massive waters fall, water-roar, the old hypnosis.
> Water has risen into the car-graveyard—it glitters
> behind the masks.
> I hold tight to the narrow bridge.
> I am on a large iron bird sailing past death.[55]

The incessant patter that opens the final movement places listeners on high alert: clock time has returned, and we are waiting, watching, and ready. Images of melting snow run the gamut from benignly melting icicles whose steady dripping sound is gently comforting (a welcome harbinger of spring), to the thunderous rush of rivers swollen with mountain snow runoff that devours banks helpless against the surge. The relentless boom of the latter can strike terror in the uninitiated, but like the former it can also hypnotize. Neither Tranströmer nor Larsen is cowed by the violence.

Soft, "lightly" "whirling" sextuplets of repeated notes churn through the first eighty seconds of the nearly six-minute final movement. They drop out, return, and ultimately propel close to half of Larsen's snowmelt. Like the first movement, the last is characterized by whirling figures, and in both movements, Larsen instructs her musicians to play "violently."[56] Driving, goal-oriented rhythms, absent from the previous two movements, have materialized with a vengeance. The meter changes sixteen times within the first ninety seconds of music. Another twenty changes will occur in the remaining four minutes. Soft, surging currents drain from all directions, simultaneously, consecutively, but continuously, and Larsen captures their action in wedge-like convergences and series of descending passages, each of which differs from what came before. What had begun as snow squalls is now turbulent, icy whirlpools (ex. 4.10).

The cold is still present and sounds in "brittle" attacks, straight tones, "biting" bow strokes, and flute accents. But a change takes place when an extended passage of "very restful" molto legato piano playing appears in the second minute of music and brief moments of cello vibrato warm the air. Starting in measure 39, Larsen instructs the cellist to play "cantabile" and then "con vibrato."[57] The piano pulses a low *pianissimo* pattern of alternating octaves, minor ninths, and major sevenths. Larsen composes throbbing signs of life (ex. 4.11).

As if to suggest the cyclical nature of seasonal snows, Larsen ends her piece with a return to the opening material of the movement. The modified A-B-A' structure is as close as she comes to a traditional form in the work. Starting at measure 48, the same *pianissimo* sextuplets and meter changes that opened "Snow-Melting Time" push the piece forward, and the same descending melodic line reappears but now in a different instrument. Throughout the movement literal returns alternate with varied recollections. But there is nothing neat or generic about a snowmelt despite Larsen's quasi-ternary form. Although the composer might have been inspired by Tranströmer's poem about a particularly memorable Swedish snowmelt, she brands her own uniquely American. Two minutes from the end, the composer introduces a "walking bass" line and then instructs her pianist to play a series of syncopated chords "boogie, biting." It seems that upper Midwest snowflakes melt to a decidedly American rhythm. Familiar sevenths and tritone chords that characterized the previous three movements return to end the final one. As the last sounds melt away in a near-inaudible (*pppp*) dissonance, the tension of Larsen's snow poem lingers beyond its audition. The snow may be gone, but its memory continues to operate on us.

Example 4.10. *Slow Structures*, movement 4, "Snow-Melting Time," mm. 1–8

Example 4.10. *(continued)*

Looking to nature for tutoring or identifying the natural world with mystical understanding suggests that Larsen might ally herself with late-eighteenth-century German Romantics or mid-nineteenth-century American Transcendentalists, whose writings frequently reference a godlike power and presence in nature. But when asked to reflect upon the sources of her understanding of nature, she granted her familiarity with their ideas but clarified that she "already knew it without them," explaining, "I mean, I look at them, and study them and know them, but I don't look to them to give me direction." Searching for the roots of her particular connections to nature, I asked the composer: "As a child, did you always think there was something religious, or spiritual, or mystical about nature, even when you were skiing, or sailing, or running?"[58] She responded:

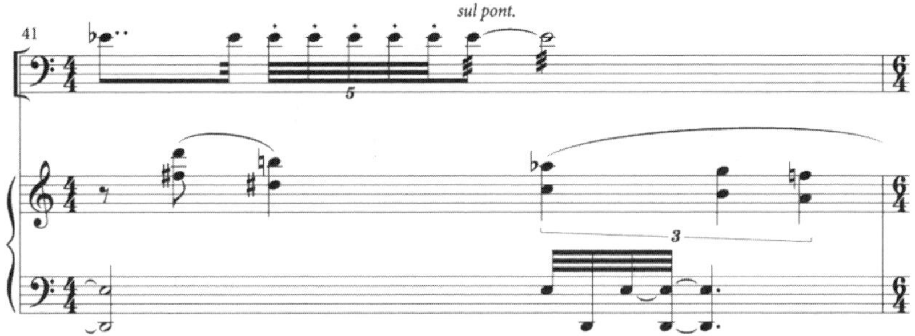

Example 4.11. *Slow Structures*, movement 4, "Snow-Melting Time," from pickup to m. 39 to downbeat of m. 44

Oh, that's a wonderful question. . . . Not religious, never, never. . . . I guess if I had to say one of the three I'd say "mystical." Just the falling of the snow, that it's happening, and there's no dominion in the falling of the snow. Or the blowing of wind; there's no dominion. There's the *beauty* of light in all of its forms, natural light, not man-made light. Or shadows: I'm a great

Example 4.11. *(continued)*

> fan of shadow, and I have not found the right place to write about shadow. So, mysticism, I always knew that outdoors is where I would go to find my natural self. I'd go down to the lake when I was really, really sad because I think it's the oscillation, and the improbability of water that becomes ice, becomes water, becomes ice: it's a great teacher. Or the trees.[59]

In 2015 Larsen was working on multiple commissions, three of which were related to nature and the environment. It is perhaps telling that chamber musicians looking for a composer sensitive to their concerns for the natural world have sought her out. Larsen has explained the projects:

> One of them is for *Nexus*, a great percussion ensemble, and they want a piece that has to do with earth's sustainability. . . . So I translated certain passages [of *Silent Spring*] into Morse code to carry the message.[60] There's the Fry Street String Quartet, a great quartet, and they're embarked on their own mission for environmentalism. So they have commissioned a piece about water. It's obvious why we're working together! I'm bound to water, and I thought this will be an interesting collaboration. It's not only the

molecular structure of water that they're interested in, but they're trying to understand how that molecular structure is being affected by the things that we add to water as culture. Now that's a piece I really can't wait to get to![61]

Then there's Ancia, a saxophone quartet founded in 1990 and based in Minneapolis–Saint Paul that has commissioned an environmental-themed piece. Given the Twin Cities' location near the source of the Mississippi and the intersection of a half dozen other rivers, it seems logical that the group would invite a piece about "the confluence of rivers and what happens at confluences, which is a very serious issue."[62] Although Larsen is a child of her local lakes, the world-traveling adult composer is sensitive to the global ramifications of water policies. She will lend her music to Ancia's cause.

As four decades of compositions reveal, the natural world infuses Larsen's thinking and music. But it also permeates her being to a degree uncommon among contemporary urban-art composers. She is a product of her particular upper Midwest place much like the walleye, the loon, and the pink lady's slipper, and Minnesotans identify her just as closely with their home state.[63] Whether her rootedness derives from empathy with the strong, stoic northern citizens who take pride in enduring winters unmatched in their severity in the continental United States, or is the product of nature's presence as a refuge, or is a foil for her indefatigable energy, or is the result of an essential DNA-binding protein that defies observation or explanation, or some powerful fusion of all the above, Larsen is fully integrated with and requires the quietude that her Minneapolis environs provide. Nature offers her a sanctuary, a classroom, a laboratory, a playground, an anchor, a stage, solace, imagery, and inspiration.

5 Larsen and the Academy Years
"My Soul Was Shaking"

FAMILY, RELIGION, NATURE, AND PLACE continued to influence Larsen during her undergraduate years. She may have stopped attending Sunday services, but she never expunged the lessons taught by the Catholic sisters: wonder, humility, spirituality, generosity, and grace shaped her core; they were overlaid with clear thinking, pragmatic efficiency, formidable tenacity, inexhaustible energy, and determination that brooks no opposition. She'll be a "cradle Catholic," even if a lapsed one, to the grave.

The natural environment of Larsen's Minneapolis childhood remained when she enrolled at the University of Minnesota; it was just four miles from her parents' home, where she continued to live. Family stayed visibly present. Although her intellectual world and circle of friends expanded, she wouldn't venture far from the upper Midwest until she was an established composer in the 1980s and traveled as a professional.

Beyond these continuities, another constant in Larsen's life was the steady-state social upheaval of the times. The year she headed to the university, 1968, had seen the Tet Offensive in January and the My Lai massacre in March, flashpoints for outraged antiwar youths. American troop levels in Vietnam reached well over half a million, their highest in the entire fourteen-year conflict.[1] Martin Luther King Jr. and then Robert F. Kennedy were assassinated in April and June that year. In August the Democratic National Convention became the scene of riots when Mayor Richard J. Daley called out the Chicago police and Illinois National Guard to quell thousands of demonstrators at and around the International Amphitheatre, the convention site. Using rifle butts, billy clubs, tear gas, and mace, guardsmen and officers roughed up and injured over a thousand people, including three dozen news reporters. Protestors gathered outside the Chicago Hilton Hotel, chanting, "The whole world is watching! The whole world is watching!" and indeed, millions of Americans were glued to their TV screens watching the Midwest political theater, just as they witnessed the mayhem occurring in Vietnamese rice fields half a world away each evening on the news. The Soviet Union used the convention melee as evidence of the U.S. government's brutality and suppression of its citizens. It became commonplace to tag war protestors "Communists." The generational divide that had cracked open in the 1950s with rock 'n' roll music and car culture became a chasm in the 1960s. Patriotism, so closely associated with military service during World War II and the 1950s, was not so easily defined in the Vietnam era.

Unrest continued in Larsen's second year in college when in November over five hundred thousand peaceful citizens gathered in Washington, DC, to protest the war.[2] Discontent reached a new high, however, after December 1, 1969, when the first of a series of draft lotteries took place: all males born between 1944 and 1950 became eligible for military service; a young man's birth date and then his first, middle, and last name initials determined the order in which he would be called to serve. Panic seized an entire generation of male college students and their friends who foresaw their educations and lives being interrupted at the very least, and the real possibility of death fighting a war that many judged indefensible and doomed. Without hesitation, the composer dates her political activism to the December 1 lottery and the complete helplessness she and her friends felt as they watched television and saw one male colleague have his birthdate pulled randomly from a rotating drum early in the evening, meaning he was headed for an induction center, and another friend, by chance have his birthdate called later, meaning he was likely free to continue his life uninterrupted. The government joined the church and patriarchal family structures as a third system that Larsen wouldn't trust. In each case she had no input and no voice; she was powerless against invisible forces and felt disenfranchised. If the Great Depression and World War II had shaped her parent's generation, the incessant threat of nuclear annihilation, social upheaval, and the Vietnam War marked Larsen's own. Roiling civil unrest provided a continuous backdrop against which her academic years unfolded.

Larsen's consciousness regarding a gendered society was ratcheted up a few notches when she entered what she described as the "monastically" ordered academy.[3] It took her a few years to fully appreciate the degree to which university life and the world of music composition, specifically, were overwhelmingly male-centered spaces. As she sees it, rituals and ranking systems endemic to academia had been passed down from the medieval church and reinforced by the military, places with little room for women in the front lines. But discovering this reality did not deter Larsen from knowing who she was (or is) or doing what she knew she could (or can) do: she is a composer—outside the academy and the old-boys network—and she has "never felt vulnerable composing" music that reflects who she is and what she believes.[4]

But before even getting to college Larsen experienced a number of events that challenged her beliefs and agency, and each took place within an academic environment.[5] During high school Larsen sought opportunities to participate in organized athletic events. Structured team sports abounded for the boys in her class, but without the guarantees of Title IX, which wouldn't become law until 1972, Larsen's public high school was not required to make similar opportunities available for girls. "Girls could play badminton, field hockey, or swim, but I swam all the time so why would I want to swim? I wanted to run!"[6] Rather than be denied, in her senior year Larsen organized a girls' cross-country team. Although the team was not hugely successful, Larsen recalled that one of the girls' team members, Suzanne Baxstresser, won an individual event.[7] This early foray into administration on behalf of a perceived need prepared Larsen for her work supporting regional composers, which resulted in the Minnesota Composers Forum. It became a signature achievement of Larsen's college years.

Larsen's musical talents were obvious to anyone watching first the child and then the adolescent as she composed, sang, danced, and played piano at award-winning levels. Although early training in the Catholic chant tradition remained her primary musical influence as a composer, her public high school chorus experience and its director, Oscar B. Dahle, whom Larsen describes as "very Scandinavian," the leader of a "choral dynasty," and with "a tremendously powerful personality," also left a mark. In a 1998 interview with Vivian Perlis, Larsen described her visceral reaction to the director and music-making *chorus* style.

> We were at odds with each other immediately. It was very interesting. I went into the choirs right away—I could read and sing and harmonize and do all those things. But why we were at odds was . . . I couldn't understand the complete subjugation of the body in the service of interpretation of music. Nor could I understand the social hierarchy of the various roles that are assigned to choral members—soprano, alto, tenor, bass, first and second, really—which is a very structured and hierarchical system. And this was all new to me—really, really new. It wasn't part of my church [musical] tradition, wasn't part of my musical upbringing. And I chafed at it. I guess because I'm a composer and a strong personality, too. And so while I did it, while I worked within the system, I also was angry about it, because I couldn't understand it. Although I loved it, too. It's also being adolescent—

that's terrible turmoil. But somehow for me it all focused around music. I was able to work out turmoil through music.[8]

Because chant with its transcending potential was Larsen's model for music, it is easy to understand her confusion with the new experience. But it turns out that it was not just a different musical style or aesthetic or Dahle's strong personality that disturbed Larsen; it was also the repertoire and her sense that the director did not respect aspects of what she held dear. As Larsen has explained:

> He loved Mitch Miller, and so we did a lot of sort of Mitch Miller kinds of arrangements. We did things that embarrassed me to death. . . . Having sung Latin chant during funeral services and seen and felt and been part of music's role in life's passages, and then to move into a tradition where we sang the Hawaiian war chant. Can you imagine a bunch of Scandinavian high school students? And not only that, we had to pluck our noses and sound like a Hawaiian guitar? Yes! And he wore a grass skirt and a hat and a ukulele and he would hula. My kindergarten teacher was Miss Yamamoto, a Hawaiian, who taught us the hula as sacred, as sacred as chant is to the Catholic Church. . . . It was infuriating, but I couldn't express any of it. I was just this seething ball of rage, but still loving music and adhering to the system. But just my soul was shaking! And I couldn't tell why. And I thought maybe it's because I liked rock 'n' roll. So I tried singing in a rock band for a little while—I quit piano. I started to begin to move, musically, inside.[9]

Larsen's outrage didn't reflect a narrow sense of what constituted good music, which was extremely broad and inclusive given her family's amateur music-making and consuming traditions, or the absence of a sense of humor, which she always enjoyed and was known for, but indicated her rejection of what she perceived as appropriating, misunderstanding, and disrespecting music, in effect, not taking the ideas behind the music seriously. To this day, Larsen has a fraught relationship with much contemporary choral music, which she thinks of not as music but as "pieces."[10]

When in the 1980s Eugenia Zukerman asked her friend what career she would have pursued had she not become a composer, Larsen replied, "Investment banker."[11] Although Zukerman was initially surprised, she appreciated that Larsen's business savvy was likely an outgrowth of this interest. She is an artist and pragmatist in equal parts in ways that recall Charles Ives and Wallace Stevens. Larsen's gifts in math and economics were not encouraged or nurtured in the 1960s, except perhaps by her father, whose career as a financial advisor later in life gave her permission to think seriously in and about numbers. A summer school experience between her junior and senior years in high school, however, suggests how limited opportunities regularly impacted young girls' lives and decided their fates. The composer has explained:

> There was a summer program in Minneapolis to keep active kids busy, and it was the Twin Cities Institute for Talented Youth. They taught a lot of things and I applied for [the program]. My first choice was economics, because I really loved math, and I love "if-then" propositions. My second choice was music. But they didn't take girls in economics at that time, and so I didn't get into economics, and I was heartbroken; but boy I know economics! So I got music, and I thought, oh, no. It turned out it was a fabulous thing! It was taught by William Lydell, who is still a very good friend. He is in his nineties now.[12]

Despite her initial disappointment, Larsen's second choice for a summer class ended up being life-changing. It introduced her to a world of musical thought that she had not encountered before. Forty years after the class, it is easy to hear in her recollections the impact that it made:

> [Lydell] was a pianist trained at Juilliard, a brilliant guy, and teaching high school at Washburn High in Minneapolis. . . . He designed a course, a theory class [where] we looked at various systems of organizing—Fux and Hindemith—and one day we got into tuning, and he gave a talk on the *spiral* of fifths, which I had learned was a *circle* of fifths, but it's only a circle on [a piano]. And I thought it was the voice of God. I thought this was the most beautiful concept, and I still do, actually, because it's infinite. And I just thought, I have to live there. That was the "ah-ha" moment, the compositional "ah-ha" moment. That opens up all music: no hierarchy, no bins.[13]

Lydell's four-week course reinforced Larsen's original experiences with music at Christ the King. The modal language of chant that she first learned there, where "do" was naturally movable, where the pitch world was as open as vocal production itself and not confined to the semitones of an equally tempered scale or the prescribed behaviors of a functional tonal system, now had additional depth, breadth, and resonance. As Larsen has explained, she "grew exponentially in understanding that music has structure, that structures contain sound, and sound contains structures."[14] There was history to build on; there were alternatives to common practices. The consolation course opened Larsen's musical mind.

Today Larsen acknowledges the serendipity of learning opportunities: "My teachers have come from unexpected places in my musical life. They have been poets, architects, painters, and philosophers. The other way I really learn is by reading scores voraciously, from Chuck Berry to Witold Lutoslawski."[15] In reality, Larsen's steady-state curiosity means she is always asking questions and absorbing ideas. And her openness to where learning takes place is a good thing, since, despite working with a number of mentors who would remain close supporters and collaborators over the years, Larsen's university experience was not always positive, productive, or confirming. On more than one occasion, she was left to fend for herself.

Larsen had not settled on a major when she started at the university. A summer job at the Clark Dodge & Company stock brokerage firm while in high school had reinforced her interest in economics.[16] In meeting with her freshman advisor, Larsen proposed pursuing an economics major and taking a few courses in music, but her advisor had other ideas: "It became very clear from working with my counselor, who was a musician, that I should do music, and then take a couple of economics classes. So I went to the U entering as a BA in voice."[17] We can only speculate why the counselor discouraged Larsen from economics: because women weren't welcome in the field as they hadn't been in the summer course; or because the advisor couldn't imagine a woman succeeding in economics; or because Larsen's musical gifts were too formidable to be denied. Once again, Larsen was directed away from economics, but here again, the decision to go with music proved fortuitous.

In 1968–69 Larsen took freshman theory classes: "I was like a duck in a pond with theory. . . . I was just writing away and composing. But you never know where your mentors come from."[18] Lois Ann Wittich, an Indiana University–trained adjunct voice teacher to whom Larsen was assigned, suggested that she write her own repertoire for her year-end jury. Using songs from Shakespeare's *The Tempest*, Larsen composed a small set of pieces. In mining Shakespeare's play, Larsen joined composers as varied as Arthur Sullivan, Vaughan Williams, Sibelius, and Tchaikovsky among others who had found inspiration for their own vocal and instrumental music in the work.[19] At eighteen years of age, Larsen contributed to the tradition and claimed a place for herself.

In hindsight, it seems only logical that Larsen would write a set of songs, but at the time she imagined herself a singer, not a composer. As she explains: "I had visions of being the next Roberta Peters. I saw her at the old Met, and I thought she was wonderful; she was a great communicator, and she was on TV, on *The Mike Douglas Show*, and all those things, so I said to Lois, I

Figure 5.1. Libby Larsen, "While You Here Do Snoring Lie." From Larsen's set of freshman songs based on Shakespeare's *The Tempest*, act 2, scene 1, Ariel's song to Gonzalo. Reproduced with the kind permission of the composer.

think if I'm going to be a singer, I better go to New York."[20] Wittich helped Larsen prepare an audition program that included "Musetta's Waltz" from *La Bohème*, and in her sophomore year Larsen's father took his daughter to Juilliard, Mannes, and Oberlin to audition. She remembers the Juilliard faculty reading newspapers and talking while she sang and the experience being "awful": she did not get in. Mannes, on the other hand "was just fine," and she was admitted with the promise that they would find her a nanny job to help her pay her way. But as the composer has explained, "I wasn't elated. I couldn't see the sky in New York. You can't get to the sun, unless you're down in Chelsea or the end of the island."[21] On another occasion Larsen volunteered that she simply "was not prepared at all to [pursue singing as a career].”[22] She auditioned at Oberlin “and had a very good time analyzing a Beethoven sonata and doing all the theory tests.” Larsen recalls the assessment of the faculty: “You probably could sing, and you probably could be a chamber singer, but no students who come here have these kinds of analysis skills. Don’t you think you should be thinking about that?” Larsen was utterly heartbroken: “I was going to be a singer! And I was crushed.”[23]

Having been steered away from economics and discouraged from pursuing voice, Larsen headed back to the University of Minnesota; if she couldn’t be a singer, she reasoned, she might as well stay there. As it turns out, it was unlikely that she would have been allowed to attend school anywhere but the university, as Larsen’s father refused to bankroll her studies at any institution but the state one in town. And this was his policy: neither of her older sisters had convinced him of their need to go away despite having been accepted at other schools.[24] The University of Minnesota was a family tradition. Having “tried to get away from Minnesota through singing,” Larsen determined to make peace with her hometown university. There too she would be discouraged from pursuing a voice major, but this time her disappointments ultimately clarified “what [she] was naturally doing anyway,” which, she reflects, “is lucky for students who can learn that early on.”[25]

During her sophomore year, Larsen met Vern Sutton, a new, young professor of opera theater. Sutton had been in Minneapolis since 1960, directing church choirs, singing, and earning two graduate degrees of his own at the university, but he was appointed to the faculty in 1967, just a year prior to Larsen’s arrival as a freshman. In 1970 Larsen auditioned for Sutton’s production of Gian Carlo Menotti’s one-act radio opera *The Old Maid and the Thief*, singing The Seekers 1966 hit song “Georgy Girl.” Although Sutton cast her as Laetitia, he nonetheless felt he had to discourage her from pursuing a career as an opera singer. As Sutton explained in an interview in 2012, it wasn’t Larsen’s voice per se that was the problem; he described it as a “fine, not an exceptional voice.” It was her extraordinary energy: “The very essence of who she is just gets in the way of being a singer. The very thing that makes her the great composer that she is, that sort of *drive* . . . it can destroy singing careers simply because people oversing, or overdo, or overexert. I just sensed that there were other ways to channel her energy.”[26]

More important, however, than telling Larsen what she was not suited to do, Sutton encouraged her to do what he recognized she did best, and he did it in a way and with an authority and affection that no one else commanded. Like Wittich, Sutton recognized and honored that she was a composer, and he invited her to compose. Sutton understood Larsen’s vocal inclinations, her sensitivity to the sounds and rhythms of American English, and her skills as a composer and orchestrator; he respected her work ethic and craft, and in an environment where most people tended to take themselves quite seriously, he appreciated her side-splitting sense of humor, which he shared. Ultimately Sutton offered Larsen a deal she could not refuse: if she would compose an opera, he would mount the production. In 1974 Larsen made good on Sutton's suggestion to consider the children's story *Charlotte's Web*. The one-act opera, *Some Pig*, became her master's thesis.

Larsen describes herself as "mostly just sleepwalking through [her] undergraduate years,"[27] but a few events stick out in her memory. Under duress, in her sophomore year she joined her mother's sorority, Pi Beta Phi, as her older sisters, LuAnne and Molly, had done before her. But the sorority's rules and requirements proved problematic. Larsen was fined regularly for a variety of infractions, the most maddening of which was having males in the sorority house after hours. Larsen and her friends needed the space to work on a sorority-sponsored project for a campuswide carnival. Despite their entry winning the carnival competition and bringing honor, glory, and a money prize to the sorority, Larsen was brought before its disciplinary board and informed that she would have to stay in the sorority house on consecutive weekends, even though she lived at home at the time. The arbitrariness of the curfew, the illogic of the punishment, the disregard for the specific situation, the ingratitude for what she and her male friends had accomplished, and Larsen's complete rejection of sorority culture with its rules, rituals, and pledges (which she had refused to sign) motivated her to finish undergraduate classes as soon as possible. She refused to serve her weekend confinement and informed the sisterhood that she would be graduating at the end of her junior year, although she would actually remain through the fall of her senior year and graduate in December, one semester early. Given Larsen's aversion to established systems and hierarchies, it is not surprising that sorority life didn't suit her. Voluntarily subjecting herself to someone else's rules was out of character for Larsen; the idea was destined to fail.

Other undergraduate experiences were more positive. In 1970 she was inducted into Sigma Alpha Iota, a national fraternal organization that recognized women of exceptional musical accomplishment. The organization maintained a cottage at the MacDowell Colony, an artists' retreat in Peterborough, New Hampshire.[28] The colony had been founded in 1907 by Edward and Marian MacDowell and offered residencies for men and women from across the arts. By 1970 it had hosted hundreds of composers, writers, poets, sculptors, and artists. Larsen wanted to see what went on there, and in 1971 she wrote to the colony asking about a summer job. She recalls,

> My mother helped me with this. I told her I wanted to go there and work in the summer, and she helped me write the letter: a brilliant letter. We sat in the kitchen, which is where all our good talking ever happened, and . . . I composed the letter, and she said "what if you phrase it this way; what if you phrased it that way." And so I sent maybe a two or three paragraph letter to Conrad S. Spohnholz, who was the general director at the time, and he answered it within the week and said, "Come and be a chambermaid."[29]

Larsen explains: "I wanted to see how [composers] moved in their composing studios. And I wanted to see what they did when they weren't composing. I was young, and female, and in 1971 there was never a thought that I was a composer. I was just this young woman hanging around."[30] She craved models of what she wanted to become, and because this was the year that the MacDowell Medal was awarded to a composer, William Schuman, many composers visited the colony beyond those who were already in residence.[31] On the actual medal weekend, Larsen recalls, "The whole Northeast came in for a big party." During her time there, she got to see Aaron Copland and clean his cabin; to observe Barbara Kolb, who had won the Rome Prize earlier that year (the first woman to do so); to be in the presence of Joel Hoffman and Robert Lombardo; and to spend time with William Woods, "a jazz guy" who taught at the University of New Mexico: "We talked about composing a lot and he actually wanted to talk about it more." Larsen recalls Stephan Wolpe, who was suffering from Parkinson's disease "desperately, desperately trying to communicate; and we did." She has vivid memories of seeing composers who had been only names to her previously. She got to study the workaday habits of a range of contemporary composers, talk at length with some of them, and make a few friends in the process. Based in part upon her observations at the colony, from the start of her career Larsen insisted that being a composer would be one aspect of a larger life.[32]

Besides the freshman communications class where she met James Reece, her future husband, another communications class provided Larsen with the first opportunity to "stand on [her] own two feet and talk." In light of her childhood experiences being quieted and silenced by her family, Larsen "felt like the whole class was an exercise in dealing with post-traumatic stress."[33] Anxiety regularly accompanied her oral presentations, but the class proved revelatory, and Larsen values that she heard herself communicate in words there. Although the composer is clear that verbalizing is never her preferred expressive mode, on more than one occasion Larsen has been praised for her articulate and moving talks on a variety of issues. Whether through the trauma of this class or something else, Larsen learned the art of verbal communication.

An undergraduate theory class provided a less stressful epiphanic moment when Larsen's assignment was to write a brief piece. Although she cannot remember the instructor, Larsen vividly recalls that the piece came to her whole.[34] She states, "I knew I must be a composer. Not that I love to do it, just that I am it."[35] Despite her ongoing interest in economics and her never-realized aspirations to be an opera singer, Larsen recognized that she was a composer. In December 1971, just days shy of her twenty-first birthday, Larsen earned a BA in Music Theory and Composition and finished her undergraduate schooling.

Done with college a semester early and unsure of what to do next, Larsen signed on with an employment agency that decided she had a talent for the insurance business. She landed a job as head secretary for the field managers at a large insurance firm in downtown Minneapolis. But her time there was unsettling for many reasons. Larsen's placement in this position offended an older employee who had been with the company for many years and assumed the job would be hers. In a world of "head guys and field managers," all men, the loss of a single female friend in the workplace was troubling. In addition, part of her job required forging signatures and others' handwriting, which she could do with ease given her training with music notation and her care with scores. But as the composer explained: "I regularly forged documents for them . . . and I thought this is unbelievably illegal . . . and I'm not going to do this." Larsen also "had the full-on experience of being a young girl secretary [enduring] a lot of harassment. . . . I just wanted to get out of it."[36] And she did: she quit after six months, but not before she had also written two one-act operas during her coffee breaks and in her free time. As she explains, "I just kept on composing."[37]

It became clear to the composer that her only reasonable course of action was to pursue a graduate degree in what she did naturally, to learn how to do research, and to polish her composing skills. The university boasted an excellent composition faculty including Dominick Argento, Paul Fetler, and Eric Stokes, and Larsen was excited at the prospect of working with them. She rented a small room in a house shared by a number of graduate students; she describes the room as "really an oversized closet." It contained just enough space for an elevated single bed, under which she stored her things, and a full-size upright piano. Larsen opted for a piano instead of a desk, which she reasoned she could find on campus if needed. Thus began her habit of composing at the piano and notating her scores while lying on her stomach dangling from the piano bench, staff paper on the floor. As Larsen reasoned: "I was small; I could fit."[38]

Despite Larsen doing poorly on the GREs and applying late, the director of graduate studies, Johannes Riedel, interviewed and admitted her to the theory and composition program in fall 1972.[39] With her next younger sister, Duffy, headed to college and a family policy of not paying for more than one degree per daughter, Larsen needed to fund her own education. She learned that there would be no support from the department that admitted her.[40] But Riedel found her a position in the physics department as a lab assistant in an acoustics of music course. As with the high school summer music class, which turned out to be the proverbial "blessing in disguise," so did her assistantship in the physics department. She had taken an acoustics course while an undergraduate in which she "made an instrument and analyzed the auditorium." She remembers, "I just loved it!"[41] Larsen's natural sensitivity to sound, which had been given a theoretical foundation in the undergraduate course, was additionally strengthened when she assisted in the physics lab. Soon after being admitted, Larsen set about producing her two small operas. As she recalls: "I got all my friends together, John Low, who [eventually] designed the Composers Forum logo, he wanted to do sets. And it was your basic Mickey Rooney–Judy Garland 'Let's put on a show!' And we did."[42] Larsen wasn't awarded an assistantship in theory or composition until 1975, when she enrolled as a doctoral student in the program.

Although she enjoyed her work in the physics department, Larsen was determined to have an assistantship in the Department of Music. Once again, she took matters into her own hands; she walked into the office of the musicologist Donna Cardamone (Jackson), who had recently arrived from Harvard, and blurted out, "I need a job." In 2012 Larsen reflected: "Can you imagine? Because I couldn't get a TA-ship in theory, she took me on as her TA in musicology, and I wasn't a musicologist. But I think she fought a lot of battles. She was the frontline of the feminist movement in the music department."[43] Larsen recalls that she assisted for almost every course that Cardamone taught and in doing so "worked with a strong, centered, no non-sense, not angry role model." She credits Cardamone with teaching her all her study skills and providing that essential model: "She just set the bar high. She was great."[44] Because an assistantship would not cover all her expenses, Larsen worked in the music library as well; at times she held down three jobs to support herself while working on her master's degree.[45] In that regard, her graduate school experience matched many of her colleagues at UM and was typical of grad students at large public universities who seldom have the luxury of financial support generous enough to allow exclusive focus on their studies. But unlike most graduate students who are embraced by faculty eager to work with serious, eager, budding professionals, Larsen sensed she was tangential to her department, and Vern Sutton speculated why. Looking back on Larsen's early years in the graduate program at Minnesota, Sutton confided: "She had some struggles at first being taken seriously by faculty."[46]

Larsen did not fit the model of the American academic composer circa 1970s. Her high-spirited, effervescent personality was unusual in a profession whose practitioners too often cultivated a persona perceived as aloof, apart from, and confidently disengaged from others. Milton Babbitt's 1958 argument that composers were specialists writing for other specialists resonated in a field that struggled to justify its existence in a newly science-oriented world.[47] Larsen's unapologetic admission that she wrote music to be understood and enjoyed by audiences put her in a minority of composers, or at least of composers willing to admit such beliefs. Her outspoken honesty would have been disquieting, her position a possible source of embarrassment for a music program striving to be taken seriously in a regional music culture that included high-powered university programs at Illinois, Michigan, and Indiana. And then there was the fact of her being a young female composition student in an overwhelmingly male world. Separating this aspect of who Larsen is from the whole of her being is an impossible undertaking, so the degree to which she met resistance because of her sex remains unknowable: correlations, regardless of their number or obviousness, are not causes. But Larsen believes that gendered attitudes played a part in her reception and the kinds of support and encouragement she received from certain faculty, even if unintentional. Vern Sutton agrees.[48]

Sutton's early encouragement of Larsen's compositional career sowed the seeds of a collaborative relationship that continues. Over the years they have combined their talents to create additional operas, songs, song cycles, shows, and musical projects of all kinds. While Sutton studied the vocal music of Baroque opera composer Nicola Porpora (1686–1768) and was an accomplished vocalist, he was also a lover of country music and musicals and shared those passions with Larsen. A talented lyricist as well as singer, over the years Sutton wrote song texts, and Larsen composed the music; they were a creative team. Both adopted aliases for their less reverent musical alter egos. "Vincent Marathon" and "Florine McKay" wrote and performed numerous show tunes and country-music-style songs, with Sutton/Marathon on the piano and Larsen/McKay composing and singing the vocals. At one performance a music faculty member complimented Larsen, saying that he had never heard her sound so good.[49] Larsen did not know and still is not sure how to take the remark. Given the tepid reception she had gotten from most faculty, she thinks it was probably intended as a put down, but it did not matter because she and Sutton were having fun making music. Larsen's nom de plume would stick until she learned that there was a real Florine McKay, and she had to invent a new one.[50] At the end of her formal training, Larsen's association with Vern Sutton resulted in her appearance on Garrison Keillor's *Prairie Home Companion*, where Sutton had become a regular. For the first national broadcast in 1978, Larsen composed "Weaver's Song and Jig." The piece included a string band (with spoons), chamber winds, additional strings, piano, and a variety of world percussion instruments. The range of Larsen's musical expression was on full display.

Graduate work provided opportunities for Larsen to develop her increasingly confident craft. She remembers being "quite interested in creating a feeling of seamless melody" and that she recognized that "the oboe is . . . an instrument where you can use circular breathing."[51] In 1973 she wrote *Circular Rondo*, a piece for oboe and guitar that shows the continuing influence of her beloved piano teacher Sister Colette, who introduced the young Larsen to the

Figure 5.2. Libby Larsen in 1978 at the premiere of her "Weaver's Song and Jig" on the first national broadcast of *Prairie Home Companion*. Garrison Keillor is to her left. Reproduced with the kind permission of the composer.

flexible rhythms, unconstrained melodies, and modal mixtures of Stravinsky, Bartók, and Japanese music. If *Saints without Tears* shows Larsen's early gift for vocal lines and text setting, *Circular Rondo* displays her budding talents as an instrumental composer.

Circular breathing, a technique that had been used for centuries by artisans hand-blowing decorative metal pieces and by many non-Western instrumentalists to spin a continuous sound, had been adopted by American jazz musicians earlier in the century. By midcentury the technique was taught regularly in university and conservatory wind studios, and today it is an assumed skill in every professional wind player's technical arsenal. Larsen wasn't a wind player, but her days as a singer made her sensitive to the importance of breath in shaping a musical thought. Although Larsen notated catch breaths in the wind part, with circular breathing techniques the line that she imagined would not have to be broken with inhalations; the melody could weave the oboe and guitar lines together "seamlessly." In *Circular Rondo*, a piece she wrote for a young faculty guitarist, Jeffrey Van, the oboe plunges and rises and curls its slow, spinning thread of sound around and through the guitar line.[52] Their partnering is simultaneously sultry and elegant. At strategic moments guitar and oboe call and respond; they couple and connect for a few notes before drifting apart. Each player makes room for the other. Larsen eventually positioned *Circular Rondo* as the middle of a group of three brief pieces that she worked on over the years 1973–74 and titled *Three Pieces for Treble Wind and Guitar* (ex. 5.1).[53]

Respecting the most basic formal conventions, Larsen's rondo alternates the undulating theme with episode-like materials. But that is the extent of

Example 5.1. *Circular Rondo*, mm. 1–10

her allegiance to tradition. Even in the slightly more animated episodes, when the guitar switches from its climbing, off-set, quasi-ostinato accompanimental figure to more squared rhythms, one has no sense that Larsen is simply filling a received musical form founded on contrast. Because the rondo theme is so thoroughly entwined in the work, there is only the faintest hint of departure and return. The piece circles round; the parts are more joined than juxtaposed. The duo supplies pitches for each other at important junctures such as when the wind plays a high B to complete the guitar pattern at measure 4, and the guitar plays a middle G to complete the wind's half-step descent pattern in measure 7. The highly chromatic oboe melody resists functional tonal thinking, even while the guitar ostinato suggests an E minor home base. Bartók's flexible modal world echoes in Larsen's duet. Although the treble wind ultimately joins the guitar in its E-ish domain with a final sustained E beginning in the antepenultimate measure, its arrival there is not a foregone conclusion. The spent momentum of the work more than the harmonic convergence dictates the end of the piece.

Despite a piu animato and accelerando two minutes into the work, Larsen's under-four-minute piece never breaks its quiet, intense, hypnotic, *Andante cantabile* spell. Three iterations of the melody control the mood. The oboe breathes a single breath: an inhalation that begins at its first entrance and a deep, satisfied exhalation at its last sound. The heartbeat-like guitar pulses along with the oboe respiration. Melodic and harmonic sevenths and tritones, intervals that will remain favorites throughout four decades of composing, are audible in this early piece. The mature composer is present in this young work. Elastic rhythms, never beholden to bar lines or accent patterns, characterize *Circular Rondo* as they did chant and as they will the majority of Larsen's later works. Fascination with pure sound can be heard in the guitar harmonics that sparkle throughout the piece. Larsen's energy bubbles to the surface in brief "dancelike" passages as if she cannot contain her joy at the beautiful work she has birthed. At twenty-two Larsen possessed a sophisticated understanding of instrumental techniques, musical line, surface and structural rhythms, balance and proportion, timbre and spacing, formal logic, and an ability to spin and suspend a soft, seductively simple sounding instrumental pas de deux. And she knew she had succeeded; her confidence is audible.

In the same year she composed *Circular Rondo*, 1973, Larsen and fellow graduate composition student Stephen Paulus applied for and received four hundred dollars from the university to explore ways "to promote the creation and performance of new musical works by Minnesota composers."[54] Their careers and American music culture would be changed forever when the Minnesota Composers Forum was born. In Larsen's interview with Vivian Perlis, she explained the circumstances of the forum's genesis and formulation.

> We [Larsen and Paulus] met in 1972. We both sang in Dale Warland's Macalester Festival Chorus, which was a community chorus based at Macalester College. . . . We just became acquainted there. Then we found ourselves at the University in a course on Russian history. And there we were again. . . . And so then we found ourselves in a lot of classes together. And just through Festival Chorus, just through talking, became friends. And discovered that we think very much alike about what composers can be or could be, what art music could or can be. And our backgrounds, at least in thinking about music in a commercial society—we had similar backgrounds: corporate dads who talked a lot about system building, one way or another, and mothers who joined the conversation and encouraged curiosity. And so we found ourselves to be kindred spirits . . . .
>
> We talked about music and culture, about composers, about how interesting it was to be writing music in all the different funny situations that we found ourselves in. We both have a good sense of humor; that helps. And we both became mutually interested in the fact that we wanted to and had actually been writing music, very seriously, for rituals that weren't particularly valued at the university. And that was puzzling to us. If we could apply the same kind of rigorous thinking to a piece that was being written for a children's choir as we were applying to our serial technique compositions at the university, why were they valued so differently? Why were our role models valuing, placing value judgments on, the compositional process, according to who was playing and hearing the music? And those conversations led on, really quickly, to "You know, we ought to be able to write music, put on concerts and put those concerts at the Walker Art Center and invite our friends, and they ought to be able to come and they ought to be able to experience these pieces. And they don't have to be musicians. They ought to be able to experience these pieces." And we found no support for that within the department at all, which was interesting.[55]

Over numerous cups of coffee at Shevlin Hall, Larsen and Paulus decided to "put together a group and . . . some concerts and . . . see what happen[ed]." But it wasn't as whimsical as that description sounds. Larsen has clarified: "We also knew that, in fact, we were very serious about this." The pair created a list of what needed to be done, brainstormed the names of possible supporters and attendees, and divvied up the tasks. But calling people out of the blue on their own behalf unnerved them both, so they quickly determined they needed a name for their endeavor, "because then [they could] call on behalf of [it]."[56] They also needed official stationery, so Larsen contacted her art school friend, John Low, who made them a logo. Larsen and Paulus worked after classes in Professor Steve Schultz's office, so they had a phone number from which to place and receive calls: there they strategized, designed programs, wrote copy, and rehearsed their best sales pitches to attract sponsors and supporters.[57] They developed a kind of patter routine where Larsen and Paulus took turns delivering their pitch. Calling people and announcing that they were with such an auspicious-sounding organization yielded unexpected positive results. In the arts-friendly cities of Minneapolis and Saint Paul, important people bought into the idea. In a short period of time, they built an audience and a following. Four hundred dollars was all they would ever request or receive from the university, and it proved to be all they needed. With a realistic set of goals, access to venues beyond the university for performances, and a sound business plan that included paying themselves and composers some token amount, the Minnesota Composers Forum was successfully launched.

The MCF met a need that plagued and continues to haunt a majority of American "art music" composers who are not affiliated with academia or an institute: getting their newly composed works rehearsed, performed, and heard by a critical mass of interested listeners in surroundings conducive to being taken seriously. When the MCF ultimately submitted official papers of incorporation, on February 25, 1975, the document listed three incorporators: Mr. Stephen H. Paulus, Mr. James S. Reece (whom Larsen would marry seven months later), and Ms. Elizabeth Larsen. Three people were named to the board of directors as well: Ms. Suzanne Weil of the Walker Art Center in Minneapolis, whose museum would become an important site of early MCF concerts; Dr. Eric Stokes, a revered and beloved faculty composer at the university, who would be the only faculty composer to lend his financial support to the fledgling organization or contribute works to its concerts; and Mr. Dennis Russell Davies, who was just establishing his career as a conductor and champion of living American composers with his first post at the head of the Saint Paul Chamber Orchestra. Russell Davies had arrived the previous year and would stay until 1980, when he was succeeded by the violist, violinist, and conductor Pinchas Zukerman. It was through Pinchas Zukerman that Larsen met Eugenia Zukerman, and the two become close friends and collaborators.

4134542

N-155 K-43, 288

ARTICLES OF INCORPORATION
OF
Minnesota Composers Forum

We, the undersigned, for the purpose of forming a corporation under and pursuant to the provisions of Chapter 317 Minnesota Statutes, known as the Minnesota Nonprofit Corporation Act, do hereby associate ourselves together as a body corporate and adopt the following Articles of Incorporation:

ARTICLE I.

The name of this corporation shall be: Minnesota Composers Forum

ARTICLE II.

The purpose of this corporation shall be: To promote the creation and performance of new musical works by Minnesota composers.

ARTICLE III.

This Corporation shall not afford pecuniary gain, incidentally or otherwise, to its members.

ARTICLE IV.

The period of duration of corporate existence of this corporation shall be:
Perpetual - continual until termination by Board of Directors (see note below)

ARTICLE V.

The location of the registered office of this corporation in this state is:
2115 West 49th Street, Minneapolis, Minnesota, 55409

ARTICLE VI.

The name and address of each incorporator of this corporation is:
Mr Stephen H. Paulus 2008 Brewster Apt. 102, St. Paul, Mn. 55108
Mr. James S. Reece 1807 Ford Prkwy. Apt. 103, St. Paul, Mn. 55
Ms. Elizabeth Larsen 3345 University Ave. S.E., Mpls., Mn. 55414

ARTICLE VII.

The number of directors constituting the first board of directors of this corporation shall be three, and the tenure in office of such first board of directors

K-43, 289

shall be 10 years, or until successors are elected and qualified. The name and address of each such first director is:

Ms. Suzanne Weil, Walker Art Center, Vineland Place Mpls., Mn.
Dr. Eric Stokes, Scott Hall, University of Minnesota Mpls., Mn. 55455
Mr. Dennis Russell Davies, St. Paul Chamber Orchestra Old Federal Courts Building St. Paul, Mn.

ARTICLE VIII.

The extent of personal liability, if any, of members for corporate obligations and the methods of enforcement and collection, are as follows:
Nonliable

ARTICLE IX

This corporation shall have no capital stock. (A) See note below.
The capital stock which this corporation shall have authority to issue is: . (B)

In Testimony Whereof, we have hereunto subscribed our names this 25 day of February, A. D. 1975.

Witnesses:

James S. Reece
Stephen H. Paulus
Elizabeth B. Larsen

Figure 5.3. Incorporation papers of the Minnesota Composers Forum, February 25, 1975.

Self-organizing composer organizations have been a staple of American music culture since the late nineteenth century. But few of them have accomplished as much or endured as long as the Minnesota (now American) Composers Forum. When Vivian Perlis asked the composer to what she attributed the forum's "enormous success and influence," Larsen reflected:

> I think it was because we were serious about creating a structure that was lasting. While we wanted to put on concerts, we actually wanted to create an organization, which was equally as interested in composing music as putting on the concert. It was another exercise in composition: how to create a structure that was strong enough and broad enough so that it could contain the spontaneity of the needs of the creators. It's very clearly what we wanted to do. We started talking right away about when we leave the organization, what do we want it to be? So we wanted to create something that stood apart from us immediately. We did all our research: we looked into nonprofit organizations, how they were set up; we read about how to incorporate; we did all the incorporation papers by hand; they're all filed.

We printed them out, did them, went to the offices, sat there 'til we got our accreditation. We sought advice from many people.[58]

Perhaps most importantly, from the beginning the forum was not focused on promoting any particular composers' works, and especially not those of its founding members or their colleagues. Larsen has clarified: "It was about the idea of composers being able to have a community in which to function. That's what it was about, and actually that's what it still is about, even though it looks very different now than it did in the beginning, which is enormously joy-making for me. Because the idea itself is a good one, and it has changed as the times have. . . . From the very beginning . . . it wasn't about a style. . . it wasn't about *our* music."[59] A review of the forum's first concert appeared in the *Minneapolis Tribune* on October 22, 1973. Michael Anthony named each of the eight composers, made brief comments about their works, and explained the group's purpose: "Performance and promotion of the work of local composers is the goal of this organization, founded in April of this year—and it deserves support." Looking forward to the next MCF concert, Anthony informed readers that the event was "the first of two such evenings at the Walker Art Center Auditorium."[60]

Figure 5.4. An early program of the Minnesota Composers Forum designed by Libby Larsen. Reproduced with the kind permission of the composer.

The Walker Art Center in Minneapolis and the Landmark Center in Saint Paul became home to their early concert series.

Larsen and Paulus looked for locations that would get music in front of receptive audiences, and given the area's reputation as a regional incubator for the arts, they were easy to find. Newly developed bank plazas complete with welcoming gardens in downtown Minneapolis provided sites for spring and summer concert series. As the forum did all of its own administrative work, members quickly learned what was required to secure sites and pull off a successful concert series outside a university setting. Their achievements attracted additional members. Larsen recalls, "Within a few months' time, many of our friends in the graduate school became part of it, and we divided up the labor. It was a very Scandinavian tradition—sort of collectivism—which we were all part of. . . . We grew according to our means. We asked everybody who joined to give us five dollars. And we said that in return we were always going to pay our performers. So five dollars in, five dollars out."[61]

As Larsen has explained, they stayed within their budget, built a business, and immediately looked for grants. She acknowledges helpful staff in the music school office who "let [them] use the mimeograph machine, . . . [and] the phone in the main office; they were the ones who made it possible for [the forum] to function." But, as Larsen reflects, "The composers at the University were not helpful at all, . . . which was interesting." Patronizing pats on the head accompanying halfhearted inquiries such as, "How's your little group going?" revealed an all-too-common attitude toward Larsen and by extension the early forum.[62]

It would not take long, however, for some faculty to get on board. Vern Sutton, always supportive, had attended early meetings of the fledgling organization in the basement of Scott Hall when the group was mainly performing members' music. He remembers participating; and he remembers the absence of others.[63] And Larsen recalls that Eric Stokes quickly lent his support and became one of the first board members. Paul Fetler eventually showed up at concerts. But Dominick Argento was unpersuaded to join the organization, despite a yearlong student campaign directed at him specifically to gain his support, and Larsen never understood why. It is possible that at the same time the Minnesota Composers Forum was coalescing, Argento was enjoying his first national acclaim. Associating too closely with a regional, student-run group might have appeared to be a step in the wrong direction. Whatever the reason, his rejection of the group's overtures and absence from their activities remains an unresolved question in Larsen's mind. Long after she graduated with her doctorate in 1978, she stayed on as administrator of the forum. In 1983, ten years after its founding, Larsen left to accept the position of co-resident composer with the Minnesota Orchestra. Her co-resident composer, as had been her cofounder of the forum, was Stephen Paulus.

The Minnesota Composers Forum was a product of its time, place, and forward-thinking founders. Larsen, Paulus, and their cohort reasoned that given the relative youth of composition faculty across the country, it was unlikely that university positions would open up during their professional careers. Something else had to happen if they were to compose for a living. The Minnesota Composers Forum could provide a network for upper Midwest composers, both independent and affiliated, to practice their art and hear it played, regardless of their official credentials. It encouraged new music by paying composers and players small amounts, awarding commissions, staging performances, and creating a community similar to that enjoyed by faculty within academic institutions. The difference was that with MCF concerts, composers were heard by larger and more diverse audiences and outside the ivy-covered walls. Had Larsen and Paulus never composed at all after 1973, they would have assured their places in American music culture by founding the Minnesota Composers Forum and providing a unique support structure for contemporary music in the upper Midwest performed outside the expected locales.[64]

Despite her increasing responsibilities with the forum, Larsen continued to study and compose. She would not repeat the pattern of many talented women musicians before her who ended up behind the scenes running organizations that showcased men (and a very few women) of equal or lesser talent. She knew she was a composer and refused to be cast as something else simply because she was so broadly competent. With final incorporation papers for the forum being drawn up and her master's program nearly done, the academic year was set to end on a high note. Her thesis project, the one-act opera titled *Some Pig: An Opera Based on* Charlotte's Web *by E. B. White*, was in rehearsal and its university premiere scheduled for June 6, 1974. Her soon-to-be brother-in-law Rich(ard) Reece, a writer and later editor of the *Catholic Digest*, created the libretto. Accurately anticipating the opera's successful debut, the university music department joined with the Minneapolis park board and planned for additional performances. As the composer has explained, they "built a theater—a rolling theater—and decided that all summer it would take the production around to all the parks. And the music department made that happen, and that was really exciting for me."[65] Within weeks of its premiere, the opera was performed at a number of local parks, and hundreds of Larsen's Minneapolis neighbors enjoyed the work. This was a heady experience for the twenty-three-year-old, who, despite the doubters, had succeeded in such a public way in her hometown.

Unfortunately, the year 1974 and the experience of seeing her first opera performed in public would be memorable for reasons other than the success of the production. Along with refining her composer's skills, helping found an enduring music organization, writing a successful opera, and earning her master's degree, Larsen was slapped with a cease and desist order and sued by E. B. White, the author of *Charlotte's Web*.[66] He accused her of having "stolen [his] story."[67] The legal order prohibited performances of the one-act opera, a project that she had worked on with her faculty advisor, Paul Fetler, and coproduced with her mentor, Vern Sutton. In the middle of the summer 1974 run, *Some Pig* was shut down.

Riding high on the applause, Larsen was stunned by the legal action. In the context of twenty-first-century sensibilities, it may be hard to fathom that Larsen had never considered she needed to obtain permission to adapt a famous children's story for a student project. Forty years ago intellectual property law was not a thriving specialty, however, and there were no courses in music business. But more troubling to Larsen than the legal action was that during the year she worked on the opera, no faculty had suggested that she needed to obtain rights, and when she was sued and turned to the university for advice and support, "they washed their hands of responsibility"; she was on her own.[68] In a 1981 interview for the University of Minnesota's alumni magazine, the composer explained, "*Some Pig* hasn't been performed since and is unlikely to be since only the payment of many thousands of dollars will pry the rights loose from Paramount Pictures which purchased them from White many years ago."[69]

Larsen's student opera might have gone unnoticed and unchallenged by E. B. White had it not been for the March 1973 release of the Hanna-Barbera animated musical film *Charlotte's Web* and White's heightened attention to adaptations of his book. Although he approved of Earl Hamner Jr., the writer of the animated film's story, White didn't hide his displeasure with the movie and in particular the way music had intruded upon his tale. In a letter to a friend, White wrote: "The movie of 'Charlotte's Web' is about what I expected it to be. The story is interrupted every few minutes so that somebody can sing a jolly song. I don't care much for jolly songs. The Blue Hill Fair, which I tried to report faithfully in the book, has become a Disney World, with 76 trombones. But that's what you get for getting embroiled in Hollywood."[70] With the film's release fresh in his mind, White's radar was set, and he seemed predisposed to disliking any musical interference in his story line.

Larsen doesn't know how E. B. White learned of her opera, but in reality it would not have been difficult for the author or anyone related to the Hanna-Barbera film or Paramount Pictures to get wind of Larsen's one-act work. The Minneapolis music scene was well known, and its progressive arts culture was carefully tracked by interested performers of all kinds across the country. Any number of people associated with Larsen's project could have drawn attention to the production unintentionally, including her faculty advisors whose careers were in their ascendancy and thus being watched. Regardless of *how* White learned, he obviously *did* learn, and the aggressive legal action came as a complete surprise to the inexperienced student composer.

Larsen's sense of abandonment by the university left a deep scar on her psyche. She saw her first public compositional achievement, one based on a beloved children's story, being taken away from her. Ultimately an attorney who was a family friend resolved the matter, and Larsen continued moving forward. Despite the many honors that the university has bestowed on her in the intervening decades, the memory of this most painful incident lingers. A program that she understood as having declined to support her with an assistantship she now saw as eager to distance itself from her altogether. As Larsen read the situation, the faculty appeared to want no association with a work that had successfully fulfilled a degree requirement at their institution.

In the course of completing her master's degree in composition, Larsen had experienced the gamut of personal and professional highs and lows. Beyond not having been awarded an assistantship in her major, among the many minor annoyances she endured was an instructor who questioned whether she had submitted another student's composition assignment as her own because the work was too good. And then, just as she had finished her degree, she was served legal papers because, as she saw it, she hadn't received what she considered basic guidance regarding permissions and copyright issues. It was hard for Larsen to decide which of the many systems she encountered was most treacherous: the family, the church, the government, or the academy. All of them seemed determined to silence or thwart her or cut her adrift.

But the obstacles were balanced to a degree by meeting and working with student colleagues and a few faculty who provided strong friendships and role models, composers who embraced and encouraged a variety of musical styles and systems and were not insistent upon her adopting a single one, and a larger regional arts community that valued the range of her musical and administrative skills. She decided to stay and shape the environment she needed. In her remaining graduate studies, Larsen successfully navigated the waters of modern American university culture, and she determined that nothing was going to deter her from realizing her goals. It is a sign of Larsen's unwavering belief in her own abilities that she persevered and continued the next year in the doctoral program. This time, however, the theory and composition department supported her.

As part of her assistantship Larsen taught ear training, which she remarked, she found thoroughly fascinating. Not in possession of perfect pitch herself but having an extremely good ear, Larsen reveled in the opportunity to strategize the most effective ways to improve her students' listening skills. She discovered the myriad ways that people of varying talents made sense of musical sounds, and she designed exercises and assignments to raise everyone's abilities regardless of their natural gifts. Finally, in the classroom, sharing her joy of music making, Larsen got to pass on, if not in content then in spirit, what she had been taught by the sisters. Like composing or building a flexible structure for the forum, teaching was another outlet for Larsen's creativity, and she immersed herself in the opportunity.

In 1977, for her final doctoral degree requirement, Larsen composed another one-act opera, *The Words upon the Windowpane*. Dominick Argento advised her, and it was produced and performed in 1978 by the University Opera Theater under the direction of Vern Sutton. By 1977 Argento was an established force in American musical life. He had won two Guggenheim Awards (1957, 1964), and recently earned a Pulitzer Prize for his song cycle *From the Diary of Virginia Woolf* (1975). With a couple of successful operas under his belt—*Postcard from Morocco* (1971) and *The Voyage of Edgar Allen Poe* (1975–76)—and a commission from the New York City Opera for which he composed *Miss Havisham's Fire* (1977), Argento was a smart choice to guide the budding opera composer. Both advisor and student had gifts for lyrical text setting and were drawn to speaking in harmonic languages that moved freely within tonal and atonal realms. Neither was confined by aesthetic trends, past or present. Although she does not speak often about her dissertation advisor, Larsen acknowledges that she learned much about orchestration, especially, from Argento, and this is audible to someone who listens attentively to her music.[71] Vern Sutton also observed that Larsen's remarkable craft and ability to synthesize multiple styles are directly linked to her work with Argento.[72]

For her story Larsen adapted an unsettling 1934 one-act play by the Nobel laureate William Butler Yeats (1865–1939). She had first encountered Yeats well before college when she read his ruminative 1916 love poem "Brown Penny." She remembered the lines: "I whispered, 'I am too young,' / And then, 'I am old enough' / Wherefore I threw a penny / To find out if I might love."[73] The famous poem about daring to love lest the opportunity be lost resonated with the composer. *The Words upon the Windowpane* treated recurring themes in Yeats's oeuvre—the collisions of past and present, heart and mind, reason and imagination, the personal and the universal, the profound and the mundane, and in this particular work reality and the occult.[74]

The setting and story fired Larsen's imagination and spoke to her in ways that she was not fully aware of at the time. Set in a room that was the site of a series of séances in a Dublin lodging house, Mrs. Henderson makes contact with a dirty, deformed, diseased "bad old man" whom John Corbet, a young, skeptical Cambridge scholar attending his first séance, identifies as the Anglo-Irish writer, essayist, pamphleteer, and celibate cleric Jonathan Swift (1667–1745). According to Yeats scholar M. L. Rosenthal, Yeats uses Swift as "the chief representative of the intellect of his epoch, that arrogant intellect free at last from superstition" to interrogate the value of the intellectual self versus the feeling self, as well as the accomplishments of the Enlightenment and the promises of democracy. Mrs. Henderson muses on the volatile concepts of youth and age and their susceptibility to thought as Corbet explains Swift's tragedy as being that in old age "his brain had gone."[75]

Beside the other-worldly subject matter and the multiple personal, political, and intellectual threads woven through the story, references within the play to the evangelical Christian song-writing duo Dwight Moody and Ira Sankey, as well multiple instances of hymn singing made Yeats's text an attractive source for a composition project. Both Yeats and Larsen were drawn to ritual and the mystical, mysterious, and spiritual realms, and prior to accepting theories or principles of any type, tested them against their personal experiences.[76] Both were known for their flexible treatment of rhythm, Yeats in words and Larsen in music. Both were accomplished administrators and founders of professional organizations among their peers: Yeats as cofounder of the Irish Literary Theatre, and Larsen as cofounder of the Minnesota Composers Forum. Larsen met a sympathetic soul when she encountered Yeats. Having learned her lesson about securing copyright permissions from the master's project debacle, when she decided to adapt *The Words upon the Windowpane*, she "got the right permissions and wrote that opera and produced it as [her] PhD thesis."[77] Although it hasn't been performed since its university production, Larsen has entertained revisiting the work.[78] In 1998 she remarked, "I think I'll find a lot of myself in it that was subconscious at the time."[79] And in 2015 I asked her what she might find. After a momentary hesitation Larsen explained:

> The struggle to be whole; to be a passionate human being; it's the combination of the Dionysian and the Apollonian; it's that particular struggle, which just because of how my brain works and who I am, has very much felt part of that struggle. Not from inside; inside it makes perfect sense. But from outside, I don't know if it has to do with gender or just being human, but there are definitions of what results from certain kinds of behavior: the results of intellectual behavior; the results of unbridled passion; the results of a conflicted soul are all in that play, and beautifully in the play. And I just resonated and still do because they're not conflicts that are solvable.[80]

Reflecting her own musical preferences and those of the 1970s, Larsen's opera employs technology to communicate the spirit voices (in the form of the auditorium's sound system), and a brief moment of *Sprechstimme*, that other-worldly half-singing/half-speaking vocal delivery technique popularized by Arnold Schoenberg in *Pierrot lunaire*. Technology would become a regular instrument in Larsen's compositions in the years to come.[81] With sounds coming from locations around the hall, and notes sliding between the twelve pitches on the staff, Larsen created a musical atmosphere that wafted and hovered, much like the channeled spirits inhabiting Yeats's story.

Larsen's decision to write operas for both her master's and doctoral theses projects was an ambitious one, and in fact it is not typical of most graduate students pursuing their composition degrees. But Larsen's love of the voice, her appreciation of American English, her attraction to gesture and theater as expressive modes, and her home base in Minneapolis–Saint Paul combined to encourage her exploration of the genre. The place, with its critical mass of adventurous musical practitioners and a theater culture that prided itself on experimentation, made opera a natural choice for a composer already inclined in that direction. Argento had been similarly energized by regional support of the arts and opera specifically. In 1963 the Walker Art Center had commissioned him to compose an opera for its performing arts program, Center Opera, and he wrote *The Masque of Angels*. Given the Walker's focus on the visual arts, the operas it commissioned "emphasized visual design," and over the years Center Opera, now Minnesota Opera, gained a national reputation for its "progressive, alternative" productions.[82] With the experience of her advisor, the support of a community, the presence of talented and eager singers and actors, and an equally energetic friend and mentor, Vern Sutton, Larsen could be confident that her creations would be realized. Just as the physical environment of the upper Midwest focused Larsen's understanding of the natural world in specific ways, so too the cultural environment of the Twin Cities with its robust opera and theater scene shaped her sense of what was typical and within her grasp. In her conversation with Vivian Perlis, Larsen considered her propensity for opera: "In fact, writing opera, to me, is as natural as breathing. It's not formidable; it's just something that I do. And sometimes I think I've suffered because of that; because it's so natural and I always have one going, I have been unable to create the event excitement about opera that seems to be part of the mythology of having operas produced at the Met. There's a whole mythology about how difficult it is to do."[83]

When the composer considered the roots of her attraction to the genre, however, she looked beyond her contemporary cultural scene and drew a line straight to her earliest encounters with music in church; she characterized "singing chant in the Catholic rituals [as] operatic."[84] Indeed, the setting, props, costuming, ritual movements, lighting, fragrances, artworks, and soundtrack of Catholic worship prepared Larsen for the full sensory world of opera like few other experiences could. The composer was spot on when she identified religion as the most impactful force on her personal and professional life. Whether composing instrumental duets whose melodies are seamless and unending, lighthearted song sets celebrating saints, or full-fledged operas, lyrical lines, flexible rhythms, and dramatic situations are fundamental to her music, and she experienced them first while singing chant in church.

In the final two years of the decade, having just earned her doctorate, Larsen composed another one-act opera named *Silver Fox*; choral music to original words and those of May Sarton; vocal works including the oft-performed *Cowboy Songs*, which set text by, among others, Belle Starr (1848–99), the notorious Texas "Bandit Queen"; and a variety of instrumental works.[85] A discussion of two pieces from those years completes this chapter: *Eurydice: Through the Looking Glass* (originally titled *Eurydice: Looking Back*), composed in 1978, and *Bronze Veils*, finished in 1979. From Greek tragedy to modern painting, everything is potentially inspiration for Larsen.

Although Larsen does not shy away from setting poetry or libretti written by male authors, by the end of the 1970s she showed a decided propensity for setting texts by women. *Eurydice: Through the Looking Glass*, "A scene for mezzo soprano and string quintet," uses the first four poems from a set of seven titled "Eurydice" written in 1916 by the much-lauded American Imagist poet H.D. Hilda Doolittle (1886–1961) had been recommended to Larsen by a poet friend as someone whose works she should know.[86] Larsen found her poetry and devoured it. When fellow graduate student Ellen Wetherbee (Rosewall) expressed a desire for new music for her graduate recital, Larsen responded with the set. As Larsen had approached and then completed her dissertation project, she contemplated an unknown future, and that uncertainty informs every moment of the *Eurydice* set. In a 2015 interview she explained:

> During that year, and in the couple years before and after, [I was] trying to understand what would happen if I just walked out on the street and said I was a composer. And so I think I was drawn to conflicted metaphors, because they're a big help. . . . So it's almost unfair to H.D., because . . . I was using her to find myself. I couldn't say that at the time, but I know it was true. The whole question of what if I look back? What if you turn back to look at me? Would I turn to salt?[87]

Larsen recognized that she "had a special affinity with H.D.'s language, a musical affinity," and understood that H.D.'s poems contained "centuries of meaning completely relevant to being now."[88] A work using Doolittle's poems simultaneously served her friend's need for music and Larsen's need for resolution to her own internal conflict. Larsen recalls Vern Sutton remarking that *Eurydice* represented "a new you," but as years of interviews have made plain, there is always more to Larsen than the energy and optimism that strike one on first acquaintance; the scene for mezzo and string quintet drew on aspects of her personality other than those that were most obvious.

Like many of Larsen's later works, *Eurydice* takes a woman's perspective, but in this case, it is a thoroughly angry, dark, and pessimistic view: there is no hope; Eurydice is doomed. Larsen explains the scene in a brief composer's note that includes the names of the three poems/pieces in the set: "*Eurydice: Looking Back* explores the myth of Orpheus and Eurydice from the point of view of Eurydice. Cast into Hell for the second and final time, because of Orpheus' inability to keep himself from looking back at her, Eurydice looks back from Hell 'Upon Orpheus' in utter rage, 'From Hell' describing its blackness, and 'To the Earth, With Yearning' for its beauty."[89]

H.D. presented a revisionist reading of the famous love story when, rather than sympathize with Orpheus for being so overcome by love that he could not resist looking back, Doolittle has Eurydice charge him with unfeeling arrogance that ultimately condemns her to a lifetime in hell. After a scene-setting four-measure *Lento-espressivo* introduction, Larsen captures Eurydice's barely controlled anger and frustration in "Upon Orpheus"; the mezzo sings a consistently legato line against anxious eighth notes that pace, *Allegro agitato*, in the strings. A quasi-twelve-tone melody positions Eurydice homeless and wandering in harmonic space; Larsen shows herself familiar with Second

Viennese School practices but never allows its systems or rules to get in the way of the needs of the story.[90] Lengthy pizzicato passages and series of accented notes punctuate Eurydice's indictment of her "ruthless" consort (ex. 5.2).[91] The vocalist moans through a precipitous descent of a major ninth in the line "I am broken." Eurydice is blind with rage, and there is no promise

Unpublished Manuscript
Text from "Eurydice" by H.D. (Hilda Doolittle), in COLLECTED POEMS, 1912-1944.

Example 5.2. *Eurydice: Looking Back*, "Upon Orpheus," mm. 1–20 of her finding peace. Larsen reveals an aspect of her own musical-emotional palette not frequently on display. To an extent Sutton is right; this *is* a new Larsen. The composer buttresses Eurydice's first-person perspective with three iterations of the word *I* sung on a high, sustained E that collapses over the course of swollen measures of six beats in an otherwise common time

Example 5.2. *(continued)*

Example 5.2. *(continued)*

world. Eurydice is as lost in time as she is in (harmonic) space. A steady stream of dissonances in the accompaniment musicalizes the tension of the vocal drama. Larsen conveys Eurydice's continuing vulnerability and despair by removing the accompanying strings in the penultimate measure; Eurydice is alone and exposed as she finishes her brief recitative. Her return to the quasi-twelve-tone melodic line that began the song speaks to her unchanged situation. As Eurydice chides Orpheus for arousing false hope with his return, she leaps to a high F on the word *past*: a last pained gasp. Soft and dissonant pizzicato strings return and seemingly swallow her.

In "From Hell" Larsen continues the dissonant sonic landscape of the first song, but now rather than reference the abyss from a position outside, listeners and Eurydice are in it. Eurydice's rage undergoes an otherworldly transformation as she sings a strangely lilting 6/8 melody, which, while still highly chromatic and characterized by unvocal leaps and intervals, nonetheless has a rocking, soothing quality. Perhaps some part of Eurydice is reconciled to her fate, or maybe she has gone mad. As in the first song, Larsen stresses important words through rhythmic devices: hemiolas for the words *colorless* and *nothingness*, among other phrases, and a hocketing presentation of the word *hesitate* (ex. 5.3). When a recitative occurring midway through the song temporarily interrupts the lulling 6/8 meter, Eurydice "hiss[es] with anger" as she queries a now-departed Orpheus: "What was it that crossed my face with the light of your glance?" The quintet hovers in the background, triple *piano*, playing "random pizzicato [notes] above the bridge" and running "*Ad Libitum*" up and down the fingerboard before the 6/8 meter returns. But the swaying, singsongy rhythmic quality of the first part of the song is newly complicated as Eurydice's anger boils up again; she is not, it turns out, completely reconciled. Although the quintet maintains its predictable duple division of the meter, Eurydice's more agitated state seeps through in a vocal line that is highly syncopated. Larsen's music embodies H.D.'s flexible scansion and Eurydice's unstable state of mind.[92]

Larsen's attunement to nature must have made H.D.'s third poem, one that spoke so longingly about flowers, especially resonant. It is the natural world that Eurydice will miss most, and it is easy to imagine Larsen feeling similarly displaced and despairing without access to nature. In "To the Earth, Yearning," Eurydice looks back at what she would have done differently had she known she would never see or smell flowers again. "If I had . . . If I could": if Eurydice had understood that her time among saffron and crocuses was limited, she imagines she "could have breathed into [her] soul . . . the whole golden fragrance." If that had been possible, Eurydice speculates, then she might have been able to endure their loss. But this "if/then" proposition is not available to Eurydice. The weight of her exile becomes audible when the first violin recalls a brief melodic fragment that Larsen had used earlier to set H.D.'s line "fringe upon fringe of crocuses." Now, without hearing the words at all, the scansion of the melody—long-short-short-long-long-short-short-long—reminds listeners of

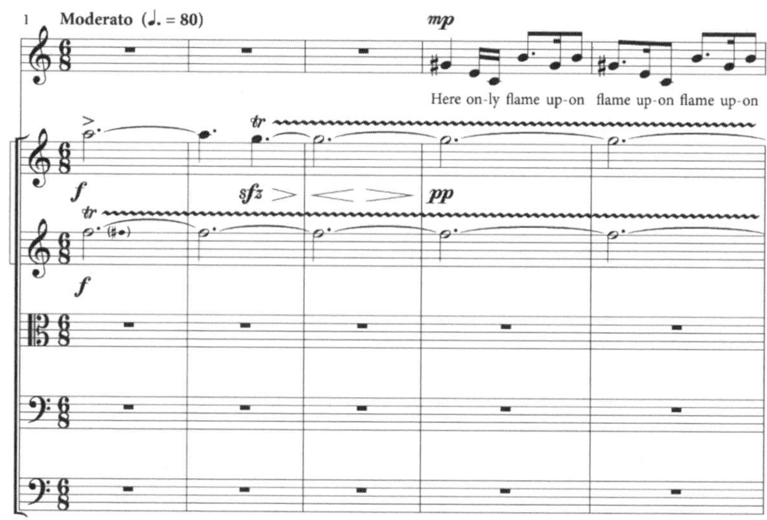

Unpublished Manuscript
Text from "Eurydice" by H.D. (Hilda Doolittle), in COLLECTED POEMS, 1912-1944.

Example 5.3. *Eurydice: Looking Back*, "From Hell," mm. 1–14

Example 5.3. *(continued)*

what has been stolen from Eurydice. As the first violin sustains its final note, the cello, then the second violin, and last the viola pick up the short-short-long "crocuses" rhythm. At the same time the flowers recede from Eurydice's view, the music dissolves into nothingness, "niente" (ex. 5.4).

Around the time of Larsen's composition, Canadian writer and environmental activist Margaret Atwood (b. 1939) had begun her own *Orpheus and Eurydice Cycle* of poems: she would work on it over the decade 1976–86. As in H.D.'s poem, Atwood's Eurydice plays a more prominent role than in the typically told tale; and like Doolittle's heroine, Atwood's Eurydice also finds Orpheus contemptible for his self-centeredness. The last line of Atwood's first poem suggests the similar sentiment felt by her Eurydice: "You could not believe I was more than your echo."[93] If Larsen's scene for mezzo-soprano and string quintet reveal "a new" Larsen, it seems the composer was right in step with another creative woman of the time who was reconsidering received wisdom and women's roles. Given the major changes in Larsen's life in the years immediately preceding the composition of *Eurydice: Through the Looking Glass*—her traumatic and triumphant graduate school experiences and achievements, and her marriage—it is perhaps no surprise that her works from that time reflect a "new" composer. In many ways, she left the decade a different, more fully realized person than she entered it.[94]

Example 5.4. *Eurydice: Looking Back*, "To the Earth, Yearning," mm. 16–17; 39–42

Bronze Veils, composed in 1979, presents a final study of the decade and a first glimpse into her intentional use of visual art as a source of musical ideas.[95] With the Walker Art Center having been an early venue for Minnesota Composers Forum concerts, and Suzanne Weil of the Walker serving on the forum's first board of directors, Larsen had already established close ties with the visual arts world before she completed graduate school. And her interest in art continues to this day as she and her husband follow and support artists whose work they enjoy.[96]

Larsen first encountered the paintings of Morris Louis (1912–62) at a show held at the Walker in 1977.[97] The museum that had supported the forum also supplied raw materials for Larsen's composerly imagination. The visual and aural intermingled in both the museum galleries and Larsen's mind. Louis, an American painter, whose exploration of "color-field" painting in the mid- to late 1950s was essential to the formation of the so-called Washington Color School, shared an outsider position in relation to the art world similar to the one Larsen occupied in relation to the composing world. With few exceptions—Los Angeles and the Ferus Gallery in particular being the most obvious—in the 1950s a majority of cutting-edge visual art trends originated in Manhattan; although Louis had spent some time in New York City, he preferred to work in Washington, DC, close by his Baltimore birthplace.[98] Louis, like Larsen (and Argento), believed that his mind was freer outside the celebrated incubator of artistry. He too understood that there was "culture" beyond New York and elected to work at those margins. Also like Larsen, he nurtured fellow artists in his immediate locale; he served as president of the Baltimore Artists Association and was close to other professionals in his area.

Although Louis wasn't ignored or dismissed because of his gender, his paintings, many of which were considered delicate, frilly, gentle, lightweight, and genteel, (feminine), were eventually devalued in comparison to the aggressive, muscular, and masculine "action paintings" of Jackson Pollack, Willem de Kooning, and Franz Kline, the acknowledged masters of their lauded technique.[99] Louis knew Pollack and his work but found greater inspiration in the paintings of another New York painter, Helen Frankenthaler, whose "Mountains and Sea" (1952) critic Peter Schjeldahl dubbed "the Rosetta stone of color-field."[100] Schjeldahl explained: "[Clement] Greenberg showed the picture to Louis and the painter Kenneth Noland, both visiting [New York] from Washington, D.C. on April 4, 1953. If color-field were a nation, that day would be its Fourth of July." Quoting Morris Louis on Frankenthaler's oeuvre, the painter saw it as the "bridge from Pollock to what was possible."[101] Perhaps the too-easy dismissal of Louis's works had roots in his acknowledging a female progenitor. Or perhaps Louis's "unapologetically beautiful and deceptively simple" paintings suggested a certain lack of "rigor" or "seriousness."[102] At least on first glance, the voluptuous beauty of Louis's paintings *veiled*, perhaps even obscured, the complex color chemistry at work. It would not be the first time that appeal, whether visual or aural, was used as evidence of superficiality or as an argument against genuine worth. Despite similarities between Louis's and Larsen's outsider status, there were significant differences that separated the painter and the composer: perhaps most basic were their temperaments. The painter's secretiveness about his work process—he allowed no one into his studio, not even his wife—and the composer's transparency regarding hers put them on opposite ends of a spectrum. Perhaps it is more difficult to hide the generating process of a finished musical composition than it is the application of media in a completed painting, although in the case of Louis's *Veils*, process is partially visible. Whatever the conscious or subconscious causes of Larsen's attraction to Louis's *Veils*, she was drawn to the works; *Bronze Veils* invited a response.

Thanks to the critical championing of Clement Greenberg (1909–94), color-field painting, and Morris Louis especially, enjoyed significant attention in the final years of the painter's too-short life. And after decades of neglect, Louis made a comeback. In fall 2014 the Mnuchin Gallery in New York devoted a month-long show to Morris Louis's *Veils*. It was, as the publicity blurb trumpeted, "the first exhibition devoted exclusively to Louis's breakthrough series in over thirty years."[103] The show included "a focused group of *Bronze Veils*."[104] In notes to her 1979 piece, Larsen explains:

> In 1977 I discovered the painting of Morris Louis at the Walker Art Center in Minneapolis, Minnesota. . . . I was fascinated by his painting technique, a process in which he poured his paint, diluted with thinners, onto a large canvas, and then tipped the canvas, guiding the paint along. When the paint dried, it created a thin veil of color on the canvas. He then repeated the process layering another color over the preceding one. The results of the process create the effect of several veils of color through which the viewer peers.
>
> I thought it would be an interesting compositional challenge to see if I could create a similar effect, but with thin veils of instrumental color. So I chose trombone, metallophones, and a few membranophones as the instrumentation for *Bronze Veils*.[105]

It may be telling that at the end of her decade in the academy, rather than reference the beauty of the artwork, Larsen's comments focused on the technique. Was beauty still suspect by academia? Would speaking of sensuous allure diminish an artwork or the observer? Is it especially dangerous for a young, professional woman to speak of beauty without risking being physicalized or trivialized herself? Given that Louis's process reveals itself only after patient and slow viewing, even for an educated viewer like Larsen, something must have preceded the revelation of his process. It is hard to accept that technique was the first thing to catch Larsen's eye.

Regardless of the original attraction, Larsen imagined creating a simultaneously aural *and* visual work, one where Louis's techniques when applied to music produced a sounding analogue, and where yet to be perfected technology allowed the silent projection of images "able to flow musically with . . . the piece" during a performance.[106] She regretted the ubiquitous noise of slide projectors; their rhythmic "shushing and clicking" would have disturbed the seamless binding of the two modalities she sought. The permeability of art and music was a given for Larsen in 1979 and remains so today as the composer continues to work with scientists and artists of all kinds in ever more creative collaborations.

Louis started with an unprimed and unstretched canvas, one that could fully absorb the thinned acrylics he poured.[107] The process married the medium to the material, making the fabric and its unique woven threads integral aspects of the work. Pouring paint on one side of the canvas, Louis tilted the stretcher, stopping when and where he sought deeper colors or the effect of allowing the vertical braces to show through.[108] He might initiate subsequent pours from the same edge as the first or from others. The intersection of vertical and horizontal flows suggests the thickened texture of musical counterpoint. As Diane Upright observes: "He probably achieved internal variations in the tapering or swelling of color planes by manipulating the angle of the stretcher and by varying the surface tautness."[109] Swelling color planes *sound* in Larsen's swelling dynamics. Gravity pulled and puddled the paints as they flowed into rounded elongated forms; colors blended in subtle and sensuous combinations; chance, carefully controlled, was partner to the painter. Ultimately Louis's manipulations and choices for the final stretching reveal aspects of his process if not precisely how or when he did things. Timing was an essential aspect of Louis's process. And to the extent possible, Larsen's slowly emerging reverberating instrumental timbres that form her initial "pour," flow and puddle in ways analogous to Louis's *Veils*. She composes color and movement, tension and translucence.

In the initial two minutes, Larsen systematically applies her instrumental colors: First a slowly reverberating vibraphone, then a suspended cymbal struck with felt mallets, then a triangle, and finally a tam-tam that is instructed to "never break sound." Within the first seven measures, Larsen has introduced all twelve tones; they blend together and softly excite the air. Although individual sounds decay and disappear before reemerging, something is always resonating; the air has absorbed their energy much like the canvas has absorbed the paint. New colors are born in the sonic confluence. A full thirty seconds elapse before a muted trombone enters "quite legato, singing" and joins the vibraphone. The trombone, while adding another metallic timbre, is noticeably different. It thickens the texture and deepens the colors. Its overtones strengthen and focus those already vibrating. The dark timbre of the trombone evokes the dark washes that Louis applied to unify the individual colors of the canvas. Until now all sounds had been struck into motion; the introduction of breath is another distinguishing factor. It is not all gravity and color; there is a human involved. Wind chimes and a bell tree complete Larsen's first application of sound (ex. 5.5).

To the extent that the properties of acrylics determined the possibilities of Louis's paintings, so do the qualities of Larsen's dominantly metallic timbres control her sonic veils. With the exception of a set of tom-toms, a woodblock, and temple blocks, the remaining five percussion instruments all ring, throb, and reverberate: Sarna bells, a bell tree, wind chimes, water gong, and a glass harmonica.

Although concepts like tone, color, and timbre share similar qualities in music and painting, time operates differently in the two arts. While viewers can focus and study individual aspects of a canvas at their leisure, moving their eyes in sync with their understanding, and free to follow the visual path the artist has created, listeners advance or stop with and within the linear temporal scheme of a piece. It pulls them through the experience at multiple, concurrent, but predetermined rhythms. In this regard, music offers less freedom to roam for a listener than a painting does for a viewer. But artists can also play with time and encourage a kind of slow seeing, and Louis's *Veil* paintings do this.[110] Viewers are drawn in and forced to slow down. Only upon closer inspection do they notice the individual pour marks at the tops and sides of canvases. To a large extent viewers *deconstruct* their initial experience over time; listeners *construct* their experience over time. Listeners' and viewers' understanding depends upon forming an impression over time.

Larsen's music draws listeners to the sounds analogously to the ways Louis's painting draws viewers into the colors, but she determines the rate at which

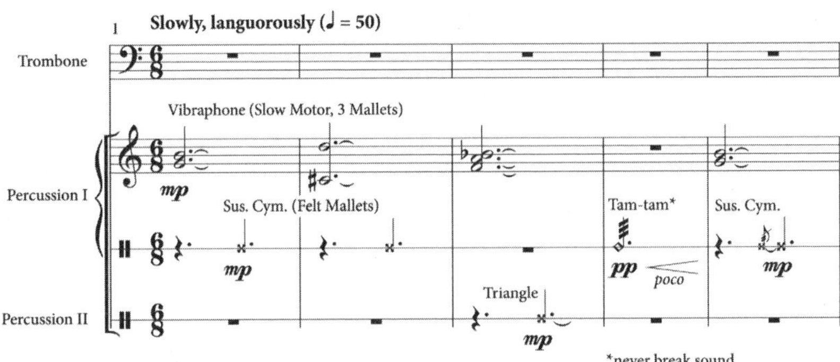

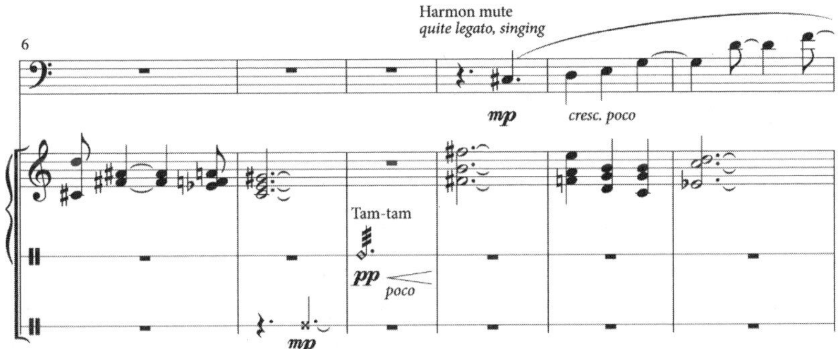

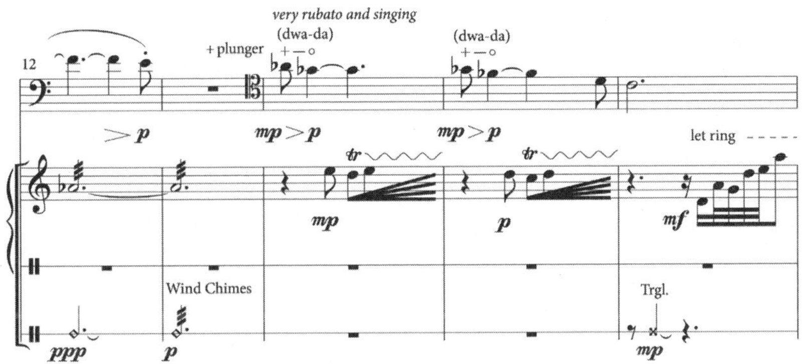

Example 5.5. *Bronze Veils*, mm. 1–29

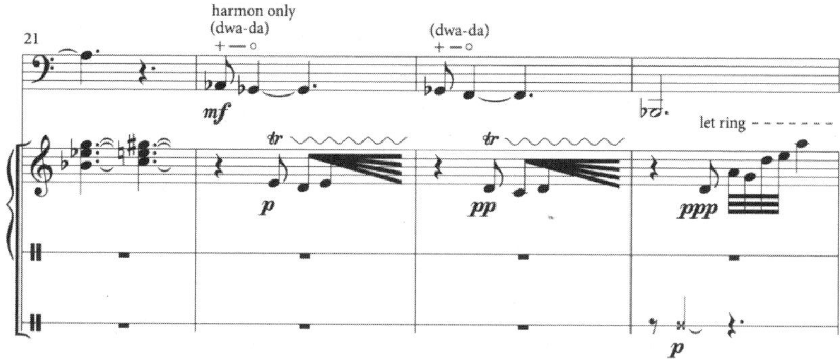

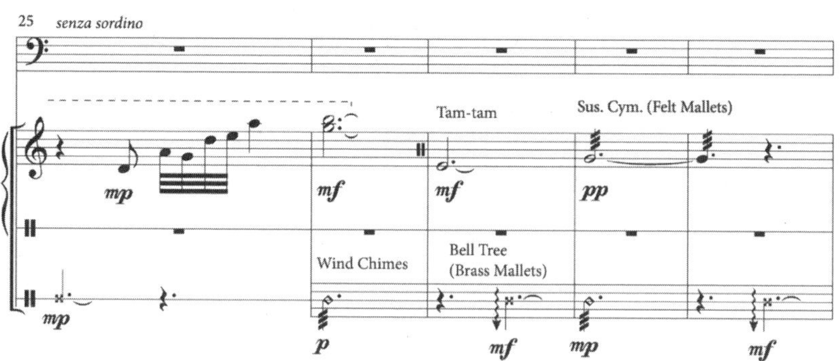

Example 5.5. *(continued)*

her audience experiences the piece. The music starts "slowly, languorously," and it is not until an accelerando beginning two minutes into the work that both the pace and the timbre undergo a significant shift. With the introduction of the woodblock, the first nonmetallophone to be heard, and Larsen's instruction to the trombonist to play *secco* (dry), we experience a new kind of sound-color: brighter, edgier, punctuated, and discrete. Tom-toms and trombone echo and shadow each other dancing upon the knock-knock of the woodblocks. Distinctly different from the resonating metal timbres, these drier sounds don't dominate the timbral field for long. They provide another layer of color but don't overwhelm the larger effect. A minute later the trombone and vibraphone interleave their sounds. Larsen's translucent counterpoint, an aural analog to Louis's diaphanous veils, preserves the clarity of each of the instruments while simultaneously blending them into a third timbre. Listeners hear sounds through each other. The jangle of bell trees, struck with brass mallets, washes over the new sound (ex. 5.6).

When the original slow tempo returns, the earlier reverberating instruments do as well; this time the icy, shimmering sounds of the glass harmonica provide a sonic glaze.[111] Larsen admits that she simply "loves the sound."[112]

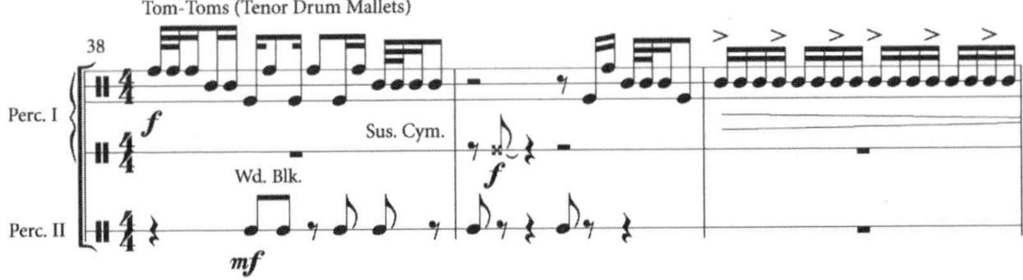

Example 5.6. *Bronze Veils*, mm. 38–42

This is no flat sonic canvas but rather a sparkling, glistening musical world. Complex combinations of timbres and pitches evoke the many-hued colors that radiate from Louis's multiple overlapping pours. Halfway through the piece, the painter's celebration of color finds an equivalent in the composer's exploration of pure sound. She invites the trombonist to "choose random pitches but maintain given rhythms" in a passage that is to be played "freely, as if short bursts of heat" (ex. 5.7).

William McGlaughlin, the composer-trombonist who commissioned and premiered the piece, goes all out. In his recording he pushes the timbral range of his instrument and imagination. The solo includes everything from recognizable pitched notes to blatts, bleeps, and splats, to ersatz electronic music effects that include wanna-be feedback and distortions. A fan of jazz, and especially of saxophonist Charlie Parker, McGlaughlin is unwilling to be outdone by the innovative improviser. Blazing-fast passages riding on virtuosic technique create a riot of color that one can hear.

In the final minutes of the piece, Larsen returns to her opening chords and timbres, but this time the volume is turned up. The original soft sounds are now *forte* and *fortissimo*. The trombone "mumble[s] and mutter[s] [triple *forte*] like Clark Terry," the master trumpeter who sputtered scat through his horn.[113] A plunger mute additionally obscures the precise "words." Everything is a blurry mix. As the trombone ascends through a final rising gesture, a figure reminiscent of its first entrance, the soloist sings "as lyrically as possible." Vibes, suspended cymbal, triangle, wind chimes, and tam tam lay down a final shimmering wash of sound, and the music fades away (ex. 5.8).

In the 1970s Libby Larsen moved out of her family home and created one of her own. She expanded her arsenal of compositional techniques, identi-

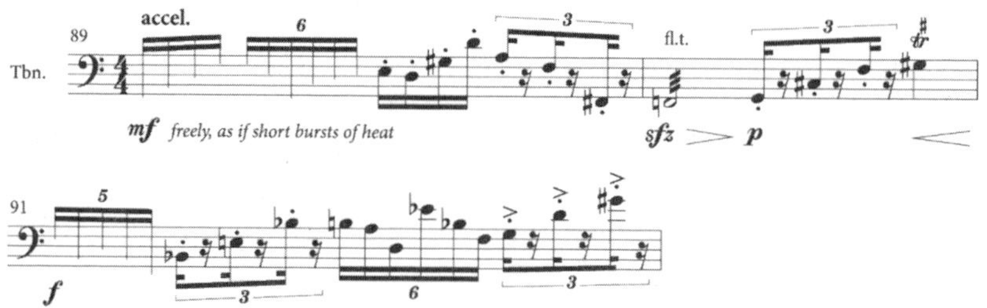

Example 5.7. *Bronze Veils*, mm. 89–91

Example 5.8. *Bronze Veils*, mm. 105–14

fied at least one female academic role model, cofounded an organization to nurture contemporary American music, established professional ties with the larger arts community in the Minneapolis–Saint Paul area, developed a range of collaborative relationships, earned three academic degrees, learned about the legal side of music making, broadened the range of her sources of inspiration to include the visual arts, all the while honing her craft. Early in the decade she began to think of herself as a composer, and by the end of the decade she knew she was one.

Like those of many people in their twenties, Larsen's aspirations were tested and realigned. Thoughts of pursuing a career in economics were replaced by dreams of becoming a singer, but they were trumped by her gifts for composition. She channeled her love of vocal music and her fascination with language into writing operas and songs.

A trip to New York, where she entertained the possibility of studying voice at the Mannes School, only clarified her deep ties to the upper Midwest. The particular qualities of the natural environment as well as the cultural scene of the Minneapolis region were what nurtured Larsen. She needed to be where she could see the sky; where she could run long distances and often; and where lengthy, deep winters focused her thinking. She learned all of this about herself in the 1970s.

As her eclectic musical voice coalesced, Larsen increasingly appreciated the impact Gregorian chant had on her mature sense of rhythm, tuning, phrasing, and acoustic space. An attraction to flexible structures, whether musical or organizational, grew out of early music lessons with the sisters and local piano teachers who understood that she would not be content with exclusively four-square meters or common-practice approaches to harmony.

Larsen's distrust of systems, which had its roots in the patriarchal power structures of her home and church, extended to the male-gendered spaces of politics, business, and academia. Systems of any kind became suspect, musical ones included. Refusing to be hidebound by any set of compositional rules or aesthetic values that excluded entire musical genres or styles or practices opened her up to unlimited sources of inspiration but also left her vulnerable to charges of trendiness and dilettantism.

During the 1970s, Larsen solidified her understanding of a number of social issues that came to the fore in the decade. As it affected many of her generation, the Vietnam War made her feel part of a larger body politic. The first Earth Day, celebrated April 22, 1970, ushered in an international movement that would reinforce Larsen's own commitment to the environment. As her consciousness was raised, she also became more aware of her woman's perspective on her life and career. Refusing to be confined by others' expectations of what she should do, Larsen determined to tack her own course, get out of line as often as needed, and do what she knew she could do. The 1980s would see Larsen come into her own.

6 Larsen and Gender
Doing the Impossible

GIVEN THE RANGE OF EXPERIENCES WITHIN her family, the church, and the academy that seemed to turn on Larsen's being female, the composer's naming gender as one of the most important influences in her life follows logically. Although she never felt that gender was the immediate cause of her parents' desire to silence her or the primary justification of various household practices, Larsen understands that the family system, a reflection of American society, was stacked against strong women of any age who acknowledged, pursued, or insisted upon their ambitions. In this structure the man was the head of the house (or the company, or the school), the wife (or the secretary) was his dutiful and subservient helpmate, and the children were there to be seen but not heard.

Disciplined silence was reinforced by Larsen's church. Despite the powerful influence exerted by the Sisters of Saint Joseph of Carondolet, the Roman Catholic Church was (and remains) an overwhelmingly male domain. Women were welcome only within circumscribed spheres, and the same holds true today. In January 2015 Cardinal Raymond Burke, former archbishop of Saint Louis and the highest-ranking cardinal in the United States, blamed "the advent of the women's rights movement during the 1960s, which pushed for female participation in the Catholic Church" (what he identified as "radical feminism") for the current crisis state of the church.[1] Burke connected everything from "feminized and confused . . . disordered men," child-abuse scandals, the declining interest of young boys serving as altar boys, and the discomfort of men within the fold to the presence of women in the church.[2] He saw it as a crisis of "manliness." Burke argued this even as he acknowledged that "girls were also very good at altar service."[3] As Terrence McCoy reported in a *Washington Post* article: "While [Burke] directs most of his ire at 'radical feminists,' he also appears rankled by ordinary women doing ordinary Church activities. To him, that act alone constitutes the dangerous feminization of the Church that has alienated, disenchanted, and made men sexually confused."[4] A thoroughly exasperated Burke observed: "Apart from the priest, the sanctuary has become full of women."[5] The reality, however, is that the church has always depended upon the largely volunteer efforts of women to keep its doors open and its local efforts alive. One can only wonder how uncomfortable the recently demoted cardinal would be if women had any real power within his church.[6]

Larsen's growing reputation as an important "woman" composer put her in a new position in the 1980s.[7] In 1980 she received an individual artist's fellowship for $10,000 from the Minnesota State Arts Board and was appointed to the National Endowment for the Arts, New Music Panel. Minnesota named her to their State Arts Board and in 1981 honored her as "Outstanding Woman of the Year in the Arts." Recognition grew when in 1982 the American Music Center elected her to its board of directors, and then she was chosen to be a member of the National Advisory Board of *Meet the Composer*. While still administering the Minnesota Composers Forum, in 1982 Larsen helped launch a new MCF initiative, Innova Recordings, a much honored, non-profit label that continues to distribute the works of American composers and performers.[8] In 1983 Larsen was named Composer-in-Residence with the Minnesota Orchestra through the Exxon/Rockefeller/Meet the Composer residencies program. Her star continued to rise in 1984, when she became vice president of the American Music Center. In 1985 she learned that her orchestra residency had been extended through fall 1986. Faculty who had not taken Larsen seriously when she was a student in their program had to reconsider the composer in the face of these accolades.

Larsen had become something of an expert witness when it came to women in the field, and the composer Janika Vandervelde (b. 1955) acknowledged as much in a 2014 conversation when she reflected on a conference she had attended that involved Libby Larsen. Vandervelde studied composition at the University of Minnesota from 1978 to 1985.[9] Prior to that she had been an undergraduate music education and piano major at the University of Wisconsin–Eau Claire and only switched to composition in the fall of her final year; the senior piano recital she had planned became a composition recital instead.[10] Vandervelde admits that she was "amazed" that she'd been accepted in composition at UMN in light of her minimal preparation and achievements at the time and the reputation of the highly regarded faculty. In addition to Argento's accolades and achievements, Paul Fetler had won his own Guggenheim in 1953 and 1960.[11]

Vandervelde was immediately awarded an assistantship and put in a classroom to teach ear training and theory as a first-year graduate student. As she has explained, she arrived at the university with little awareness that gender mattered, and her own experiences didn't suggest that it was an issue. She "felt very connected to everyone"; she "got pulled in[to]" a program where "graduate students supported each other."[12] In hindsight she realizes that the Composers Forum had much to do with creating the comradely atmosphere that greeted her, and of course, Larsen shared major credit for its creation. Vandervelde formed an especially close bond with faculty composer Eric Stokes, whom she characterizes as "the most controversial [faculty member] in terms of style—very eclectic, a bit of a conceptualist—gave enormous amounts of personal time to his students, more than any of the others."[13] She also enjoyed working with the "humanist" Dominick Argento, who could write twelve-tone "music that didn't sound atonal."[14]

The absence of any women composers among the faculty did not register as problematic for Vandervelde when she arrived, but her consciousness changed when a new Harvard PhD named Susan McClary was appointed. Donna Cardamone Jackson, an earlier Harvard graduate, was already a respected presence. According to Vandervelde, Cardamone Jackson was always professional and objective, and over her thirty-eight years at the university, she worked in the background quietly changing the culture by making opportunities available for the likes of Libby Larsen. There was nothing polarizing or controversial about the revered Cardamone Jackson. But McClary was a different story. Throughout her fourteen-year tenure, McClary created waves in the department and the community; factions developed in response to her presence even while she earned a University Teaching Award.[15] Larsen and McClary would impact Vandervelde in different ways.

Vandervelde and Larsen had known each other only through forum activities at the university, but in 1982, after Larsen was out in the world composing, building her career, and administrating the forum, the two women traveled to and then roomed together at a conference hosted by Rice University and the Houston Symphony. Vandervelde described "Current Trends in Contemporary Women Composers: Post-Feminism" as a "life changing experience."[16] In panel sessions that featured Larsen, Joan Tower, and Joan La Barbara, Vandervelde first became aware of the disparaging ways women and their music were routinely treated by the orchestra world, and it was happening at the very conference.[17] As part of the event the Houston Symphony performed a concert of all women's music—a remarkable undertaking at the time for a nationally recognized symphony. She heard Larsen explain that despite her music being programmed and making herself available during rehearsals, she had had no voice at all in the preparation of her piece; the orchestra did not take her or the music seriously. Vandervelde recalled that "one of the percussionists was seen throwing wads of paper around and goofing off."[18] If Larsen's growing reputation and McClary's presence at the university did not immediately change Vandervelde's perspective, the conference did. She would thereafter be acutely aware of the gendered realities of American musical culture. McClary became her musicology mentor, a champion of her compositions, and later a collaborator.[19] Even after McClary accepted another position, the two stayed close. Regarding Larsen, Vandervelde speaks warmly of her continuing, inspiring presence in the Midwest: "Always available; always open to discussion; paving the way; a bit of a mentor; she kept a lot of people here."[20]

Just as Larsen has never confined herself to a few musical styles, sources, or topics, when it comes to women-related subjects, the broad range of her interests shows in the variety of writers and poets she has set. From Julian of Norwich, a fourteenth-century anchoress and mystic, to Elizabeth Barrett Browning, from Virginia Woolf, to Eleanor Roosevelt, Mary Oliver, and Rita Dove, Larsen's literary sisterhood embraces centuries and cultures. On occasion Larsen writes her own texts as Libby Larsen, but she has also used the aliases M. K. Dean, Aldeen Humphries, and early on Florine McKay, each of whom has her own tone and temperament.

This chapter tracks Larsen's growing reputation. It looks at works that reflect her life as a socially conscious composer who is also a woman, daughter, sister, wife, and mother. Larsen speaks from and through her position as a woman, but her ideas and music acknowledge the larger human condition.

Moving beyond her hometown meant increased exposure, scrutiny, and criticism, some of it personal, but it also provided Larsen with the space she needed to enlarge her thinking and test her ideas. As she extended her professional sphere, Larsen also expanded her personal world: the most life-changing event was the birth of her daughter, Wynne, in 1986. Mesmerized and dazzled by this new person, Larsen also faced challenges of a different kind brought on by Wynne's appearance. Even with the assistance of Phyllis Veravice, who first helped Larsen care for her newborn for a few hours each day, Larsen suffered from insomnia for months; her mind wouldn't turn off despite its exhaustion. With her sleep routine interrupted, physical energies depleted and scattered, and the hours available for focused concentration on composition severely curtailed, Larsen was compelled to develop a new relationship to time. As motherhood denied Larsen the extravagance of unlimited hours for self-cultivation, she learned how to go deep into the time she had. Precious minutes around the edges of infant care became dilated, infinite occasions. Larsen explains: "I moved from horizontal time to vertical time in the creative process when my daughter was born. It took me about a year to learn how to create in vertical time. Vertical time means while it appears to be scraps of time on the surface of daily life, it actually is not. That's only clock time. So instead of luxuriating in the hours of consideration, if I had twenty minutes, I went deep so that the twenty minutes could have felt like twelve hours."[21]

Adjusting her understanding of time in relation to her creative work impacted not only Larsen's daily habits and practices but also the nature of time in her music. The present grew in a way she had not experienced previously. Larsen's mastery of stillness in music is attributable, in part, to her ability to go deep into vertical time. As she observes: "If you actually focus and work in vertical time, you just don't exist in the time plane that we've constructed to civilize our lives."[22] Although motherhood is not a prerequisite for developing this discipline, in Larsen's case it was a powerful catalyst. Her desire to *be* the snow, the stillness, the wheat, the fragrance, and the gearbox can be understood as manifestations of this practice of rejecting an imposed linear conception of time and sinking in to the moment.

While developing this more mindful relationship to time, Larsen also tended to her physical being. Recognizing the connection between her physical and creative energies, Larsen took a running course offered by the American Lung Association and joined its running club, the ALARC, the goal of which was to complete a marathon. In 1988 Larsen ran her first marathon, and by 2015 she had run thirty-three of them. Attention to her reasoning and experiential selves reflects a holistic understanding of music and life.

Surveying the large repertoire of Larsen's women-themed works reinforces the confluences of religion, the natural world, the environment, and gender in her thinking. *In a Winter Garden* focuses on a religious woman in the midst of a particular natural world. In her 1987 homage to Georgia O'Keeffe, *Black Birds, Red Hills*, Larsen considered a different natural environment and the painter's exploration of "the flow of time and color on her beloved red hills of New Mexico." Larsen observed that O'Keeffe "became fascinated with the effect of time on the rocks, noting that time has turned them into objects which are precious to look at and hold."[23] In 1991 Larsen combined environmental themes and religion with a celebration of the original earth mother, Gaia, in *Missa Gaia: A Mass for the Earth*. She involved poets and writers from across time and culture to make a pan-gendered, religious-environmental statement.

In other works, Larsen claimed a place for women inside Christianity more specifically. Her multiple settings of the words of the medieval anchoress Julian of Norwich in pieces written in 1979, 1999, and 2003, of the seventeenth-century

Spanish sister Juana Inés de la Cruz in works composed in 2003 and 2005, and of the poet and painter Sister Mary Virginia Micka, who had just retired as professor emerita from Saint Catherine's University in Minneapolis in 1993, show Larsen seeking out the voices of historical religious women in her own tradition.[24] Larsen recovered her beloved Saint Mary when she wrote *Canticle of Mary* in 1994 and brought the venerated mother of God into the twenty-first century with *Rodeo Queen of Heaven* in 2010. In 2012 Larsen reclaimed the "other" Mary when she finished *The Magdalene*, a set of songs for soprano and piano, whose texts come from the *Pistis Sophia*, a third-century Gnostic source. It is enticing to speculate that Larsen identified with "bad girl" Mary Magdalene, a woman Larsen described as "a personification of the Gnostic belief in gaining wisdom through questioning."[25] She honors silenced, disenfranchised, and defamed religious women and gives them voice with her music. Her works become a personal homage to them all.

Larsen's women-celebrating works are not, however, purely self-serving acts of rescue and rehabilitation. Valuable and powerful as these compositions are, their motivations are more complex. Behind many of these pieces is also the composer's continuing search for role models. The youthful Libby combing the shelves of her school's meager library for biographies of women is still looking for stories of people like herself: women who refused society's circumscribed role. Too late now to show Larsen how to choreograph a career, or carve out a place, or balance the competing demands on her time, many of the women Larsen has showcased in her music confirm the choices she has made: they corroborate that she got it right. She is clear: women need to recognize and honor who they are; women's choices are not limited by others' expectations; it is not mandatory that women regard themselves as iconoclastic when they insist upon a larger life; ambition, achievement, and even anger are OK. Normal is OK.[26] By writing these pieces Larsen has created a library of models for today's young girls.

Collectively these compositions embrace the range of Larsen's rich, reflective, and occasionally irreverent life. They honor international superstars and local heroines, the extraordinary and the prosaic. They insist upon the rightness of women's choices to be devoted family nurturers, or accomplished careerists, or both. They explore the attachments of mothers and daughters and the variety and reach of loving relationships. And they question and examine those relationships. At times, Larsen good-naturedly mocks social mores while simultaneously delivering a strong message. The lighthearted touch that characterizes her 1976 *Saints without Tears* returns in 2001 even as she makes a point regarding society's foolish and repressive ideas about women's behavior. As she explains, *Hell's Belles*, a set of four songs for mezzo-soprano and a five-octave handbell choir, organizes "around the narrative of an independently spirited young girl . . . who grows into womanhood, even more independently spirited . . . and moves into old age with spit and vinegar, . . . finally defining the chariot that swings low for her on her own terms!"[27] The composer's note could be describing Larsen herself. Another piece from that same year, *Love after 1950*, shows a similar blend of playfulness and social commentary. Although musical expressions of self are no more dependable than autobiographies as truthful accounts, Larsen's compositions provide at the least faint outlines of her "figure under the carpet" and perhaps more importantly reveal what Patricia Hampl has characterized as the "brave desire to place the self in the world."[28] Larsen's music embodies how she aspires to place herself.

In 1987, within a year of Wynne's birth, Larsen wrote *ME (Brenda Ueland)*, a cycle of eight songs for high voice and piano based upon the memoir of Brenda Ueland, a native Minnesota memoirist, and a friend of Patricia Hampl.[29] Ueland's book had been suggested to Larsen by Bruce Carlson, who knew Hampl. He was the director of the Schubert Club of Saint Paul, Minnesota, which commissioned the work. Benita Valente premiered the piece that year in Saint Paul.[30] Larsen's relationship with Valente endured for years and so did her association with Carlson. Through his acquaintance with Stephen Paulus, Carlson knew early on that the forum needed an office. Although it had a small off-campus space in Minneapolis, the organization needed a more permanent location, and Carlson offered a corner room in the Schubert Club. Larsen commuted there for the ten years she administered the forum. The years sharing a building meant that Carlson and Larsen became well acquainted. But despite Carlson's familiarity with the composer, he likely did not appreciate the degree to which Ueland's and Larsen's life stories overlapped. Just as H.D.'s poems about Eurydice resonated with Larsen at the moment of her leaving the university, Ueland's memoir spoke to Larsen in the vulnerable months after first becoming a mother.

Writer, editor, and feminist Brenda Ueland (1891–1985) was a devoted child of Minneapolis; the city was imprinted on her free-spirited being even when she moved to Greenwich Village and lived in New York for close to fifteen years. From the beginning, it seemed her return was inevitable. Ueland, like Larsen, was at home in the natural environs of the upper Midwest, and they were both drawn especially to the lakes. In her chapter "Childhood," Ueland recalls "walking home on a soft midsummer night from the Lake Harriet band concert."[31] These were Larsen's memories as well.

Both Ueland and Larsen also enjoyed strenuous physical activity. Throughout her life Ueland took daily nine-mile walks, and when she was over eighty years old she set a swimming record for women in her age category. Larsen always ran and still trains conscientiously for the races she runs. Toni Lindgren, one of Larsen's assistants, has commented that not long after going to work for Larsen the composer bought her a pair of running shoes and coaxed her to get outdoors and use them. Lindgren attributes her improved fitness to Larsen's encouragement and the composer's example of regular physical activity.

Ueland and Larsen shared their Norwegian cultural heritage, as well as large numbers of siblings and similar places within their family constellations: Ueland was the third of seven children and Larsen the third of five. They each also had one child, a daughter. Larsen could identify with all these qualities even if other aspects of their lives differed significantly.[32]

When Larsen chose lines for songs from Ueland's *Me: A Memoir*, she followed the basic eight-chapter outline of the book and set the author's life, but she also set aspects of her own life.[33] Although the composer may have picked those passages that resonated with her own experience or provided the chance for personal reflection, this was not purely or primarily an act of soul-bearing musical ventriloquism. The sounds and rhythms of words and lines and the story they conveyed played an equally large role in her choices; she was a composer creating a musical work, albeit a personally resonant one. Numerous omissions of individual words, ones that challenged the laws of scansion, euphony, or rhyme—"refulgent" and "pellucid" for instance—bear witness to the priority Larsen gives to the aesthetic needs of the piece. As Larsen explains in her note to the score, she was driven by the *musical* story she could tell about "Brenda's passion, lyricism, optimism, and buccaneer spirit."[34]

Larsen's stylistic palette is characteristically large and diverse; free recitatives, Viennese waltzes, passages of "Leporellic" pattering, lengthy sections of intoned text, and rapturously legato lines convey the range of Ueland's "fiery, if not disciplined, personality" and Larsen's musical response.[35] Noteworthy, perhaps, there is no reference to boogie-woogie specifically in the entire thirty-seven-minute cycle, although Larsen's fourth song, "Greenwich Village," includes all kinds of syncopations and jazzy rhythms in its "saucy" opening passage.[36] *ME* requires the singer to be reflective, jaunty, and stentorian; innocent, horrified, arrogant, and matter of fact; a child, an adolescent, and an adult. In this cycle the author *is* the speaker, and she talks directly to listeners through the composer's adapted words and the singer's voice; there is no intermediary beyond the composer's music; the directness heightens the sense of intimacy.[37]

As with Larsen's earlier vocal music, there is little that is simply tuneful, and there are no strophic settings, although Larsen does repeat especially important lines of text. Her respect for the unique qualities of individual words steers her away from strophic forms with their one-size-fits-all melodic lines. Larsen's instinctive sense of the music that inheres in American English, a language that contains its own melodic and rhythmic character, is always audible. A deep understanding of musical declamation enlivens both music and words. She regularly employs dissonant pitch pairings, even when the scene being depicted is relaxed and stable, and her rhythms are similarly rich with juxtapositions of duple and triple divisions as the norm. She moves around and through bar lines effortlessly. The free-flowing pitch and temporal space of chant, where the music grew out of the words, and not vice versa, is still at the heart of Larsen's composerly thinking. If *Saints without Tears* is humorous and lighthearted, and *Eurydice* seethingly serious and sober, *ME* sounds the voice of a more reflective, perhaps philosophical composer. It is hard to know how much is Larsen simply responding to Ueland's story and how much is Larsen expressing a new aspect of her being, but there is something different about this work. Written in the year immediately after she gave birth, the piece may illuminate new thoughts that Larsen was entertaining about gender. An examination of two songs from the cycle, "Childhood" and "Art (Life Is Love . . .)," provide glimpses into the musical language, tone, and character of Larsen's 1987 compositional voice and one example of the place gender occupies in her oeuvre.

When Ueland writes that her first memory was "running up and down [her family's] long porch with a child of [her] own age," the composer sets the line with brightly galloping, energetic music that hardly needs the words to be envisioned (ex. 6.1). It turns out that imagining the scene was a goal of hers as Larsen explained in an interview: "I've been toying around . . . more and more in songs that I compose, wanting to make a complete visual listening experience, if at all possible, in the theater of the mind."[38]

Larsen selects Ueland's memory about her kindergarten class, which turns out to have been as enchanting an experience for the child Brenda as it had been for the child Libby. Listeners are transported back in time as the vocalist chatters about the "long, low tables" and "the galumphing games on the shiny floor," and "shiny beads" and "colored paper" and all the activities that keep five-year olds' hands busy. She cannot help but think of it all as "a lovely thing, a lovely thing" (ex. 6.2). In Larsen's setting, the

Example 6.1. *ME (Brenda Ueland)*, "Childhood," mm. 11–15.

warm memory elicits a rising, sweeping melodic gesture in whose repeat the soprano reaches her highest note yet. It is as if the author, composer, and singer are all lifted up and transported to the past through music: as they are moved, so are listeners.

When Ueland recalls swimming, Larsen's music responds with glistening and rhythmic sounds much like those that accompanied the child runner. But this time, rather than sound innocent against the cycling accompaniment, the singer swoons "rapturously," even sensuously at the recollection of bodies pulsing and slipping through the lake water (ex. 6.3).

The lake was a talisman for Ueland as it became for Larsen, who sets "the lovely sunsets in the evening when the lake was yellow as glass" over cascading passages of consonant sixths that float "very legato." Mention of the lake, however, stops the incessantly busy accompaniment that had characterized the piece to this point; Larsen wants to linger for a while. The music quiets, changes from

Example 6.2. *ME (Brenda Ueland)*, "Childhood," mm. 72–76.

the previous duple to a "relaxed" triple meter, and carries singer and listeners to the edge of the lake complete with a "creaking . . . rusty oarlock" and gentle "bell-like" sounds from a distant buoy (ex. 6.4). The fogginess of memories find their musical equivalent in an accompaniment that is muted, and a vocal line where the soprano is directed to sing "lontano, extremely legato" (as if from a distance, very smoothly). As Ueland remembers the voices of her parents and their friends calling to each other rowing on the lake in the evening, Larsen draws upon her own memories of sounds coming "over the water with the slow, musical clun(k) of the oarlocks."[39] She momentarily stops the action on her soundstage and drops down into this richly reverberant place.

"Art (Life Is Love . . .)" is the seventh song of the cycle. Its text comes from Ueland's chapter titled "Home Again," a section of the book filled with

Example 6.3. *ME (Brenda Ueland)*, "Childhood," mm. 88–93.

Ueland's reflections on the importance of creative work. Larsen's significantly different title signals more than a simple rewording of Ueland's text. With this change the composer appears to be more willing to acknowledge her presence and creative contribution than in any of the other songs so far. In her memoirs Ueland quotes "Francesca," a young Minneapolis violinist who lived with her family for a time, and whom she credits with showing her "something about music and God."[40] Lines such as "the way you can help everyone most is to do your own work," and vivid imagery that includes "pouring yourself into some work of your own," likely resonated deeply with Larsen, whose days were fractured by a thousand and one competing demands.[41] Larsen starts her song with "Memento vivere" (Remember to live!) sung three times; she will repeat the same phrase another three times close to the end of the song. Each iteration lingers longer and climbs higher; while quoting Ueland, one wonders whether Larsen is also reminding herself to keep herself alive.

Example 6.4. *ME (Brenda Ueland)*, "Childhood," mm. 98–117.

Example 6.4. *(continued)*

And then Larsen skips pages of Ueland's chapter to get at a passage about Vincent van Gogh, one of Ueland's heroes. The author puts great store in his thoughts: "Van Gogh thinks . . . that love is the creative thing. . . . you love a man and you want to create him, you want to create him—have a child."[42] It is hard to imagine either Ueland or Larsen embracing Van Gogh's rationalization for motherhood as a desire to create "a man," but Larsen easily believes in the creativity of love and the love of creativity. The perpetual motion accompaniment, while different in its details from that which first appeared in "Childhood," recalls its energy and mood. When Ueland announces, "Van Gogh loves the sky and has to paint it," the soprano sings long legato lines over an undulating piano figuration that includes sparkling individual treble notes grabbed by the left hand.[43] The music lover in Ueland compares Van Gogh's paintings with the works of composers: "We love beauty, . . .then we create it in music, . . . in ourselves."[44] It requires no stretch to understand why these lines might have appealed to Larsen (ex. 6.5).

In another parallel to "Childhood," when Ueland turns her thoughts to the lake, Larsen's music slows down just as it had earlier. She tells the vocalist to

Example 6.5. *ME (Brenda Ueland)*, "Art (Life Is Love . . .)," mm. 9–26.

Example 6.5. *(continued)*

sing "calmly," and the pianist to play "very legato." The first mention of the lake had signaled a meter change, and this one does as well. More chordal writing and rocking rhythms characterize this place in Larsen's thinking. With Larsen's music, the author, composer, and listener can go back "home again."

The seventh song ends with a "brilliant," "vibrant" statement of Ueland's creed that Larsen culls and adapts from the final chapters: "That we live forever. That love is the creative thing. That life is love. That perfection is in all—and we should love it in all. That I must love people. That I must love myself. That God is a person. That I must love myself, my reckless, arrogant, joyful self. I believe that we live after death again and again and again." A perpetuum mobile accompaniment builds excitement and momentum, and the song eventually ends with an elated "Ah . . . "

Perhaps at this particular moment in Larsen's life, when so much of her attention was focused on her newborn, and when her previously ordered life was challenged at every turn with domestic duties and professional obligations, the composer needed the assurance that Ueland's life and memories provided. Larsen's note to the score hints at such: "Her biography is not particularly different from anyone else's biography, consisting of those events which seem insignificant . . . but are really the most important things that happen to us in life. These are the experiences which form our substance. Ueland's gist is to confirm in us the true art into which we are all born, the art of living."[45]

Ueland's homespun wisdom and celebrity assured Larsen that it was possible to be a working mother from the upper Midwest and not lose one's self in the process. Her model of a feminist woman who refused limitations of thought or action was what Larsen needed in 1987. Choosing to have a child and be a professional woman was a radical thing for Ueland in 1921, and it remained the case for Larsen sixty-five years later. For a variety of reasons, most of her women composer contemporaries did not elect motherhood. Perhaps Larsen needed to believe that focusing on her family was OK; it would not derail her life. Ueland showed her how one woman did it.

Having a child altered Larsen's life suddenly and dramatically. There was no way to deny the subject-hood of this new person; coos, gurgles, and screams became part of the daily soundscape. Professional obligations could be rescheduled or temporarily shelved, but there was no way to postpone attending to this particular life project. Motherhood forced Larsen outside herself in a way that she had not experienced before. Over the next few years, she wrote directly about mother-daughter relationships in her *scena*, *Songs from Letters* (1989), and in the set *Notes Slipped under the Door* (2001), the latter a collaboration with Larsen's friend Eugenia Zukerman and Eugenia's daughter Arianna Zukerman.[46]

Songs from Letters, among Larsen's most often performed, recorded, analyzed, and discussed works, shows her sensitivity to the drama inherent in any family relationship. Adapting lines from several of Calamity Jane's letters to her daughter, Janey, Larsen elevates what might be passed over as "insignificant," and confirms her belief that everyday interactions may be among the "most important things that happen to us in life." Certainly by the end of the set, Calamity Jane is seen as valuing her relationship with Janey, distant and unconventional as it might be, and the pictures of Janey with her father as among her most meaningful possessions, even as she goes blind and can barely make out their features. Like *ME (Brenda Ueland)*, *Songs from Letters* shows Larsen's musical-emotional range. The five songs provide opportunities for intimate reflection, proud recitations of accomplishments, parental advice, references to a gunfight, and angry outrage. By the late 1980s Larsen's attention to declamation, intonation, and sympathetic text setting had become a hallmark of her style, and in 1996 *USA Today* identified Larsen as "the only English-speaking composer since Benjamin Britten who matches great verse with fine music so intelligently and expressively."[47]

In a 2003 interview with Andrea J. Mitternight about *Songs from Letters*, Larsen explained her approach to creating vocal texts. The following excerpt picks up where the composer is searching for the right word to describe how her text-selection process works; she has just rejected the word *prune* but is unable to find an adequate substitute.

> What are the words that really want to be highlighted through intonation? And so, when I look at prose, I look at it with a pencil, and I will very lightly underline the words that, if I were to eliminate everything else from that paragraph, the essential words would be there.
>
> And often times I find . . . you don't need to sing the adverbs: you don't need to sing the adjectives. You need to sing the nouns and the verbs. The verbs are very important because that's where the tempo and progression [reside], it really comes out of the verbs, not the nouns. And so the nouns and the verbs will rise up off the page, and the adjectives and the adverbs will ask whether or not they really need to be set.
>
> Now an interesting thing is the articles, like "the," and many of those don't need to be set. What's really interesting though is that the conjunctions, "but," "and," "or," those you have to be very careful about, you know? Because in prose, the "buts" and the "ands" and the "ors" are where the

> meaning lies. And so I look very carefully at the conjunctions and try to understand if the "buts" and "ands" and "ors" are ironic or if they are self-defensive mechanisms, which often an "and" clause is a self-defensive mechanism in an explanation. . . . Now secondary to that process is to try and find end rhyme.
>
> It's a lot of work, you know, it's a lot of work, but that's where you find the music. That's why the music comes out of the words.[48]

Larsen found a dozen of Calamity Jane's letters in Karen Payne's edited collection *Between Ourselves: Letters between Mothers and Daughters*. Payne explains: "In 1877 [Calamity Jane] began keeping a journal in the form of letters to her daughter, Janey, who was then 4 and living in New York in the care of an old family friend, Jim O'Neil. Calamity Jane was an occasional guest in the O'Neil household, but Janey never knew that the exciting woman who told her all those stories was her mother. She never knew that Wild Bill Hickok, who figured prominently in most of the stories, was probably her father."[49] Payne's background sets the scene for Jane's September 1880 letter to her daughter, which Larsen adapted. The beginning reads: "Janey, a letter from your Daddy Jim came today and another picture of you. Your birthday is this month, you are 7 years old. I like this picture of you . . . . Your expression [is] exactly like your father's . . . . Your picture brought back all the years I have lived with your Father and recalled how jealous I was of him."[50]

To arrive at the text for "So like Your Father's (1880)," Larsen eliminates words, substitutes her own, and subjects others to repetition; in the process she removes extraneous information, strips away the sounds that get in the way, emphasizes what she feels is most important to the drama and the music, and shapes Calamity Jane's words to suit the needs of her *scena*. The process resulted in something like this:

> Janey, a letter ~~from your Daddy Jim~~ came today and a~~nother~~ picture of you. ~~Your birthday is this month, you are 7 years old. I like this picture of you . . . .~~ Your expression ~~[is] exactly~~ like your father's **<like your father's>**. . . ~~Your picture~~ brought back all the years. **<Janey, a picture of you . . . like your father's, brought back all the years.>** ~~I have lived with your Father and recalled how jealous I was of him.~~[51]

Texts for the second and third songs, "He Never Misses (1880)" and "A Man Can Love Two Women (1880)," also come from the same lengthy letter, but altogether Larsen sets fewer than a quarter of its four-hundred-plus words in her first three songs combined. She is ruthless when it comes to sculpting her text. Larsen's aphoristic "pruning" reveals the extent to which she listened to the words, found the sounds she wanted, took possession of the materials, and made the drama her own.

Eleven years later, Larsen moved from setting a historic, mythologized mother-daughter relationship to setting one that she had watched develop over many years. With *Notes Slipped under the Door*, Larsen drew upon her friendship with the flutist Eugenia and the soprano Arianna Zukerman to compose another mother-daughter homage, one that was particularly meaningful to all three women because of its fidelity to their personal experience.

The Larsen-Zukerman friendship had its roots in a musical collaboration begun in 1980. When they met, Zukerman (b. 1944) was mother to two daughters, Arianna (b. 1972) and Natalia (b. 1975), and Larsen was yet to have Wynne. As Zukerman explains, they developed an instant rapport. "We became good friends, really good girl friends. . . . We knew each other well; we were emotionally intimate; we could read each other's temperature; we were very tuned to each other; with [Libby] there was a lot that didn't need to be said."[52] Looking back over the years, Zukerman acknowledges how much she enjoyed working with a woman with whom she had so much in common: "We shared similar interests, were devoted to our children, and very driven by excitement over our work."[53]

The text to *Notes* written by Eugenia Zukerman in 2001 imagines an adolescent girl writing brief messages to her mother and slipping them under her door as a way to vent, share, plead, manipulate, bargain with, and get around too uncomfortable in-person conversations. "I love you so much," says the child in Zukerman's text, and one can feel woven into the notes every mother's hope that her child returns her love. Zukerman captures the tenor, tone, and tactics of the budding woman-child in direct, declarative prose that contains both honest expression and disingenuous protest. Its credibility is likely the result of being based upon a real-life practice of note exchanges in the Zukerman household. "A Kiss, That's All," "My Throat Hurts," "The Rock We Used to Sit On," "What Could Possibly Happen," and "Anything I Put My Mind To" are written from a child's perspective, and that child, the soprano Arianna Zukerman, brings her real life experience to the role. The flutist/writer Eugenia becomes (as she was) the responding parent. Larsen explains:

> Through the simplicity of the texts, we become partners in this dialogue of life passages—this exhilarating explosion of life independence for the child and the wrenching letting go for the mother. I've composed the music with an ear towards the new and innocent emotions of the child, giving the

orchestra clean and clear textures and tempi. I created a dialogue between the flute and soprano but while the soprano is always in direct dialogue, the flute line is a complicated blend of direct dialogue, internal reaction, supporting line and patient guide.[54]

With her own daughter turning fifteen years old, Larsen was in the throes of that sometimes wrenching, always "complicated" process of letting go herself. If in *ME* Larsen identified with Brenda Ueland, in *Notes Slipped under the Door* the composer pulled from her own ongoing experience and that of her good friend; the music becomes biography by proxy.

The soprano-daughter speaks her mind in simple flowing lines or matter-of-fact barely sung statements, while the flute-mother alternately holds her breath, nods her head, offers brief comments, dodges the daughter's slings, defends herself against the daughter's wrath, tries her best to get a word in, and reflects on what her child has said. *Notes* is every bit the *scena* of *ME* or *Songs from Letters*; Larsen has created another theater of the mind complete with the dance of a mother-child relationship, a choreography that she was learning. Given Larsen's penchant for stripped-down texts, Zukerman's clean, unencumbered "notes" were the perfect starting point for her music. But even so, she eliminated the occasional word, circled back to repeat crucial lines, and made the text precisely what she needed. In all cases the alterations are for purely musical reasons: none of them changes the emotional or dramatic content of the note's message.

Larsen's set takes on its own dramatic shape: the first and last songs form a soft and gentle arch that contains Zukerman's loving texts. The "Dear Mommy" motive, a heartfelt octave leap (approached by a leading tone)—heard at the opening of the first song and intermittently throughout the set—returns prominently in the final song and enfolds the group like an audible embrace. The petulant, comic, fast-paced, and highly rhythmic second and fourth songs offer contrast and relief while they simultaneously propel the drama forward. Both songs also provide moments for virtuosic displays by flutist and singer. Each character knows her persuasive powers and is not afraid to use them: the singing child with soaring stratospheric vocal flights and the flutist mother with displays of musical imagination and technical agility. Larsen reminds us this is not just any mother and daughter: these are the Zukermans!

The set is anchored by the third song, "The Rock We Used to Sit On." Here is a child's wistful reflection on a time when she and her parents walked in the woods "on hot summer days in the country." It is not clear whose memories these are: the child speaking the lines or the mother who wrote them. The ambiguity increases their effectiveness. In the child's romanticized memory of her family, she sat together with her parents on "that magical rock" and dreamed of where they wanted to go: "You wanted to go to Timbuktu. Daddy wanted to go to Africa. I always wanted to go to Disneyland."[55] On the other side of a divorce, however, the daughter wants only "to go back to that magical rock, so the three of us could be together again."[56] In the fifteen-minute set, the third song takes the longest—over four minutes—occupies the middle position, and is the temporal heart of the set. To this point, however, there was no reference to a second parent, and this song will remain the only one that mentions "daddy." In doing so it becomes the emotional center as well, perhaps an apt reflection of the complex thoughts and feelings that accompany the dissolution of a family and their very long resonance. Although Larsen had no personal experience with divorced parents, or being divorced herself, she has expressed anger, puzzlement, and regret over the distance she felt from her father. Divorce finalizes and legalizes an estranged relationship, but it is not a prerequisite for a child to feel separated from a mother or a father or for parents to feel separated from each other. In this song listeners hear the composer working from her imagination, experience, and deep empathy with her friends.

In an article Geoff Gehman wrote about the 2001 premiere of the work with the Lehigh Valley Chamber Symphony, he quoted Zukerman talking about her collaboration with Larsen: "One of the nice things about [*Notes*] is that it opened the door to talk about mothers and daughters. You can share with [Libby] because not only will she understand, she will illuminate."[57] Zukerman and Larsen welcomed the opportunity to talk with each other about their lives, the professional as well as the personal aspects. Like the most effective lieder and art songs, *Notes Slipped under the Door* draws out, expands upon, and illuminates the meanings and emotions contained within the words. In this particular work, Larsen illuminates her own life as well.

Women from every corner of American culture and beyond exerted their influence on Larsen and her music, and always she was drawn to strong, fearless, accomplished, independent women; motherhood was not a requirement. The painters Mary Cassatt (1844–1926) and Georgia O'Keeffe (1887–1986), so different from each other, both inspired musical replies, as did many others. This chapter concludes with discussions of *Black Birds, Red Hills*, Larsen's 1987/1996 response to six paintings by Georgia O'Keeffe; two song sets, *Love after 1950*, which Larsen composed in 2000 (simultaneously with *Notes Slipped Under the Door)*, and *Hell's Belles*, written in 2001; and a final tribute to one of the first named, nonconforming women who hailed from a different time and culture, Mary Magdalene. Larsen's setting of chapters from the *Pistis Sophia* in her work *The Magdalene*, premiered in 2013. The multivalent quality of Larsen's music is especially obvious in *Black Birds, Red Hills* and *The Magdalene*. Both pieces could have been discussed in earlier chapters: the former in the chapter on nature, and the latter in the one on religion. But Larsen's empathy with the modern painter and the early religious leader is at the root of her attraction to the subjects in the first place. Both women defied gendered stereotypes.

In notes to the 1997 Innova Recording *Dancing Solo: Music of Libby Larsen*, Todd E. Sullivan observes that Larsen's "distinctive style" drew from a variety of musical cultures and idioms, as well as "a deeply rooted visual impulse." Larsen's homage to Georgia O'Keeffe, *Black Birds, Red Hills*, bears witness to that impulse. The piece was commissioned by the University of Alabama for Thea Engelson (vocalist) and Scott Bridges (clarinetist). It was originally conceived as a multimedia work for soprano, clarinet, and piano accompanied by slides of O'Keeffe's paintings and text taken from the artist's remarks set to song. But copyright issues required Larsen to remove the vocal part, which she rewrote for viola; she kept the clarinet and piano parts.[58] She ultimately eliminated the slides as well. As Larsen explained, "I technically could not supply them or encourage their use in performance."[59] It is unique among the pieces discussed in this chapter for its existence as a purely instrumental work. Rather than be guided by words that tell a story, create a dramatic scene, or argue a point, goals that are all well served by texts, Larsen's revised *Black Birds, Red Hills* is more a purely sonic study of six paintings by Georgia O'Keeffe. We listen to their colors, join what Larsen calls their "flow of time," and experience musicalized impressions of the works.[60]

There are similarities to what she had done in 1979 with *Bronze Veils*, her first significant musical response to visual art, but there are important differences as well. In *Bronze Veils* Larsen employed techniques analogous to the painter's when she systematically layered metallic instrumental timbres upon each other to deepen and nuance the opening shimmering cymbal and slowly oscillating vibraphone sounds.[61] When Larsen thickened musical textures she suggested equivalents of Louis's subtly crosshatched intersections of color pours. By contrast, *Black Birds, Red Hills* is not about copying O'Keeffe's process or technique but instead is about capturing the paintings' effects. We "see" with our ears, a practice familiar to those of the radio generation, or to others denied their sight. Larsen's "portrait of six paintings" is born of her recurring desire to "be" her subject. She endeavors to go beyond the limitations of her consciousness to inhabit an Other or something else; at some level this is the ultimate empathetic act. She traverses expressive modes as she does musical styles and genres. Why should paintings speak only to the eye? Why music only to the ear? In *Black Birds, Red Hills*, Larsen heard the paintings as easily as she saw the music and invited others to consider them with new eyes and ears.

In a live commentary that Larsen delivered at a performance of the work in South Dakota in 1988, she explained the origins of the piece. She referred to its genesis corresponding to centennial celebrations of Georgia O'Keeffe, who had recently died.[62] Then she spoke more specifically about her compositional process. Her remarks reveal the continuing influence that the natural world exerted on her thinking, even as she focused her attention more specifically on this iconic, strong woman and her art. O'Keeffe's paintings of the Southwest environment reinforced Larsen's love of her own place. As is typical with any new project, Larsen read everything she could find by and about her subject. She poured over books and studied as many of O'Keeffe's works as possible. Larsen explains that she looked for points of contact with the painter and discovered that "just about *everywhere* she and [Larsen] touched aesthetically and spiritually!"[63]

Unsurprisingly, the first point of contact that Larsen discovered was O'Keeffe's sensitivity to the natural world: the painter, so closely associated with her place, touched the composer, so closely associated with her own. Larsen explains: "Georgia O'Keeffe is a painter who notices the details of landscapes where one might be bored, or where one might find no beauty at all; Georgia O'Keeffe is the kind of artistic eye that looks down at the ground and sees a black rock, and finds in that black rock 17 paintings . . . or in a flower, the perspective of a flower that no one else has seen." She sums up their aesthetic and spiritual bond when she observes, "Georgia O'Keeffe is a painter who loves the land."[64] It is hard to imagine a stronger connection between Larsen and anyone than an attachment rooted in the land, even if O'Keeffe's desert Southwest was unlike Larsen's lake-filled upper Midwest in just about every way: from land formations and weather patterns, to colors and seasons, there was little common ground. But as Larsen pointed out, O'Keeffe's dry landscape was "absolutely verdant in its artistic possibilities." In this regard the painter's desertscape was analogous to Larsen's snow-shrouded upper Midwest, which could just as easily be regarded as silent and motionless by those bored with its seeming sameness or blind to its allure. Larsen saw and heard its unlimited potential for artistic realization. Both women were tied to their adopted places, and both of them reveled in the finest details of their surroundings.

Larsen's *Black Birds, Red Hills* announces its dual focus in the title: this is a study of O'Keeffe's natural world and its color palette. Larsen explains that in viewing the artist's landscapes, she was struck by the preponderance of red and black; the colors and the place became synonymous in her mind. Radiant light illuminating the foothills and mountains, the stones, birds, and even the doorways of buildings intensified the colors; it is likely that the whiteness of Larsen's world intensified the colors of O'Keeffe's. They became Larsen's unifying theme. In this regard *Black Birds, Red Hills* is like *Bronze Veils*, where color was the primary concern. But Larsen's "portrait of six [O'Keeffe] paintings" goes beyond color to become a study of time and place, and flow and stillness as well;[65] these more temporal elements become audible in the musical portrait. Ultimately Larsen created names for her movements based on six paintings, each of which referenced colors and a natural setting: "Pedernal and Red Hills," "Black Rock with Blue Sky and White Clouds," "Red and Orange Hills," "Red Hills and Sky," "A Black Bird with Snow-Covered Red Hills," and "Black Bird Series (In the Patio IX)."[66]

Visitors to the desert Southwest know the unique effect the clear, dry air has on the look of the surroundings, especially that seen in the distance: colors are deeper, edges are sharper, and contrasts are starker. The absence of visually distorting humidity means objects appear discrete, almost in relief one to the other rather than blended; they look like cutouts, layered on top rather than melded together. O'Keefe captured this multilayered effect in her many images of "Pedernal," the angular, narrow 9,800-feet-high mesa visible from her Ghost Ranch home in Abiquiu, New Mexico. And Larsen foregrounds O'Keeffe's favorite mountain in the title of her first movement, "Pedernal Hills," where she maintains the discrete features of the landscape in the distinctive timbres of the piano, clarinet, and viola; they sound separate even as they share many materials and layer on top of one another.

Listeners hear the distant undulating hills without pictures or words to suggest them. The "shadowy, wafting" rolling motions introduced triple *piano* by the piano, are immediately taken up by the clarinet.[67] Larsen's washes of sound evoke O'Keeffe's practice of smudging pastels and blending oils to achieve subtle hues and gradations.[68] The viola, by comparison, presents both timbral and material contrast; it resists the surrounding oscillating movements for its own simpler, more declarative climbing line. And this too has a visual analogue: in dozens of paintings and pastels O'Keeffe separates the more distant and angular Pedernal from the foregrounded foothills by setting it off with color, and delineating the edges of the adjacent forms.[69] Perhaps with the viola part Larsen sought to compose her own Pedernal mesa standing separate and more delineated, as O'Keeffe painted hers.

Analogies between O'Keeffe's and Larsen's works can be drawn for each of the movements that show the many connections between the painter and the composer; a few will make the point. Black rocks inspired multiple O'Keeffe paintings and supplied the name for Larsen's second movement as well. The single black rock regularly situated at the center of O'Keeffe's canvas has sounding equivalents in the clear focus of Larsen's second movement, a tightly integrated two-minute work that grows out of the opening two measures and their accented and staccato articulations. The hard sheen of the stone becomes Larsen's motivic fragments that glint off one another similarly to the way the white clouds painted at the top of O'Keeffe's canvas reflect in the rock's lustrous black surface. There is as much clarity and edginess in this movement as there is softness and lyricism in the first. If the first contemplates a distant scene, the second movement looks at something close up; we can imagine walking around the stone, turning it over, and investigating every aspect (ex. 6.6).[70]

In discussing her third movement, Larsen refers to "the V shape" of the hills just outside O'Keeffe's window: "[O'Keeffe] describes this shape as the arms of two great hills which reach out to the sky and hold it, suggesting to me an abstract cradle."[71] And that is just what listeners hear: Larsen composes a musical cradle—a soft and gentle, rocking lullaby—that invokes the quiet rhythms of O'Keeffe's simple shapes. Given O'Keeffe's thorough identification with the land, it is not clear whether she or the red hills are embracing the sky. Perhaps she and the land and the sky are one, and they are parts of a single, mutual embodiment. Such thinking would not have been alien to Larsen.

Bell-like sounds in the upper register of the piano ring rhythmically and mark the passage of time. Like Louis's *Bronze Veils*, O'Keeffe's *Red Hills and Sky* invites slow seeing; its depth of color, gradations of tone, and few careful lines only reveal their complexity and power through careful consideration. Viewers discover that the painting is abstract and realistic in equal measure. This is a patient painting, and Larsen responds with a patient composition. She creates room and time to hear the landscape in a musical texture that is open, spacious, and unhurried. Echoes and unison passages provide sounding analogues to the large- and small-scale symmetries that hold the painting in perfect balance. O'Keeffe and Larsen evoke a harmony of relationships: the women to the earth, the hills to the sky, and the music to the painting. The unchallenged E major chord that closes the third movement provides a

Example 6.6. *Black Birds, Red Hills*, "Black Rock," mm. 18–24.

unique moment of conventional resolution within the set of pieces; without suggesting a key center for the larger work, it matches the feeling of centeredness and repose that emanates from the painting.

Time, whose passing Larsen presaged in the slow chiming bells of the third movement, takes center stage in the fourth movement, "A Black Bird with Snow-Covered Red Hills." O'Keeffe's painting shows a stylized, oversized black bird in flight within the same enveloping arms of the red hills featured in the previous movement. A few basic contours delineate its shape and the scene, and we see the contours of the hills echoed in those of the bird's wings. The bird appears to have grown out of the land. A faint red tint, perhaps alizarin crimson, glows underneath the snow that covers the slopes, which helps distinguish them from the infinitely deep blue-gray-white sky that rests in the valley.[72] As a viewer's eye moves to the top of the canvas, the sky becomes more cobalt, more definite, more defined. For all its subtlety and service to shape, O'Keeffe's mastery of color is no less laudable than Louis's. The black bird flies through a band of blue sky at the top of the canvas and dominates the viewer's experience. The color helps frame the scene. The undulating form is simultaneously suspended in time and soaring through it; there's enormous power in its supple, graceful, curving silhouette. If the third movement contemplated the place and its peacefulness, the fourth movement revels in its energy and life force expressed by the bird. Larsen wakes the winter world with a series of clarinet trills, and the black bird soars. Trills and tremolos pulse through the movement. The piano's constantly rippling accompaniment supplies the sonic air currents that keep the bird, and the viola and clarinet, aloft. Larsen's instruction to the pianist to play "very lightly" guarantees a sensation of effortlessness, an apt musical analogue for the elegant and graceful shape that suggests the bird. The directness of Larsen's musical portrait matches the clarity of O'Keeffe's painted composition.

With this piece (and her seven-song set *Mary Cassatt* composed in 1994), Larsen paid tribute to American visual artists, and the choices of her particular subjects were not surprising. O'Keeffe and Cassatt were among her very first models of strong, independent, creative, artistic women: the women she first read about in the early 1970s.[73] Larsen writes serious studies that reflect her respect and gratitude for the brave artists and their remarkable achievements.

But as she had shown herself capable of doing in early works, Larsen never lost her capacity for well-aimed irreverence, and she hits her mark in the song set *Love after 1950*, a project commissioned in 2000 by Artistic Circles for the mezzo-soprano Susanne Mentzer. Like its near-contemporary *Hell's Belles*, *Love after 1950* challenges tired attitudes toward women, but neither set is so lighthearted that it disguises its serious intent or message. In an insider's reference to Robert Schumann's 1830 song cycle *Frauenliebe und Leben* (A Woman's Love and Life), the composer characterizes her *Love after 1950* as "the new woman's *Frau, Love 'em and Leave 'em*."[74]

In *Love after 1950* Larsen and Mentzer strove to capture "the pathos and humor of just plain living the life of an artist/mother in our complicated world"; they "wanted songs that are little real life-dramas."[75] Larsen's "theater of the mind" is at work in this set as it was in *Notes Slipped under the Door*. The collaborators found poems by five twentieth-century women (an African American, three white Americans, and a Scot, all still living but one) that captured the tone of the times. As Larsen puts it, "The English chosen by the poets is voraciously contemporary."[76] Their modernity invited Larsen to speak in a range of popular musical idioms that showcased her multilingual style: poems by Rita Dove, Julie Kane, Kathryn Daniels, Liz Lochhead, and Muriel Rukeyser summoned a blues, an [anti-] torch song, a honky-tonk, a tango, and a propulsive, coursing dance respectively. The poems take the singer and set from adolescent infatuation to mature reflection. Along the way love is romanticized, men are objectified, beauty regiments are savaged, lost love is mourned, and a woman finally recognizes the source of her own strength.

Beyond being attracted to the five poems because of their honest language and dramatic coherence, Larsen found specific musical qualities in each of them that resonated with her physical being. She described their "sense of rhythm" and linked it to "the ways contemporary bodies move while dancing."[77] Larsen's somatic relationship with music and her kinetic engagement with the world governed her attraction to the poetry as well. Similar to the way she heard the music in O'Keeffe's paintings, she hears the music in these late twentieth-century poems. It becomes clear that regardless of the origins of her source materials or a project's programmatic goals, when Larsen composes, musical considerations trump all else. The sound and logic of the music guides everything, whether it is the excision of select words in a poem or prose passage, the repetition or reorganization of others, or concerns for the larger rhythm and flow of a multimovement piece, Larsen works from her position as a composer, and in this piece from her position as a woman who composes about being a woman.

Love after 1950 is a musical study, "an interior monologue about love."[78] It examines women's expectations, relationships at various stages of their lives, and vulnerabilities regarding matters of the heart. Whether considering individual songs or the set as a whole, however, *Love after 1950* is also an exploration of the inseparableness of life rhythms and musical rhythms.

"Big Sister Says, 1967: (a honky-tonk)" is the third song of the set; it follows the warm and sensuous "Boy's Lips (a blues)" and playfully ironic "Blond Men (a torch song)." It opens with the words "Beauty hurts," a line that returns six more times, and then multiple other times in slightly varied forms: "looking good hurts," and "it hurts." It is the fastest and most flamboyantly dramatic song of the entire group and comes complete with composer instructions to howl and to sing "in pain, as if your hair is being pulled."[79] The "cocktail piano" of the torch song has been replaced by a honky-tonk piano, and Larsen wants the pianist to play it like "(Jerry Lee Lewis)" pounding the *fortissimo* chords and exciting the crowd with a showy glissando.[80] There is nothing shy or retiring about this tirade. Larsen's favorite boogie-woogie accompaniment starts as the singer begins her rant about the torturous beauty routines regularly practiced by young women in 1967, when a teenage Libby was among the sufferers.

In Kathryn Daniels's poem, "Beryl," the sadistic older sister, insists that looking good is hard work and it hurts, and then proceeds to yank and pull her younger sibling's hair into submission: as any survivor of the time will attest, the self-inflicted pain bordered on the masochistic. Large, soup-can sized, bristly rollers were standard equipment and had to be worn while sleeping if they were to do their job straightening or waving one's hair, and Beryl passes along this wisdom. Plucking and tweezing eyebrows, taking a razor to "tender armpit skin," and using "stinking depilatory cream" were also routine procedures in the late-sixties "beauty" regimen.[81]

Among Daniels's most expressive lines (and Larsen's most empathic settings) is the poet's characterization of an eyelash curler as "a medieval-looking padded clamp." Nervous tremolos in the piano right hand and a ticking ostinato in the left simultaneously build dramatic tension and musical momentum as the line and the tool come closer to their targets. Larsen stops the pianist on a dissonant chord cluster at the word *medieval*, leaving the singer free to control the pacing and delivery of her text. The slowly enunciated descending vocal line ends with a rest, and the voiced plosives in *padded* and *clamp* have time to sink in. Larsen hears the power of the words and wants her listeners to as well. In the unaccompanied "freely" declamatory measure that follows, the singer recovers, girds her loins for what is to come next, and reminds listeners once more that "looking good hurts." The boogie bass starts up again, and the soprano wails a sustained "Ow" over the top. The pained cry is Larsen's only original addition to the text; she was drawing upon her own experience (ex. 6.7).

Beyond rearranging the order of lines, repeating a number of phrases, and adding her own howl, Larsen remains largely faithful to Daniels's text.

"BIG SISTER SAYS, 1967"
Beauty hurts, big sister says,
    yanking a hank of my lanky hair
    around black wire-mesh rollers
    whose inside bristles prick my scalp
    like so many pins. She says I'd better
    sleep with them in.
    She plucks, tweezes, glides razor
    blades over tender armpit skin,

Example 6.7. *Love after 1950*, "Big Sister Says, 1967," mm. 47–61/beat 1.

Example 6.7. *(continued)*

> slathers downy legs with stinking
> depilatory cream, presses straight lashes
> bolt upright with a medieval-looking
> padded metal clamp. *Looking good*
> *hurts,* Beryl warns. *It's hard work*
> *when you're not born beautiful.*[82]

Larsen sets the entire poem with the exception of the final line, "when you're not born beautiful." Instead she ends with the phrase that began the poem and the song, the simple declarative, "beauty hurts." This is the message she wants to leave with her listeners. In 1967 when the ultrathin, heavily made-up, chisel-haired, androgynous-looking model Twiggy set the standard for beauty, it is possible that Larsen rejected the idea that any woman was "born beautiful" or recognized as such.[83] It might also be that the sounds of Daniels's final line didn't serve her musical purposes for the song or the set. The middle song needed to provide contrast, something fast-paced and lighthearted, and momentum to push the set forward. The final hissing sounds of the word *hurts* made their own comment on the torturous practices that had been enumerated. The fourth and fifth songs would provide time and space for quieter, more introspective reflections. With "Big Sister Says, 1967" the set reaches its rhythmic and dynamic apex; the final two songs complete the arc and end the set in the soft sounds of its beginning, even if they do not return to the emotional state of the first song.

Larsen's *Love after 1950* is a dance suite of songs. It explores women in relation to their own and others' changing attitudes and locates love inside the era's most iconic musical styles. The final freely, sensuously, "dazzling" song pays homage to one of the nation's most notoriously iconic dancers, Isadora Duncan.[84] Duncan's strong, confident, intuitive, self-styled practice situated her outside tradition, a place where Larsen chose to reside herself. Duncan's insistence upon naturalness challenged inherited aesthetic values in general and balletic disciplines, postures, and poses more specifically. Her copiously draped, barefooted body that simultaneously covered and exposed her in ways antithetical to convention, questioned notions of what constituted beauty and dance. Larsen built her set using the blueprints of traditional multimovement musical architecture complete with its temporal, dynamic, and mood contrasts and thereby delivered the formal unity, logic, and coherence listeners expected. However, her choice to conclude the set with Muriel Rukeyser's 1973 poem "I Make My Magic" introduces ambiguity to the closed form and possibilities for the new woman, much as Duncan did in the world of dance decades earlier. Rukeyser (1913–80), a poet of optimism, joy, and political conscience, suited Larsen, who possessed the same qualities.

At a colloquium celebrating the centennial of Rukeyser's birth, the poet Alicia Ostriker commented upon the musical quality, "the profound song" of her words:

> Some of Rukeyser's writing is clear and direct. Much is not. I begin to read and am immediately in danger of drowning. The writing is not merely fluid; it is oceanic. It cannot be paraphrased. At the writing's surface, I am not on the shore at ocean's edge like Whitman in "Out of the cradle endlessly rocking," on solid ground listening to the birds and the sea-mother. At the writing's surface I am already in a lifeboat, surrounded in all directions by measureless waves. The waves of language slap and surge and pull, making their music. But it is beneath the surface that the meanings wait for me. To read Rukeyser is to learn to breathe underwater. Underwater, where life on our planet begins.[85]

In the preface to her 1978 *Collected Poems*, Rukeyser spoke of "two kinds of reaching in poetry, one based on the document . . . the other informed by the unverifiable fact, as in sex, dream, the parts of life where we *dive deep*."[86] "Diving deep" is how Larsen described her entry into vertical time, that space where she could disengage from clock time and inhabit an infinitely expansive moment to do her work. There she swam and floated in her music unmoored from the demands of quotidian life. Years later diving deep regularly allowed the composer to plumb the depths of her art and her consciousness; she learned to dive and surface at will.

In an earlier book, *The Life of Poetry*, Rukeyser questions what poetry accomplishes. Her answer could be applied equally well to music: "A poem invites you to feel. More than that: it invites you to respond. And better than that: a poem invites a total response." She acknowledges the role of the intellect but insists that the "response is total, . . . reached through the emotions . . . through what we call feeling."[87]

Rukeyser clearly understood the emotional appeal of poetry and music and spoke of their relationship with sensitivity and insight. "The meanings of poetry take their growth through the interaction of the images and the music of the poem. . . . The music involves the interplay of the sounds of words, the length of the sequences, the keeping and breaking of rhythms, and the repetition and variation of syllables unrhymed and rhymed. It also involves the play of ideas and images."[88] Larsen could have written the same.

Ostriker's watery references drew upon Rukeyser's many uses of liquid metaphors as well as the ceaseless flowing cadences of her poetic language. In "I Make My Magic," Rukeyser's image of the "straining dark underwater" likely resonated with the water-wise-and-loving composer; she would have known and felt its ever-present undulations, even in moments of seeming stillness.[89] In her final song, "I Make My Magic," Larsen meets Rukeyser's liquid language with continuous, roiling music. Larsen instructs the pianist to play "darkly, smoothly." "Dazzling" glissandos wash over the rhythmic vamp (ex. 6.8).

The poet and the composer maintain their focus even if "with uneasy patience."[90] As the piece moves toward its "ecstatic" close, the piano music is overtaken by the "dazzling" glissandos.[91] The piano becomes as a harp. Although the piece closes with a rolled, shimmering *pianissimo* chord high in the upper reaches of the piano, the music and the idea of coming to a "sunlight magic" linger beyond our hearing. The composer's biography might not be as obvious in *Love after 1950* as it was in *ME (Brenda Ueland)*, *Songs from Letters*, or *Notes Slipped under the Door*, but it is there in Larsen's selection of texts, their contemporaneity with her own experiences, and her insistence, as in Rukeyser's closing poem, that she makes her own magic according to her own rules.

The next year Larsen was inspired by the words of three American women, writer Gertrude Stein (1874–1946), actress Tallulah Bankhead (1902–68), and tennis champion Billie Jean King (b. 1943). They provided a lyrical counterpoint to the nursery rhyme "There Was a Little Girl."[92] She treated them as a group in her 2001 set *Hell's Belles* written for Frederica von Stade, another extraordinary American woman. In the first song, named after the nursery

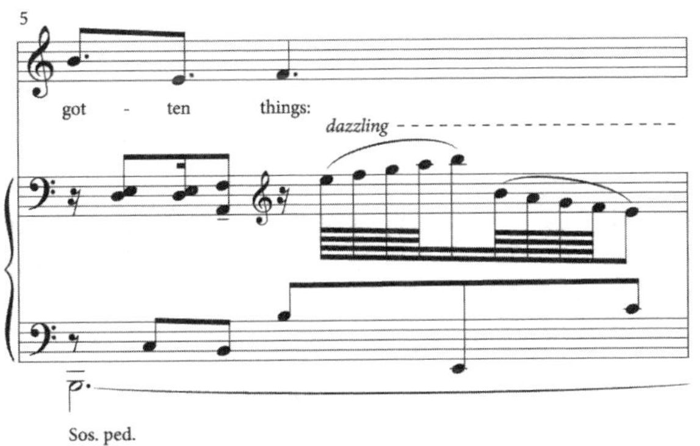

Words by Muriel Rukeyser.

Example 6.8. *Love after 1950*, "I Make My Magic," mm. 1–5.

rhyme, Larsen juxtaposes lines about the "very good" and "horrid" girl with pithy pronouncements from the feisty rule-breaking trio: Bankhead observes, "If I had my life to live over again, I'd make the same mistakes, only sooner." Billy Jean King advises, "Be Bold. If you're going to make an error, make it a doozy," and Stein concludes, "There ain't no answer. There ain't going to be any answer. There never has been an answer. That's the answer."[93] In the remaining songs of the set, Larsen takes pleasure in pointing out that none of the women cowed and leaves it to listeners to understand that it is because of their nonconformity that they succeeded beyond anyone's expectations.

As an etymology search makes clear, original meanings of the phrase "hell's bells" vary widely.[94] Whether used as a mild swear, an exclamation of surprise, a statement of disappointment, or an idiom that suggests a clanging in one's head after having been clobbered, none of the earliest uses comes close to Larsen's take on the term: a group of gals (belles) who must have seemed like emissaries from the underworld to those who wished that women would stay in their (domestic) place and toe the line drawn by society. That Larsen wrote the set for mezzo-soprano and a five-octave handbell choir adds to her unique spin on the phrase. Bells shake, shudder, shimmer, ring, clang, and clamor for the duration of the fourteen-minute set.[95] Choked and stopped bells, open and oscillating bells, those struck with hard mallets or soft mallets or set ringing with no mallets at all, their sounds fill the atmosphere. Larsen examines the wide world of pealing bells similarly to the way she explores the possibilities of women's lives. Freely vibrating sound, always a favorite subject and material in her compositions, is given additional programmatic meaning in this set: these belles resonate.

In the remaining three songs of the set, Larsen privileges other freethinking females. The second song, "Footlight Wisdom," was inspired by an interview with Olive Logan (1839–1909), a nineteenth-century American actress, author, journalist, and suffragist who detailed the various ways theater directors determined a young woman's likeliness for success on the stage: "Will you expose your arms . . . your bosom . . . will you wink at men and appear . . . every night before the gaze of thousands of men, wearing nothing but this pair of satin breaches, ten inches long?"[96] And over and over the director inquires, "Is your hair dyed yellow?" (ex. 6.9). Logan concludes that if you respond in the affirmative, you'll get the job. Larsen's song, a nostalgic, "wistful" waltz, is among her most conventionally tuneful and rhythmic works explored in this chapter; memorable motives that return at relatively regular intervals make their own comment on the traditional nature of society's expectations of women. But an attuned listener will hear the singer-actress subtly chafe at convention as occasional well-placed hemiolas appear within the ¾ meter.

In a third song, "When I Am an Old Woman," Larsen references Jenny Joseph's famous 1961 poem "Warning" to celebrate the freedom older women can enjoy and the behaviors they can indulge in to "make up for the sobriety of [their] youth."[97] Wearing purple "with a red hat which doesn't go" seems an answer to the oppressive dictates regarding what constitutes beauty that

Example 6.9. *Hell's Belles*, "Footlight Wisdom," mm. 18–35.

Larsen showcased in her earlier song "Big Sister Says, 1967." In keeping with Joseph's emancipated, unyielding older woman, Larsen's song is metrically freer. It stands in stark contrast to "Footlight Wisdom" with its seemingly harmless, but insistent, prescriptive, and ultimately oppressive waltz rhythm.

The last song, "The Magic City Golden Transit," was inspired by a published interview with Alabama-born American visual artist and poet Armor Keller (b. circa 1960).[98] Its subject is "an art car that is gold leafed and jeweled inside and out." As Keller explained, she collected "thousands of Barbie Doll shoes . . . and thin sheets of gold" and covered her 1980 Toyota station wagon with them and with mirrors.[99] Her car glistens and glimmers from any angle, much like the shimmering, ringing bells that fill the soundscape. The airwaves vibrate; the result is "mobile magic." One can only imagine how much this poem must have resonated with Libby Larsen, whose family hobby was cars and who found her own freedom sitting behind the wheel of the '57 yellow T-Bird! It is likely not coincidence that this final song text reinforced the message of Muriel Rukeyser's "I Make My Magic," the last song of Larsen's *Love after 1950* composed around the same time. By 2000, as Larsen turned fifty, she was an established force in American musical culture—a composer, advocate, administrator, and educator—and without taking herself too seriously, she recognized her achievements. Focused energy, hard work, and steely determination rather than anything supernatural had brought her to that position; she had earned the right to make her own musical "magic."

More than a decade later, Larsen created an eleven-minute *scena* for soprano and piano setting words spoken by Mary Magdalene; she wanted this early, most-favored and most-maligned religious woman heard in her own voice. To that end, in *The Magdalene* Larsen set verses from an ancient Coptic manuscript that Mary of Magdala knew well, the Gnostic sacred book *Pistis Sophia*.[100] Mary Magdalene would become the embodiment of *Pistis Sophia*. Mary Magdalene, Martha, and Mary the mother of Jesus were among three women named multiple times in the Gospels, and Mary Magdalene was noteworthy among them for having more than a first name, an unusual situation for a female; like Jesus of Nazareth, and John of Judea (more commonly known as John the Baptist), she was identified by her presumed place of origin, suggesting perhaps that she was an independent woman of wealth and not in need of identification through her patriarchal lineage.[101]

In the first three centuries of the Christian era, Mary Magdalene was honored as Christ's chief disciple and even regarded as the "apostle to the apostles" because of her personal witness to his death and resurrection and her role as messenger of the news to other followers.[102] But with the crowning of Emperor

Constantine in 306 and the gradual institution of Roman law and practices throughout all aspects of society, women were increasingly unwelcome in public leadership roles; they were removed and silenced. Over time Mary Magdalene's historical position changed from that of a revered disciple to that of a wanton woman. In a sermon on the Gospel of Luke delivered by Pope Gregory I (540–604) in 591, a year after he assumed the papacy, Gregory cast Mary as a public sinner and a repentant prostitute and institutionalized that reading within the Western Church. As Sister Christine Schenk, CSJ, explains: "Henceforth, Mary of Magdala became known in the west, not as the strong woman leader who accompanied Jesus through a tortuous death, first witnessed his Resurrection, and proclaimed the Risen Savior to the early church, but as a wanton woman in need of repentance and a life of hidden . . . penitence."[103] But she was never hidden in her lifetime. Despite a 1969 revision to the Roman Missal issued under Pope Paul VI that corrected Gregory's misidentification of Mary Magdalene as a penitent prostitute, the earlier pope's reading and characterization of this singular woman persisted. Large numbers of Catholic Church leaders and laity continued to diminish Mary Magdalene's historic role, defame her character, silence her voice, and keep her in her place, a place she never occupied while she was alive. Here lies one of the cornerstones of Western attitudes toward women that has stayed in place for millennia and limited the roles available to women if they dared to think about moving outside the home: they could be cast as virgins (as Mary the mother of Jesus), or whores as Mary Magdalene.[104]

In the last few decades, as large numbers of progressive Roman Catholics have questioned a variety of church doctrines and practices and especially those impacting the role of women and minorities within the institution, Mary of Magdala is gradually regaining some ground vis-à-vis her historical leadership position. Rather than take church fathers at their word and accept their readings and rulings as handed down over millennia, a variety of contemporary scholars have revisited documentary evidence regarding Mary Magdalene, including her recorded activities in the Gospels and extracanonical writings. They have considered their findings against the myth of her depravity and within the context of the Eastern Church's continued veneration of the Magdalene. Why was she removed from her original position within the *Western* Church and denied her achievements? Whose purposes were served? Feminist religious scholars, including Jane Schaberg, see Mary's demise as a deliberate act on the part of the Roman Catholic Church to discourage female leaders or at least contain women within its ranks.[105] As the modern Catholic Church endures a seemingly endless series of sexual scandals and revealed abuses, rehabilitating Mary Magdalene might seem a minor effort in the larger scheme of things. But as a public figure who endured defamation, ostracization, and silencing by those in power, her story speaks to thousands of others who have suffered a range of abuses at the hands of trusted religious leaders. Larsen's piece is her personal response to the historic misidentification of Mary Magdalene as a weak, sinful woman; it has become a public response on behalf of all who have withstood mistreatment at the hands of a misguided Church.

Given Larsen's early childhood experiences within the church, it is easy to understand her attraction to Mary Magdalene as the subject of a musical work. Within the elite discipleship, Mary Magdalene was distinguished by her intelligence, her thirst for knowledge, and her leadership. Larsen empathized with this gifted and insatiably curious religious woman. She could also understand the Gnostics' feeling of oppression. Fifty years after Vatican II, Larsen still objects to the idea that clerics alone decided religious practices or ways of knowing. With her piece Larsen acknowledges and celebrates the Magdalene's role in early Christianity. She demonstrates the continuing resonance of her own early religious training in her adult life and honors an iconoclastic woman who was unafraid to question authority and lead by example.[106]

The Magdalene brings together three powerful forces in Larsen's life: religion, gender, and an urgent need to question systems. In addition, the composer's continued sensitivity to visual imagery is evident in her original conception of the piece, which included the projection of the sung text on the body of the singer "so that the words 'I' and 'for my God' are directly centered on her."[107] Although technical problems have prevented the simultaneous realization of both aural and visual aspects in any performance of *The Magdalene* to date, the piece remains, as in Larsen's conception of *Black Birds, Red Hills*, a multivalent, theatrical work.[108]

Larsen selected verses from chapter 33 of the *Pistis Sophia* that describe Mary's interactions with Christ during one of his many returns. The composer explains: "Mary steps forward to tell the story of the *Pistis Sophia*, [she is] a personification of the Gnostic belief in gaining wisdom through questioning."[109] Mary speaks a version of Psalm 68, which, Larsen explains, she repurposes "to describe the oppression of the Gnostics by the rule-oriented orthodox Christians."[110]

The singer assumes three roles: the narrator, the Archangel, and Mary Magdalene. She is costumed in a simple sackcloth-like garment. Lighting is an essential component of the work; it sets the mood and suggests Mary's in-

Example 6.10. *The Magdalene*, score page 1, mm. 2–3.

ner light. Both the narrator and the Archangel sing only in English, and their lines tend toward chant-like recitation; their music is relatively contained. Occasional melismatic flourishes on individual syllables or words intensify their meaning, but this is not their story (ex. 6.10).

Mary sings in both English and Coptic. It is as if the real mysteries of ancient Christian practices belong to her; she alone is privy to their full meaning. When the vocalist sings in Coptic, Larsen envisioned that English translations would be projected. The score is filled with large black *X*s above the staves indicating when the text appears and when it goes "out." Mary's religious ecstasy is apparent at her first entrance. Her line soars and grows and encompasses whole tone, octatonic, and diatonic scales; her "inner light" cannot be contained within a single common pitch pattern. The harmonic language sounds vaguely Eastern but wholly unique to this piece (ex. 6.11).

Larsen's initial piano accompaniment consists of recurring minimalist patterns that set Mary's more emotive part in high relief. Occasional flourishes mimic her impassioned line, but on the whole, the piano never gets in the way or upstages Mary's declamation. The accompaniment plays a more dramatically evocative role in Mary's first Coptic interpolation when she pleads with God to "save me . . . for the waters cover my soul. I'm sinking in the slime of the deep." Mary enters "the watery depths."[111] Water, such a familiar medium for Larsen, is musicalized in a low, swirling, *pianissimo* accompaniment that rushes underneath Mary's Coptic verse. Without understanding Coptic, we can hear the turbulence of Mary's soul. Given the dramatic delivery of the music, we can feel her anguish in the singer's performance (ex. 6.12).

As she has done in numerous religious pieces, Larsen weaves chant in unexpected but thoroughly organic ways into the texture of her pieces. The same chant that was heard in *Rodeo Queen of Heaven* appears numerous times

Example 6.11. *The Magdalene*, score pages 3–4, mm. 9–12.

Example 6.11. *(continued)*

in *The Magdalene*. It is a sounding touchstone for Larsen, a link to her youth (ex. 6.13). The chant returns at the end of that section of the piece hanging unfinished at the bar line (ex. 6.14). Mary's remaining song consists of soaring vocalizations on "Ah"—at one point traversing an octave from C above middle C to "high" C—and the words "Hear me, O Lord. . . Hear me." On her final uttered "hear," Mary climbs a minor ninth to a high D-flat before ending on high C. With her last words it is as if she has transcended earthly realms or musical gravity. The space reverberates with the celestial sound. The final words of the piece are given to the Archangel, whose entrance is heralded, as it was twice before, by a rising E Phrygian modal scale.[112] Although Larsen resists locking her piece into a key, and Mary's music is more tethered to D-flat than any other pitch, E emerges as the most important pitch anchor of the work. Its centrality is reinforced when it provides the root of the final (major) chord that closes the piece. *The Magdalene* lifts upward as the Archangel "bless[es] the name of God in song" and asserts that "they who love his name shall dwell [in a city . . . in the light]" (ex. 6.15).

The piece was jointly commissioned by pianist Jeffrey Peterson, a faculty member at Baylor University, and soprano Rebecca Wascoe, a faculty member at Texas Tech University. Mary Magdalene as the topic of an extended piece for voice was originally Wascoe's idea, but she knew of Larsen's ties to religion. She had first come in contact with Larsen's music while an undergraduate student in a music history course and was immediately drawn to it. She eventually wrote her doctoral treatise at the University of Illinois on Larsen's vocal works. At the time of the commission for *The Magdalene*, the two women had enjoyed a relationship that went back a number of years.[113] Larsen knew Wascoe's voice, and Wascoe was "fluent in Larsen."[114] Both women were also drawn to the idea of a work about a strong, religious, female figure. As Wascoe recalls, "We said 'Mary Magdalene' at the same time."[115] Once they had decided

*Dashed barlines indicate no metric stress. Solid barlines indicate metric stress.

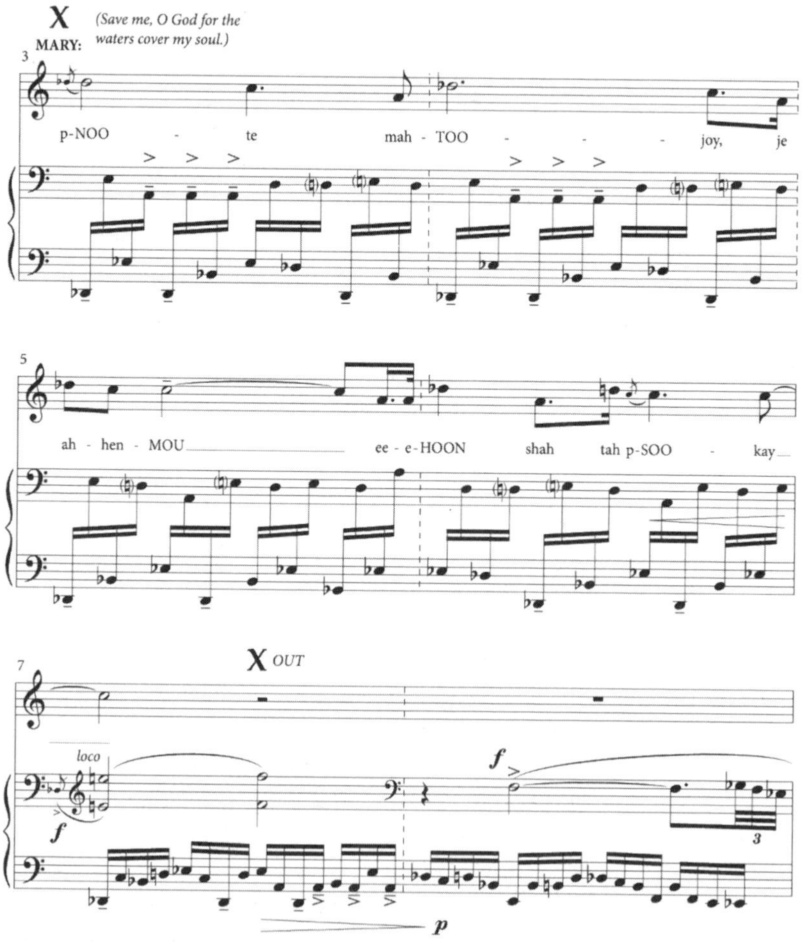

X (Save me, O God for the waters cover my soul.)

MARY:

3

p-NOO - te mah - TOO - - - joy, je

5

ah - hen - MOU ee - e-HOON shah tah p-SOO - kay

7

X OUT

loco

f

f

3

p

Example 6.12. *The Magdalene*, score pages 6–7, mm. 1–8.

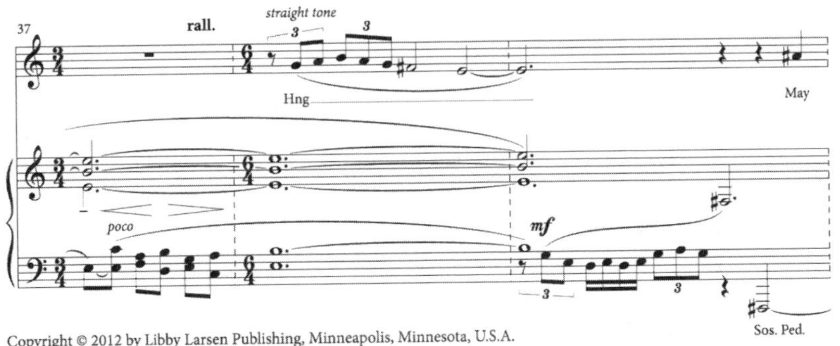

Example 6.13. *The Magdalene*, score page 11, mm. 35–39, chant melody.

Example 6.14. *The Magdalene*, score page 16, mm. 68–69.

upon their subject, the two women created a list of about thirty books and articles that they read over the next year. They settled on the *Pistis Sophia* as the essential text but left Larsen to chose the precise chapters and verses that she would set. Larsen and Wascoe and eventually Peterson worked together on the project.

Example 6.15. *The Magdalene*, score page 22, mm. 109–11.

Beyond the commission from Peterson and Wascoe, additional funding from Baylor University, Mississippi State University, and an alumnae chapter of Sigma Alpha Iota, the professional music fraternity that Larsen had joined while a student at the University of Minnesota, rounded out the commissioners. An article announced the impending work in Baylor University's *Research Tracks*; it discussed the specificity of the composer's vision of the song cycle, all the way down to "instructions for stage lighting and the vocalist's costume."[116] Once Larsen had started thinking of her song sets as theater pieces, she continued along that path, and *The Magdalene* was another example. The theater of Larsen's mind was staged for others to see.

The work premiered in February 2013 at Baylor, a Baptist-affiliated Christian research university in Texas known for its conservatism regarding many aspects of Christian doctrine.[117] As might be expected, the work was not greeted enthusiastically by leaders of the George W. Truett Theological Seminary at Baylor, who declined the opportunity to meet with Larsen, despite her offer to speak with them during her residency at the university.[118] As a seminary "centered in the gospel of Jesus Christ and consistent with historic Baptist commitments" and grounded in the belief "that the sixty-six books of Holy Scripture are inspired by God's Spirit and are the sole supreme authority under God for Christian believing and living,"[119] it follows that a work whose text originated in the *Pistis Sophia*, which gave voice to an insatiably curious and questioning woman and endorsed personal revelation as well as accepted doctrine would not be warmly embraced or encouraged by the theological school. As recently as 2000, Southern Baptist Conference leadership voted against women serving as pastors.[120]

As Peterson has observed, despite the seminary's stance, the premiere of the piece took place before a packed audience, students and colleagues loved the piece, and the reception was tremendous.[121] It is hard to imagine Larsen finding a more supercharged venue within mainline Christianity for the unveiling of a work about the erased, ignored, and maligned Mary. And it is also hard to imagine a more empathetic composer than Larsen to take on the subject. In a conversation with Peterson regarding his work with Larsen on *The Magdalene*, he spoke of her passion for researching her projects and her deep understanding of her collaborators; he also spoke of "how much and how beautifully she speaks for this woman."[122] Indeed, in giving voice to the Magdalene's "hear me," Larsen makes a powerful plea for Mary, but beyond that she speaks for herself, the young child who had been bribed to remain silent, and for anyone else who has felt stifled or suppressed by society. With deep empathy for her subject, Larsen "becomes" Mary; the women "meld" together. Like so many of her pieces about women, there is biography in this piece as well.[123]

Over the next year Peterson and Wascoe performed *The Magdalene* throughout Texas, in Oklahoma, and in Paris, France, and according to Peterson, always to enthusiastic audiences.[124] Wascoe recalls that the Parisian audience, in particular, embraced the piece.[125] That Baylor University ultimately decided not to fund a grant proposal that would have underwritten a recording of the work has not deterred the trio from going ahead with their project. They have a contract with Albany Records to record *The Madgalene* "along with several other unrecorded pieces," and it will come to pass.[126]

7 Larsen and Technology
Challenging the Concert Hall

ON FEBRUARY 16, 2014, the Fort Worth Opera announced that it would postpone indefinitely the long-awaited world premiere of Libby Larsen's time-traveling opera *A Wrinkle in Time*, a greatly expanded update of the fifty-minute version that she had composed for the Delaware Opera in 1991. Referring to the original production, Larsen explains, "At that point the technology was crude compared to present day technology. I used an EMAX II to create tech sound and we amplified through traditional cluster speakers."[1] The 2014 opera would have "anchored the [Fort Worth] company's 2015 festival."[2] Throughout preparations for the premiere, Larsen repeatedly questioned the general director, Darren K. Woods, about the company's "ability to produce the sound, and he always responded: 'Do what you need to do, and we'll make it happen.'" Larsen enjoyed a relationship with Woods and the Bass Hall site as a result of having worked with their sound technicians to design the sound for their existing system.[3] When plans fell through and Woods was asked why this "signature piece" was removed from the lineup, he cited the bottom line: "It cost so much because its technology . . . hasn't been seen in Bass Hall before. The theater had to be equipped with surround sound. There was video equipment that is only now being invented. I mean, this is a fantastical story where a woman turns into a unicorn . . . so people had to vanish and appear in different places, so there was probably $300,000 to $400,000 of technology that doesn't exist in our hall, or any other hall."[4] Without anticipated funding, the opera was beyond the reach of the company. The news came as a major disappointment to Larsen (and Woods), who had dreamed of staging an operatic adaptation of Madeleine L'Engle's children's story for years.

The technological challenges that Woods cited in 2014 accrue additional meaning in light of a plenary address that Larsen had delivered seventeen years earlier to the National Association of Schools of Music (NASM): Her talk was titled, "The Role of the Musician in the 21st Century: Rethinking the Core." Although it was directed to educators, Larsen's talk argued that everyone in music needed to catch up with contemporary practices lest they be left behind, deemed irrelevant, or find themselves unable to engage.[5] She spoke of the current age of electronic music and mass media; our obligation to recognize and honor "produced" sound as well as acoustic sound; the fluid and variable venues that host a range of musical events; new forms of notation; the rich diversity of musics experienced by any cross-section of the public; and the necessity to learn about sound production and recording studio practices, mixing boards and microphones, wet sounds and dry sounds, MIDI keyboards, and electric drums and computers.[6] It was as if Larsen anticipated the Bass Hall dilemma in 1997.

Larsen spoke as an acoustic composer, but one who had made a conscious decision to take on collaborative partners to bring new sound and media possibilities into her music. She had begun mixing acoustic and produced sounds in her own works starting in the late 1980s with her opera *Frankenstein; or, The Modern Prometheus*. In 1989 she received a fellowship from the Bush Foundation to study with Morton Subotnick, one of the nation's most highly regarded electronic composers; she worked with him over the course of a year. Because Larsen realized she "didn't have the skills to create tech sound that were equal to [her] skills in acoustic sound, for *Frankenstein* [she] worked with [audio engineer] Tim Stiles."[7] A description of the "Instrumentation" needed for the work illuminates her multisensory imaginary at the time:

> Sound enhancement needed for proper electro-acoustical mix, flute (doubles piccolo), oboe (doubles English horn), clarinet (doubles bass clarinet), bassoon (doubles contrabassoon), horn, trumpet, 2 percussion, timpani, keyboard (piano, DX7 synthesizer), string quintet. Other requirements: Video and slide projection system needed to project details of eyes, hands, etc. on various layers of the scrim. Sound system needed to project backstage chorus into the hall and to amplify body microphones and mix orchestral sound.[8]

As part of a 1999 "Science of Sound" project at the Science Museum of Minnesota, Larsen wrote *All around Sound*, a work for the Minnesota Orchestra and an actor-mime. Along with standard pairs of orchestral instruments, the score included a metal folding chair, a large red rubber ball, a brake drum, and a bicycle bell, as well as prerecorded found sounds. Larsen cued the *musique concrète* sounds on a CD and interleaved them in the five-part work.

Imagining a work that requires cutting-edge technology is nothing new in the world of music; on the contrary, the desire for the next thing has been the engine behind the development of instruments and techniques since recorded time. Starting in the twentieth century, however, technology itself increasingly became a driver of new technology: Luigi Russolo created a "Futurist's Orchestra" with his noise-intoning Intonarumori. Six families of noises produced a range of fundamental sounds that he believed characterized the modern era. Léon Theremin invented a two-antenna etherphone to produce a controllable infinite pitch spectrum of sounds like those generated by sirens. Harry Partch took a different tack when he looked backward to ancient Greek culture for what he needed, and found and built instruments—themselves works of visual art—that could deliver the microtonal pitches and unique timbres he heard during his years of wandering and in the voices of his hobo chums. Prior to them all, in 1901 Thaddeus Cahill had developed the telharmonium (also known as the dynamaphone), an organ that turned electrical signals into sounds that were then broadcast through a self-contained speaker system within a building; the instrument anticipated Hammond organs, and even Muzak, or what is commonly referred to as elevator music.

Perhaps most celebrated for imagining new sounds in the twentieth century is Edgard Varèse, a composer Larsen holds in the highest regard. In an article published in 1917 in the Dadaist journal *391*, Varèse remarked: "I dream of instruments obedient to my thought and which with their contribution of a whole new world of unsuspected sounds, will lend themselves to the exigencies of my inner rhythm."[9] Varèse spoke "of "sound-masses, of shifting planes . . . taking the place of linear counterpoint" and observed that "when these sound-masses collide, the phenomena of penetration or repulsion will seem to occur."[10] Years later, in a lecture he delivered in 1936, Varèse spoke of a fourth dimension for music: "sound projection—that feeling that sound is leaving us with no hope of being reflected back, a feeling akin to that aroused by beams of light sent forth by a powerful searchlight—for the ear as for the eye, that sense of projection, of a journey into space."[11] Given the extraterrestrial nature of *A Wrinkle in Time*, where human beings and otherworldly creatures are transported through "tesseracts" (wrinkles in time and space) to confront the mind-controlling, disembodied brain IT on the planet Camazotz, one can appreciate the fundamental role that technology plays in Larsen's operatic "journey into space." It is not an add-on or an accessory; it is the essence of the story and the acoustic-theatrical world she imagined.

Larsen's fascination with the spatial dimensions of sound shaped *The Words upon the Windowpane* when she composed sound projecting from multiple locations. Studying Ives's music with Johannes Riedel deepened her appreciation of the affective possibilities of spatial considerations, as would a residency by Henry Brant at the University of Minnesota, which gave Larsen a chance to perform a number of his spatial works.[12] Brant admired Ives's uses of multiple ensembles positioned separately as sound sources in *The Unanswered Question*. Larsen recalls, "I got to know Henry and he joined the Minnesota Composers Forum. Visits from Olivier Messiaen, Lou Harrison, and Donald Martino also made deep impressions. I think I connected with each composer's use of the physical space [of a] concert hall as part of the music."[13]

Larsen's sensitivity to the spatial qualities of sound was always a part of her perception and thought, even if she did not have a name for it. Singing chant in highly reverberant spaces meant that sound mixing in the air was an essential aspect of music and constitutive to the mystery of the spiritual experience. Listening to voices and ambient sounds as they bounced, echoed, and wafted across Lake Harriet conditioned a young Larsen to be at home in polyvocal acoustical environments; she swam in the water and the sounds as well. But Larsen's interest in sound and space does not require operatic-sized projects to materialize; minimal materials and shorter pieces provide ample opportunities to explore. As Larsen has explained, spatial concerns were the essence of her 1993 piece *Fanfare for the Women*, a two-minute solo work for trumpet. "At the premiere the trumpet soloist stood alone, in the center of the basketball court. The music is composed to create layers of tonality which overlap in space, especially in a vast space with a long acoustic decay, and it was extraordinary to watch and hear this fine musician as she spun the sound into space and time."[14]

Larsen's interests lie not only with the effects of space and time on sound but also with the active roles musicians assume projecting, releasing, and spinning a "sound into space and time." Sounds affect and are affected by space, and people affect both sounds and spaces. It turns out that Larsen's nature-related compositions are not the only works that explore her understanding of her place within a larger, mutually interactive and dependent environment. Larsen has a role in her acoustic environment as well: she is a collaborator with the space around her. She determines what best serves the sound ecology of a piece and a place and pulls from all possible sources. Exploring creative possibilities of all sounds is part of her work as she writes music that probes Varèse's fourth imagined dimension of sound: projection.

In a 2015 conversation Larsen revisited issues related to sound projection and acoustic environments when she mulled over the conditions of most existing concert halls.[15] She spoke of traditional acoustic design that is focused on delivering maximal clarity, balance, impact, and effect when sound originates on a stage at the front of a hall and is projected toward a seated (and immobile) audience whose arrangement has been determined with that single sound source in mind. The hall becomes a particular kind of sounding box. With luck, performers on stage hear themselves similarly to the way audiences do hundreds of feet away, although this is seldom the case. But what happens when a composer wants an audience to be in the middle of multiple colliding sound masses or shifting planes of sounds originating from different points in a hall? What happens when a single sound source or acoustic "sweet spot" is not the reality or the goal? Larsen acknowledges that producers are more accustomed to engaging with mixed sound worlds in theatrical works—opera, dance, theater—than they are in purely instrumental works, but physical-acoustic challenges persist regardless of the genre. Larsen's all-encompassing multimedia concept for *A Wrinkle in Time* pushes against the acoustics of a hall designed for a more traditional sonic imagination; *Wrinkle*, like many of her other works, rejects conventional categories and boundaries. That a number of her multimedia pieces have had to be performed without all their components is frustrating, but Larsen is confident that ultimately technological obstacles are solvable, and her works will be realized full and complete, and as she originally imagined them.

She takes heart in knowing that Varèse's 1917 dream "instruments" became realities with the development of widely available magnetic-tape technology immediately following World War II.[16] In *Déserts* (1950–54), his first work using what was then new technology, the tape recorder acted as another instrument in the ensemble. With *Poème électronique*, an eight-minute piece completed in 1958 for the Phillips Pavilion at the Brussels Worlds Fair, Varèse created a piece generated solely by electronics that was synchronized with photographs and paintings and projected into the pavilion space through 425 speakers. *Poème électronique* may be "the first piece of 'surround sound' and certainly of multimedia as we understand the term today."[17]

Sound is one part of a multidimensional world that Larsen seeks to create; it is one aspect of a larger conception that often includes visual, theatrical, and even imagined olfactory components in addition to music. In this regard Larsen is like Harry Partch, many of whose pieces were carefully choreographed or used film or ritual-like performance practices, and for whom the visual aspect of music making was essential.[18]

Although Larsen thinks beyond sound, she is not beholden to any other single sense either.[19] In her multisensory being, Larsen embodies the fully engaged "sensorium."[20] Technology has allowed neuroscientists to see the physical simultaneity of our sensory perceptions and to track their journey to consciousness. It is not that humans naturally privilege sight over sound or smell over touch, but that time and culture train individuals to value one over the other. Stimuli attain their maximum effect, however, when they are understood as happening together. Larsen values them all. Her attunement to words, sounds, smells, rhythms, motions, gestures, all things visual, and more generally the energy (the "life force") that surrounds her reveals itself in Larsen's empathetic ability to "be" the subject. Multimedia works are the logical outgrowth of the ways she registers her world.

Three recent pieces testify to the integral role technology plays in Larsen's multimedia sensorium: *Now I Pull Silver* for solo flute and computer-driven imagery; *O Magnum Mysterium*, a hybrid piece that uses SATB chorus and prerecorded materials; and *Emergence*, a work for string quartet, narrator, and visual imagery.[21] They reflect where at least a portion of Larsen's creative energies have been focused of late. The pieces also reveal the continuing influence that nature, religion, and gender exert upon her thought and music.

In 2004 Larsen composed *Now I Pull Silver*, a work for amplified solo flute, laptop-driven projected real-time shifting fractal imagery, and a prepared CD, for which she performed all the sound.[22] The silver of the title comes to life quite literally in the sounds of the sterling flute. The instrument that inspired so many of her earliest works remains a favorite. The disc contains manipulated spoken voice—the actress Katherine Ferrand reciting A. E. Stallings's poem "Arachne Gives Thanks to Athena"—including barely audible echoed words, Silvertone lap guitar, kalimba, and brass wind chimes. In *Now I Pull Silver* Larsen creates a musical-theatrical enactment of Stallings's poem, which tells the mythological story of the peasant girl Arachne, who boasted that she could weave as beautifully as the goddess Athena. Arachne's punishment for challenging Athena's artistic prowess was to spend the rest of her life as a spider. Arachne accepts her fate with grace knowing that in her spider incarnation she contains within herself an infinite source of raw material and more "hands" to weave her creations than in her human form. She is self-sufficient and complete, a system all her own. She takes comfort in the realization that "if [she is] not beautiful" herself, she is "beauty's maker."[23] The idea of who and what determines beauty (female or otherwise) returns in an unexpected way and goes far beyond the world of eyelashes, hair, and smooth skin railed against in "Big Sister Says, 1967." A photograph preceding the first page of the score shows the otherworldly visual effects created by fractals that Larsen imagined as the flutist/Arachne weaves a web of sound.

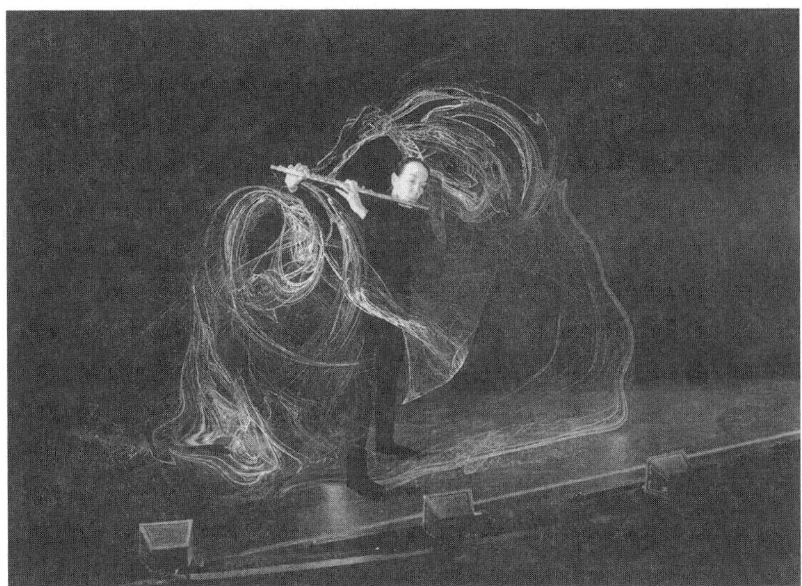

Figure 7.1. Libby Larsen, *Now I Pull Silver*. Imagined fractal imagery in performance. See score, *Now I Pull Silver*, copyright © 2008.

Larsen uses a combination of modern and traditional sounds and sound effects to tell the ancient tale; she is not opposed to employing tried techniques to vivify the story. When Arachne refers to the "lines I pulled from my own belly," the Silvertone lap guitar responds with a series of barely audible upward slides. The sound is as thin and silky as the spider's filament. Larsen instructs the flutist to "skitter, as a spider casting the web" over the sounds of wind chimes that start and stop to a rhythm all their own. The composer uses the kalimba to articulate Arachne's movement; its pinging tones are the sounding equivalents of coordinates in space. Listeners can imagine Arachne tying knots at strategic "arrival points" in her airy, gossamer web.[24] Larsen paints gestures the way Renaissance composers painted words.

Despite its judicious use of inherited techniques, the piece challenges traditional notions of what constitutes a musical work. Is this a dramatic recitation with accompaniment or some version of a song?[25] The delivery style recalls Schoenberg's *Pierrot lunaire*, although Larsen doesn't indicate any pitches for her speaker. Despite that difference, there is a similarly fantastical quality to both works. Hints at pitches are reserved for the flutist, and here Larsen uses Schoenberg's *Sprechstimme* notation of "x"ed note heads on

Example 7.1. *Now I Pull Silver*, page 3

pitches. They always accompany Larsen's "wings" instruction to the flutist, where the performer depresses the appropriate key pads without blowing into the instrument: listeners hear soft, popping, vaguely pitched sounds.[26] With the exception of a brief section of triple *piano* notes that Larsen wants to be played "loco"—where we hear discrete, tongued, whistled pitches—the flute alternates between the winged passages and whistle tones, a majority of which oscillate randomly within stated parameters. She notates the whistle tones with "W. T." above the staff, and indicates oscillations with delicate, wavering lines (ex. 7.1).

With *Now I Pull Silver*, Larsen enters the theater of her mind and invites us in. Whether to categorize the piece as a musical work or a melodrama is irrelevant to the composer. She describes the piece as "a sonic soliloquy for interior flute and prepared CD." A dynamic compass of *pp* to *ppp* emphasizes the interiority of Larsen's expression. A listener wonders for whom the music sounds; to whom is Arachne speaking? As the composer explains: "While spinning her web, Arachne speaks the words of the poem as if she were speaking either to herself or to any being within intimate distance. She casts her filaments or whistle tones . . . as she almost, but not quite, inaudibly scuttles from anchor point to anchor point." Larsen clarifies her wish for an almost silent, internal music when she explains that as spiders cast "their webs largely unnoticed, the piece should be listened to on headphones with eyes closed or in half-light when performed live."[27]

Larsen's allowance for closed eyes begs a number of questions, the first of which is why she includes fractal imagery or any visual component at all. Can the piece be complete without the visual? Perhaps the composer wants listeners to dive deep into their own inner theaters and create their own imagery. Does the piece even need an audience? Perhaps the piece *is* truly a soliloquy for the performer, the spinner of the sounds, and does not require additional listeners. Might the fractal images lead a listener's hearing? Perhaps the visual images are tracings of the flutist's sounding movements, and Larsen intends to reinforce one sense with another. Perhaps practical exigencies suggest that it is wiser to have a piece that does not require high-tech go-with-its if it is ever to be performed at all.

But perhaps there is another explanation for Larsen's apparent willingness to forego the visual element: Just as Arachne contains within herself all she needs to spin her web, it is possible that any part of Larsen's piece contains the whole of the piece. Like the pine tree seedlings that Larsen and her fellow scouts decided were simultaneously now and then (the present and the future), in Larsen's theater of the mind, the sounds contain the imagery and the imagery contains the sounds. There is no separation of components; regardless of whether they are both present, they are always both there. Perhaps the piece does not need to sound at all.

The quiet interiority of *Now I Pull Silver* recalls a conversation with the composer in 2009 when Larsen pondered her decades-long creative trajectory. She spoke of an early set of pieces, now lost, that she had titled *Soft Pieces* and of starting with "pieces of a more 'inward' and contemplative cast, which she distinguishe[d] from her public 'display' pieces."[28] She characterizes the "display" pieces as typically "commissioned, event-oriented works that are linear and teleological." She explained that these works "often involve large performing forces." Her "inward pieces," on the other hand, are typically softer, smaller works of a more personal nature even though they may also be commissioned."[29] Larsen thought a long time about her exploration of the ideas of outward and inward music and in a second day of conversations observed: "I realized that I have a twenty-year arch going that I didn't know I had going, an investigation. . . . Where I'm going, is to be quiet."[30]

Now I Pull Silver is a delicate sound world; it is lacy and shimmering. There is an evanescent quality to the music that suggests the chimerical quality of spider webs. In the right light they are obvious and well defined, beautiful works of the most artistic engineering, but approached from the "wrong" angle, they are completely invisible; neither their artistry nor technical achievement can be appreciated. When fully intact they are remarkably strong and resilient, they bend and flex and allow for the entrapment of victims many times their weight, but when breeched they are rendered wholly ineffective. In *Now I Pull Silver* sounds waft in and out of our hearing. The musical framework seems infinitely accommodating. The exotic timbres of the kalimba, the endless reverberations of the chimes, and the slippery sounds of the lap guitar evoke another world that is not quite in focus or fully accessible; it is chimerical as well. In this piece, technology allows Larsen to push the boundaries of her imagination while she demonstrates the timelessness of Greek mythology. The idea of listening on headphones with eyes closed relieves the piece of the necessity of a public performance or communal enjoyment. In this way the piece participates in the solitary listening practice that characterizes so many of today's musical experiences, and that Larsen commented on in her 1997 NASM talk. These are experiences made possible by technology, experiences not beholden to the exigencies of a concert hall. Technology allows Larsen to create new visual imagery, new sounds and sound effects, to listen in new ways, and to turn even further inward in a super-quiet world that she hears.

Despite the composer's observation that she is heading toward quiet, the group of pieces considered in this chapter shows Larsen continuing to write both small, intimate works and large, public pieces, although the larger compositions, her operas for instance, go well beyond entertainment or display as she often tackles serious questions with them.[31] A piece that straddles the ideas of interiority and display is *O Magnum Mysterium*, written in 2011. If Larsen's use of A. E. Stallings's poem "Arachne Gives Thanks to Athena" for *Now I Pull Silver* demonstrates her ongoing attraction to the works of women writers and women's issues, *O Magnum Mysterium* shows the continuing presence of a mystical, spiritual dimension in the composer's life. In fact, with its Latin text and Christmas story, the piece embodies the never-to-be-erased religious school experiences from her childhood. On the title page, just underneath the Latin text, Larsen includes her own awestruck statement about the great mystery of Jesus's birth:

On the first Christmas night, what must it have been like when the skies exploded with heavenly light and erupted with the sound of angels? It must have been terrifyingly beautiful, furiously ecstatic and powerfully peaceful. Time must have stopped and in this moment suspended in eternity, the angels taught us how to sing. In this setting of the text *O Magnum Mysterium*, The Archangel quietly shepherds us into a twelve-fold Alleluia—heaven and earth singing together at the Birth.[32]

Beyond revealing the continuing joy that the Christmas story brings Larsen, the composer's remarks confirm her multimedia understanding of the world, her natural propensity toward unboundedness and reconciling seeming opposites, and her awareness of the temporal and timeless dimension of experience. The visual and the aural (light and sound) appear simultaneously; beauty is terrifying and peace is powerful; and time cedes to eternity. Out of this all-encompassing, super-rich, multisensory moment comes song: music results from ecstasy.[33] That Larsen shares her heartfelt engagement is not surprising to anyone who knows her; on the contrary, it is unlikely that she could contain it.

Larsen's multimedia *Mysterium* is another work that employs technology, as well as unexpected instruments and traditional voices in the service of her musical vision: machine and human come together. For this piece she collaborated closely with English tenor Paul Phoenix of the King's Singers at the Floating Earth Studios in London.[34] The performing forces include two choirs, although only one of them is the traditional choral ensemble. Choir 1 is a seven-track recording that consists of an overdubbed solo tenor voice, sitar, vibraphone, and bells that are mixed and then "performed through a laptop computer and speakers." Choir 2 is a traditional live SATB ensemble.[35] Larsen describes the choir 1 music as "a collaborative effort of a tenor, percussionist, sitarist, computer programmer, two sound engineers, and [herself]."[36] The second (live) choir music is her unique creation. The two forces embody different aspects of experience that ultimately come together. The prerecorded material "is set in shape, time and dynamics," so it is unchanging; the music for choir 2, on the other hand, varies significantly each time it is performed, and Larsen wants this. Her "aim is for the [live] choir to revel in the freedom of human breath, phrasing and timing." She is after "immediacy, fragility, even fallibility . . . relief against the technical precision of the nine-note ostinato pattern" present in choir 1.[37] But even while musicalizing the idea of what is fixed and what is mutable, Larsen allows for additional flexibility within the prerecorded tracks. In the composer's notes, she clarifies that the volume of the ostinato is adjustable, and both voice and the bells can be muted and their parts taken by live players if preferred, which allows for unexpected variety in the soundscape. Additionally, the choir 1 recording contains speaker controls that can customize balance to a particular acoustic environment. Technology allows Larsen to decide her limitations and design her freedom.

She creates a quietly ecstatic sound world via the prerecorded nine-beat, D-flat major arpeggiated vibraphone ostinato that immediately grounds the piece; at the third iteration of the pattern, Phoenix's otherworldly recorded tenor voice enters intoning "O magnum Mysterium, et admirabile sacramentum" (O great mystery, and wonderful sacrament) on F. The pure voice of the Archangel hovers weightlessly over the ostinato; it conjures the heavenly host (ex. 7.2). Larsen intensifies her pitch world with the presence of a two-beat E-flat that acts as the fulcrum of the ostinato as it overlaps one measure to the next. The vocalist's F and the E-flat in the ostinato rub against each other at regular intervals producing a shimmering tension that grows more luminous when the prerecorded solo voice splits into four parts (E-flat, F, G, and B-flat) on the final syllable "tum," and a Sarna bell ringing D-flat joins in slightly behind the vibraphone beats. Although the piece is thoroughly anchored in the key of D-flat, the vibrating metalophones fill all available pitch space with their resonance. The whole world glistens and glimmers while the ostinato pulses steadily, unperturbed. Only after eternity is made apparent, does Larsen introduce the fully human sounds of choir 2.[38] They take their lead from the chanting Archangel and repeat his words "O Magnum Mysterium" *pianissimo*; they become part of "heaven and earth singing together."[39]

In *O Magnum Mysterium* Larsen reconciles the chant tradition to which she was born with the four-part choral tradition that had so riled her sensibilities in high school. She also harmonizes Western and Eastern sounds when she writes a part for sitar, which appears for the first time approximately a minute and a half into the seven-minute work. Entering with its own strummed, arpeggiated figure that matches the D-flat major orientation of the softly clanging ostinato, the sitar also introduces a new source of lyricism. Numerous glissandos showcase the unique tuning and timbre of the North Indian instrument.[40] Its appearance signals Larsen's refusal to be confined by expected sounds or cultural traditions. Immediately following the sitar's first appearance, the recorded tenor soloist reenters on the word *Beata* (blessed). But it is not clear exactly where the instrument's sound ends and the singer begins; the movement from strings to voice is seamless, perhaps a metaphor for the unity of humanity with heavenly and earthly realms.[41] Or perhaps

Example 7.2. *O Magnum Mysterium*, mm. 1–14

Larsen is suggesting that the hope for peace is as much a reality in the East as it is in the West.[42]

As Larsen builds her "twelve-fold Alleluia," individual parts, acoustic and produced, peel away from the ostinato and its controlling nine-beat pattern. Although it had dominated the first two-and-a-half-minutes, when a greatly overdubbed choir 1 starts its "Alleluia" followed by the four-part choir 2 moments later, a total of twelve parts start circling each other in a kaleidoscopic array of meters that includes the germinal 9/8 as well as patterns of 2/4, 3/4, 4/4, 5/4, 6/4, 7/4, 5/8, 6/8, and 7/8. Like whirling dervishes chasing religious ecstasy, "alleluias" swirl for close to a minute while a D-flat chime continuously "rings out."[43] Seconds after the three-minute mark, the sitar begins a euphoric solo that excites the ensemble to a *forte* dynamic level for the one and only time in the entire subdued seven-minute piece. For a brief period of time, the dynamic level can't be contained. But having reached the peak of its outward display, the piece returns to its more inward and contained expression of joy. The SATB choir coalesces into a traditional choral ensemble moving together, creating beautiful, round vocal sounds; the sitar expends its energy exploring the range of its technical and emotional possibilities. As the piece nears its end, the voices of choir 2 join their "alleluias" with the pitches and rhythms of the vibraphone ostinato—live and recorded media align, the human and the technological merge—the sitar returns to its ascending slide that reinforces the D-flat harmonic world, and the chime strikes its final ringing D-flat.

All participants would seem to have been fully transported into the eternal realm were it not for the brief appearance at minute six of an unexpected fragmentary quotation in the bass line of choir 2. The sequential, descending dotted pattern starting at the pickup to measure 93 recalls any number of Christmas carols, but the composer explains that it comes specifically from "Gesù Bambino" (ex. 7.3). The original idea to include a fragment of the carol came from the singers: knowing the text, with its references to snow, a winter night, and the Christmas rose, it must have resonated with the composer, whose earlier work *In a Winter Garden* celebrates those same meaningful signs.[44]

Larsen's musical paean to the great mystery combines the transcendent and the mundane. It gives the last words to the live chorus but the last sounds to the long-resonating chime. Choir 1's recorded voices go silent before they complete the word *alleluia*; the vibraphone pattern stops on the pivotal E-flat; the SATB chorus finishes its alleluia, although the bass part ends on the fifth of the D-flat major chord rather than the root; and Larsen instructs the

Example 7.3. *O Magnum Mysterium*, mm. 91–96

recorded chime to "let ring out, continue after choir stops."[45] With the sound of chimes continuing beyond human audition, Larsen reminds listeners of humanity's transience within eternity. Although not the notion of sound projection that Varèse had in mind, it is Larsen's take on the idea and one specific to the message she wants to communicate with this multimedia, technology-infused, mystical work.

In 2014 the Fry Street Quartet commissioned Larsen to write music that Rebecca McFaul, violinist with the group, hoped would "connect, empower, and inspire action." The piece, titled *Emergence: String Quartet No. 4*, is the

Example 7.3. *(continued)*

second piece in the Quartet's Crossroads Project, an open-ended series of multimedia works "conceived as an education project" that, according to the group's Web site, explores "nature, humanity, and the paths that lie before us."[46] More specifically the Crossroads Project seeks to educate listeners by raising environmental consciousness through the combination of music, visuals, and spoken text: "It's performance art, and performance science."[47] As Bradley Ottesen, violist with the group observed, they provide "a living, breathing metaphor [for] the complexity of natural systems right there on stage."[48] The quartet—which includes McFaul, Ottesen, cellist Anne Francis Bayless, and violinist Robert Waters—joined with Robert Davies, a physicist, to bring awareness of the current environmental crisis into the minds and hearts of audiences.

The first collaborative piece in the project involved the Fry Street Quartet and Davies, all faculty at Utah State University, with composer Laura Kaminsky and artist Rebecca Allan of New York City among others. The goal was to have Kaminsky's music and Allan's abstract paintings, pictures of Lyman Whitaker's wind sculptures, and environmental photographs by Garth Lanz and Lu Guang reinforce one another and function as parts of a single entity: to become an ecosystem of their own. The group aspired to combine art and science "in service of genuine understanding."[49]

Excited and encouraged by the reception of that first effort, the quartet commissioned Larsen to work with them on a new iteration of the project. McFaul had become acquainted with Larsen's music in the mid-1980s, when she was attending a one-day-a-week music school in Minneapolis and Larsen was composer-in-residence at the Minnesota Symphony Orchestra. But she and the other members of the Fry Street Quartet first met Larsen in person in 2011, when the composer spoke at a Utah State University convocation. As McFaul remembers, "She came, and she just lit up everybody she was in contact with."[50] The group was inspired by her energy and imagination. McFaul, in particular, was taken by the way Larsen spoke of the creative process: "It was brilliant, and mesmerizing. . . . Who wouldn't want to be in the wake of her energy and imagination? I told her, 'I've been listening to your work for thirty years.'"[51] Upon getting to know the quartet, Larsen expressed interest in working with them. Collaborating with the environmentally sensitive activist ensemble appealed to the composer, whose concerns for the natural world had already inspired dozens of her works.

McFaul's passion for raising environmental awareness runs deep, as became evident when she explained the original impetus for the project: her feeling that "we're betraying the students we're working with by not talking about this issue." She continued, "This issue is something they're saddled with. . . . I just felt that this is unconscionable. And I was also about to turn forty, and I was waiting for the adults in the room to do something; and I thought, Oh my gosh, that's me."[52] McFaul and her physicist husband, Robert Davies, appreciate that it is one thing to understand rationally what is happening to the environment, but it is another thing to feel it. Their hope is that combining appeals to the head and the heart will strengthen their own and others' belief in what is the right thing to do, and ultimately that that belief will inspire action.[53] McFaul's and Davies's environmental consciousness is shared by others in the quartet, each of whom is active in individual and community efforts aimed at stimulating positive behavioral changes; all members of the quartet acknowledge their complicity in the problem. But McFaul wonders aloud: "How do we live in a way that's consistent with what we know?"[54] This kind of reflection, awareness, and willingness to take on big questions speaks directly to Larsen, who, despite her seeming spontaneity, also thoughtfully considers her actions and choices and their resonance. She knows that music rooted in principles can move people to think and act. Artistic projects become politically charged because they reflect what matters.

The quartet collectively described the Kaminsky *Rising Tide* collaboration as beautiful and haunting but leaving audience members overwhelmed with the question "what do we do?"[55] McFaul and the quartet recognized that despair is not productive; they needed to provide listeners with hope that they could imagine a sustainable future that was inspired and exciting; and that's why they wanted to work with Larsen. The "sense of possibility" the quartet witnessed in her convocation speech convinced them that she was the person to help them suggest a way. As McFaul admitted, "We want her energy and her voice to speak to this issue, . . . we need her." The violinist felt fortunate to have Larsen "aboard."[56]

The multifaceted nature of the Crossroads Project is not new in the arts world. In the Christian Era liturgical dramas, court ballets, and the earliest operas all included both aural and visual components, as well as dance and spoken text. As Larsen has argued, the mass was a multisensory theatrical experience. The concept of *Gesamtkunstwerk* as adopted by Richard Wagner and Sergei Diaghilev's broadly collaborative Ballets Russes productions are famous nineteenth- and twentieth-century manifestations of the urge to combine the arts.[57] Although Wagner might have believed his music-dramas included some kind of instructive component—perhaps using German folk tales to express what he believed were universal truths—neither he nor Diaghilev privileged the pedagogical. Davies and the FSQ's Crossroads Project, on the other hand, are clear in their purpose to educate audiences; Davies identifies himself as a physicist-educator, and all four members of the quartet are artist-teachers at Utah State University. Although Larsen does not compose any of her music *solely* to teach, argue a point, or make a statement, she admits that she has "been political about ecology through [her] music." Regarding a 1992 piece the composer explains: "In the *Marimba Concerto: After Hampton*, in the orchestral part I embedded Morse Code for 'save the rain forest' in the percussion part." About *Missa Gaia*, which she composed in the same year, she says: "It *is* ecology, and meant to be about ecology."[58]

Bringing together a composer, four musicians, one physicist, photographers, visual artists, and audio and visual engineers, all of whom have access to the latest technology and high hopes for exciting an action-inducing response among audiences, is as daunting a prospect as it is an ambitious one. It also takes on a life of its own and moves in unexpected directions.

Larsen met and talked with the musicians and Davies multiple times to understand individual and mutual roles and goals in the endeavor before ever setting pen to paper. Since the visual and texted parts of the project would not be finished prior to the music's scheduled premiere at Utah State in February 2015, and Larsen understood too well the possibility that promised technology may not materialize, she composed a work for the quartet that was free standing and complete by itself. Like *O Magnum Mysterium* and *The Magdalene*, Larsen's music for *Emergence* embodied the spirit and aspirations of the entire multimedia project as she heard them.

Guided by her grasp of the quartet's aesthetic and didactic aspirations, and not wanting her music to be vulnerable to later additions of still-unknown imagery or narration, Larsen composed a set of short movements that provided moments to stop, start, and synchronize with yet-to-be-developed visual and texted components. She also composed a musical statement that was full and complete on its own. Thinking beyond a single expressive mode and working with imposed restrictions excited her imagination equally. The resulting virtuosic piece is just under twenty-five minutes long and divides into five discrete but related suite-like sections. The music makes sense free of any programmatic associations that might be applied. Knowing the general thrust of the project and its desire to deliver a more hopeful message about nature and the environment, Larsen structured sounds that evoke fully functioning, healthy organic processes; if they have not yet become a reality on planet earth, they are her goal in the music. The tight motivic relationships that weave together individual movements and the larger set musicalize Larsen's natural ecological thinking. Like *Missa Gaia*, Larsen's *Emergence* is about ecology, human, musical, and environmental.

Considering the purely musical aspect of *Emergence* provides insights into how ideas spark and excite Larsen's imagination. McFaul explains that from the group's first conversations with Larsen they wanted to "hang the narrative on the water cycle."[59] She recalls the composer saying, "I am bound to water." Here was something they all understood. Together they discussed aural and visual characterizations of water as the original life-support system, "but then it shifted towards transformation, flexibility, adjusting, cycling through." The temporality of music had the potential to more powerfully reinforce these themes than a study of a system. (It is also easy to imagine Larsen chafing at the idea of composing about any system.) McFaul spoke of the quartet's desire to "create a performance experience that inspires an internal transformation," to lead listeners to "internalize the reality that we have the possibility to transform how we orient ourselves." Music's motion served the idea of transformation.

With the first few *pianissimo* notes, Larsen transports listeners into a wide-awake sound world; she creates a pulsating place. A soft, cycling motive comprised of delicate, discretely bowed sixteenth notes courses through the first minute of the piece. All members of the quartet take their turn with the idea; there is a quiet but incessant energy to the music. The motoric quality evokes myriad images: a distant machine, the patter of rain, people busily going to work, a clock marking time. All of them suggest motion and change. The music invites a range of visual images and texts.

Occasional harmonics played by each of the instrumentalists feather the soundscape; the entire world is abuzz and then unexpectedly pauses to tune itself before heading in a new direction. In measures 18 to 21, Larsen stops all forward momentum for a few seconds while she has each performer play his or her own pair of open fifths, first *forte* and then *piano*. The droning, tuning gesture recalls traditional Western musical evocations of pastoral scenes, but it has additional meaning inside the context of the imagined project. The moment to retune becomes a metaphor for people taking stock of their lives and developing a more harmonious relationship with their environment. The retuning drone will return multiple times throughout the work (7.4).

A minute into the three-and-a-half-minute movement a second section of nonstop sixteenths commences, but this new pattern is characterized by sliding, skipping, and bouncing sounds; they contrast with the more detached and regularized pattern of the first motive. Larsen turns attention to a different set of voices in the soundscape. The texture of the piece thickens and grows more varied as fugal and fiddle evocations coexist with dots and dashes of pitches. Larsen's complex soundscape captures the complex environment and problem. A third section starts just after the two-minute mark, recalling the first rhythmic motive. As the movement heads toward its end, players are instructed to "ricochet" off their final notes. Sounds reflect and refract in an atmosphere of hidden forces. The entire movement is a triumph of rhythmic counterpoint that gently but relentlessly swirls itself to exhaustion in a final soft crunching cluster of sound that slows and fades to its end. The dissonant close portends not only the final sounds of the larger piece but also the unresolved problems besieging the planet.

Example 7.4. *Emergence*, movement 1, mm. 14–21

Although Larsen maintains a predominantly soft dynamic palette throughout the second movement, it has an urgency (and dissonance) that is largely absent in the more static, if energetic, sound world of the first movement (ex. 7.5). In this regard, Larsen acknowledges the most basic rules governing large-scale musical structures, where contrast between consecutive movements is assumed. Over the four minutes of this movement, Larsen gradually increases the tension, which will come to a head in the third and fourth movements; once again they change moods.

Fiercely attacked, *fortissimo*, sustained notes pile up at the beginning of the third movement; although the intense music might reflect nothing more than the exigencies of a multipart musical form that has reached some climactic moment, in this particular context it augurs and embodies the

Example 7.5. *Emergence*, movement 2, mm. 22–35

Example 7.5. *(continued)*

climatological crisis that Larsen seeks to dramatize. It abounds in instructions to the players that reveal the composer's own dramatic intentions for the work. Within seconds of the opening, she invites pandemonium with her instruction to players that they should use a "free bow" and become "progressively chaotic" over a period of seven seconds, and another seven seconds, then ten seconds, and finally fifteen seconds, which she specifies with precise timings. This is discomforting music and designed to be so. Tuning gestures halfway through the movement allow players to regroup once again, and Larsen instructs performers to play them "warmly."[60] But the third movement is not about humanity living in harmony with the planet; it is not ultimately optimistic. In the final measures Larsen asks her players to make "keening," "mourning," "plaintive" sounds (ex. 7.6). It is easy to hear Krzysztof Penderecki's *Threnody to the Victims of Hiroshima* hovering in the ether over the entire movement.[61] Comparing that instant, man-made firestorm with the more gradual one we are now experiencing

Example 7.6. *Emergence*, movement 3, mm. 51–66

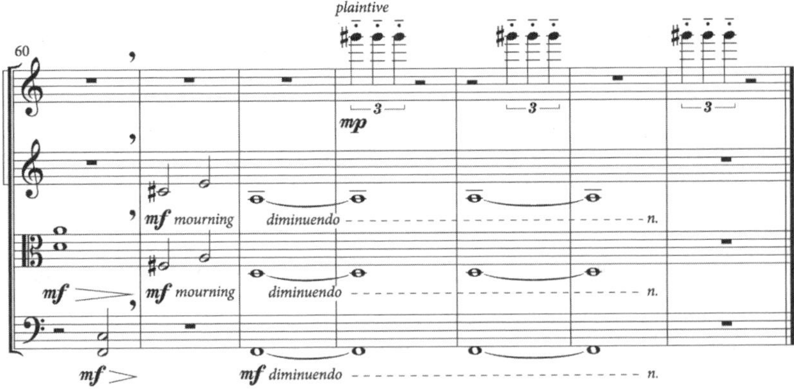

Example 7.6. *(continued)*

with global warming would be hard to ignore for an audience familiar with the 1960 work.

The first violin opens the fourth movement with a relatively tranquil iteration of the folk tune "The Water Is Wide." (In retrospect listeners can understand the pattering sounds of the first movement as Larsen's musicalization of rain.) For a few moments, it appears that the composer is going to clear space for a hopeful message. But even though viola, cello, and then second violin comment "warmly" on the folk tune, each added instrument introduces new levels of dissonance.[62] By the time the tune is passed off to the cello, the air is filled with tense clusters of major and minor seconds. When the first violin introduces a fragment of another tune, "Old Man River," and the second violin takes her turn at "The Water Is Wide," the two melodies converge in a tense, "moiling" counterpoint (ex. 7.7).[63] Even a return of the initial tune in the first violin, this time doubled at the octave, fails to impose order on the acoustic environment. What had started out comforting in its familiarity becomes overwhelmed in the churning violence of Larsen's music. Listeners wait for sounds of hope, but hope is not easily mustered.

Whether understood as part of a didactic environmental project or as an autonomous, abstract piece of instrumental music, by the end of the fourth movement Larsen's quartet requires signs of impending closure and resolution or admission that none is forthcoming. Beyond a certain point, ceaseless musical tension loses rather than gains in power; its strength is neutralized and turns on itself. Given the emotionally charged nature of discussions circling around the environmental crisis, it would be easy to toy with an audience, to lead it to the brink of despair and then, at the last moment, swoop in with

Example 7.7. *Emergence.* By Libby Larsen, Mvt. IV, mm. 25-38

Example 7.7. *Emergence*, movement 4, mm. 25–38

Example 7.7. *(continued)*

the needed harmonic exit. But despite her optimism and good humor, Larsen is not one to toy with her music or with people when the stakes are so high. There will be nothing neat or tidy about the way out. Knowing the limits of tension and release within this art of time, Larsen delays the denouement of *Emergence*, not to manipulate her audience but in order to write music that is honest with itself and with the concept. A clear-eyed appraisal of the crisis reveals that there are no easy answers, and Larsen provides none in her piece. Hopeful as she is by temperament, she is also disarmingly honest. Her final movement will suggest hopefulness but not certainty; it will point toward solutions but offer no guarantees. Danger and conflict are audible companions of hope. What becomes clear is that solving the crisis will require all stakeholders to come together.

Larsen returns to the simpler and more transparent sounds and texture of the first movement. The overwhelming, chaotic strife that characterizes earlier sections is gone. Echoes of "The Water Is Wide" linger in the very "slowly, unfolding" fifth movement. There is a sense of caution about the whole movement. Instruments quietly and gently hand off phrases and build upon what the other says; they take turns to speak. In contrast to the thick textures, multiple meters, and dense rhythmic counterpoint that characterizes previous movements, here the voices work together within a single, if elastic, metrical scheme. They bend with one another. Although the dynamic level never rises above *mezzo piano*, there is a weighty seriousness to this movement. Larsen insists that the dire environmental situation is best approached with quiet resolve, perhaps with listening more than talking. As the piece approaches its end, the instruments exhale a series of deep and dissonant breaths; the quartet ultimately comes together on a final, soft, unison D. This is not an expression of tonal supremacy or triumph over adversity, however, and it does not announce success. The close to Larsen's quartet confirms a cautious, common determination not to give up; and that is as hopeful as she is willing to be at this point.

The final movement is awash in Larsen's favored major and minor sevenths and seconds, neither of which provides traditional resolution, although their prevalence in jazz and blues chords has lessened their suggestion of tension over the years. At times they sound almost sweet. Optimism and hope, as much as they are present, are located beyond the harmonic realm and most audible in this movement's louder dynamic level, rising arpeggiated and scalar figures, and a determined homorhythmic texture that alternately suggests a hymn and a march. The unison D that finishes the piece may be as close as Larsen gets to suggesting a positive resolution (ex. 7.8).

It is easy to imagine accompanying visuals that capture activists coming together to protest or to plant trees, or to join in marches to build support for policy change. And such an event took place September 21, 2014, when over four hundred thousand concerned citizens came together in New York City to join the "People's Climate March."[64] Although Larsen's intimate music for a string quartet could not provide the soundtrack for such a massive outdoor event, it captures the spirit of determination heard in the speeches and participants' remarks at the march. With *Emergence* she adds her voice to a larger multimedia effort. That she was pleased with the September 2015 premiere of the project, which she only got to see and hear after the fact, has deepened her satisfaction with the role her music can play in such joint ventures.

Like religion, nature, the academy, and gender, technology is a steady presence in Larsen's compositional work. From the earliest graduate school efforts to

Example 7.8. *Emergence*, movement 5, mm. 35–41

her most recent pieces, Larsen's musical thinking responds to the opportunities technology presents. Educating herself to understand as much as she can of its minute operations, she often employs technology to conjure the transcendent, fantastical, or that which is just beyond the human grasp. Larsen regularly pushes against the limits of the possible, as her many not-yet-fully-realized pieces attest. In some cases, technology needs to catch up with her.

Larsen's engagement with technology was recognized in 2003, when she was named the Harissios Papamarkou Chair in Education and Technology in the John W. Kluge Center at the Library of Congress. In residence at the same time as John Hope Franklin, the Presidential Medal of Freedom–winning historian, Larsen devoted her time in Washington to developing an original theory that made use of the library's unique collections and resources.

During her five-month tenure, Larsen explored her theory that "every time our culture changes its major mode of transportation—of goods, ideas, and people—we change our mode of thinking about what the concert hall is."[65] The composer explains: "And so I traced modes of transportation from the late 1700s to 1992, and I was actually able to support my theory." As she connected technology and music performance—how we transport music and audiences—Franklin "worked on human technology, from slavery to robots." As he drafted "a book about human technology and its use in the development of the country," she tracked "the development of the telegraph and the radio, and discovered where we got our canon." The two became friends encouraging each other's work.

By 2003, Larsen was comfortable in her role as a recognized and lauded composer, but the Library of Congress provided a different kind of validation, one that she had not sought or realized that she missed until then. She explains, "What was important to me about the experience, at least at that point in time, was that I felt validated as much for my brain as I did for my compositional skills. I was taken on by the Library of Congress to represent them, and I did." Larsen traveled around the country giving a speech she titled "The Concert Hall That Fell Asleep and Woke Up a Car Radio." She recalled with a laugh, "I gave it everywhere except the symphony orchestra leagues, the ones in the most trouble." She enjoyed the opportunity to think and speak about something theoretical and to exercise that part of her brain and being. Although Larsen never completed the book she envisioned coming out of her residency, technology continues to be a force in her musical imaginary. Because Larsen is unable and unwilling to separate from all the influences acting upon her, technology broadens her reach and stimulates the entirety of her thoroughly integrated sensorium.

8 Larsen and the Collaborators, Larsen and the Critics

IN MARCH 1979, AT THE RIPE AGE of twenty-eight and just a year after receiving her doctorate, Libby Larsen was the subject of a thirty-minute film, part of the series *Encounters with Minnesota Artists* broadcast on KTCA, the Twin Cities public television station.[1] It had to have been a heady experience for the young composer. In footage that captures Larsen composing, conversing, and attending rehearsals, viewers see her reflect on the act of "arranging sound in time." They learn of her concerns regarding the "segmented" woman composer and hear her thoughts about living a balanced life.[2] The collaborative spirit that had propelled student opera projects and the creation of the Minnesota Composers Forum is on full display. More than thirty-five years later, that same spirit remains integral to Larsen and to her lifelong creative project, and this is affirmed by those who have worked closely with her over the decades.

As a group Larsen's collaborators have applauded her eclecticism, her productivity, her music's appeal, her desire and ability to write for a range of performers and situations, her choice to live and work outside consecrated cultural centers, her independence from any single aesthetic ideology, her rejection of the myth of the isolated, genius composer separated from society, and her willingness to do the grunt work promoting American music culture. All agree on Larsen's gifts for rhythm and setting American English in natural-sounding lyrical lines.

They also regularly cite her energy, determination, fearlessness, and creativity, essential qualities for a successful, freelance art-music composer. In a September 2014 interview, John Duffy, composer, and founder and director of Meet the Composer, went beyond the usual string of descriptors and singled out Larsen's curiosity and resoluteness as defining qualities. Having chosen to tack a course different from those charted for women born in the mid-twentieth century, Larsen often had to "man the tuits" on her own, and resoluteness served her well.[3]

Duffy and Larsen had much in common, not least a passion for fostering American music. In 1974, a year after Larsen and Paulus created the Minnesota Composers Forum, Duffy founded Meet the Composer, a joint project of the New York State Council on the Arts and the American Music Center. From the start, it operated without any academic affiliation and provided grants, commissions, and residencies and underwrote educational programs that brought composers and audiences together. At its core was Duffy's belief in music's role in society and the need for the composer to be in the middle of it. In the early 1980s Meet the Composer chose the Minnesota Orchestra to be a part of its orchestra residency program; and it was Duffy's program that funded Neville Marriner's selection of Larsen and Paulus as Composers-in-Residence starting in 1983. Duffy and Larsen met at the beginning of her residency. He explains: "Her music delighted me; I found her to be a unique person. . . . She goes deeper than most composers." Observing her high energy, he "cautioned her not to cover so many bases; not to wear herself out."[4] Duffy and Larsen took a liking to each other immediately but soon discovered they had crossed paths years earlier, unknowingly. Duffy had composed the score for a 1960s production of *A Midsummer Night's Dream* at the Guthrie Theater in Minneapolis, and a teenaged Larsen had been there. As Duffy characterizes that occurrence: "We had a mystical, mysterious experience quite early on, so our roots, in a certain sense, go way back to the sixties."[5] When they met (again) in the 1980s, they started as if they'd been old friends.

Over the years Duffy and Larsen collaborated closely through her participation on the board of Meet the Composers and via the John Duffy Composers Institute, which partners with the Virginia Arts Festival. In 2014 Duffy announced that he had handed over the administration of the institute to Larsen, whom he describes as "a person I trust, have faith in, honor, and love."[6] In 2012 Larsen and Duffy, along with fellow institute faculty members Tania Leon, Fred Ho, Michael Colgrass, and Frank J. Oteri, worked with seven young fellows—all aspiring opera composers—numerous singers, and musicians of the Virginia Symphony Orchestra to share their insights, expertise, and passion for writing opera; they mounted concert versions of the fellows' works in progress.[7]

Formal and informal discussions among the faculty and participants where ideas and mentoring float freely in all directions are prized aspects of the institute. Matt Frey, one of the fellows, spoke of getting to ask fundamental questions including, "Why we do opera? Why is it important to the world?"[8] Jake Runestad, who had studied privately with Larsen years earlier, observes that the faculty members "know what questions to ask." Leanna Kirchoff, the only woman among the seven fellows, appreciates the opportunity "to bounce ideas off one another." Ethan Greene admits that prior to coming he had written a children's opera and some songs but in attending the institute "pretty much [he] learned how to write for the voice," noting, "I don't think I understood the voice, understood breath, understood vowels, the tessitura . . . I really had no idea."[9]

Among the conversations that took place was a private one between Duffy and Larsen; it was provoked by his 1998 opera *Black Water*, which was based on the 1992 Joyce Carol Oates novel of the same name. The story is a thinly veiled telling of the Edward Kennedy–Mary Jo Kopechne tragedy, when in the summer of 1969 the senator drove his car, in which Kopechne was his sole passenger, off a bridge at Chappaquiddick Island after a late-night party. The senator managed to extricate himself from the car and swim to safety, get to a hotel, change clothes, sleep a few hours, and greet people the next morning to inquire about the regatta results of the previous day before reporting the accident to police nine hours after it occurred. Despite an official statement that Kopechne drowned, according to testimony by John Farrar, the professional diver who recovered her body, she likely suffocated over a period of hours in the submerged, overturned car.[10]

Duffy felt these events challenged him "to find a musical means to express the horror that can result when cowardice overpowers conscience."[11] A conversation with Larsen about the opera illuminated an aspect of her character that Duffy believed was not always evident to others. Larsen had confided to him that she "found it very difficult to sit [through the opera] while this violence was going on, especially in this case toward a woman." Duffy continued: "She asked 'is it possible to do a music drama or theatrical works that do not show violence? Can we find a metaphor for the violence, or somehow not show it?'" He concluded, "We talked about that a lot, although we didn't come to any conclusion."[12]

According to Duffy, Larsen "feels that opera is a social art; the composer has the power in her to make a statement, to right a wrong, to make people aware of social justice and so forth. It would seem to me that naturally in trying to reach an audience and performers that she would be sensitive to this point."[13] Larsen's belief in music as "a social art" capable of inciting action is fundamental to her thinking as a composer, and Duffy shared that belief. It may, however, be beyond the core goals of many composers, and perhaps especially those whose security protects them from considering the social ramifications or usefulness of what they do. Larsen's compulsion to write music that connects with, reflects upon, and speaks to society is driven neither by pragmatism nor careerism; it is not, at its source, born of her need to make a living. Larsen is compelled to compose music that speaks to society because it is what she believes music does. Finding ways to engage is fundamental to that belief.

Duffy's opera raised additional issues for Larsen. It is a commonplace that female characters regularly endure physical violence and meet untimely deaths in operas; they are raped and strangled, stabbed and bagged, shipped out to sea to die, and kicked to death. These fictional but sometimes also distant historical figures appear removed from contemporary life; the likeliness of a modern woman meeting a similar fate seems remote. The death of Kopechne, however, a twenty-eight-year-old Catholic-school graduate who was a secretary, teacher, civil rights activist, and sports fan, was no fiction. In her college yearbook picture, she looked like tens of thousands of young white women at the time. The story was splashed all over the news and touched millions of people who watched accounts of the "incident" unfold on television; and it touched Larsen. Duffy's 1998 opera *Black Water* would have recalled news headlines from Larsen's late teens and personalized violence against women for her. That the honorable senator in the novel and in real life escaped both the automobile and any punishment for Kopechne's death tested credulity and stunned all but the most cynical. Powerful men, whether on stage or in Senate chambers, disposed of women in violent, horrific ways either by accident or design, and then they carried on. The realities of the nation's gendered society were reenacted on operatic stages with such regularity that audiences accepted their storylines as inevitable. Larsen wondered if there wasn't another way. Her sensitivity to the issue touched John Duffy deeply.

In considering her creative process, Duffy observed that when Larsen composes operas, she buries herself in research; she has a "monumental curiosity." She learns all she can about her subjects and their situations. "She just grabs hold of something and won't let it go until she gets it to the ground and fully comprehends it." She "does an extraordinary job getting the right melodic figure to show character. She has such commanding craft; she is so thorough." This practice makes the subjects more real for her. Duffy explained that as part of her research for *Every Man Jack*, her opera about the alcoholic author Jack London, Larsen undertook several nights of drinking "so that she knew what it was to be an alcoholic. This is how she finds these pieces of character traits." Duffy, of course, appreciated that Larsen's strategic, fully controlled exercise in excessive drinking could not replicate the experience of an alcoholic, but he cited this example as illustrative of the lengths to which Larsen will go to understand her subjects.[14]

Thinking of the results of her process, Duffy explained: "If one can accept in each other that you can be playful, and you can be serious, that you can play jokes, and at the same time that you can be honorable and tender, then there's a whole gamut of emotion that is open to us. I think that Libby has that almost *regal* gift, to be able to express that in her music and in her character."[15] When asked to describe her in a few adjectives, Duffy reeled off "playful, fearless, honorable, skillful, wild sense of the absurd, tender, gentle, sweet spirit, and relentless."[16] Obviously, John Duffy was not impartial where Libby Larsen was concerned, but his reading of her, rooted as it is in decades of professional and personal interactions, makes his insights especially valuable.

Dozens of Larsen's collaborators arrive at similar conclusions regarding her character, compulsions, and composerly gifts. To repeat their assessments risks tipping this study toward hagiography. But even if collaborators are not unbiased sources of information, they are credible witnesses, especially when they have known the subject in different capacities and at various times through decades of her career.

Larsen has crossed paths with many conductors as she takes commissions, collaborates, composes, records, and attends performances in the United States and abroad. In the early 1980s, she worked with Pinchas Zukerman and William McGlaughlin through the Saint Paul Chamber Orchestra, and over the years she developed close relations with Sir Neville Marriner, JoAnn Falletta, and Marin Alsop. Larsen's association with Falletta began in 1986–87 with the conductor's tenure as music director of the Bay Area Women's Philharmonic, the professional San Francisco–based orchestra that thrived from 1981 to 2004. At Falletta's request, Larsen arranged *Four on the Floor* for solo piano and double string orchestra. It was premiered by the Virginia Symphony Orchestra in 2014. She met Marin Alsop a few years before the Monarch Brass in Oklahoma City commissioned *Brass Flight* for its 1996 summer season. The relationship continues to the present: in 2015 Larsen finished her orchestral work *Earth (Holst Trope)* for Alsop and the Baltimore Symphony Orchestra. In reflecting upon her many conductor associates, she named Marriner, Alsop, Falletta, Zukerman, McGlaughlin, and Joel Revzen as responsible for her large-scale orchestral works "and hence, a national reputation, and the critics, like Lipman, responding to them."[17]

Two conductors whose relationships with Larsen go back decades include Philip Brunelle, director of VocalEssence based in Minneapolis, and Joel Revzen, conductor of numerous symphony orchestras and opera companies and for the past ten years a member of the conducting staff at the Metropolitan Opera. Although in their interactions with Larsen both regularly focus on the music and the technical challenges of bringing it to life, each has also enjoyed various escapades with the composer involving less artistic endeavors. These encounters flesh out a composer whose prodigious output suggests she does little more than work.

Brunelle remembered a trip he and the composer took to Cairo while working on Larsen's choral symphony, *Coming Forth into Day (Symphony No. 2)*.[18] He had hoped that Madame Jehan Sadat, an accomplished writer and the widow of Egyptian president Anwar el-Sadat, would consent to write the text for the piece; ultimately she declined. He recalled an outing that he and Larsen took to the local bazaar, where one of Madame Sadat's friends acted as their guide; and then Brunelle spoke of camels. He unearthed a photograph showing Larsen and him smiling broadly astride camels. But that was before the camel driver threatened to cut the animals loose if the two didn't turn over all their money; they acquiesced. A cropped version of the photo, showing Brunelle alone atop a camel, became a billboard advertising the symphony around the Twin Cities.[19]

Figure 8.1. Libby Larsen and Philip Brunelle atop camels in Cairo. Reproduced with the kind permission of Philip Brunelle.

Revzen recalled skiing with Larsen, admitting, "Libby, of course, skied me off the mountain doing acrobatics and aerobatics on skies."[20] Serious and playful experiences get mixed together and are all part of Larsen's essence, and according to both conductors, they find their way into her music. Larsen has no reservations about embracing new adventures or having fun.

Revzen has conducted and recorded a number of Larsen's works, but perhaps among the most celebrated of their projects to date is *The Art of Arleen Auger*, for which composer and conductor received Grammy awards in 1993 for the Best Classical Vocal Recording. Revzen is grateful for having introduced Larsen and the soprano Auger in 1988, especially when it turned out that Auger was terminally ill and wouldn't have many more opportunities to sing and record. When Auger confided to Revzen that she'd "love to commission an American composer to set *Sonnets from the Portuguese*," he encouraged Auger to talk with Larsen. Almost immediately, the two women began reading through and selecting poems from Elizabeth Barrett Browning's set of forty-four love sonnets.[21] Larsen's recollections of their initial conversations suggest the many ways in which the soprano and the composer resonated:

> Arleen spoke to me about her love of the art song repertoire. She talked about love, and life, and her desire that I compose a work which spoke about the finding of mature love. She wished to create with me a cycle of songs which were in contrast to the young girl's feeling for the promise of love in *Frauenliebe und Leben*. Arleen told me that the poetry she most loved was Elizabeth Barrett Browning's *Sonnets from the Portuguese*. She admired the fact that within the stylized and romantic language, lived a creative woman grappling with issues [that] seem still to engulf modern women. What part of her voice must she sacrifice to the lover and the world? Will the sacrifice be reciprocated? Can her essence survive? Browning at times soars to heights of daring—demanding the world take her as she is—at other moments her self-confidence wavers. Ultimately she realizes—as we must—that love and death demand constant faith in the leaps life requires.[22]

The two women sprawled out on Larsen's living-room floor in Minneapolis with copies of Browning's poems scattered around them. As the two made difficult decisions regarding what to include and how to handle challenging passages, the composer's daughter, Wynne, and Auger's personal manager, Celia Novo, provided food and occasional ideas. Creating music at home with family close by—Larsen looked back on that day and concluded: "For me that afternoon was the essence of why a composer lives to work."[23]

Auger and Revzen previewed the set at the 1989 Aspen Music Festival with the Festival Orchestra. In 1991 they did another preview, this time closer to Larsen's home with the Saint Paul Chamber Orchestra. They recorded this performance with the intention of using it to secure an official premiere performance, but the Saint Paul recording became the master from which the Koch disc was made. Auger became too ill to take on the official premiere and died of a malignant brain tumor in June 1993, the same year the disc won its Grammy. It stands as a memento of a brilliant and heartfelt collaboration between a composer, a performer, and a conductor, all of whom loved their project.

Revzen and Larsen made two other discs with Koch: in 1997 the London Symphony Orchestra recorded her first and third symphonies, *Symphony: Water Music* (1984) and *Lyric* (1995), as well as *Overture: Parachute Dancing* (1983), and *Ring of Fire* (1995). In 2000 Koch released a mixed orchestral and vocal disc with Revzen conducting the Scottish Chamber Orchestra. It included her fourth symphony, *String Symphony* (1998), and two sets of songs sung by Benita Valente: *Songs of Light and Love* (1998) and *Songs from Letters* (1999). Having learned the intricacies of multiple works by Larsen, Revzen is well qualified to comment upon the qualities of her compositional achievements.

Revzen's favorite Larsen piece is her *String Symphony*, a work that was commissioned by the Minnesota Orchestra as part of a series designed to celebrate its centennial in 2002–3. In notes that accompany the CD, Larsen recalled the power of hearing *Scheherazade* when she was a young girl and "closing [her] eyes and trying to breathe in the music." As a mature composer she wondered what the melody of American English sounded like, and whether it could "be best expressed through orchestral strings."[24] The *String Symphony* is her answer. Revzen believes "it has everything. It's jazzy, it's electric in places, it's *very* difficult . . . very challenging rhythmically, and texturally." Revzen was committed to getting the textures and the balances "right." He wanted to "capture all of her rhythmic energy." On reflecting upon Larsen's musical gifts, he identified the oft-cited "remarkable sensitivity to language" and an acute sense for orchestration as among her greatest strengths: "She orchestrates absolutely astoundingly. She knows exactly how to place [instruments] and how to balance them; and how to use instrumental color to illustrate the essences of her pieces." Revzen confesses that he used to think Larsen had a particular gift for wind and brass instruments, perhaps to the exclusion of other instrument families, "but then [he] got involved with the *String Symphony*, which just put that on its ear. The way she was able to write for the complexity and yet clarity of these string instruments, with *enormous* rhythmic ingenuity, was just plain brilliant, just genius." He concludes: "Libby's creative genius just goes from soup to nuts. I think that containing it sometimes is the challenge. Paring it down to its essence is sometimes hard."[25]

As with other collaborators, Revzen is intimately familiar with Larsen's energy: The consensus is that she absorbs and wrings out everything in sight. As Revzen puts it: "Her antennae are always completely up. I don't think they ever come down. . . . You feel like you're in a tsunami of thought."[26] But it is this energy, always on the brink of consuming one, that—if it doesn't exhaust people—excites them to work harder, better, and more boldly in whatever project they undertake with the composer; she generates and attracts energy. She is an exuberant.[27]

Larsen's work with choral conductor Philip Brunelle offers different insights into the reach of her composerly life. In the fall of 1969, the start of Larsen's second year at the University of Minnesota, Brunelle was appointed music director at Plymouth Congregational Church in Minneapolis, where he established the Plymouth Music Series. From his position there the Plymouth Music Series became VocalEssence, which includes the thirty-two-voice professional Ensemble Singers and the one-hundred-voice volunteer chorus; over the years it has won the ASCAP–Chorus America Award for Adventurous Programming five times.

Prior to meeting Larsen, the conductor had heard of her through Minnesota Composers Forum activities. They started working together in 1978 on an area-wide project where Brunelle, Larsen, and the MCF joined forces to involve area churches with the annual convention of the American Guild of Organists, which would be held in Minneapolis in 1980. Brunelle imagined individual churches commissioning regional composers to write anthems suited especially to the size and ability of their choirs. Using contacts she'd developed and administrative skills that she'd honed at the MCF, Larsen matched composers and churches; Brunelle arranged for an anthology to be published. Ultimately twenty-nine churches participated, and "on the Sunday of the convention every church sang its anthem."[28] According to Brunelle, he and Larsen "just naturally got along together," and he immediately assessed that "she was one of the vibrant spirits around [there]."[29] In 1982 the Plymouth Congregational Church commissioned its own anthem from her, *Double Joy*, a work for divisi choir, handbells, and organ, and Larsen dedicated it to Brunelle.

But their collaborations didn't stop at short pieces. Brunelle and VocalEssence commissioned *In a Winter Garden*, and he encouraged her as she composed her second symphony *Coming Forth into Day*. When Brunelle wanted to commission a work from Larsen to celebrate her fiftieth birthday, she agreed and suggested Jenny Lind as the subject. She had become interested in the Lind/Barnum relationship years earlier while composing *Seven Ghosts* for VocalEssence's 1995 season.[30] With Brunelle's encouragement, Larsen wrote a full-length opera, *Barnum's Bird*, based upon the 1850–51 tour of Jenny Lind that had been arranged by master showman P. T. Barnum. The opera allowed Larsen to explore contemporary attitudes that equated (or confused) art and commodity and entertainment. Larsen's "Composer's Notes" to the score read as a prompt for a philosophical meditation on the subject: "the story of art: in service of humanity on the one hand, and in service of commerce on the other."[31] The opera was co-commissioned by the Odyssey Commissioning Program of the Plymouth [Church] Music Series and the Library of Congress in 2001 to honor the library's bicentennial.[32]

Both Brunelle and Revzen described Larsen using terms seldom applied to women. Joel Revzen spoke of her "brilliance" and "genius" for string writing. When it comes to composing, Brunelle sees her "as a real visionary, and there are just not a lot of them out there."[33] But neither Revzen nor Brunelle shied away from using these terms to describe Larsen; it appears they don't think of her in typically gendered terms. And this is true even as Brunelle spoke of Larsen's "collaborative spirit" and the fact that "she cares deeply, deeply about people" as essential to what makes her tick.[34] Caring and collaboration are qualities historically gendered female. Has Larsen challenged gendered expectations so successfully that she has overcome long-ensconced linguistic conventions? She and many composing women would be ecstatic to think that was the case.

Brunelle attributes Larsen's collaborative successes to her striking a unique balance between knowing what she wants and listening to others: "She's flexible and willing to listen to comments." He elaborated that it's unfortunate when "people who would do a piece of hers [don't] know that they could have a dialogue [with her]."[35] Over the course of our interview, Brunelle kept returning to Larsen's "real human spirit," which he remarked informs everything she does. He contended, "She and Stephen would never have started the Composers Forum if they hadn't cared about how composers are seen in the bigger world out there, there's no question about that. And over the years [as we've] worked on so many projects together, we find ourselves asking 'What about this composer? How can we help them?'"[36] But when asked what he believed Larsen would want to be remembered for, he didn't name her humanitarian inclinations. Brunelle speculated: "It seems to me she wants to be known and respected as a composer, not as a woman who is married and has a daughter [and who also composes], so that should not enter into the equation. . . . She is first and foremost a composer. She also happens to be a woman. . . . It's not about 'you'll like me better if you knew about my family.' She doesn't want that. She just wants people to know [her music] because it's *her*, and her passion for life, and her passion for people, and working with them and exciting them."[37] As was true at the family dinner table, Larsen's passion to engage, her need to be heard, is what drives her.

Libby Larsen has described James Dunham as "a muse for twenty years," but when I quoted the composer to the world-famous violist, he chuckled and countered: "*She's* a muse to all of us; we inspire each other."[38] Dunham, a "founding member of the Naumburg Award winning Sequoia Quartet, and subsequently violist with the Grammy Award winning Cleveland Quartet" has premiered, recorded, and played a number of Larsen's works; he's a champion of new music.[39] Dunham's eclectic musical experiences and tastes make him an ideal performer of Larsen's music, something he discovered when the Cleveland Quartet commissioned "Schoenberg, Schenker, Schillinger." The piece, with each of its movements in a different style, suited a performer who has played and "likes all kinds of music."[40] Dunham relishes the idea that his *vocal* debut at Tully Hall consisted of scatting a section of the viola part in the "Schillinger" movement and explained how that came about: "Due to my love of jazz, I discovered a passage that seemed to me a perfect foil for simultaneously playing and scatting the line. I demonstrated it for the quartet as a curiosity and told them not to tell Libby, thinking it was fairly inappropriate, especially for a composer I had yet to meet . . . ! Of course, as soon as we got to that spot, they all said: 'Guess what James can do!' And as we now know Libby, she thought it was great!" Dunham values her openness to ideas, her eagerness to collaborate, and her lack of intellectual rigidity and wishes "more composers were like that."[41]

At the same time, Dunham appreciates that she knows her mind and is not afraid to articulate and defend strongly held beliefs. He recalled a public forum where Larsen spoke about her work and an audience member challenged her insistence that she needed to hear her music live. But Larsen, according to Dunham, "startled some of the younger composers when she didn't budge" and proceeded to enumerate all the reasons why computer-generated playback was an inadequate substitute for live sound and the act of making music. Her insistence on live performance follows logically from her commitment to music making as a social act. Echoing John Duffy's assessment of Larsen's thoughtfulness, Dunham observed: "She goes deep, and she goes deep fast, if you let her, and if you're willing."[42]

A final observation Dunham offered illuminated what he understood as Larsen's exceptional craft. He recalled a rehearsal conversation he had with Larsen and mezzo-soprano Susanne Mentzer. The three were preparing *Sifting through the Ruins*, a piece Larsen had written for voice, viola, and piano commemorating the September 11, 2001, attacks. Mentzer remarked that the motion between the final two movements seemed abrupt and asked whether Larsen could write "a little viola cadenza to connect the movements." Dunham expressed his deep admiration that Mentzer had detected that something was missing but then utter amazement that Larsen "wrote it out on the spot, on a scrap of paper, a cadenza that connects the two movements. She heard the sounds, the connections. It's second nature, but it's more than that." He reflected: "I need to frame that piece of paper."[43] The work was premiered at Aspen in the summer of 2005 by Dunham, Mentzer, and renowned collaborative pianist and coach Craig Rutenberg. Over a decade later Dunham described the piece as "stunning and devastating." And clearly just recollecting the performance was emotional for the violist. As Dunham recalled, when the piece was over and the three musicians looked up, they saw the audience on its feet; "everyone was standing; applauding *pianissimo*."[44] Speaking with James Dunham, I was struck by the complete respect this world-class musician has for a composer who has "gifted him" with her music.

Knowing a public personality, even over a period of years, doesn't guarantee that one knows the more private person: the individual who is juggling family and work, children and parents, doctor and dentist appointments, cars that need oil changes, and the thousand and one tasks that require tending to get through the day. Disturbing, sometimes horrifying revelations regarding the private behavior of seemingly exemplary citizens—mild-mannered authors, heroic athletes, wholesome entertainers, and respected people from every sector of society, even the priesthood—are now commonplace. It made me curious whether I would find a disconnect between the public Larsen and the one most people don't see. Is the person who appears upbeat, open-minded, and indefatigably generous with her time and energy someone else when not on stage? Is she ever *not* on stage?

Toni Lindgren has been one of Larsen's assistants for over four years. Regarding their relationship, Lindgren is clear that "Libby is the head honcho; she's the shot caller," but Lindgren also observes, "Libby really treats us with a lot of respect; she talks to us as if we're equals."[45] Having observed Larsen interact with three assistants over the years, I can vouch for Lindgren's characterization of the association as mutually respectful; there are no uncomfortable signs of rank or hierarchy. Lindgren majored in environmental science in college, but she is also a guitarist who regularly tours with a band, so she knows music. Her engagement with both the arts and sciences, and environmental issues in particular, feeds and excites Larsen's boundary-crossing interests. Lindgren and a newer assistant, Jason Senchina, also bring up-to-date technology skills to the business side of Larsen's music-making endeavors, which is increasingly important with the growth of Larsen's publishing company, which started in 2007.[46] When a Web presence is a must for independent artists and musicians, having assistants who can focus on it frees Larsen to tend to what she does best: compose. Lindgren's writing and interpersonal skills, as well as her inclination to be self-motivated and detail oriented, make her an ideal coworker for the composer, who is the same way; she sees her job as "trying to take as much pressure off Libby as possible so that she's free to be creative."[47]

Over the years Lindgren has watched Larsen as she undertakes new projects. Larsen's steady state of wonder, a quality that others have commented upon, is obvious to Lindgren as well: "She's constantly learning, and I've never gotten the impression that she thinks she has all the answers; she's always researching new topics of interest and asking us questions about what we know. I forget that there's an age difference. She's so enthusiastic and ready for new experiences; she's very open-minded." Given the tempo of Larsen's life and the constant demands placed on those in the third-floor office in the house, Lindgren observes, "If we get along and there's positive energy up here, then she can be productive and feel good about what she's doing downstairs."[48]

In so many ways Lindgren's observations echo those of others who have worked closely with the composer, and this is especially true when it comes to the composer's humility. Lindgren explains: "I was really surprised when I started working for her. I had never worked for a composer before, and I imagined that there'd be some ego involved, but I have yet to see it . . . and I've worked for her for a while."[49] In a relationship that could easily devolve into a more typical boss-worker model, and especially when the boss enjoys a degree of globe-trotting celebrity, Lindgren points out that Larsen has never acted the role of the typical composer-artist.

This is true despite Lindgren's observation that Larsen has strong opinions and shoots from the hip. She admires Larsen's perceptiveness of everything going on around her and the accuracy with which she sums up situations: "Having a conversation with Libby is a little scary at times; she knows how to read between the lines and is very sensitive to body language and the energy of a room."[50] It may be, according to Lindgren, that in the time she has worked for Larsen she's seen the composer "mellow out a little bit" and take more time before reacting to things, which may be the result of some "big life events" happening, like "losing her mom in the spring of 2014." But she also speculated that it may be related to having someone write a biography; it "makes you think twice about things . . . and become more introspective."[51] Lindgren's observation is a reminder to me that writing a biography of a living subject is not only a story about a subject's life but also becomes a part of a subject's life story; it changes the subject in subtle but tangible ways.

I asked Lindgren what she had learned about Larsen from working with her, and without skipping a beat she responded, "[Larsen] is one of the most driven and ambitious people I've ever met." In contrast to her own experience "coming from the Midwest where people tend to be passive," she explained, "Libby is very direct. If she thinks something, she'll say it, which is a necessity for success in the business world." Ambition, traditionally a quality denied women, is not out of place or character in Lindgren's reading of Larsen. It makes the composer's work possible; it is part of who she is. Lindgren commented upon Larsen's commanding organizational skills and the ways she stays on top of things: "She has an ability to learn something from everyone around her. She pays attention, and when you speak she's always listening."[52]

But Lindgren has taken away other lessons from being in Larsen's world, and they have changed her. The idea of Larsen's energy, a consistent observation among interviewees, is a rondo theme for Lindgren as well. The young Libby who was driven to run and sail and bike and ski is still present in the sixty-five-year-old woman. Referring to Larsen's marathon habit and a recent 5K win, Lindgren admitted, "Libby has more energy than I do. Working with her has shown me that keeping your body healthy is one of the most important keys to success. She's inspired me to get active, because she's demonstrated to me that your mind and body are deeply connected. What she accomplishes in a day is the result of being incredibly intelligent; she [also] takes great care of her health, which allows her to produce an amazing amount of work. Libby refuses to accept age as an excuse, and just keeps her mind and body going. . . . She's just getting started."[53]

Despite Larsen's success, longevity, and devoted chorus of champions, no public figure is universally lauded. Those in the arts are especially vulnerable to challenge by others who embrace different values, tastes, and agendas. Criticisms often reveal more about the critic than the subject being discussed, and this situation complicates evaluating the legitimacy of the assessment whether positive or negative. And then sometimes what presents itself as a focused critique is in reality a discussion of something only distantly related. That said, considering criticisms of Larsen's work and aesthetic suggests the range of the concerns they raise. As might be expected, what Larsen's most vocal critics found irksome was often what her most ardent champions praised.

Although Larsen enjoyed favored status within her upper Midwest cultural enclave, she wasn't immune to its criticisms. In the *Twin Cities Reader*, a free weekly area tabloid, Larsen was invited to "Get Out of Town." The January 1992 issue featured brief write-ups on fourteen local celebrities. Previous years' evictees included Robert Bly, Garrison Keillor, Kim Basinger, and Yanni. The column on Larsen was accompanied by a photo of the pageboy-ed composer and the caption "New-music mascot." In the paragraph that follows, Larsen is called a "fashionplate," "feminist," and "trend hopper." Like typical nineteenth-century reviews of public women, the critics go first for her physical appearance. Using "feminist," in the ostensibly pejorative stream of descriptors, they criticize her insistence on writing women into history. Gender remains a primary mode of attack. "Trend-hopper" is followed by the charge that "Libby Larsen has been on the cutting edge of every fad to wash its way through the local classical music scene."[54]

Without any discussion of her music, the column is more a launchpad for clever lobs than a forum for serious debate. But even the negative assessment suggests Larsen's presence in the region; it also hints at more serious criticisms that will recur in others' assessments of her work: her practice of writing music that appeals to a variety of listeners, and her agile eclecticism composing in multiple styles and genres.

Beyond the suspect nature of appeal, the *Twin Cities Reader* rebukes Larsen's compositional fecundity: "every month seems to bring a new Twin Cities premiere of a new Larsen piece." The half-dozen authors who contributed to the article also challenged her choice to remain in Minneapolis rather than try "her luck on either coast." They encouraged her to get "off the Minnesota bunny slopes."[55] One wonders whether any of the evictees was seriously offended by the judgments of the youthful band of Twin City writers, the majority of whom ultimately stayed in the very region they disparaged for the duration of their careers, or whether it was something of a badge of honor to be singled out for expulsion.

Criticisms came from other quarters as well. In 2000 Allen Gimbel (b. 1956), an American composer and tonal music theorist, reviewed a CD of Larsen's music conducted by the American Joel Revzen. He remarks on the "awfully British" sounding first movement of *String Symphony (Symphony No. 4)*, and a second movement whose "ten and a half attractive minutes" go on too long.[56] It is hard to know if he is accusing Larsen of feigning Britishness or not sounding American enough. He observes that the third movement is inoffensive but faults it because "the music . . . does not take enough risks." And then the issue of Larsen's regionalism comes into play. Although the music doesn't excite Gimbel to seek out a second hearing, he is "sure the piece was a success with Minnesota's generally conservative concert-going audience." He finishes the review with a patronizing jab that the set *Songs of Light & Love* "will find its proper place at university chamber recitals," and that *Songs from Letters* is emblematic of the entire CD, where "nothing is left to the imagination, and a single hearing will suffice."[57]

In a 2001 review of a Koch CD conducted by Marin Alsop, the same critic took on the issue of Larsen's appeal.[58] Regarding the *Solo Symphony*, Gimbel attacks "the pops concert audience," who "may delight in condescending snippets of funk, waltz, swing, square-dance, tango, and jig," and instructs "less gullible listeners, and Ms. Larsen herself" that they "would do well to listen to Kalevi Aho's Seventh Symphony for a more rewarding musical experience of this sort."[59] It is unclear what Gimbel finds instructive in the Finnish composer's symphony or the experience he is alluding to. He finds the third movement "utterly monotonous" and chides the composer for the fourth movement and its "predictable, bravo-inducing climax." Gimbel concludes, "This is a truly terrible piece that does little for the reputations of those involved." Regarding *Marimba Concerto*, he criticizes Larsen for "hiding" the "weaknesses" of the final movement "by bringing the percussionists forward and asking them to interact in movement in addition to their musical performance." Gimbel notes that he was "glad [he] wasn't there to see it" and expresses dismay that the audience *likely* "roared with approval." The reviewer sums up his assessment by calling Larsen's "accessible modern music . . . a peculiar kind of Show Biz," which he finds "disturbingly invasive." Although a CD review may not be the forum for a detailed analysis, a reader is left wondering whether Gimbel's criticism of Larsen's music reflects a fundamental aesthetic disagreement or the fussing of a jealous contemporary; the tone gets in the way of knowing. In the case of the *Marimba Concerto*, Gimbel neglected to acknowledge Larsen's liner notes, which discussed modern audiences who "listen more visually," and how this reality influenced her decision to foreground the percussionists. She *intended* to explore the visual relationship between the soloist and the larger ensemble and lead listeners to hear with their eyes.[60]

Other critics had different complaints. A 2007 issue of *American Record Guide* includes a review of Larsen's opera *Every Man Jack* by Paul Hertelendy. He challenges Larsen's concept for the piece and her decision to compress Jack London's real-life operatic biography, "a compendium of sheer adventure—a little Ernest Hemingway, a little Teddy Roosevelt, some Don Giovanni, a bit of Captain Ahab, combining several careers," into a "single make-believe night of withdrawal from reality by the alcoholic London." He questions the composer's move "away from traditional opera" and toward something more vaudeville-like. He notes her "attractive, readily sung melodies" but regrets their sparse "characterizations from the nine instruments in the pit." Hertelendy sees London's life as grand opera and wants "a bigger-budget production." Larsen's lean score and "fragmented form" are inadequate to the work he envisions.[61] Like Gimbel, Hertelendy concedes the attractiveness of Larsen's music, but both men want more.

An earlier conceptual challenge was launched at Larsen's theater piece *The Nothing That Is*, a work for baritone solo, two narrators, chorus, and chamber ensemble that premiered at MIT in 2004. Peter Catalano found Larsen's "contemplation of faith in [a] supreme being through faith in numbers" to be overreaching. He regretted that her lyrical gifts were underserved by "a text that is impervious to musical expression," although he applauded Larsen's transformation of notes taken from the Apollo 13 logbook "into a portentous chant" whose "repetitions become a kind of dirge-like litany, creating a mystical or ritualistic atmosphere."[62] Catalano imagined what Larsen was after and saw the potential in the work even if he believed it was not fully realized in its present form.

As a group the critics mentioned above took issue with Larsen's fecundity and eclecticism; they were unhappy with her music's accessibility, attractiveness, and appeal, which they associated with its regional reach, and what might be its unrealized potential. But none of them suggested that she was symbolic of all that ailed American music culture as did Samuel Lipman (1934–94). He is important to this study not only as a critic of Libby Larsen's music but perhaps more importantly as an extreme example of an attitude that was prevalent in American culture at the time. His assessments speak for one side of an ever-widening schism in the nation's arts scene that responded to larger social realities of 1980s America. Larsen's growing reputation threatened a critic predisposed to favoring European pedigrees and old-world values. As much as Larsen represented something new, she embodied the enemy.

The California-born pianist came to New York in 1955, when he debuted at Town Hall. But Lipman quickly left performing to concentrate on writing, first as a music critic for *Commentary* and then for the *New Criterion*, the magazine he founded and published with art critic Hilton Kramer starting in 1982. Lipman became a cultural advisor to the Reagan and G. H. W. Bush administrations and served as a member of the National Council on the Arts from 1982 to 1988. He disapproved of multiculturalism, affirmative action, and cutting-edge art.[63] He derided the idea "of art and culture to accomplish radical social and political goals" and more generally what he characterized as a trend toward reducing art to entertainment. He summarized his disdain in a criticism of "An American Dialogue," a private report issued by a consortium that included the NEA, the Rockefeller Foundation, and the Pew Charitable Trusts. Lipman took issue with the idea that "the purpose of the arts" was to make "a profound impact on American society and the changes that are shaping it."[64]

> The exact nature of this "profound impact" becomes clear in the way "An American Dialogue" treats the hitherto exalted status of European-based high art. These imperishable masterpieces, along with the artistic traditions derived from them, are now to be regarded as no more than one kind of ethnic manifestation; in preserving and extending those traditions on the American shore, European immigrants of the past, like peoples everywhere, were merely indulging old instincts and tastes, having brought "with them their hunger and demand for European-style performing arts events."[65]

Lipman rejected the idea that non-European cultures might produce equally "imperishable masterpieces. . . . But, the report tells us, we should not grant favored status to this kind of cultural and artistic expression [traditional European-based high art], for we now know that art is itself made up of a 'breadth of genres, styles, sources, venues, artists, art forms, and expressions,' and that the art of all peoples is equally worthy of preservation and presentation."[66]

Lipman attacked "the egalitarian rhetoric of the advocates of multiculturalism" and argued that "beneath the slogans of equality lurk implicit, and sometimes explicit, hierarchies of favored cultures, often chosen with political ends in mind."[67] But Lipman's 1990 argument for apolitical cultural high-mindedness is complicated by a March 1985 *Commentary* article he wrote in which he identifies music as "a Jewish art" that "served as a vehicle of assimilation," preserved a distinctly Jewish identity, and acted "as a vehicle for Jewish survival."[68] The critic appears oblivious to the political assumptions undergirding his own aesthetic platform and reluctant to extend the advantages of music's social and cultural power to others.

In an August 1985 article in the *New Criterion*, Lipman reacts specifically to comments that Larsen made during an intermission interview conducted at the premiere of her *Symphony: Water Music*, which had been broadcast on Minnesota Public Radio. Lipman's self-assured voice rings out in the first sentence of "Music and Musical Life: The Road to Now":

Despite all the warning signs in musical life—a shortage of significant new music, lowered standards in performance, and the declining commitment and sophistication of audiences and patrons—it is the fashion today to see serious music in America bursting forth at every moment and in every place. In order to sustain the fiction of a splendid present, it is necessary to treat music in this country as if it were an activity without a history.[69]

He laments "our extravagantly ballyhooed but nonetheless unanchored present" and is explicit about his preference for "the finest European masters," whom he refers to as "such giants." He praises émigré conductors and performers, "the great European talents" who enriched American musical life. He lists a few composers of whom he approves, Copland among them, but more often he names those he disparages, including the post–World War II avant-gardists whose "era . . . would now seem past in every way, were it not for the damage it did (and continues to do in the academy)."[70]

Women don't fair especially well in Lipman's world unless they fill more traditional roles as vocal performers, patrons, teachers, or writers. Thea Musgrave's 1985 opera, *Harriet, the Woman Called Moses*, falls short because it "has such a thin effect to make *qua* music."[71] Lipman "admires" Laurie Anderson for her "ability to make a success, onstage and in recordings of [her] musical shortcomings." Larsen's music and aesthetic, however, become exemplars of all that is wrong with American music. In that regard she shares Lipman's wrath with Lejaren Hiller and Pauline Oliveros, who were among Lipman's damaging "honor roll" academic avant-gardists.

Lipman spews slurs and insults, and few are safe from the verbal attack: George Crumb is his candidate "for the Pied Piper of the young"; David Del Tredici's *Alice in Wonderland* is "warmed over *Salome*." John Adams's and Nicholas Thorne's music is "unbuttoned vulgarity," and John Corigliano is "musically complaisant."[72] He declares that neither Steve Reich nor Philip Glass has "succeeded in winning any audience at all from traditional music lovers or from the most respected performers of traditional music."[73] Lipman takes on "the rise of a California school of composition which, as in the music of Robert Erickson played at an Alice Tully Hall concert this past spring, seemingly attempts to provide a music to enjoy hot tubs by."[74]

According to Lipman, Larsen's *Symphony: Water Music* is "a large-scale work evidently based on images of Minnesota's many lakes. . . . Despite its ambitious scoring . . . the work itself at its best moments did no more than echo Thomson's earlier, and vastly more successful, attempts to write a quasi-original, folk-like music. At its less successful moments, it sounded like note-spinning done to accompany a nonexistent nature film."[75] He appears to fault its being derivative, programmatic film music. But Lipman doesn't name which Thomson work he has in mind or how Larsen's piece resembles it; he never discusses Larsen's piece further, perhaps because it was not what interested him most. Lipman was incensed by her remarks about being a composer in America at the close of the twentieth century.

In the interview Larsen had explained that she considers "the audience who is going to hear the piece" and acknowledged "that music lives in the moment," which means she "very much want[s] to have it understood now," rather than "a hundred years from now." This incited Lipman, who interprets her comments as a confession of her short-sighted preference for "identifying a market."[76] When Larsen distinguished between academically trained composers who chose to write for "a very small number of people . . . interested in the process of composing" and her own choice "to make [her] living, if possible, and to write [her] music and create [her] art in the concert situation," Lipman censures her for "such egoistic, career-oriented activity."[77] When she rejected the idea that her essential job as a composer was to educate the public "in the nature of music,"[78] he takes her to task for abdicating her "duty": "It would still seem a mistake, in reacting against the excesses of the musical avant-garde, to give up the idea of education and to replace it entirely with a gospel of amusement." Lipman lectures Larsen: "There is more in music education, after all, than delivering an unpleasant and unwanted message to an unwilling audience. Its purpose is the teaching of civilization and beauty; the need exists all the more after the misfires in music composition over the last forty years."[79]

The critic positions music's educative and entertainment qualities as mutually exclusive: "But in the absence of education, all that is left is entertainment—the mindless pursuit by the audience of empty satisfactions and trivial delights, and by the artist of glamorous success and bloated fame."[80] Readers don't have to work hard to figure out which glamorous artists he believes suffer from unwarranted success or fame.

Lipman is frustrated with the direction contemporary American musical culture is headed and disparages even those musicians one assumes he might favor. Van Cliburn's 1958 Tchaikovsky Competition win in Moscow was noteworthy, but the pianist's "foundering" career by the mid-1960s was an indicator of our national musical poverty and "another sign . . . of the continuing primacy of foreign influence in our performing life." Itzhak Perlman is "the Luciano Pavarotti of the violin," but Lipman faults him for "being the most famous virtuoso of the day without at the same time having had any effect on the playing of other violinists, either in style or repertory."[81] Lipman summarizes the nation's destitute musical culture by noting that the "authentic-performance movement is headquartered not in the United States but in England and on the Continent." He castigates critics for prose that is either "infused with academic musicology" or "an unattractive combination of musical and literary incompetence."[82] He criticizes the American music business for forcing the nation's composers overseas to be recorded because of high costs in this country.[83] On this last point, American composers, including Larsen, would agree.

In September 1993, Lipman wrote the first of a final quartet of articles for the *New Criterion*. This one criticizes members of the American Symphony Orchestra League, including Larsen, for their report "Americanizing the American Orchestra." He chides the authors for providing "not remedies, exactly, but the optimistic suggestions of a group of experts for carrying our orchestras into the multicultural twenty-first century."[84]

On three occasions he singles out the promotion of blacks as exemplary of the larger problem: "It is not enough to have, say, black musicians: they must also play music written by blacks."[85] His comment disparages not only black performers but also entire repertoires of American music closely associated with African American culture and artists whose works would not find a place in Lipman's canon of masterpieces but whose styles regularly appeared in Larsen's compositions.

Lipman speaks of "the anti-white and anti-European culture bias . . . evident throughout" the report and names Larsen among a "cabal of liberal foundations, uncommitted board members, and opportunistic administrators in and out of government . . . an inside network" responsible for wanting to "indoctrinate" audiences in the politically correct transformation of society.[86] According to Lipman, intolerant and parochial musical radicals dared to push for diversifying all aspects of national symphonic life and to question traditional practices and programming choices of symphony boards. He compares their techniques to those used by "totalitarian societies" eager to promote a political agenda but fails to acknowledge the extreme, elitist agenda of his own aesthetic or argument or the powerful network of tastemakers he represented.

Lipman's stance regarding what constituted "masterpieces" and how to guarantee "the future of great music," and his belief in the primacy of Western European cultural values remained intact throughout his life. Larsen's outspoken advocacy of a US-American musical culture that encourages and supports the widest variety of creators and traditions stood 180 degrees from Lipman's vision of a Eurocentric "highest civilization."

* * *

Larsen had a different agitating effect on another stratum of contemporary music culture when she visited the University of Illinois School of Music in spring 1990, and it, like her childhood dinner-table experience and the *Some Pig* episode, stands out as life changing. The initial response came from a group of computer and electronic music (electroacoustic) composers and their students at the university. Ironically they were members of the academy-damaging avant-garde that Lipman had disparaged and lumped together with Larsen as responsible for the demise of American music culture. The environment of the Illinois music school, shaped to a large degree by a monotheistic high-modernist musical culture and an all-male composition faculty that was typical of many schools at the time, illuminates the ways in which the academy, gender, and aesthetics could converge.

Faculty composers had been attracted to the school by Lejaren Hiller (1924–94), who founded the Experimental Music Studios in 1958.[87] Students were drawn to a faculty that included James Beauchamp, Herbert Brün, Salvatore Martirano, Sever Tipei, and Scott Wyatt. Followers of the charismatic German-born Brün (1918–2000) became known as "The Brünettes."[88] As the university's Experimental Music Studio's Web site boasts, many advances in computer and electronic music composition were accomplished at the school.[89]

Larsen's formal invitation to visit the university came from the chair of the composition faculty, William "Bill" Brooks, an Illinois DMA who had studied with Brün among others. But the idea to bring Larsen to campus had originated with Heidi Von Gunden, the only female faculty member in the theory and composition department at Illinois.[90] She had studied with Pauline Oliveros, one of Lipman's "damaging avant-garde forces." Though Von Gunden was trained as a composer, the terms of her employment limited her teaching to theory and academic classes only; she never taught composition.

In spring 1989 Von Gunden taught a course on "Women and Music"; she was troubled by the paucity of works by women composers on concerts at the school and expressed her concern to Brooks, who was arranging the next year's concert series. Von Gunden had recently heard a recording of Larsen's *Symphony: Water Music*. She was moved by the piece and especially impressed with its orchestration, which reminded her of pieces by Robert Erickson, another of her former teachers (the one Lipman had associated with hot tubs). Von Gunden suggested Larsen as a short-term resident composer. Brooks canvassed the faculty and hearing no objection wrote a proposal to Meet the Composer to fund the residency. Elizabeth Hinkle-Turner, a DMA composition student at the time, speculates that Brooks may have anticipated Larsen's impact, but believing that she could handle any opposition, he purposely invited her to stir things up. She also believes that Brooks knew Larsen would "be nice."[91]

At a dinner that included Larsen, Von Gunden, and Patricia Repar—a second of three female doctoral composition students—Von Gunden informed Larsen of the often controversial nature of the Composers' Forum.[92] She felt it was only fair to tell the "so young and almost elfin[-looking]" guest what awaited her.[93] Hinkle-Turner, now a successful composer who is proud of her University of Illinois doctorate and studies with Herbert Brün, looked back on the forum ritual from a distance of twenty-five years and recalled: "The atmosphere was really intimidating. Composers would sit in a chair on a stage with a spotlight on them; the stage of the recital hall was not up above the audience; it was down. It was like you were in this pit or cistern looking up at your accusers."[94] According to forum protocol, Larsen would offer remarks, and the audience would respond with comments and questions. Larsen said she understood and welcomed the challenge.

Larsen had come to Illinois directly from a residency at Austin College in Sherman, Texas, where her piece *Overture: Parachute Dancing*, a work commissioned by the American Composers Orchestra in 1983, had been played. She began her Illinois Forum talking about that experience. Larsen explained the title's reference to a Renaissance court spectacle where dancers used brightly colored umbrellas (parapluie) to float down from the ledge of a wall "into the midst of the spectators" at the end of their performance.[95] She spoke about her career as a professional composer outside the academy who wrote on commission. She shared her belief in music as communication and as a social act, and her vision of the composer as an integral part of society. She offered practical insights, among them the need to recognize the abilities of performers and take rehearsal time into account when writing for specific groups. She reflected on the idea of being a "generous" composer, one who acknowledges "the composer's choice concerning the performer's and the listener's access to the music—its pitch, shape, motion, and architecture." While she readily admitted that "a composer of any genre has no responsibility to compose music that can be understood, there is a choice involved."[96]

Larsen had reason to feel confident. By 1990 she had written chamber music, song cycles, multiple operas, band and choral music, concerti, and two symphonies. She had been a composer-in-residence at a major US orchestra, and her works were performed regularly. She would be commended for "her innovative use of synthesized sounds" in her opera *Frankenstein; or, The Modern Prometheus.*[97] As part of the residency, two of her works, *Four on the Floor* and *Pinions* (a violin concerto in three movements), were performed in a + Series concert arranged by Brooks.[98] He had been a freelance composer between academic appointments and knew the worlds inside and outside the ivory tower. He had worked with John Cage and played in the 1969 premiere of Cage's and Hiller's HPSCHD, a multimedia, acoustic/computer-generated musical event; he was also an outspoken supporter of women composers. Larsen and Brooks had similarly broad and practical perspectives regarding what composers could be and do, and both welcomed a variety of ideas and voices. If Larsen's residency hadn't originated with Brooks, he was a supportive participant once she arrived.[99] She had reason to believe her thinking would be valued. What Larsen expected to be a stimulating and positive exchange of ideas at the Forum morphed into something increasingly personal; and it continued after Larsen left campus. Issues raised by her visit resonated in two additional forums in the following weeks.

Hinkle-Turner describes her initial reaction to Larsen's remarks: "This was like the worst thing you could talk about with all of us 'modernists,' all of us worshippers of Stockhausen, and Babbitt. [To talk about] writing music that was accessible . . . that you have to think about your audience. To us it was 'Oh, no!' . . . We were trying so hard to be Pierre Boulez."[100] Hinkle-Turner recalls getting increasingly incensed by what Larsen said: "People were kind of squirming in their chairs, and I opened my mouth and said: 'So are you saying that in order for us to get audiences . . . we have to write cute pieces about parachutes?'" In 2015 Hinkle-Turner characterized the wording of her question as "something absolutely horrible" and pointed out that she immediately apologized for how "offensive and condescending" she sounded. But she also remembers that her question "set everybody off," noting, "When I said that, the floodgates opened. It was the catalyst for the 'lively discussion' that followed."[101] Larsen was clearly offended by Hinkle-Turner's use of the word *cute* to describe her music. Others took issue with the idea that writing music purposely designed to require minimal rehearsal time could ever be a desirable goal. Comparing such compositions to fast food and calling it microwave music became a joke in the department.

Hinkle-Turner remembers that "everybody left genuinely upset and uncomfortable," but she also wonders whether it wasn't exactly what Brooks wanted to happen:

> He wanted to stir things up by bringing in someone who was enjoying more mass appeal than all of us who had been raised in the John Cage, Harry Partch, Karlheinz Stockhausen, Pierre Boulez, Milton Babbitt, "Who Cares If You Listen" kind of background. . . . He was throwing someone in the mix who was from a world that we just didn't know about. He wanted us to have that conversation, because it was a different conversation than we were having before, which was very influenced either consciously or unconsciously by the "Brünettes" and Sal Martirano and his crew. . . . For better or worse, they had a big influence on everyone.[102]

The degree to which Hinkle-Turner perceived the program's ideology as more or less uniform can be gleaned from a project she completed for her minor in ethnomusicology at Illinois. In "What Is New Music," Hinkle-Turner used the Illinois program as a case study for what she described as "the 'groupthink' thing they had going on there."[103] In a conference at Middle Tennessee State University in 1993, where both Hinkle-Turner and Larsen were panelists, the once-outraged graduate student had a chance to interact again with Larsen. Without changing her aesthetic stance, Hinkle-Turner thanked Larsen for providing her with a model of a "normal" person who was also a composer, who had a child, and who managed to have a life like the one she wanted.[104]

Brooks has "only the vaguest memory of the particulars" of Larsen's residency, in part because it was more the rule than the exception that forums were contentious. He explained that after the composer made his or her comments,

> one or another [of the audience] . . . would begin the attack, so to speak. And this happened so consistently that I have only the vaguest memory of particulars. It happened to George Crumb, it happened to Charles Wuorinen, it happened to Libby; it would happen all the time. . . The thing with Charles Wuorinen degenerated into a near riot. . .. Libby was probably very forthright about her ability and her willingness and her desire to write music for the occasion, and this was, of course, anathema to heavily politicized rhetoric that followed from a critical examination of the social implications of pandering to tastes.[105]

Brooks acknowledged the legitimacy of such criticisms in certain situations but also understood that in "Libby's case it would have completely missed the point because the working assumptions were utterly different."[106]

Brooks described the questioners' tactics:

> The method used by the group tended to push things by way of caricature and exaggeration. In this situation, Libby being the clear-headed and forthright person she is, it's easy to imagine the escalation as sort of automatic: she says something, it's exaggerated; she responds by clarifying; things build up. And she's not a person to necessarily yield the ground for diplomatic reasons; she would yield the ground if she thought she was in the wrong or if she thought the other person had a point. But she's not going to yield ground just because she doesn't want to cause a fuss. [Whatever was said was likely] critical to the borders of tolerable. To me [what happened] doesn't seem unexpected, but to her, she was completely blindsided. Like "where did this freight train come from?"[107]

As Hinkle-Turner recalled, Larsen got "super-offended" by her comment and responded that she didn't write "cute" music. For a woman composer who had fought gender bias during her academic studies, and whose diminutive size attracted such descriptors, having her music described as "cute" likely seemed the worst kind of characterization. That it came from a young woman composer would have been additional unfathomable treason. Hinkle-Turner wasn't familiar with *Parachute Dancing*, whose full orchestra, oversized percussion arsenal, and generally large and dissonant sound precluded any suggestion of "cute," but as she observed, she felt disappointed by Larsen. Prior to Larsen's residency, the only woman composer Hinkle-Turner knew beyond her student peers was Pauline Oliveros, and much as she respected Oliveros, she didn't see her as a model for herself. She explains: "I was finally meeting a successful woman in the field, and she was espousing that I compromise my aesthetic, and that was really hard for me to take. Hence my initial hostility."[108]

The absence of women composer models made Larsen's visit all the more important for Hinkle-Turner. It also revealed a larger problem with educational environments so lacking in variety. As women composition students at American universities still understand, it is impossible to model yourself on someone who isn't there, and no single person can be a model for everyone. It is no surprise that Hinkle-Turner devoted a significant section of the introduction to her book *Women Composers and Music Technology in the United States: Crossing the Line* to the question of professional models and the difficulties encountered by "young female composers" seeking "a mentor and friend in the academic and musical community."[109]

Larsen discovered that her forum remarks had inspired responses at subsequent Composers Forums that spring when she received a copy of the text of a public talk delivered April 9 by Heidi Von Gunden. The talk, titled "Heidi Von Gunden discussing Sever Tipei discussing Libby Larsen," complete with Von Gunden's handwritten editorial revisions, was a response to Tipei's Forum talk given March 26, which in addition to presenting his piece *Many Worlds* touched upon Zen, morality, math, science, his musical aesthetics, and "that person."[110] Without ever naming Larsen specifically in his talk, references to the speaker who had been a forum guest two weeks earlier made Larsen's identity clear. In her own talk Von Gunden expressed disappointment that there had been no serious discussion of aesthetic differences between the two composers' positions, as everyone was aware they occupied different ends of a spectrum. Beyond disappointment, however, Von Gunden voiced her shock and humiliation over a comparison that she believed had been implied. Using a reference to Jean Paul Sartre's 1946 play *The Respectful Prostitute*, Tipei had characterized "that person" as a "respectable whore." Von Gunden pointed out that Larsen's phrase "generous composer" had also been turned against her, transforming the composer's idea of generosity into something "immoral."

Von Gunden was incensed and informed those present that the use of the word *whore*, even in an indirect association with Larsen, was gender harassment. Reminding the audience that sexual harassment was one of the university's most pressing concerns, she read aloud the then-legal definition of the term, which included a clause referring to humiliating or offensive statements. She also read from a paper by Barbara Reskin, a professor of sociology and director of graduate studies at Illinois at the time, that addressed the structure of Western universities, whose values reflected the needs and behaviors of the men who had founded them. Von Gunden finished her forum talk with data on the number of women at universities across the country who had experienced some form of sexual harassment, the most common form being belittling or offensive remarks, and a statement that she and the women in the division were awaiting an apology from her colleague.

In Hinkle-Turner's words, "aesthetic viciousness" was just a part of the very contentious atmosphere of the program at the time, and Tipei's disagreement with Larsen was rooted in an aesthetic difference of opinion. But belittling, gendered language, regardless of its indirection, turns conversations away from ideas. Hinkle-Turner believes that the absolute judgmentalism and compartmentalization that had characterized the program through the 1980s was on the wane when she arrived in 1986, but it hadn't disappeared completely and neither had the "very strange, misogynistic atmosphere. It was a horrible, hostile atmosphere. Women were not being taken seriously musically or intellectually."[111] Her memories of being the only female in a class where the professor began the first session of the semester with a dirty limerick and later having to endure meetings with a professor in an office with postcards of naked women in her sight line created a culture of discomfort. She concludes: "You had to develop really thick skin."[112] Unfortunately, the Illinois music school wasn't uniquely parochial or misogynistic; while the examples Hinkle-Turner cites seem extreme, perhaps, they were more the rule at the time.

Although a quarter century has dulled Larsen's memories of the experience and her wrath at learning of the follow-up forums, in a 2014 conversation Larsen admitted that she had been "blindingly angry at the time."[113] It's hard to imagine equivalent gendered epithets being hurled at Crumb or Wuorinen, regardless of his compositional philosophy or choices. Brooks observes that if you wanted to attack a man for doing the same thing "you'd call him a hired hand; or [say] he's just doing his job. You could be dismissive, but it would be hard to gender it."[114]

The Illinois Experimental Music Studio (EMS) had been founded in the same year that Milton Babbitt's *High Fidelity* article "Who Cares If You Listen?" (originally titled "The Composer as Specialist") appeared. Babbitt advised "that the composer would do himself and his music an immediate and eventual service by total, resolute, and voluntary withdrawal from this public world to one of private performance and electronic media, with its very real possibility of complete elimination of the public and social aspects of musical composition."[115] His focus on writing for specialists lives on today in the Illinois Computer Music Program, where its homepage states: "The Computer Music Project (CMP) on the fifth floor of the Music Building is a site where serious—even witty—composition faculty and students can meet to share ideas and information. They can use the facility for composing, research, and teaching—but also to present their work to each other and prepare it for professional meetings."[116]

For Larsen, identifying music creation with a metaphorical fifth floor, disregarding the social aspects of musical composition, or writing only for initiates to the practice or those attending professional meetings are ideas alien to her beliefs: in understanding music as communication, it is the public she intends to reach. Living as a composer without the security of a university salary, retirement fund, studio space, equipment budget, or support structure also forced a consideration of the practical functions of music. Although Brooks explains that it was "standard operating procedure to grill the visitor," he also concedes that in Larsen's case such language would have represented an extremely personal "ad hominem attack" even when considered within the self-consciously political and combative rhetoric that characterized the program at the time.[117]

As late as the final decade of the twentieth century, a successful woman composer who bucked aesthetic orthodoxies or defied gendered stereotypes and earned a living through her artistic work could be berated like women actresses and performers of earlier centuries. Whether the disagreement was anchored in genuine philosophical differences or not, the gendered language used to express the dissenting opinion contained more than a simple challenge to the quality of ideas, reasoning, or ideology. It reflected the larger society's values. Rather than focus on the soundness of an argument, project, position, or performance, potentially productive discussions too often devolved into personal, gendered invective if they were started at all.

Upon learning of the follow-up forums, Larsen's associates encouraged her to litigate, but she moved on, taking lessons from the experience with her. In letters cordially thanking people at the university for their hospitality, Larsen admitted to feeling "changed (maybe older!)."[118] Correspondence between Brooks and Larsen in the months that followed refers obliquely to the incident. Brooks is "sorry for any unpleasant issues." He hopes she'll come back some time in the future, when, he promises, "We'll spare you the arena this time."[119] On the upside he wrote: "I have to report that your visit stirred up more controversy than anything I've seen since coming back here in 1984—controversy which is, I think (I hope!), much needed and very beneficial." And then referring to the verbal beating she sustained: "I hope the bruises didn't take too long to heal; from my point of view it was worth it (easy for me to say, of course)."[120]

In the years immediately following Larsen's residency, a number of events took place at the School of Music that circled around the idea of women and composing and the relationship of composers to worlds beyond the studio. In this regard, the Illinois program was progressive. In 1991, Susan Parenti, a composer who had earned her DMA at Illinois in 1986, initiated a project called "Composing the Music School: Proposals for a Feminist Composition Curriculum."[121] She referenced her personal experience of being a university composer for three years: "one of two persons to use the women's bathroom on the composition floor of the University of Illinois." She asked, "Why do music departments not attract young women to study composition?"[122] In light of Larsen's and Hinkle-Turner's experiences, answers might not be hard to imagine. But Parenti was interested in exploring behaviors that went beyond the dramas acted out in the small fiefdoms of individual academic departments; her sights were set on understanding behaviors that were systemic in society.

In early January 1992, Parenti organized a gathering of eleven "composing women" that included Hinkle-Turner, Patricia Repar, and Lucinda Lawrence; the latter two women were composition students of Bill Brooks. Parenti observed that women needed to stop performing the roles of coordinator, moderator, and "interior designer" and become instead the architects and builders of university curricula. Courses that perpetuated images of composers as lone individualists struggling competitively among their male cohorts had to be opened up to embrace other models as normative. Language that assumed male prerogatives as natural ones needed to be retired. Programs that encouraged the removal of composers from society rather than their service to community had to be reconstructed. The all-knowing, always serious expert persona associated with new music composers (who were assumed to be male) was ultimately destructive of imaginative development; Parenti wished "to reclaim the Fool."[123]

The year 1991 had seen the publication of Susan McClary's *Feminine Endings: Music, Gender, and Sexuality*, followed quickly by dozens of essays, articles, and books by as many scholars that explored various aspects of women's roles in music culture. The time was ripe for change, and whether Larsen's visit was the cause or not, Hinkle-Turner observed that after her forum "there were a lot of students who came in who did not fit the mold," adding, "Bill Brooks brought a different conversation to that floor; I don't think he realizes." In looking back at her remaining years in the program, Hinkle-Turner concluded, "I would say that Libby's forum was probably the last nasty one."[124] And for Larsen, ultimately the experience strengthened her aesthetic values, made her a more articulate spokesperson, and prepared her for a range of encounters. She would never again be blindsided.

* * *

Observations and assessments by collaborators and critics provide valuable insights into Larsen's impact on contemporary American music culture, but they still only get at her public being. An interview with Libby Larsen's daughter, Wynne Reece (b. 1986), supplies the most intimate portrait of the composer. The chapter ends with her thoughts.

Reece, a young attorney and successful business owner, explains that she always knew her mother was a composer: "There was no time in my life or at least in my memory that I can think of her as anything *but* a composer."[125]

Putting things in context, she explains: "From what I understand, my mother was already well known before I was born, and then she won a Grammy in 1993, further establishing her place in the classical arena." But in their personal interactions, Reece understood her mother as "a parent foremost for the first eighteen years of [her] life: setting boundaries, teaching [her] the importance of chores, daily interactions with people from all walks of life, and being independent at a young age." In comparison to mothers of her friends, Reece reflects, "I can't cite many places where she was different from other working mothers, other than she traveled a lot, but that was her work, and I understood that. In fact, I feel fortunate to have had a mother who traveled so much, as it allowed me to see the world too!" More recently Reece and Larsen "get manicures and pedicures together, *always*." And "once a year, usually over a holiday, [they] go to New York or Chicago and see some shows, dine at [their] favorite local spots, and go shopping."

Reece saw her mother and father, who both were given to putting in eighty-hour work weeks, sharing parenting responsibilities. "When one of them couldn't make it to something then the other made sure to. And so it wasn't one or the other being any *more* present." Reece credits her only-child status with allowing her to travel everywhere with her parents, both of whom were often on the road because of their professions. Reece remembers trips to France, England, Italy, and China, and they "never did the stereotypical tourist stuff."

> We went off the beaten path. We tried to soak up culture, as best a tourist can; we went to the local watering hole instead of . . . the Hard Rock Café in France. I'll never forget this corner pâtisserie in Annecy, France, which my mom sent me into after teaching me how to buy bread in French; it was so wonderful. And that's [traveling for culture] something that I have carried with me as one of the most valuable things that they gave me while I was growing up; they worked really hard to inform me of different cultures, and different socioeconomic classes [and to teach me] there's so much more to life than what we see daily. And that's been invaluable. Knowing that there is more than one can possibly discover in a lifetime and valuing differences is probably one of the most treasured lessons that they bestowed upon me.

By her own accounting, Reece developed "a worldly perspective from a young age," concluding, "Today I think I've been to forty-eight states and seventeen countries, which is a lot!"

When possible, vacations were combined with work trips. But even on a world stage, Reece observed very little change in her mother's behavior except perhaps that she was more "composed." But she compares it to her own work as an attorney: "When I go into a courtroom . . . there's more thought that goes into what and how something is said; there's just a different level of composure."[126] She observes that being more composed in public settings is normal. Normal is, of course, relative and depends upon a host of economic, educational, and cultural conditions, but in the case of Libby Larsen, who she is in her most private family moments and how she presents herself to the world seem remarkably consistent.

Reece was thoughtful in talking about the importance of her parents' shared backgrounds and values.

> They're both self-made, humble and generous beyond words. When they were married they were quite poor; in fact they told me stories about saving up their five dollars or so to get a steak once a month. I think that it [being self-made] can go two ways. If you start out with nothing and make a lot of money, it goes one way or the other, and I am beyond proud of the direction that they went—caring so much for others. Also, I must note, that being *immersed* in the arts world, it's rare to run across an artist who has really made it big. But that doesn't make anybody's art less important. And so, I don't know exactly where it [their appreciation for all] comes from, but both of them really focus on the *value* of the person rather than what it is that they have. And that comes out in both of their work. My dad has done pro bono work for as long as I can remember.[127]

Reece matter-of-factly talked about her parents' similar work ethic: "They'd rather *earn* $1,000.00 than have someone give it to them; and they have instilled that in me." And she also reflected on their belief in doing work that you're passionate about: "It has to be something that you really, truly can put your heart into. Otherwise there's going to be some edge missing." Raising their daughter, Libby Larsen and James Reece taught her to pursue what she was passionate about doing. Their shared belief in hard work, giving back to their community, and valuing people for who they are and what they've done rather than what they have or the circumstances of their birth has created a partnership and a family system that nurtures and supports all its members. Differences in style between the gregarious composer and her more reserved husband are transcended by love, respect, and a common core of beliefs, ones that they were born with and have cultivated together over forty years.

* * *

Can a daughter's characterization of her mother be trusted? Is the child simply caught up in a family romance of her own making? Is the lawyer selecting her evidence to argue a best case? It's possible, but the consistency of character that Larsen's collaborators and intimates have observed is hard to ignore or deny. She knows what she believes and who she is. She understands making music as a personal, social, artistic, and expressive act. She acknowledges the power of music as a communicative tool. She participates in collaborative processes as one player among many. The breadth of her interests, influences, and passions and her respect for a wide range of genres, styles, and cultures are audible in her music. Hers is not the aesthetic of a romantic artist locked away creating esoteric works for a few initiates. Although she respects another's right to do that, it is not who she is. When asked to name her favorite composers and performers, Larsen listed J. S. Bach, Hector Berlioz, Chuck Berry, James Brown, Harry Partch, Sergei Prokofiev, Maurice Ravel, and Big Mama Thornton. She thinks of Thea Musgrave, Pauline Oliveros, and Miriam Gideon as models. She loves the music of Charles Ives and was stunned by the beauty of Rimsky-Korsakov's *Scheherazade*. Larsen grew up on chant and boogie-woogie and Broadway musicals. She's written operas, symphonies, chamber music, and song cycles and sets that enjoy a popularity matched by few living composers.

Is the attractiveness of her music a liability in the world of "art" music? Does her eclecticism suggest that she is without a unique, personal voice and given to following trends? Does "appeal" reflect the absence of rigorous aesthetic standards required of serious new music? Does her nonstop productivity mean Larsen doesn't spend enough time perfecting any single work? Some likely believe the answer is yes to all the above. Many remarkable musicians disagree. Regardless, Larsen isn't waiting on anyone's approval. She writes her music. Every piece is Larsen, an American composer who is one with the rhythms and melodies of her native tongue and the constantly changing social milieu in which she finds herself.

Conclusions
Reflections on a Life and the Process of Telling It

IN THE SAME INTERVIEW I REFERENCED in the preface to this book, Leon Edel observed: "The subject of a biography has never had a chance to bring order to a life so constantly lived and involved in action. It is the biographer who finds the frame, sorts things out, and for better or worse tries to bring order into a life story—create a sense of sequence and coherence."[1] Not all of what Edel said applies to a biography of Libby Larsen—for instance, Larsen has brought some order to her life in a remarkably complete and well-organized personal archive—but enough does to make his observation ring true to my experience. Having played and listened to hours of Larsen's music, read pages of prose by and about her, spoken with the composer numerous times, and published essays and chapters on a handful of her pieces, I knew from the start there was more to her story than was contained in the multiple file cabinets and shelves of library-quality preservation boxes.

When Larsen shared what she thought were the most important influences in her life, neither of us envisioned her answer as the organizing scheme of this biography; that only emerged over time. The themes that seemed integral to Larsen as she looked back on her life it turns out were thoroughly intertwined as she has lived it. They provided an organic coherence that was truthful to the subject I came to understand.

Family, whether the one she was born into or the one she created with her husband and daughter, grounds Libby Larsen. Finding her place in the center of five siblings and a traditional 1950s-style hierarchical household became an apprenticeship in self-discovery and identity creation. Larsen's need for deep and lasting human connections expressed itself first in her caring relationship with her younger sister Duffy and then in an enduring marriage and the decision to have a child. Recognizing that beyond the successful career she was enjoying, she wanted "what [her] sister had: a child," speaks directly to the impact of family upon her character and choices.[2]

Family, that most basic and complex of social units, is a theme that threads through decades of musical works; Larsen is drawn to exploring mother-child relationships. She continued to fathom its depths in 2015 with *The Birth Project*, a set of eleven songs for two sopranos and piano that premiered in June that year. Larsen set poems and prose by seven women who wrote about their experiences announcing their pregnancies, having ultrasounds, contemplating due dates, giving birth, and coping with death. Texts projected during the performance interleaved ancient and modern remedies "To Cause a Women to Be Delivered" and dubiously helpful suggestions for what to do during labor: "Look to your labor coach and health care team for encouragement and support."[3] Larsen captured the gamut of emotions that often attend this uniquely female creative experience: feelings of aloneness, awe at the miracle taking place, and pride attending the physical achievement.[4] Family also connects with other important themes Larsen named: religion, nature, gender, and even the academy, where professional expectations and timetables originally designed with traditional male life patterns in mind continue in the second decade of the twenty-first century to make it especially difficult for professional women who want to have children to do so.

Religion was the word Larsen first used to reference experiences with the spiritual world. That world originally manifested itself with the Sisters of Saint Joseph of Carondolet. They modeled a version of an accepting, loving family and cultivated her spiritual being. In an interview Larsen explained their impact and achievement: "To bring the mystical and the holy to the daily life, that's the influence of the nuns. To struggle, strive, and live to lead a sacred domestic life."[5] The seeds of Larsen's driving ambition were nurtured by the nuns, who struggled and strove daily to live sacred lives. Larsen's observation that the sisters gave generously of themselves to all students echoes in the composer's oft-commented-upon openness and availability. She makes time for people. The eighty-hour work weeks that Wynne Reece saw as typical for both of her parents when she was growing up reflect a family culture of hard work and service.

The ongoing presence of early religious training in Larsen's life shows in the dozens of pieces she has created that treat spiritual-mystical themes. Chant, with its metrically free rhythms and melodies, informs both her vocal and instrumental music. Recitative is her natural mode of vocal expression, and when paired with a heightened sensitivity to American English, the result is vocal lines that illuminate both words and emotions. In a review of Larsen's song cycle *ME (Brenda Ueland)*, Gregory Berg spoke of Larsen's "almost uncanny ability to breathe life into a text." He called it "the work of a mature genius and a stunningly accomplished craftsman."[6] Berg is one of many critics who appreciates Larsen's lyrical gifts. Her inclination toward gesture and movement frees her from slavish adherence to the habit of bar lines: they're there for the performer's convenience. Larsen's intimate, bodily engagement with sound means that she feels the rhythms and architecture of music at micro and macro levels.

When organized religion failed the composer, she left the sanctified confines of the church and went outdoors. The natural world became her spiritual home. Its multiple collaborative systems and cycles reinforced her understanding of the ways things could work: ecology trumped any single hierarchy. Like the purest belief systems, the natural world taught humility, patience, wonder, and awe, the rewards of listening and looking carefully; it also impacted how Larsen thought about music.

The spaciousness of the outdoors provided a kind of acoustic environment that was different from the one she had experienced in the enclosed, if reverberant, church sanctuary. There was a natural counterpoint of pulses, colors, sounds, and smells that spoke simultaneously to Larsen's sensorium; here was the original multimedia, multimodal staged performance art.

The climate and topography of Larsen's upper Midwest home provided specific models and materials for her music. Cold, whiteness, northern light, the sounds and muting effects of snow, winter's slowed-down time, water in its many moods and forms, the fragrance of a long-awaited flower all find their way into Larsen's nature-inspired music. With *DDT*, a percussion piece that premiered in 2015, Larsen has ramped up her musical activism. She uses Morse code to tap out words from Rachel Carson's *Silent Spring*.[7] For Larsen, the natural world continues to be the site of spiritual and moral contemplation and of responsibility.

The composer felt welcomed and nurtured by the natural world but for the most part not by the academy. Too often a stronghold of aesthetic groupthink and gendered policies and practices for much of the twentieth century, the university was no place for strong-willed female composition students. Larsen didn't fit any of the models. On occasion the institution advised against her inclusive aesthetic. Larsen's omnivorous musical appetites and her refusal to hew to a single style resulted in more than one warning that she'd never succeed unless she reined herself in; and here gender had nothing to do with it. The composer recalled a graduate school theory teacher, Dorothy Gross, who believed that her music couldn't survive because the "work was too eclectic."[8] A few years later, in 1980, Larsen's stylistic heterogeneity disturbed Joseph Horowitz. In a *New York Times* review of *Ulloa's Ring*, Horowitz commented that "despite the recurrence of motivic cells, the structure and style of the piece ultimately eluded this listener."[9] Of course Larsen was not interested in *a* "style," and the form would emerge from the needs of the idea, not be imposed by a ready-made structure. By the end of the century, eclecticism seemed to be no problem. In 1997 Todd E. Sullivan applauded Larsen's music as a "classical vernacular stylistic amalgam."[10]

Despite its reputation as an incubator for new ideas, university composition departments have too often been preserves for ensconced practices. This was the case at the turn of the twentieth century when newly established U.S. music departments imported and then perpetuated nineteenth-century German ideals, and it was the case at the end of the twentieth century when high-modernist, midcentury values held sway well beyond their natural expiration dates. Too often what masqueraded as high-minded, modernist aesthetics was little more than an updated version of romantic notions of the composer as the isolated genius advancing the cause of music beyond the understanding of the uninitiated. Larsen confronted a version of this situation during her 1990 Illinois residency, but she could have experienced it elsewhere as well. Although she has always acknowledged that there is a place for acoustic research and specialists' music, she flatly rejects the idea that cutting-edge sound experiments are the only valuable musical practice or perspective. For those inside the academy, there is a lot at stake preserving the status quo—faculty lines, dedicated studio space, equipment budgets, and prestige within rarified circles of practitioners—but the idea of a status quo is anathema to Larsen's understanding of music's purpose or to her larger sense of how to live a meaningful life. She demonstrated deep self-knowledge when she decided never to pursue a university position; she couldn't have fit. When Larsen presented an alternative model of the modern composer at the 1990 residency, her ideas were greeted with nothing less than moral panic. She threatened the culture that held sway; aesthetic preferences were cast in ethical terms. In 2015 the entire episode seems almost quaint.

Regardless of her rocky relationship with the academy, Larsen learned important lessons there, and they continue to impact her work as a composer. In an interview in late 2015 Larsen reflected on the influence of her composition teachers. Regarding Dominick Argento, Larsen observed: "I wouldn't say he was ever my mentor, but I studied his orchestration, and he was a great orchestration teacher. He always wrote for performance, never just as a theoretical exercise." And Larsen does likewise. She confided that she still thinks of Paul Fetler "every time [she puts] too much on the page," adding, "He was a great teacher for beginning composers. I learned that less is more and how to balance unity and variety, tension and release."[11] A number of

Larsen's most moving pieces are remarkable for their spare scores. She had a couple of lessons with Eric Stokes; his "eclectic aesthetic that embraced fluxus, dada, post-fluxus" reinforced her inclination to be ecumenical in her musical thinking. Vern Sutton, Larsen explained, is someone she still thinks about a lot and whom she credits with having enormous influence not only on her but on composers throughout the area. She spoke of his broad musical abilities and his generosity, humility, and integrity, as well as his scholarly approach to projects. More than one of Larsen's collaborators commented upon the extensive research she undertakes educating herself about her subjects. From consulting experts, to reading everything she can find, to trying to get as close as she can to simulating her subjects' experiences, Larsen is driven to get inside her materials, to become her subject, and Sutton provided an encouraging model of how to do this.

At a time when women academic models were scarce, Donna Cardamone-Jackson provided Larsen with that rare specimen. Forty years after they worked together, Larsen's gratitude is audible:

> Donna Cardamone-Jackson took me on as her TA. Imagine the risk she took as a new untenured faculty member! For two or three years I worked with her as she taught courses on Stravinsky, 20th century music history, general lectures, and graduate level music history. I also took every graduate course she taught. From her I learned how to research, how to write well, how to hold my own in an academic conversation, how to manage time, how to make drip coffee, how to cook Italian food, and how to be comfortable in my own skin as a professional woman. She always treated me as a colleague.[12]

While Larsen was still a student, and before *entrepreneurial* was a buzzword, she honed her skills cofounding the Minnesota Composers Forum with Stephen Paulus. She and Paulus imagined that building the forum would be similar to composing a symphony: both were large forms designed to endure, and their structures needed to be strong but flexible enough to contain a range of creative possibilities. In the first decade of its existence, with Larsen as the daily administrator, the forum found financial partners, awarded individual grants to composers, underwrote regional concerts, built relationships with community organizations, published the *Minnesota Composers Forum Newsletter*, and created a record label, Innova Recordings. After Larsen was named co-resident composer of the Minnesota Orchestra she left her position with the forum and focused her energies on composition. But she admits that it was very difficult to let go: "I had a hard time."[13]

A few years after turning over the reins, she learned that the forum would change its name. The composer explained: "When Keith Bradshaw showed up at my door to tell me in person that the name of the Minnesota Composers Forum had been changed to the *American* Composers Forum, I just thought, Minnesota is not a *place*; *it's a state of being*. It's a state of mind—creative, constructive, cooperative. And when that happened . . . I thought that it was really gone."[14] For Larsen the original name announced not only what the Forum *was* but what it *was not*. Larsen explained, "In my mind, it was not New York, nor did it want to be New York. And I know many, many, many New Yorkers, who would like to be Minnesota." Larsen credits her husband with helping her let go and understanding that "when leaders change then two things can happen: the [founder] can really get in the way and ruin everything, or they can enjoy the ways that new leadership is taking the organization."[15] She decided to walk away and watch.

Under the leadership of Linda Hoeschler, the executive director from 1991 to 2003, and John Nuechterlein, who has been at the helm since then, the American Composers Forum has raised its profile, secured ongoing funding, and expanded its reach. As Hoeschler explained, it provides composers with the opportunity to have their music heard. She reflected: "I think [the ACF] continues to be successful . . . because it keeps coming up with new ways to do it."[16]

In a video celebrating the fortieth anniversary of the forum, Larsen, Hoeschler, Nuechterlein, Carol Barnett (one of the original student founders of MCF), and a variety of contemporary composers associated with the forum reflect on what the organization has done, is doing, and where it is headed. It is hard not to notice that of the ten composers interviewed, eight of them are women.[17] The forum appears not to have a problem with women who compose. This is in contrast to the number of women composers with positions in university faculties, where percentages hover around 15 percent.[18] The forum's reach continues to expand: in November 2015 ACF sent an artist delegation to Havana, Cuba, to participate in the Festival de Música Contemporánea de La Habana (Havana Contemporary Music Festival). Larsen's creative, constructive, and cooperative organization is still thriving and providing opportunities for composers on a scale that not even she imagined. What had started as a Minnesota state of mind is now a hemispheric one.

Gender continues to influence how Larsen thinks and works and the projects she takes on. It is thoroughly interwoven in compositions that often focus on nature or family or religion as well. Being with Larsen for any extended period of time only illuminates the ways gender impacts daily life; the personal and professional lives are nested within each other. With a few exceptions, our interviews regularly took place in Larsen's home, in her living room or seated at her kitchen table; over the years the kitchen became the preferred place. Unintentionally we gravitated to this traditionally female-gendered domestic space.[19] We would sit looking out on her backyard, which was filled with greenery and flowers in the blooming season and covered in white the rest of the year. The garden is a favorite place where Larsen takes pleasure in digging in the soil, in weeding and planting. With no off-site office to sequester her work from her daily routines, the two are intimately interwoven. Signs of musical activities are all around, on tables, walls, on the piano, in the third-floor office, in neat stacks on the floor, on shelves in the basement. There's no mystery why a listener can hear her life in her music; they are inseparable. Being in her home is being in her music.

On one occasion during an interview, the composer excused herself to take her mother to a doctor's appointment. She had anticipated the interruption, however, and presented me with two large boxes of photos that I was free to look through while she was gone. Larsen returned about ninety minutes later, and we resumed our conversation without missing a beat. The vertical time she had discovered as a new mother served her well as she tended her parents.[20] During another conversation, preparations for that evening's book club meeting, which she was hosting, meant that the doorbell rang a number of times with various people dropping off food, flowers, or wine. Larsen greeted each person and received what they'd brought, and then we continued our conversation. On a third occasion, prospective collaborators—a dancer and a physicist—arrived at her front door fresh from the airport. Larsen and her assistants had prepared the dining room for their work the day before by pushing back all the furniture and covering the windows with blackout curtains. They needed space to rehearse a possible sequence for *A Wrinkle in Time* that involved the dancer moving across the width of the room while interrupting sound-producing light signals. When the dancer requested some kind of flexible objects that she could weave through her hair to randomly break the light signal, Larsen charged to her office supplies cabinet and returned with a fistful of eighteen-inch plastic spiral coils, the kind she used to bind oversized scores, and the dancer proceeded to create the ultimate deely bobber; antennae quivered and bounced in all directions. Caretaking, problem solving, and juggling work and dozens of distractions are Larsen's modus operandi, as it is with many professional women. Like Ives, the fabric of Larsen's life weaves itself whole.

Technology has supported and facilitated Larsen's career, and not just in her composing work. She discovered the importance of media as she and Paulus advertised forum events and learned how to get the word out. When the internet first emerged, she worked with Jeff Crane, a University of Minnesota voice student, to design libbylarsen.com; she secured its domain name July 9, 1999, and it debuted shortly afterward. The kind of advertising that academia provides music faculty via departmental Web pages, concert announcements, focus stories, special features in university publications or over university-owned radio and television stations, specialized publicity offices, and the all-important easily accessed contact information is not automatically enjoyed by freelancers. Papers, documents, and various resources collected by universities in their libraries and special collections are not immediately available to unaffiliated contemporary composers or artists. Freelancers can be invisible. They need to be their own agents, archivists, publicists, and promoters. Larsen and her assistants have built on Crane's original work, and in 2015 the team set about redesigning the site "to be interactive by today's standards—plus some."[21]

When Larsen talked about her original motivations for a Web site, she explained that "it was for a gendered reason; it actually *was* for a gendered reason," and then she clarified:

> At that point in time . . . you couldn't find women composers in the Dewey Decimal system under their names, or under "composer." You had to look for "women" subcategory "composer." . . . I just thought that the archival system of the monastery is one that has not been accessible to women. That's a thousand-year-old tradition. So I just thought, fine: I'm going to build my own library. This is new. So when we built [the original site] our first vision was that it's a cathedral with chapels. And then that morphed into it's a resource library with a gift shop.[22]

Larsen's reference to monasteries, cathedrals, and chapels testifies to the lingering power of her early religious training and its imagery. Technology, gender, and religion may appear to be strange bedfellows, but for Larsen there's a natural connection.

Larsen is an acoustic composer, but she has regularly argued for and used electronically created and manipulated ("processed") sounds and various kinds of media in her compositions. She works with engineers and electroacoustic composers to realize her multimedia projects and always in a collaborative relationship, listening to others ideas, describing what she imagines, imagining new possibilities, and helping to shape the result.[23] In 1995 Larsen worked with Tim Stiles on *Western Women*.[24] The chamber-sized score included a sampler. In 2005 Tom Mudge helped her with sound manipulation in *Now I Pull Silver*. But since the early 1980s, her most frequent technical collaborator is Russell Borud, a Saint Paul–based recording engineer who has overseen the sound on several of Larsen's recordings. Larsen embraces the possibilities of technology and regards it, as she explained in her 1997 talk at NASM, as another instrument in the modern orchestra. She advocates for its use across styles and genres, and as with the 2014 *Wrinkle in Time* production debacle, has suffered because of its integral presence in her works, which sometimes creates insurmountable problems.

When asked to talk in a general way about the sources of her eclectic musical aesthetic, Larsen went straight to her American roots. What emerged was the realization that Larsen couldn't have become any other kind of composer being born where and who she was. She explains:

> If I were to draw a line backwards in American music from my own esthetic to its roots, I'd reference a lively conversation between one of my office associates, Grace Edgar, and me. We were discussing definitions of American music and its roots. My perspective was grounded in the effects of electricity on the Western European Leipzig tradition, American Tin Pan Alley, and Non–Western European music traditions. Grace suggested the idea of looking at American composers associated with the Western European Leipzig tradition and drawing lines backwards from their work to late nineteenth-/early twentieth-century American masters. She placed composers in either what she called the "Copland pile" or the "Ives pile," both of them concerned with notation. Given this perspective, I'd say that my own line goes backwards through John Cage, Carl Stalling, and Edgard Varèse to Ives. I think of these four composers in particular, as composers who heard the world. Really listened to the world, and integrated sound and time in a way that *is* sound and time, in a way that is directly communicative and very abstract: deeply abstract. But it's inseparably twined with another, non-notated line I learned by ear as a child through radio, TV, and records: Chuck Berry, Burl Ives, Big Mama Thornton, Little Orley, Billie Holiday, and Louis Armstrong.
>
> Stalling is so associated with visuals, but I love to listen to his music without visuals. And what I hear is sound bites, and they're not necessarily representative of anything. A Hawaiian guitar is a Hawaiian guitar, and it's a sound bite. And I hear Carl Stalling working with the sounds that are in the world within his own form. It's not collage; it's Stalling. You can put Porky Pig in it, but you don't need to; it's as if he's always walking down the street and listening. It's [like] Ives; only it uses technology mixed with acoustic sound. He was a genius, a genius. Totally original.[25]

When Larsen reflected on Ives, she focused on his sense of time and tied it to Transcendentalist thinking, a product of his nineteenth-century New England background. She recognized that standardized time didn't take hold until later, and then it was driven by commercial, not aesthetic forces. She observed that Ives could live in both worlds and did, and so does Larsen. She is grateful to Johannes Riedel for introducing her to Ives: "I think it was the way he would describe Ives. Whenever he talked about Ives, it always made sense to me. It just made sense. It just *makes* sense. When I listen to Ives, I feel like I'm embodied and moving through all the perspectives while I'm listening to it." She responded viscerally to the way Ives could put her in a place. "I'm not in the Copland pile" she concluded. "My sensibility is Ives."[26]

Varèse invited Larsen to think about sound and, together with Ives, about how sound comes at a listener and envelopes and moves around her. She embraced the limitlessness of Varèse's imagination. Cage forced the question: what is music? Together the four American composers confirmed what Larsen already knew about herself: She lived in the whole world of music—acoustic, electronic, abstract, programmatic, high art, and popular—and she would bring them together in her work.

Larsen's US American identity is seldom discussed separate from her democratic artistic sensibilities and then most especially in relation to her use of vernacular sources, their rhythms, and her musicalization of American English. But in fact Larsen's Americanness undergirds all aspects of her being, starting with her attachment to her upper Midwest American home. It also manifests itself in her valuation of the individual—a person outside the crowd, on the margins. Besides being optimistic, outgoing, and direct, qualities often associated with an essentialized view of Americans, Larsen assumes personal freedom as a given: her right as an individual to design and pursue the life she wants, to "step out of line" to achieve her goals if that's what it takes.

She also believes that the arts play a central role in society, that they speak to and for a society, and that they are essential to the health of a society. To that end she understands the relationship between the arts and economics and rejects the idea that artists should gift their work or be happy with appreciation and applause. There's a strong pragmatic streak in the idealistic composer: She expects to be paid for making music and has created a framework and a system where she is.

But perhaps as important as the foregoing qualities, what might mark Larsen as US American more than anything else is her recognition of the importance of individuals within communities. This idea, a recurring theme in discussions by American historians whose specialties range from Puritan practices, to utopian societies, to cowboy culture, provides the overriding framework for understanding Larsen's worldview.[27] Whether interacting with her family or in the relationships she forms with her collaborators, Larsen naturally operates as a member of a community rather than as an isolated individual. The young girl who organized a cross-country team and then cofounded the Minnesota Composers Forum, and who now sits on boards and councils of multiple organizations, foundations, and agencies is most fully herself when she brings Larsen, the individual, to any communal effort. This quality reflects in her understanding of her place within the natural world.

* * *

A biography that relies heavily on personal interactions and conversations with a subject may be especially vulnerable to that person's performance of herself or himself and to reporting the story she or he wants to be told. How has Larsen performed Larsen over the seven-year period of our interactions? How has she consciously or unconsciously shaped, selected, or edited the persona she presents? What are a biographer's safeguards against becoming simply the puppet of a masterful ventriloquist? Of course, the carefully selected and preserved letters and documents of a long-deceased person can present just as selective a portrait, and in that case the absence of the subject eliminates any opportunity to expand or correct one's understanding or reconcile contradictory versions of the person through ongoing observations. Whether a subject is present or absent, biographers, like all historians, need corroborating evidence, and then they must trust their own vision.

Observing the composer over a period of years interacting with family members, multiple assistants, her friends, long-term associates, her collaborators, a number of performers, audience members, a variety of students, the proprietor of a local bookstore, wait staff at neighborhood restaurants, and young teachers at what had been her elementary school has given me an eyewitness perch, and a picture has emerged of a woman comfortable in her skin. Larsen is consistently Larsen: the same person in running clothes or concert dress. If she is performing a persona, she and it have melded.

Photographs of Larsen from over a sixty-year period, both candid and posed, are another way of understanding Edel's "figure under the carpet." With the exception of obligatory elementary school pictures taken by a photographer tasked with providing snapshots for proud parents to carry in their wallets, hundreds of pictures of Larsen capture the multifaceted composer I have come to know: a reflective, intelligent, ambitious, focused, optimistic, energetic, and joyful person.

Ultimately, however, a biography that doesn't offer some insights into what drives an individual fails in its duty to illuminate a subject's actions and achievements beyond their mere occurrence. What drives Libby Larsen today, and is it the same as what drove her in 1973 or 1990? What explains her seemingly limitless vitality? Is her inexhaustible energy a symptom of some undiagnosed condition like hyperactivity? The composer expressed her dismay that were she a child today, she'd likely be medicated to calm her down. Is her generosity, especially when it comes to sharing her time, the sign of a need for approval, or being liked, or the desire for power? Is her creative fecundity evidence of a fundamental fear that if she stops composing she will cease to be, or perhaps worse, be forgotten? Or are such readings only the most recent updates on the crazy woman in the attic trope, the stock character eccentric female, the amiable, dotty aunt with an artistic streak who must be pathologized? In a much-lauded study on exuberance by the MacArthur Award–winning clinical psychologist Kay Redfield Jamison, the author suggests another reading.

> Exuberance is an abounding, ebullient, effervescent emotion. It is kinetic and unrestrained, joyful, irrepressible. It is not happiness, although they share a border. It is instead, at its core, a more restless, billowing state. Certainly it is no lulling sense of contentment: exuberance leaps, bubbles, and overflows, propels its energy through troop and tribe. It spreads upward and outward, like pollen toted by dancing bees, and in this carrying ideas are moved and actions taken.[28]

Jamison traces the word *exuberance* to its Latin roots and the concept of fruitful, abundance. "At its core," Jamison explains, is "a concept of fertility." When applied to nature exuberance "is defined by lush, profuse, riotous growth; it is an overflowing, opulent, and copious abundance."[29] More than one of Larsen's collaborators commented upon feeling as if they were in the presence of an intense force of nature. And after years working with the composer, I understand the analogy.

The child who needed to be heard still has lots to say, but now she has as many opportunities to speak as she wants. She can pick and choose her forums. Beyond a surplus of energy, Larsen enjoys an abundance of musical giftedness, curiosity, and creativity. She combines confidence with a continuing concern for confirmation. She learned the habit of generosity from the sisters at Christ the King and takes pleasure in being able to give, because it's the right way to be. But she is also generous because it puts her in contact with people, and as much as Larsen relishes a quiet moment to dive deep, she also needs to be in the thick of things. Her belief that music is a social activity grows naturally from her understanding of her place in the world: both are parts of a larger endeavor whose purpose is to improve our common lot. The sisters' lessons continue to resonate. Larsen composes because it is who she is and what she does. She can't help herself. And it turns out that many thousands of musicians and music lovers, and not a few scholars, are grateful that's the case. As Larsen might say: *Onward!*

Notes

Preface: An Inauspicious Beginning

1. See Edel, "Art of Biography."

2. I first came upon this phrase in Nancy Milford's book *Zelda*, where Milford talks about the individual perspectives of Scott and Zelda Fitzgerald: "Both of the Fitzgeralds would corrupt and alter the story by seeing it through their private angles of vision" (224). For a better-known use of the phrase, see Doris Kearns, "Angles of Vision."

3. Stanley, *Auto/Biographical I*, 155.

4. In our first telephone conversation dedicated specifically to the biography, April 16, 2012, Larsen excitedly closed with "Oh Denise, what a journey is ahead!"

5. See Edel, "Figure under the Carpet," 16. In addition to writing the Pulitzer Prize–winning biography on Henry James, Leon Edel wrote extensively on the practice of biography.

6. There are, of course, exceptions, but women who were not queens, empresses, or politically powerful by dint of their associations were largely invisible.

7. April 16, 2012, telephone conversation with the composer.

8. Lisle, *Portrait of an Artist*, 334.

9. April 16, 2012, telephone conversation with the composer.

10. For one of many uses of the phrase "muse of the jazz age" to describe Zelda Fitzgerald, see http://www.flapperjane.com/July%20August/zelda.htm. Accessed June 17, 2014.

The 2014 feature film *Big Eyes* told a related story. Painter Margaret Keane ultimately proved she was the artist responsible for the "Big Eyes" pictures claimed by her husband, Walter Keane. The difference between the Fitzgeralds and the Keanes is that both F. Scott and Zelda were accomplished people.

11. In the same decade, the composer Pauline Oliveros more fully embraced and lived her lesbian sexual identity.

12. See Heilbrun, *Writing a Woman's Life*, xvi.

13. Ibid., 31.

14. In November 2012, Libby Larsen had two assistants, Grace Edgar and Toni Lindgren. Each person worked about twenty hours per week maintaining Larsen's Web site, researching sources for current projects, proofing her scores, and answering requests for information, permissions, materials, and music.

15. Kearns, "Angles of Vision," 91, 103.

16. In a conversation March 28, 2009, the composer remarked upon the central-ness of her Upper Midwest perspective and her sense that she could, figuratively, look out in every direction across the nation and Canada. "Groupthink" is a term first used by Yale psychologist Irving Janus in the 1970s to describe the practice of consensus thinking among otherwise intelligent people that results in unintended and avoidable consequences. For a history of the term, see Lassila, "Brief History of Groupthink."

17. Personal conversation with the composer, November 12, 2012.

18. Edel, "Art of Biography."

19. Larsen, *Songs from Letters*, unnumbered page.

Prologue: A Polyphonic Life

1. I am grateful to Michael Broyles for his references to LaRue and Reese. See Broyles, *Emergence and Evolution*, 5; LaRue, *Guidelines for Style Analysis*, vii; and Reese, *Music in the Renaissance*, xiii. Reese comments: "If there were such a thing as polyphony in prose, it would obviously be a godsend to the writer of history, whatever it might be to the reader."

2. Charles Ives quoted in Bellamann, "Charles Ives," 48.

Chapter 1. Libby Larsen and the Cultural Moment

1. Libby Larsen visited Florida State University as a guest of a doctoral musicology seminar led by the author. The referenced remark was part of comments Larsen made May 1, 2014: "I try to understand what was it that made 1950, well 1948 to 1962, so radical. Which in my mind is the most radical portion of that century; and it was government."

2. Telephone conversation with the composer, April 16, 2012.

3. There are numerous online sites that speak to the Cuban missile crisis. For a discussion of Kennedy's address and a timeline of events, see "Kennedy Announces Blockade."

4. Larsen spoke passionately about the first draft lottery in a personal conversation May 1, 2014.

5. Larsen's piece was one way to make Carson's message her own.

6. The Levitt brothers could build thirty four-room houses each day, thanks to a method that divided "the construction process into 27 different steps from start to finish." Levittown was followed by a number of other developments in Pennsylvania and New Jersey. See Rosenberg, "Levittown."

7. I'm grateful to Larsen for suggesting the connection between military and academic cultures, which I would not have made on my own.

8. See "Doomsday Clock." Martyl Langsdorf, an artist and the wife of Alexander Langsdorf, a scientist who had worked on the Manhattan Project, created the clock image for the *Bulletin of Atomic Scientists*.

9. Telephone conversation with the composer, April 16, 2012.

10. For a chronology of readings of the Doomsday Clock, see "Doomsday Clock: Timeline." The clock began as a measure of nuclear danger; today it also reflects the threat of environmental disaster.

11. The use of the word *merely* is not intended to minimize the personal devastation wrought by accusations of Communist sympathies slung by Senator McCarthy. It would take until December 2, 1954, for the US Congress to condemn McCarthy's conduct as "inexcusable," "reprehensible," "vulgar and insulting," conduct "unbecoming a senator." In the four years of McCarthy's investigations, two thousand government employees lost their jobs, and hundreds of careers and lives were ruined by his innuendo and accusations. A disproportionate number of his victims came from the arts, film, and entertainment industries. Beyond Communist sympathizers, a second group targeted by McCarthy was homosexuals. See "McCarthy-Welch Exchange."

12. See "Alan Freed Biography."

13. RCA Victor introduced the 45 in 1949 as a cheaper and less space-consuming alternative to the larger twelve-inch 33 1/3 vinyl disc unveiled by Columbia in 1948.

14. Jack Weinberg, a graduate-student leader of the Free Speech Movement at UC Berkeley, uttered this remark to a reporter for the *San Francisco Chronicle* who had implied that student unrest was being covertly incited by Communists. Weinberg insisted that it wasn't Communists but all those who had political power: generally those over thirty. Weinberg didn't intend the phrase to sum up the entirety of his feelings, but it was quickly adopted and crystallized the sense of fear and distrust a younger generation felt toward its elders. See *Daily Planet* staff, "Don't Trust Anyone over 30."

15. *All in the Family* (1971–79) was the first television sitcom that presented fully human (still all white) characters wrestling with real contemporary issues; bigotry was a recurring theme throughout the series. *The Cosby Show* (1984–92) was the first series that portrayed an upper-middle-class, professional, African American family. Although the show never engaged in edgy conversations, from time to time the five children in the Huxtable family introduced serious issues. Although Henry Louis Gates admitted to liking the show, in an article that appeared in the *New York Times,* November 12, 1989, he criticized it for suggesting that America's racial problems had been solved. Gates objected to the series for suggesting that it was "well, truly representative." See Gates, "TV's Black World Turns."

16. See https://www.socialexplorer.com/explore/maps for statistics on the 1950 racial makeup of Minneapolis, accessed June 15, 2015.

17. For the text and signatories of the manifesto, see "Southern Manifesto" at *Kdentify*. For an article about manifesto, see "Southern Manifesto" in the March 26, 1956, issue of *Time* .

18. As the series of highly publicized police interactions with unarmed black youth and men in 2015 and 2016 has demonstrated, racism continues to exist, as do numerous practices that deny human beings equal rights on account of any

number of real or imagined differences. Laws that prohibit discrimination mean that many racist activities have become more clandestine and less easy to address or litigate against. Attitudes take more time to change than laws.

19. On February 1, 1960, a Woolworth store lunch counter in Greensboro, North Carolina, refused to serve four male African American college students. Their peaceful request spurred a wave of sit-ins at similar venues and on college campuses across the nation. May 1961 saw waves of black and white "Freedom Riders" board buses to force desegregation in the South. Buses were shot at and torched, and the peaceful passengers were dragged from the vehicles and beaten. Television cameramen, many of them suffering violent attack themselves, recorded the events. Broadcast of their footage on national television brought the realities of racial injustice to entire new audiences. October 1962 witnessed rioting as James Meredith, an African American male, entered the University of Mississippi escorted by federal marshals.

20. Among the most celebrated defectors in the arts were ballet dancers Rudolf Nureyev (1961), Natalia Makarova (1970), and Mikhail Baryshnikov (1974), and composer Maxim Shostakovich (1981). Athletes included figure skaters Ludmila Belousova and Oleg Protopopov (1979) and Gorsha Sur (1990); tennis player Martina Navratilova (1975); gymnast Nadia Comaneci (1989); and numerous chess, hockey, and football (soccer) players. For a well-cited list of East-to-West defectors from the 1940s to 1990, see http://en.wikipedia.org/wiki/List_of_Soviet_and_Eastern_Bloc_defectors, accessed June 20, 2014.

21. See David Mitchell's remarks expressed as Waldorf educational philosophy in "Essential Phases of Child Development."

22. Mississippi NAACP field secretary Medgar Evers (b. 1925) was murdered in his driveway on June 12, 1963; President John F. Kennedy (b. 1917) was assassinated November 22, 1963, while riding in a motorcade in Dallas; Muslim cleric and activist Malcolm X (b. 1925) was gunned down as he prepared to give a speech in Manhattan on February 21, 1965; minister and civil rights activist Martin Luther King (b. 1929) was killed April 4, 1968, the day after he gave his "I've been to the mountaintop" speech in Memphis; and two months later, on June 5, 1968, former senator and attorney general Robert F. Kennedy (b. 1925) was shot in Los Angeles moments after winning the California Democratic Primary—he died the next day.

23. Personal conversation with the composer, November 13, 2012.

Chapter 2. Larsen and Family: Needing to Be Heard

1. "Chatterbox" is Libby's description of herself. Personal conversation with the composer, May 1, 2014.

2. Personal conversation with the composer, November 12, 2012.

3. Ibid. Italicized words are those Larsen emphasized.

4. Larsen made this point in a May 2014 open forum at Florida State University.

5. Interview by Vivian Perlis, February 20, 1998, file 282a–c, Oral History of American Music, Yale University, New Haven, Conn.

6. Personal conversation with the composer, November 12, 2012.

7. See http://global.oup.com/academic/product/john-mirks-festial-9780199590377, accessed May 12, 2014. An edition of *John Mirk's Festial* based upon the British Library MS cotton Claudius A. II, vol. 2, was published in 2011 by Susan Powell, chair in Medieval Texts and Culture at the University of Salford.

8. Larsen never interpreted her parents' silencing techniques as being consciously driven by gendered thought. The senior Larsens abided by larger social behaviors and assumptions of what was appropriate, and church teachings reinforced society's practices.

9. Libby explained that her father was often addressed this way.

10. Personal conversation with the composer, November 12, 2012. All quoted passages in this paragraph come from this conversation.

11. Larsen used the phrase "golden boy" to describe the way her father was perceived during his early years at the Pillsbury Company. The young Dr. Larsen worked on methods of freezing yeast.

12. Personal conversation with the composer at her home, November 12, 2012. The italicized words indicate Larsen's spirited verbal emphasis. My addition of the words "in motion" is an attempt to describe the whirring sound that Libby made as she whirled her index finger next to her head.

13. Interview with Vivian Perlis, February 20, 1998.

14. Despite the different paths that Larsen's kindergarten classmates have taken over the decades, she has remained friends with several of them, and they see each other regularly around town. Her past is constantly visible in her present.

15. Personal conversation with the composer, November 12, 2012.

16. The Minnesota province of the Sisters of Saint Joseph of Carondelet is in Saint Paul. In 2014 approximately half of their fourteen thousand members were working in the United States. For a brief description of the Sisters of Saint Joseph of Carondelet, see http://www.csjalbany.org/, accessed July 5, 2014. For a more thorough discussion of the history of the order, see http://www.csjoseph.org/our_heritage.aspx, accessed July 10, 2014.

17. Personal conversation with the composer, November 12, 2012.

18. Ibid.

19. See http://libbylarsen.com/index.php?contentID=232 for Libby's posted answers to a number of commonly asked questions, accessed July 5, 2014. On this site Libby characterizes the removal of Gregorian chant as "a huge mistake . . . to move away from the Guidonian system to a rote, repetitive one."

20. Personal conversation with the composer, September 3, 2014.

21. Personal conversation with the composer, November 12, 2012.

22. http://libbylarsen.com/index.php?contentID=232, accessed July 5, 2014.

23. Personal conversation with the composer, November 12, 2012.

24. The information in this paragraph is a combination of Libby's remarks during a personal conversation and those she posted on her Web page: http://libbylarsen.com/index.php?contentID=232, accessed July 5, 2014. Personal conversation with the composer, November 12, 2012.

25. Personal conversation with the composer, November 12, 2012. Despite the regular drama acted out by student and teacher, it is clear from Larsen's recollections that she felt her teacher loved her.

26. Ibid. The italicized word "good" suggests Larsen's tone as she offered a qualified endorsement of Sister Rosanne.

27. Ibid.

28. In a personal conversation on November 13, 2012, Larsen proudly acknowledged that her sister Duffy "is the great sailor now. She's the one who made the choice to sail." The composer respects people who decide to do something and then do their best.

29. Interview with Vivian Perlis, February 20, 1998.

30. Ibid. Regarding Alice Larsen's taste for stride boogie, Larsen observes that her mother "went to Central High School in Saint Paul." She notes, "I think her ears were much more diverse, . . . so it wasn't white versions, it was not covers; it was authentic. Big difference."

31. Telephone conversation with the composer, April 16, 2012.

32. Personal conversation with the composer, November 13, 2012. A new and enlarged band shell has replaced the one that was there when Larsen was a child. Summer concerts still regularly take place there.

33. Larsen explained that *tuits* is her own made-up word. "Man the tuits" is a stand in for "all hands on deck, everyone to their posts, do your job, get it done."

34. Personal conversation with the composer, November 13, 2012.

35. Fuller, *Woman in the Nineteenth Century*, 174.

36. Personal conversation with the composer, November 12, 2012.

37. Personal conversation with the composer, November 13, 2012.

38. Personal interview with Alice and Bob Larsen, November 13, 2012, in Minneapolis.

39. Personal conversation with the composer, March 28, 2009.

40. I discuss this incident and its ramifications more fully in *Music and the Skillful Listener*, 243.

41. Larsen describes her family as "rawboned," and pictures of family members attest to their lean and spare physiques. Personal conversation with the composer, November 13, 2012.

42. Alice Larsen's father owned a business in Saint Paul selling automotive parts, so car culture, albeit a different aspect of it, was an integral part of her family life before she married Robert Larsen.

43. When I was speaking with the Larsens about the Thunderbird, Robert Larsen asked me if I was familiar with this piece. It was the only one of their daughter's hundreds of pieces that either parent named. It clearly occupied a special place in their memories. Personal conversation, November 13, 2012.

44. "Short Ride in a Fast Machine" is the name of a hugely popular fanfare for large orchestra written by composer John Adams and premiered by the Pittsburgh Symphony Orchestra in 1986.

45. The piece was recorded in Saint Paul, Minnesota, in 1987 on the Innova label, the record label of the Minnesota Composers Forum.

46. Larsen, *Four on the Floor*, unnumbered page preceding score.

47. See Bogdanov, *All Music Guide*, 234, for the characterization of Jerry Lee Lewis as "the Killer."

48. See score, p. 17. *Marcato* indicates a louder and more forceful attack on a note or chord. Larsen's comment suggests that she is more interested in the feeling of thrust than a particular pitch collection or chord.

Chapter 3. Larsen and Religion: The Tie That Binds

1. In her conversation with Vivian Perlis in 1998, Larsen clarified that she has "resisted writing sacred music in favor of writing spiritual music, because . . . [she couldn't] reconcile the church with the spirit easily." See: interview by Vivian Perlis, February 20, 1998, Oral History of American Music, Yale University, New Haven, Conn.

2. Personal conversation with the composer, November 12, 2012.

3. Telephone conversation with the composer, April 16, 2012.

4. Telephone conversation with the composer, September 3, 2014.

5. Rone, "'Voice Cries Out in the Wilderness,'" 10.

6. Ibid., 11.

7. Telephone conversation with the composer, September 3, 2014.

8. Personal conversation with the composer, September 10, 2014.

9. Biery, "New Music for Organ," 76.

10. Telephone conversation with the composer, September 3, 2014.

11. Ibid.

12. See "Marian Antiphons and Hymns" for a discussion of Marian antiphons and their use throughout the liturgical year. The Web site also includes audio files of "Alma Redemptoris Mater," "Ave Regina Caelorum," "Regina Coeli Lætare," and "Salve Regina," the four most famous Marian antiphons.

13. Telephone conversation with the composer, September 3, 2014.

14. Email correspondence from the composer, July 14, 2014.

15. Personal conversation with composer, November 12, 2012.

16. See the obituary for Rev. Duffy that appeared in the *Nebraska Register* ("Rev. James A. Duffy [obituary]").

17. Telephone conversation with the composer, September 3, 2014.

18. The event was especially traumatic for Alice Larsen, who feared that her daughter was condemning her soul to hell and that the marriage would not exist in the eyes of God. Personal conversation with the composer, November 13, 2012.

19. See Schnittke, "Polystylistic Tendencies in Modern Music."

20. Kent Kennan referred to the bassoon as "the clown of the orchestra" in his book *The Technique of Orchestration*, 89.

21. In this regard, the song *is* like chant where musical rhythms reflect those of the words.

22. See Souvay, "Elias," for a lengthy discussion of the prophet Elias.

23. See "Saint Teresa of Avila" for a brief characterization of the saint. Perhaps Larsen could identify with Saint Teresa's reception in a male-dominated world.

24. See *Saints without Tears*, by Libby Larsen, 13. The words enclosed in quotation marks are Larsen's instructions in the score.

25. Larsen acknowledges that her many uses of boogie-woogie suggest the influence of her mother, but they are not any kind of homage. Personal conversation with the composer, September 10, 2014.

26. In 1965 Steve Reich was inspired to write *It's Gonna Rain* based on the melodic quality of the streetside sermons of a black preacher, Brother Walter.

27. *Holy Roller* was premiered in 1997. See *Holy Roller*, "Composer's Note."

28. See Burkholder, *All Made of Tunes*, 137–266.

29. Ives used both "Shall We Gather at the River" and "God Be with You 'til We Meet Again" in his orchestral works. When in previous conversations I suggested to Libby that a number of her musical works reminded me of Ives, she was delighted.

30. See Larsen, *In a Winter Garden*, "Instrumentation," unnumbered page following title page.

31. Telephone conversation with the composer, September 3, 2014. Larsen talked especially of Sisters Marilyn and Leo Irene waging their individual battles with faith because of Vatican II.

32. Telephone conversation with Patricia Hampl, October 21, 2014. Hampl's Catholicism speaks in the pages of her many poetic memoirs, perhaps especially in *A Romantic Education* (1981), *Virgin Time: In Search of the Contemplative Life* (1992), and *The Florist's Daughter: A Memoir* (2007).

33. See Larsen, "Program Notes by Libby Larsen," in *In a Winter Garden*, unnumbered page following title page.

34. "Doomsday Clock: Timeline."

35. See "Program Notes by Patricia Hampl," in *In a Winter Garden*, unnumbered page.

36. "Patricia Hampl: 'The Florist's Daughter.'"

37. "Program Notes by Patricia Hampl," in Larsen, *In a Winter Garden*, unnumbered page.

38. Larsen instructs Sister to sing her line "dramatically." Larsen, *In a Winter Garden*, 7. All text is written by Patricia Hampl.

39. The "Christmas Rose," also known as the "Winter Rose" and the "Snow Rose," can withstand extremely cold temperatures making it especially valued in cold climates. See "Christmas Rose."

40. All quoted passages in this paragraph come from Hampl's text in *In a Winter Garden*.

41. See Von Glahn, *Music and the Skillful Listener*, 252–65.

42. Regarding "a *mass* for our times," see Larsen, "Program Notes," in *Missa Gaia* (1992). Larsen composed *Missa Gaia* as she was becoming increasingly aware of environmental and feminist issues and their potential connection. Italics are

mine. For "a modern treatment" and "the sum and summary," see *Catechism of the Catholic Church*, lines 1324 and 1327. Cardinal Jorge Mario Bergoglio, archbishop of Buenos Aires and cardinal of the Roman Catholic Church of Argentina, was elected to the papacy in March 2013. He took the name Francis, the first pope to do so.

43. From the transcript of "The Pope and the Sin of Environmental Degradation."

44. Ibid.

45. See White, "Historical Roots of Our Ecologic Crisis," for a thoughtful explanation of the complicity of Christianity in today's environmental condition.

46. See Larsen, Program Notes to *Missa Gaia*.

47. The "natural overtone series" has its basis in the sympathetic tones that result from striking any fundamental pitch on an acoustic instrument. The series of overtones occurs consistently and is explained by experiments first attributed to Pythagoras in the fourth century BC.

48. Larsen uses lines from Wendell Berry's poem "Closing the Circle."

49. Larsen, *Missa Gaia* (1995), unnumbered page.

50. Telephone conversation with the composer, September 3, 2014.

51. According to the *Merriam-Webster's Collegiate Dictionary*, a santo is "a painted or carved wooden image of a saint common especially in Mexico and the southwestern United States."

52. Larsen, *Rodeo Queen of Heaven*, composer's note. For a color photograph of the artwork, see Lopez, *Rodeo Reina del Cielo*.

53. Telephone conversation with the composer, September 3, 2014. I have italicized words that the composer emphasized in her speech.

54. Ibid.

55. Enhakē premiered *Rodeo Queen of Heaven* at Carnegie Hall, May 3, 2010. The group originated as a graduate student ensemble at the Florida State University College of Music in the first decade of the twenty-first century. At the premiere, enhakē included Wonkak Kim (clarinet), Brent Williams (violin), Jayoung Kim (cello), and Eun-hee Park (piano).

56. See Larsen, *Rodeo Queen of Heaven*, "Composer's Note."

57. Larsen, *Rodeo Queen of Heaven* (2010), 11.

58. Ibid., 35–36.

Chapter 4. Larsen and Nature: Tutoring the Soul

1. Personal conversation with the composer, September 10, 2014. Larsen's conflation of nature and religion and then of music and the sacred recalls arguments of the nineteenth-century Transcendentalists, and specifically of John Sullivan Dwight, who viewed all music as sacred. Larsen is familiar with both but arrived at her understanding free of reading about the group or its musical spokesperson.

2. Ibid.

3. Ibid. Italicized words suggest Larsen's spoken emphasis.

4. Larsen's gingko tree was a favorite of many who lived close to the park. When it toppled in a storm, a self-appointed salvage team cut it into pieces and distributed them among neighbors as reminders of this beloved tree. Larsen was given the *V* of a crook. In 2012 Larsen showed me where "her" tree had stood. Another gingko tree has been planted in its place.

5. Personal interview with the composer, March 28, 2009. Larsen is cognizant of nature having been gendered by others speaking about it—mother nature, mother earth—but she doesn't see one gender exerting control in the natural world. The ecological relationship requires all genders equally.

6. *Symphony: Water Music*, premiered in 1985, was one of Larsen's first sustained explorations of the medium of water in composition.

7. Personal conversation with the composer, November 13, 2012.

8. Email correspondence from the composer, November 25, 2008.

9. Personal conversation with the composer, September 10, 2014. The italicized phrase reflects the composer's emphasis in her speech.

10. Email correspondence from the composer, November 24, 2008.

11. Personal conversation with the composer, September 10, 2014. Larsen refers to Ms. Zukerman as "Genie," an indication of their close friendship.

12. The Schubert Club of Saint Paul goes back to 1882 and continues to support concerts by classical virtuosi from around the world, to offer lessons to children in the surrounding area, and to commission works by American composers. A number of Larsen's pieces have some connection to the Schubert Club, either through commissions or performances. See http://schubert.org/about/, accessed September 30, 2014.

13. "Notes on the Title," copy of the manuscript shared with me by the composer, September 2014. Italics added.

14. Quoted in an article by Merrie Leininger, "Alexandria Symphony Orchestra presents 'Atmosphere as a Fluid System,' by American composer Libby Larsen." April 28, 2010. See http://alexsym.blogspot.com/2010_04_01_archive.html. Accessed October 21, 2014.

15. Phone conversation with and follow-up email from Eugenia Zukerman, October 22, 2014.

16. Personal conversation with the composer, September 10, 2014.

17. The term *soundmark* comes from R. Murray Schafer's book *The Soundscape*, 274. Schafer's "soundmark" refers to "a community sound which is unique or possesses qualities which make it specially regarded or noticed by the people in that community."

18. Full breaks in the sound occur on only three occasions within the piece: around minutes 4:27, 6:25, and 8:46. Timings are approximate and keyed to the recording of the work that is available at libbylarsen.com.

19. *Niente* is one of Larsen's favorite instructions. She explains that she is seeking more than a quiet dynamic level. She seeks the disappearance, the evaporation of sound. It is more like the complete dissipation of an entity rather than a quieting of the entity.

20. She also boxes the gesture at its eighth iteration, when it is sounding simultaneously with a flute swirl. This occurs around 11:04 in the recording.

21. The elusiveness of an identifiable "structure or style of the piece" formed part of Joseph Horowitz's criticism of *Ulloa's Ring* when it premiered in New York, Saturday, October 11, 1980. See Horowitz, "Flute."

22. *Deep Summer Music*, composed in 1983, is another example of Larsen's music being inspired by her Minnesota home. See my essay "Musical Actions, Political Sounds."

23. See libbylarsen.com for a recording of Larsen's audio program note for a performance of *Aubade* at South Dakota State University, March 14, 1988, accessed October 9, 2014.

24. Larsen, *Aubade*. A composer's note typed on the page facing the first page of handwritten score. I am grateful to the composer, who shared a manuscript copy of the piece with me.

25. Phone conversation with Eugenia Zukerman, October 21, 2014.

26. Patricia Hampl, written response to questions regarding her collaboration with Libby Larsen on *In a Winter Garden*.

27. See Stevens, "Snow Man."

28. The concepts of "display piece" and "inward piece" are Larsen's own. She originally expressed these ideas in a personal conversation, March 28, 2009. For a fuller discussion, see my *Music and the Skillful Listener*, 244.

29. See Larsen, *Concerto: Cold, Silent Snow*.

30. Personal conversation with the composer, March 28, 2009.

31. Larsen, *Concerto: Cold, Silent Snow*. See also Bly, *News of the Universe*.

32. Bly, *News of the Universe*, 8–17. Bly traces the decline of the mysterious in nature to before the Christian era, so does not hold Descartes responsible for originating a nature-subjugating attitude. He also sees correspondences between the diminished roles of nature and of women. For one of the earliest and most thorough examinations of women~nature correspondences, see Ruether, *New Woman, New Earth:*.

33. Bly, *News of the Universe*, 2.

34. Ibid., 4. Italics are mine.

35. For information on the origins of the Good News Bible (Good News Translation), see https://www.biblegateway.com/versions/Good-News-Translation-GNT-Bible/, accessed October 20, 2014.

36. See Larsen, *Slow Structures*, "Composer's Note."

37. Northern Minnesota shares its border with the provinces of Manitoba and Ontario, Canada.

38. See Larsen, *Slow Structures*, "Composer's Note."

39. Ibid.

40. Larsen, "Program Note," in *Slow Structures for Flute, Violoncello and Piano*.

41. See Larsen, *Slow Structures*, "Composer's Note."

42. See Haryana, "How to Write an Object Poem."

43. Larsen, *Slow Structures*, "Composer's Note."

44. Larsen, "Program Note," in *Slow Structures for Flute, Violoncello and Piano.*

45. See Haryana, "How to Write an Object Poem."

46. Larsen, "Program Note," in *Slow Structures for Flute, Violoncello and Piano.*

47. Ibid. The Emerson and Longfellow poems are accessible online at http://www.poetryfoundation.org. Tomas Tranströmer (b. 1931) is a Nobel Prize–winning Swedish poet and psychologist whose work often focuses on nature, especially the long Swedish winters. His five-line poem "Snow-Melting Time, '66" appears in *Half-Finished Heaven*, 55.

48. "Ferociously" is Larsen's instruction to the instrumentalists.

49. "The frolic architecture of the snow" is the final line of Emerson's poem "The Snow-Storm."

50. These are Larsen's instructions to the instrumentalists.

51. Larsen, "Program Note," in *Slow Structures for Flute, Violoncello and Piano.*

52. The third movement consists of five eight-measure phrases with the final one extended by three measures. Its asymmetrical length joins the uneven measure lengths of the other movements: neither the movement lengths nor their forms are conventional. Consistent with her interest in the "mystical understanding of how time operates on us as human beings," Larsen devotes more time to slow tempi than is typical of traditional multimovement works.

53. The words *whitely*, *frozen*, *suspended*, and *shimmering* are Larsen's instructions to the instrumentalists on how to play their parts.

54. Merton, *Asian Journal of Thomas Merton*, 117. The most read and influential American Roman Catholic of the twentieth century, Merton (1915–68) speaks from within the religious tradition that trained Libby Larsen.

55. Tranströmer, "Snow-Melting Time, '66," 55.

56. See measure 17 in both movements.

57. The words in quotation marks are the composer's instructions to players.

58. Personal conversation with the composer, September 10, 2014.

59. Ibid. The italicized word reflects Larsen's verbal stress.

60. Larsen used Morse code in an earlier piece, *Marimba Concerto: After Hampton.* In that work she embedded the rhythm of dots and dashes for "save the rain forest" in the percussion part of the concerto.

61. Composer's remarks at an open forum at Florida State University, May 2, 2014.

62. Ibid.

63. The walleye is the Minnesota state fish; the loon is its bird; and the pink lady's slipper is the state flower.

Chapter 5. Larsen and the Academy Years: "My Soul Was Shaking"

1. In 1968, 536,100 American troops were on the ground in Vietnam. See "Vietnam War: Allied Troop Levels 1960–73."

2. See "Nov. 15, 1969 Anti-Vietnam War Demonstration Held."

3. Larsen has often described the university as "monastic." See her interview with Jennifer Kelly in Kelly, *In Her Own Words*, 309. In a personal interview on November 13, 2012, Larsen called the academy "a monastic encampment" and described composition as "a monastic art form: born in the monasteries."

4. Personal conversation with the composer, November 13, 2012. Larsen's full statement was "I have never felt vulnerable composing; never, not once."

5. Larsen used a variation on this phrase when describing her initial reaction to high school chorus, which I discuss later in the chapter.

6. Personal interview with the composer, November 13, 2012.

7. Telephone conversation with the composer, November 12, 2014.

8. Interview by Vivian Perlis, February 20, 1998, Oral History of American Music, Yale University, New Haven, Conn.

9. Ibid.

10. Larsen made this distinction at an open forum at Florida State University, May 2, 2014.

11. Telephone conversation with Eugenia Zukerman, October 21, 2014.

12. Open forum at Florida State University, May 2, 2014.

13. Ibid. Italics indicate those words that Larsen emphasized in speaking. In a published interview with Tina Milhorn-Stallard, Larsen also identified attending a performance of Rimsky-Korsakov's *Scheherazade* with her mother as another epiphanic moment. See Slayton, *Women of Influence in Contemporary Music*, 204.

14. Interview by Vivian Perlis, February 20, 1998.

15. See http://libbylarsen.com/index.php?contentID=232, accessed July 5, 2014.

16. Larsen worked at Clark Dodge, located in Minneapolis, in the summers before and after her senior year in high school.

17. Personal conversation with the composer, November 12, 2012.

18. Ibid.

19. Among the most recent *Tempest* progeny are Paul Moravec's Pulitzer Prize–winning chamber work, *Tempest Fantasy*, written in 2001–2, and Thomas Adès's 2004 opera, *The Tempest*.

20. Personal conversation with the composer, November 12, 2012.

21. Ibid.

22. Interview by Vivian Perlis, February 20, 1998.

23. Personal conversation with the composer, November 12, 2012.

24. It wouldn't be until the fourth daughter, Duffy, went away to Montana State University in Bozeman to study nursing that any of the Larsen girls attended schools other than the University of Minnesota.

25. Personal conversation with the composer, November 12, 2012. Robert Larsen's accompanying his daughter on her audition trip is curious given his commitment to her attending the University of Minnesota.

26. Personal conversation with Vern Sutton, November 11, 2012.

27. Telephone conversation with the composer, November 12, 2014.

28. In 1916 eleven existing chapters of SAI voted to build a cottage at the colony, and in 1919 it opened. See "MacDowell Colony."

29. Personal conversation with the composer, November 12, 2012. According to MacDowell Colony scholar Robin Rausch, "Spohnholz was listed as the General Director at the MacDowell Colony in the 1970s. Today MacDowell has an executive director and a resident director. It is not clear if Spohnholz was serving both those roles at this time." Personal email correspondence from Robin Rausch, November 21, 2014.

30. Personal conversation with the composer, November 12, 2012. It is telling of the gendered assumptions of the time that Larsen understood she would never be mistaken for a composer because of her sex.

31. The MacDowell Medal is awarded cyclically to practitioners of various arts; only every few years does it go to a composer.

32. In various interviews when Larsen has been asked about models of female composers, she has named Thea Musgrave and Pauline Oliveros, but neither of them fit her sense of who she wanted to be. Early in her young adulthood, Larsen determined that she wanted to be a composer, but she also wanted what her sisters had: children. She had to make her own model.

33. Personal conversation with the composer, November 12, 2012.

34. On different occasions Larsen has thought the instructor was Paul Fetler or Dominick Argento. The precise piece she composed is also unclear. In early conversations, Larsen thought the piece was *Circular Rondo*, but dates on that score put it at 1973, when she was enrolled as a master's student.

35. See Kelly, *In Her Own Words*, 305.

36. Personal conversation with the composer, November 12, 2012.

37. The two operas were *Lovers* and *Psyche and the Pskyscraper* based on O. Henry short stories. For a discussion of the genesis of these works, see Larsen's February 20, 1998, interview with Vivian Perlis.

38. Personal conversation with the composer, November 12, 2014.

39. Johannes Riedel (1913–1996) was director of graduate studies 1960–1981. He was one of Larsen's first champions in the music school and a beloved mentor who studied, wrote about, and taught the music of Charles Ives.

40. It is possible that Larsen's late admission meant that assistantships had already been decided.

41. Personal conversation with the composer, November 12, 2012.

42. Interview by Vivian Perlis, February 20, 1998.

43. Donna Cardamone Jackson taught musicology at the University of Minnesota from 1969 until 2007, when she retired. She was a scholar of sixteenth-century Italian vocal music and an ideal mentor for a young composer so predisposed to the voice.

44. Personal conversation with the composer, November 12, 2012.

45. Ibid.

46. Personal conversation with the Vern Sutton, November 11, 2012.

47. For the most infamous statement of this position, see Babbitt, "Who Cares If You Listen." Although the title was not Babbitt's own, the attitude reflected in it represented that of many composers and academic composition programs. Whether the article created, widened, or simply acknowledged the gulf that existed between modern, high-art composers and audiences is impossible to know.

48. Personal conversation with Vern Sutton, November 11, 2012.

49. Personal conversation with the composer, November 12, 2012.

50. Larsen has also used "M. K. Dean," a name printed on a coffee mug that she purchased at a neighborhood yard sale. Larsen's third alias is Aldine Humphries. In an interview with Deborah Crall, Larsen described Humphries's texts as "just verg[ing] on cheesy, with humor." See Crall, "Context and Commission," 278.

51. Personal conversation with the composer, November 13, 2012.

52. Van mentored Larsen on the technical possibilities of the guitar.

53. The oboe part is playable on a variety of treble winds, including flute, B-flat clarinet, or alto saxophone.

54. The statement of purpose is taken from the official articles of incorporation that the Minnesota Composers Forum submitted to the state on February 25, 1975. Papers were officially filed March 19, 1975.

55. Interview by Vivian Perlis, February 20, 1998.

56. Ibid.

57. Stephen Schultz was a professor of music education at the University of Minnesota from 1970 to 2000.

58. Interview by Vivian Perlis, February 20, 1998.

59. Ibid.

60. Anthony, review.

61. Interview by Vivian Perlis, February 20, 1998.

62. Ibid. Larsen referred to this incident in her interview with Perlis. The male-dominated composition world and larger patriarchal society rendered such behavior commonplace. Larsen's gender and diminutive stature frequently drew patronizing remarks and interactions from male faculty. Given Stephen Paulus's gender and height, no one would have (or could have) considered patting him on the head. Physical realities can exacerbate gendered interactions.

63. Personal conversation with Vern Sutton, November 11, 2012.

64. For a brief history of the MCF and its later-day incarnation as the American Composers Forum, see "In the Key of Now."

65. Interview by Vivian Perlis, February 20, 1998. Larsen heard one performance of the opera before heading to New York City for a summer trip.

66. E. B. (Elwyn Brooks) White (1899–1985) was an American writer best known for his contributions to the *New Yorker*; his many children's books including *Stuart Little* (1945), *Charlotte's Web* (1952), and *The Trumpet of the Swan* (1970); the collection of essays *One Man's Meat*; and the writer's guide *Elements of Style*, which he revised after the death of William J. Strunk. See "E. B. White Biography."

67. Libby Larsen quoted in Vaughan, "We're Bullish on Libby," 41.

68. At this point in our conversation, Larsen pantomimed the common hand gestures for "see no evil, hear no evil, speak no evil." November 12, 2012.

69. Larsen quoted in Vaughan, "We're Bullish on Libby," 41.

70. Quoted in Burr, "Bard of the Barn." The "Blue Hill Fair" refers to a yearly fair that took place in Blue Hill, Maine, close to where White had a summer home.

71. Personal conversation with the composer, April 28, 2015. At a recent performance of Argento's opera *Postcard from Morocco* (Tallahassee, May 30, 2015), I was struck by Argento's exquisite movement from a guitar passage to a tenor vocalist's line. The two timbres seemed to grow in and out of each other. Larsen had created a similarly sensitive and seamless motion from a tenor vocalist's line to a sitar passage in her *O Magnum Mysterium*, a piece I discuss in the chapter on Larsen and technology.

72. Personal conversation with Vern Sutton, November 11, 2012.

73. Yeats, "Brown Penny." This poem is in the public domain.

74. Yeats had attended séances, so he had personal experience with what he wrote into his play.

75. The phrases "bad old man," "the chief representative . . . ," and "his brain had gone" come from Yeats, "Words upon the Windowpane," 158–71.

76. See Auden, "Yeats as an Example."

77. Interview by Vivian Perlis, February 20, 1998.

78. Vern Sutton commented that an archival film was made of the university production. I have not viewed it.

79. Interview by Vivian Perlis, February 20, 1998.

80. Telephone conversation with the composer, February 25, 2015.

81. Although *Sprechstimme* was not a popular vocal technique in the 1970s, all aspects of Schoenberg's compositional practices, methods, and theories, including twelve-tone techniques, were widely taught at the time, and Larsen learned them.

82. See "History," *Minnesota Opera*, for more on the Minnesota Opera and Dominick Argento's role in its early days.

83. Interview by Vivian Perlis, February 20, 1998.

84. Ibid.

85. In 1889, trading on Myra Maybelle (or Belle) Shirley Starr's (1848–89) then recent unsolved murder, Richard K. Fox published a dime novel titled *Bella Starr, the Bandit Queen, or, the Female Jesse James*. It was the first of a number of books, movies, television series, and musical works referencing the oft-married mother of two, who was a close friend of Jesse James. See http://www.tshaonline.org/handbook/online/articles/fstbl, accessed December 17, 2014.

86. Telephone conversation with the composer, February 25, 2015.

87. Ibid.

88. Ibid.

89. The composer's note appears at the bottom of the typed title page of Larsen's handwritten score.

90. The first statement of Larsen's melodic line contains a single repeated pitch C before all twelve tones are sounded. The second iteration goes through all twelve

pitches without repeating any. Beginning in the second half of measure 14, however, the mezzo line ceases to bend to twelve-tone rules. It is at this point that H.D.'s repeating text suggests a more repetitive musical line. Starting at measure 17, at the lines "I am swept back" the mezzo seems sucked into a whirlpool of circling pitches.

91. H.D. lines include: "So for your arrogance / So for your ruthlessness."

92. As with many of Larsen's vocal lines, what looks like a difficult rhythmic setting is actually Larsen following the accent patterns of words.

93. See "Margaret Atwood's Orpheus and Eurydice Cycle."

94. In 1976, her second year in the doctoral program and the year after she married, Larsen sought out a therapist. As the composer put it, she "needed to learn how to live more truthfully as herself." Perhaps *Eurydice* is the result of Larsen acknowledging her anger at all that had tried to stifle her over the years. Personal conversation with the composer, September 12, 2014.

95. *Bronze Veils* is the first piece that Larsen published with E. C. Schirmer. The name "Veils" for the series of Louis paintings was coined by William Rubin. See "Morris Louis."

96. Larsen's Minneapolis home is filled with glass art of all kinds. She commissioned artist Peter Zelle to create large, colorful glass sculptures that stand outside her living room and dining room windows. On cold and snowy winter days, the two glass sculpture "trees" provide sparkling bits of color that reflect in the house. In addition, a large family collection of glass jack-in-the-pulpit sculptures is displayed in a wall of shelves in the living room; it also collects and reflects light throughout the Larsen-Reece home.

97. Readers are encouraged to explore Louis's paintings on any one of a number of online sites. http://www.wikiart.org/en/morris-louis is a good starting point, accessed January 6, 2015.

98. See Hunter Drohojowska-Philp's book *Rebels in Paradise* for a study of West Coast avant-garde art, and especially the pop art movement. Andy Warhol had his first pop art commercial show at the Ferus Gallery in 1962.

99. The term *action painting* was coined by art critic Harold Rosenberg in 1952. He explained its evolution: "At a certain moment the canvas began to appear to one American painter after another as an arena in which to act—rather than as a space in which to reproduce, re-design, analyze or 'express' an object. . . . What was to go on the canvas was not a picture but an event." See "Action Painting."

100. Schjeldahl, "When It Pours."

101. Ibid.

102. See Ebony, "David Ebony's Top 10." Distinctions between "the beautiful" and "the sublime" have roots in eighteenth-century landscape painting and Edmund Burke's "Philosophical Inquiry into the Origins of Our Ideas of the Sublime and the Beautiful" (1757). Beauty is associated with grace, charm, and delight, while the sublime speaks to the mind. For a succinct discussion of the connotations of the terms, see L. Smith, "beautiful, sublime."

103. "Morris Louis."

104. Ibid.

105. See Larsen, *Bronze Veils*, "Composer's Notes."

106. Ibid.

107. See Upright, "Technique of Morris Louis."

108. Seeing shadowlike impressions of the supporting stretcher braces suggests *pentimento*, a term used in art to describe the visible traces of a previous work that had been painted over. See http://www.merriam-webster.com/dictionary/pentimento, accessed January 6, 2015.

109. See Upright, "Technique of Morris Louis," unnumbered page. See also "Morris Louis."

110. There is a large literature on visual perception. For one discussion of the issues at stake, see Holcombe, "Seeing Slow and Seeing Fast."

111. The glass harmonica is a crystallophone, an instrument that produces its sound by exciting the glass, often by rubbing it with a moistened finger. In 1975, two years before the Louis exhibit at the Walker, the Bakken Museum, also in Minneapolis, acquired an original glass "armonica." Although a shipping accident destroyed the original glass disks, today children can try their hand playing a replica of Benjamin Franklin's musical invention. See http://www.thebakken.org/best-days-ben-franklin-day, accessed January 9, 2015. Larsen's glass harmonic calls for disks tuned to ten different pitch classes with octave duplication of three of them.

112. Telephone conversation with the composer, February 25, 2015.

113. The quoted phrase is Larsen's instruction to the trombonist.

Chapter 6. Larsen and Gender: Doing the Impossible

1. See McCoy, "Former Highest-Ranking U.S. Cardinal."

2. Ibid., McCoy quoting Cardinal Burke.

3. Ibid.

4. Ibid., McCoy summarizing Cardinal Burke's position.

5. Ibid., McCoy quoting Cardinal Burke.

6. Ibid. According to McCoy, Pope Francis demoted Burke "to a ceremonial post with the charity group Knights of Malta."

7. I specify "woman" composer because this is often how Larsen was categorized at the time despite her discomfort with the delineation and the marginalizing effect it had.

8. See "History," *Innova Recordings*.

9. Telephone conversation with Janika Vandervelde, November 20, 2014.

10. Vandervelde's senior recital of original works parallels Larsen's freshman jury of original songs in that both women debuted as composers at their universities in unexpected ways.

11. Only after it was announced that Stephen Paulus had won a Guggenheim fellowship in 1982, did Larsen learn that Argento and Fetler had encouraged and

supported his application. None of the three had mentioned Paulus's application, which Larsen found curious given her continuing interactions with Paulus during this time. Larsen had never applied nor been encouraged to. Paulus's death in 2014 leaves that incident unresolved in Larsen's mind.

12. Telephone conversation with Janika Vandervelde, November 20, 2014.

13. Ibid. Larsen had also characterized Stokes as a giving teacher in her interview with Tina Milhorn-Stallard. See Slayton, *Women of Influence in Contemporary Music*, 204–5.

14. Telephone conversation with Janika Vandervelde, November 20, 2014.

15. In February 1987, the year McClary won the teaching award, the original version of her article "Getting Down off the Beanstalk: The Presence of a Woman's Voice in Janika Vandervelde's *Genesis II*" appeared in the *Minnesota's Composers Forum Newsletter*. Soon afterward, McClary's own music theater piece "Susanna Does the Elders" was performed at Southern Theater in downtown Minneapolis. It shocked the proudly progressive, but always polite upper Midwest town. The multitalented musicologist-composer-teacher was broadly threatening.

16. Telephone conversation with Janika Vandervelde, November 20, 2014.

17. Ibid. Meredith Monk had originally been scheduled to participate in the conference, but after she cancelled, Vandervelde took her place.

18. Janika Vandervelde interview in Kelly, *In Her Own Words:*, 411.

19. McClary's feminist reading of Vandervelde's *Genesis II* appeared in McClary's *Feminine Endings* and catapulted the young composer into national prominence.

20. Telephone interview with the composer, November 20, 2014. It was coincidental that Vandervelde was in Minneapolis at the time of our phone conversation and planning to be at Larsen's house the next evening attending a reception Larsen was holding for area composers.

21. See Kelly, *In Her Own Words*, 300.

22. Ibid.

23. See Larsen, *Black Birds, Red Hills*, "Composer's Note."

24. On March 13, 2014, Sister Mary Virginia Micka, a member of the Sisters of Saint Joseph of Carondelet, celebrated her seventieth year with the Sisters of Saint Joseph. See http://thecatholicspirit.com/special-sections/jubilees/religious-women-men-celebrate-jubilees/, accessed January 15, 2015.

25. Larsen, *Magdalene*, "Composer's Note." In her composer's note Larsen explains: "The Gnostics seek a balance between the religious laws of the orthodox and the intellectual originality of the Gnostics, between the accepted and the revelatory." Larsen would likely have been a Gnostic had she lived in the third century.

26. Experimental composer Elizabeth Hinkle-Turner first met Libby Larsen in 1990. She decided a few years after that initial encounter that the greatest lesson Larsen taught her was that despite flamboyant and "weird" artistic types who dominated the composition world, "being normal was OK." Telephone conversation with Hinkle-Turner, April 15, 2015.

27. See the composer's liner notes for the CD *Grand Larsen-Y*.

28. Patricia Hampl, introduction to Brenda Ueland's *Me*, xii. It is another sign of the closeness of the Minneapolis arts scene that Hampl became friends with Ueland as she prepared the new edition of *Me*, and that Larsen and Hampl collaborated on multiple works of their own.

29. The capitalization of both letters in the word *me* is inconsistent between the cover and title page of the score, which show it as "Me," and the title on the first page of the score and on Larsen's Web site, which show it as "ME." I choose to use "ME" because that is how Larsen refers to her work in her composer's note. I also believe the fully capitalized title reflects Larsen's need at the time to assert herself to herself. Inconsistencies also exist in Ueland's book.

30. Valente premiered another Larsen song cycle in 1998, *Songs of Light and Love,* on poems by May Sarton, and in 2000 recorded *Songs from Letters*, whose text quotes from Calamity Jane's letters to her daughter, Janey.

31. See Ueland, *Me*, 38.

32. Ueland was married and divorced three times and spent many years living in New York City, two of the most obvious differences between the women.

33. Not all of Larsen's song titles follow Ueland's chapter titles, but five of them do: "Childhood"; "Greenwich Village"; "Marriage," which Larsen amends with "Divorce" to acknowledge Ueland's marital history; "Work"; and "The Present." Larsen collapses Ueland's two chapters "High School" and "College" into her song "Adolescence" and selects lines from Ueland's chapter "Home Again" for her song "Art (Life Is Love . . .)." She introduces the set with a song that adapts Ueland's opening lines "Why I Write This Book."

34. Larsen, "Composer's Note," in *ME (Brenda Ueland)*. Italics are mine.

35. Ibid. Leporello's catalog aria in Mozart's *Don Giovanni*, is one of the most famous patter songs in the operatic repertoire.

36. Larsen instructs the vocalist to sing "saucily." See Larsen, *ME (Brenda Ueland)*, 29.

37. Listeners may feel a greater intimacy with Ueland, whose relatively contemporary story set in Minneapolis is centuries closer than Eurydice's mythological tale set in the underworld for instance.

38. Larsen referred to "the theater of the mind" in an interview with Andrea J. Mitternight. Mitternight, "Original Work," 196.

39. In Larsen's song "Childhood," the *k* of *clunk* is pronounced on the second beat rest of measure 116. See Larsen, *ME (Brenda Ueland)*, 18. Larsen employed an Ivesian technique when she deftly inserted an augmented version of the incipit of "Good Night Ladies" into the right-hand piano part. Ives often tucked appropriate tunes into accompanimental passages.

40. See Ueland, *Me*, viii.

41. Ibid., 282–83.

42. Ibid., 296.

43. Ibid.

44. Ibid.

45. See Larsen's note to score, *ME (Brenda Ueland).*

46. In a 2003 interview with Andrea J. Mitternight, Larsen explained her choice of the word *scena* to describe her grouping *Songs from Letters*: "I consider them to all belong to each other, and it's really more of a *scena* than it is a framed cycle." See Mitternacht, "Original Work," 199.

47. See Stearns, "Contemporary Sounds in Indiana." Stearns wrote these remarks in reference to Larsen's setting of Elizabeth Barrett Browning's poems in her *Sonnets from the Portuguese.*

48. Mitternight, "Original Work," 199.

49. Payne, *Between Ourselves*, 129.

50. Ibid., 130.

51. Bolded text indicates Larsen's added words or repeated lines.

52. Telephone conversation with Eugenia Zukerman, October 21, 2014.

53. Ibid.

54. See Larsen, *Notes Slipped under the Door*, "Composer's Notes."

55. Text by Eugenia Zukerman. Shared by the author in an email October 21, 2014.

56. Ibid. Text for "The Rock We Used to Sit On." Eugenia and Pinchas Zukerman were married from 1968 to 1985.

57. See http://tinyurl.com/hcdmzmv, accessed December 13, 2016.

58. *Black Birds, Red Hills* was performed in Washington, DC, at the National Museum of Women in the Arts. See libbylarsen.com for a description of the piece. A second purely instrumental work with women as its theme is Larsen's solo trumpet *Fanfare for the Women*, which she wrote for the opening of the University of Minnesota Women's Sports Pavilion in 1993. Unlike Larsen's nature-related pieces, most of her women-related pieces are song settings.

59. Email correspondence from the composer September 4, 2015.

60. Larsen uses the phrase "flow of time" in her composer's comments about the piece.

61. The final pour actually resulted in the bronze tone of Louis's *Bronze Veil* paintings, whereas Larsen's bronze (metallic) sound is present from the very beginning of her piece.

62. Georgia O'Keeffe died twenty months shy of her one hundredth birthday on March 6, 1986.

63. From the Audio Program Note (Libby Larsen, South Dakota State University, March 14, 1988) found at http://libbylarsen.com/index.php?contentID=242&profileID=1240, accessed December 20, 2014. Italics indicate the composer's emphasis.

64. Ibid.

65. The full title of the work is *Black Birds, Red Hills: A Portrait of Six Paintings of Georgia O'Keeffe.*

66. See O'Keeffe, *Georgia O'Keeffe*. Each of the paintings' titles foregrounds color, although Larsen reduced the title of her first movement to "Pedernal Hills," perhaps assuming that anyone familiar with New Mexico would know the color of the foothills of Pedernal.

67. The terms in quotation marks are Larsen's.

68. O'Keeffe's 1936 Pedernal and Red Hills is a 20" x 30" oil painted on canvas.

69. How O'Keeffe achieved the precise effect of separated forms is not clear. It's possible she used a buffer that stopped the paints from seeping across a particular point on the canvas. I am grateful for conversations with the artist Irene Trakas who helped me understand O'Keeffe's potential techniques.

70. Todd E. Sullivan's stresses the more temporal aspect of Larsen's work. See Sullivan, *Dancing Solo*.

71. See "Composer's Note" to the score, in *Black Birds, Red Hills* (1996), unnumbered page. O'Keeffe's paintings are viewable at multiple sites online.

72. It would make sense if O'Keeffe used alizarin crimson; the color is closer to purple than orange on the color wheel, so it provides an easier blend with the more blue-gray color of the sky that it abuts. I am again grateful to Irene Trakas for our many conversations about color and its creation in the six O'Keeffe paintings Larsen consulted.

73. *Mary Cassatt*, written in 1994, included a solo trombone and orchestra as well as fifteen slide projections of the artist's paintings. In this work and *Black Birds, Red Hills*, Larsen thought across media.

74. See Larsen, *Love after 1950*, "Composer's Note." Larsen named her set *Love after 1950* in honor of the year of her birth and the changes that would occur in male-female relationships in the following decades.

75. Ibid.

76. Ibid.

77. Larsen, *Love after 1950*, "Composer's Note."

78. See Larsen, "Composer's Note," in *Love after 1950* (2001), 2.

79. Ibid., "Big Sister Says, 1967" instructions to the singer at measures 8 and 17 respectively. Despite Larsen's treatment of the poem, Kathryn Daniels originally intended it as a serious reflection on the era.

80. Ibid. Larsen writes "Jerry Lee Lewis" in parenthesis over the piano part in measure 5.

81. Ibid.

82. Reprinted with the kind permission of the poet Kathryn Daniels.

83. Twiggy (Leslie Hornby) had been named "The Face of 1966" by the British newspaper the *Daily Express*. See http://www.twiggylawson.co.uk/biography.html, accessed February 9, 2015.

84. Larsen uses the word "dazzling" nine times to describe how the pianist should play a series of fast-paced runs. See Larsen, *Love after 1950* (2001), 27–33.

85. See Ostriker, "Learning to Breathe under Water."

86. See http://tinyurl.com/j6ve4l8, accessed July 13, 2015. Ostriker explains that she "cherish[es] this quote, this image." I have italicized "dive deep."

87. See http://www.english.illinois.edu/maps/poets/m_r/rukeyser/life.htm, accessed February 7, 2015. See also Rukeyser, *Life of Poetry*, 8.

88. Rukeyser, *Life of Poetry*, 31–32.

89. See my *Music and the Skillful Listener*, 244–49, where I discuss the second movement of Larsen's *Symphony: Water Music*, "Hot, Still," as an example of the energy present in moments of supreme quietude and stasis.

90. See Larsen, *Love after 1950* (2001), "I Make My Magic (Isadora's Dance)." These are the composer's instructions at measure 27.

91. Both words in quotes are Larsen's own.

92. See "There Was a Little Girl." Henry Wadsworth Longfellow's nursery rhyme goes: "There was a little girl, Who had a little curl, Right in the middle of her forehead. And when she was good, she was very good indeed, but when she was bad she was horrid."

93. See Larsen, *Hell's Belles*, 1. There are several variants of Stein's remark but not enough to change its meaning. Author, attorney, agnostic Vincent Bugliosi contends that Stein's statement is the essence of agnosticism. See Bugliosi, "Why Do I Doubt?" These quotations can be found at www.brainyquote.com under each woman's name.

94. See http://tinyurl.com/zge5hej, accessed February 12, 2015.

95. Larsen wrote *Hell's Belles* at the suggestion of James Meredith, founder and conductor of the Sonos Handbell Ensemble, who commissioned the piece for Frederica von Stade. Larsen characterizes the piece as "the brainchild" of the three of them. "We toyed with several ideas and then lit on the idea of wild and sassy women–Hells' Belles." See Larsen, "Program Note," in *Hell's Belles*, unnumbered page.

96. An interview with the actress appears in Edgerly, *Give Her This Day*, 118–19.

97. Jenny Joseph's poetic "ode to nonconformity," "Warning," was voted the most popular poem in the UK in 1996. Joseph wrote the poem when she was just twenty-nine, perhaps anticipating a time when she would feel free of society's dicta regarding women's behavior. See Eve, "Jenny Joseph's 'When I Am an Old Woman.'"

98. See Larsen, *Hell's Belles*, 24, for excerpts from Armor Keller's interview as it appeared in Root, *Women at the Wheel*, 55–57.

99. See http://www.artcaragency.com/gallery/magic-city-golden-transit-art-car-by-armor-keller/ for references to the "magic city golden transit," accessed February 12, 2015.

100. Personal interview with the composer, November 2012. Mary Magdalene likely spoke a version of Coptic, which was derived from the ancient Demotic Egyptian script and language. It flourished beginning in the second century CE. See Gabra and Torjeson, "Claremont Coptic Encyclopedia."

101. Many biblical women were identified by their connection to "the house of" their father. Current research questions the exact nature of Mary's relationship to Magdala, but no other theory for its attachment to her name has gained much traction.

102. See "Mary of Magdala" for an overview of Mary of Magdala's leadership role in the early Christian Church, her recasting as a prostitute beginning at the time of Constantine's becoming Holy Roman emperor, and contemporary rehabilitation efforts to reclaim her rightful place as "apostle to the apostles," the person who

announced Jesus's resurrection to the rest of his followers, and who was his most trusted confidante.

103. Ibid. CSJ is the abbreviation for Congregation of Saint Joseph.

104. Beyond virgin or whore (Jezebel), African American women's choices also included "mammy": the self-less woman who lovingly reared her master's children, invariably at the expense of spending time with her own.

105. See Schaberg, *Resurrection of Mary Magdalene.*

106. For information on efforts to "provide all Roman Catholics the opportunity to participate fully in Church life and leadership," see http://www.futurechurch.org/, accessed February 16, 2015. FutureChurch was started in 1990.

107. See Larsen, "Performance Notes," in *Magdalene* (2012), unnumbered page of score.

108. I am grateful for the insights of Jeffrey Peterson, commissioning pianist for *The Magdalene*, who has performed the work multiple times without any visual component beyond the costuming and staging for the singer.

109. See Larsen, "Composer's Note," in *Magdalene* (2012), unnumbered page of score. The *Pistis Sophia* is simultaneously a text and its personification in the person of Mary Magdalene.

110. Ibid.

111. See Larsen, *Magdalene* (2012), 6. The Coptic text was translated by Philip Sellew, a professor of ancient languages at the University of Minnesota.

112. Ibid. See measures 1–3; 13–15; and 99 for instances of the Phrygian mode that announces the Archangel. See Novack, "Significance of the Phrygian Mode."

113. Wascoe earned her DM from the University of Illinois in 2008 with a treatise on Larsen titled "Libby Larsen and the Song Cycle, a Discussion of 'My Antonia.'"

114. Telephone conversation with Rebecca Wascoe, February 27, 2015.

115. Ibid.

116. See Baylor University, "OVRP Grant Supports Commission."

117. According to http://www.baylor.edu/truett/index.php (accessed January 8, 2017), Baylor's current student body includes members of a variety of religions as well as students who are unaffiliated or are professed atheists. Regardless, chapel remains a requirement for freshmen and transfer students, and Christian values and heritage still drive the mission of the school.

118. Their rebuff recalls Larsen's experience with the Houston Symphony thirty years earlier when she attended a rehearsal of her piece and no one invited her input.

119. See http://www.baylor.edu/truett/index.php?id=99488, accessed January 8, 2017.

120. See "Southern Baptist Convention Passes Resolution."

121. Telephone conversation with Jeffrey Peterson, February 19, 2015.

122. Ibid.

123. In a phone conversation with the composer, February 26, 2015, Larsen used the word *meld* to describe her connection to Mary Magdalene.

124. Telephone conversation with Jeffrey Peterson, February 19, 2015.

125. Telephone conversation with Rebecca Wascoe, February 27, 2015.

126. Email communication from Rebecca Wascoe, June 14, 2015. There are hopes for a 2016 release.

Chapter 7. Larsen and Technology: Challenging the Concert Hall

1. Email correspondence from the composer, September 4, 2015.

2. See Xayhaothao, "Fort Worth Opera Shelves World Premiere."

3. Email correspondence from the composer, September 4, 2015.

4. Xayhaothao, "Fort Worth Opera Shelves World Premiere."

5. For the full text of this address, see "Role of the Musician" at http://www.libbylarsen.com.

6. Ibid. *Produced* is Larsen's term for all sounds created using electronic equipment.

7. Among Larsen's sound collaborators are Tom Mudge (*Now I Pull Silver*), and Russ Borud, with whom she has worked multiple times, including on *A Wrinkle in Time*. Email correspondence from the composer, September 4, 2015.

8. See Larsen, *Frankenstein*.

9. Excerpts from this article and other lectures appear in "The Liberation of Sound," in Schwartz and Childs, *Contemporary Composers on Contemporary Music*, 196–208, here 196.

10. Ibid., 197.

11. Ibid.

12. In 1986 Henry Brant's work *Northern Lights over the Twin Cities: A Spatial Assembly of Auroral Echoes, for multiple ensembles & 6 conductors* premiered at the sports arena in Saint Paul, expanding the idea of spatial composition well beyond the concert hall.

13. Email correspondence from the composer, September 4, 2015.

14. See Larsen, "Composer's Note," in *Fanfare for the Women*.

15. Telephone conversation with Libby Larsen, February 26, 2015.

16. Magnetic tape was developed in Germany in the late 1920s but not available outside that country until Allied soldiers captured German recording equipment. See http://foldoc.org/magnetic+tape, accessed February 23, 2015.

17. See http://www.ipsden.u-net.com/course/EM3.html, accessed February 23, 2015.

18. In his manual for performers Partch explained: "At no time are the players of my instruments to be unaware that they are on stage, in the act. . . . When a player fails to take full advantage of his role in a visual or acting sense, he is muffing his part—in my terms—as thoroughly as if he bungled every note in the score." See Granade, *Harry Partch*, 37–38.

19. See my discussion of Larsen's rejection of sensorial boundaries in *Music and the Skillful Listener*, 267–73.

20. *Merriam-Webster's Collegiate Dictionary* defines *sensorium* as "the parts of the brain or the mind concerned with the reception and interpretation of sensory stimuli; broadly: the entire sensory apparatus." In 1991 Walter J. Ong published an essay, "The Shifting Sensorium," in *The Varieties of Sensory Experience.* I am grateful to Michael Broyles for calling my attention to the Ong essay. For additional discussion of the larger field of sensory studies see Howes, "Expanding Field of Sensory Studies."

21. Despite numerous preliminary conversations with members of the Fry Street Quartet about their hopes for *Emergence*, Larsen's role in the endeavor was solely as composer of the piece, which became the soundtrack of their work. Larsen pointed to a single moment of true collaboration with the ensemble when they collectively agreed to throw out a sixth movement and move what had been the second movement to the fifth and last position. The script and visuals were added after Larsen had completed her music.

22. Readers are encouraged to visit libbylarsen.com to hear a performance of the work by flutist Nina Assimakopoulos, accessed March 11, 2015. For a study of fractal patterns associated with music, see Brothers, "Nature of Fractal Music"; and Brothers, "Structural Scaling in Bach's Cello Suite No. 3." See also http://www.harlanjbrothers.com/, accessed March 12, 2015.

23. A. E. Stallings, "Arachne Gives Thanks to Athena," as quoted by Larsen in the score to *Now I Pull Silver.*

24. "Arrival points" is Larsen's phrase. See Larsen, *Now I Pull Silver*, 4.

25. For a systematic study of the tradition of women's recitation practices, see Kimber, *Elocutionists.*

26. "Wings" is the word flutist Katherine Borst Jones used to describe the airy, nonspecific gesture.

27. Larsen, "Program Notes," in *Now I Pull Silver.*

28. *Circular Rondo* might qualify as one of these inward pieces.

29. See Von Glahn, *Music and the Skillful Listener*, 244 and 265, for the full remarks that Larsen offered on the topic.

30. Ibid., 265. All quoted passages in this paragraph come from a March 29, 2009, interview with Libby Larsen. As I had observed in *Skillful Listeners*, the ramification of heading "to quiet" are significant for a composer.

31. Larsen observes that if there is a recurring theme in her operas it is people faced with difficult and sometimes impossible situations and choices. *Some Pig*, *Mrs. Dalloway*, *Every Man Jack*, and *A Wrinkle in Time* are all obvious examples.

32. See Larsen, *O Magnum Mysterium*, title page.

33. As much as music can induce ecstasy, it can also be the result of an ecstatic state. See Jamison, *Exuberance*, especially chapter 6, "Throwing Up Sky-Rockets," 155–61, for a discussion of the connections between music, dance, and ecstasy.

34. Email correspondence from the composer, September 4, 2015. Larsen and Phoenix plan to produce a "full-length recording for headphone concert experience." Russ Borud is the sound technician on this piece in the United States.

35. See Larsen, "Composer's Note, in *O Magnum Mysterium.*

36. Ibid.

37. Ibid.

38. This situation recalls Ives's chamber work *The Unanswered Question*, in which the composer establishes eternity in the form of a slowly moving string choir part before introducing the questioning trumpet and fighting answerers, the woodwinds. In that piece, eternity, although not always audible, continues unperturbed as well. Ives's scene fades from our hearing at the close of the piece much as Larsen's second choir dissolves and a D-flat chime is instructed to "let ring out" after the choir stops. In both cases the composers juxtaposed ideas of eternity and transience; the divine and the human.

39. Larsen, "Composer's Note," in *O Magnum Mysterium*.

40. Larsen appears to enjoy the sliding sound quality of the sitar, which is not unlike the sound of the Silvertone lap guitar that she used in *Now I Pull Silver*.

41. See measure 22 for this overlapping moment.

42. It may be significant that the responsorial chant *O Magnum Mysterium* allows Larsen to honor "the Blessed Virgin" (Beata Virgo), who gave birth to Christ. Larsen once again recovers the Queen of Heaven ostensibly driven out of the church in the 1960s.

43. See the composer's instruction to the bell player at measure 40.

44. John McDermott's opening lyrics read: "When blossoms flower e'er 'mid the snows / Upon a winter night, / Was born the child, the Christmas rose, / The king of love and light." See http://www.lyricsfreak.com/j/john+mcdermott/gesu+bambino_20074347.html, accessed June 17, 2015. The song was originally an Italian carol composed by Pietro Yon in 1917.

45. By ending on the fifth, A-flat, instead of on the root D-flat, Larsen has the basses linger on the first note of the ostinato pattern as if it is beginning again: A-flat, D-flat, F, D-flat, E-flat, D-flat, F, D-flat/A-flat . . . This is the same choice Ives made in his ostinato-based work *Central Park in the Dark*.

46. See www.thecrossroadsproject.org, accessed March 19, 2015.

47. Ibid., video interview with Robert Davies and members of the quartet.

48. Ibid.

49. Ibid.

50. Telephone conversation with Rebecca McFaul, September 14, 2014.

51. Ibid.

52. Ibid.

53. Ibid.

54. Personal interview with the Fry Street Quartet and Laura Kaminsky, October 3, 2014.

55. Ibid.

56. Ibid.

57. The term *Gesamtkunstwerk* first appeared in an essay written in 1827 by the German philosopher and theologian Karl Friedrich Eusebius Trahndorff (1782–1863).

58. Personal interview with the composer, March 29, 2009. Italics indicate the composer's spoken emphasis.

59. All quoted passages in this discussion come from a telephone conversation with Rebecca McFaul, March 31, 2015.

60. See the third movement measures 37 through 40 for a series of open fifths, this time played between instrumentalists rather than by individual players.

61. Penderecki named his work *8′37″* but explained that when he first heard the work performed the more associative title emerged. *Threnody* (*Threnos*) received the UNESCO award in 1961. See http://culture.pl/en/work/threnody-to-the-victims-of-hiroshima-krzysztof-penderecki, accessed January 9, 2017.

62. Larsen uses the word "warmly" often in *Emergence*. Despite the context of the piece and its focus on global *warming*, Larsen is not making a comment on the environmental crisis with this term. Instead she is encouraging heartfelt, expressive playing from the performers.

63. "Moiling" is Larsen's instruction to the cellist to play her "Old Man River" fragment turbulently, violently agitated.

64. See http://peoplesclimate.org, accessed March 26, 2015, for a number of videos related to this event and other activities associated with environmental activism.

65. Telephone conversation with the composer, September 7, 2015. All quoted passages that follow come from this conversation.

Chapter 8. Larsen and the Collaborators, Larsen and the Critics

1. See "Encounters with Minnesota Artists—Libby Larsen."

2. Ibid.

3. John Duffy, born June 23, 1926, passed away December 22, 2015, after a lengthy illness.

4. Telephone conversation with John Duffy, September 8, 2014.

5. Ibid.

6. Ibid.

7. For a discussion of the institute and interviews with the seven fellows, see Runestad, "Giving Life to New Opera."

8. Ibid.

9. Ibid.

10. See Anderson "Diver Hints."

11. For audio files from the opera as well as a number of reviews, see http://www.johnduffy.com/blackwater.html, accessed April 6, 2015.

12. Telephone conversation with John Duffy, September 8, 2014.

13. Ibid.

14. *Every Man Jack* is based upon Jack London's 1913 autobiographical novel, *John Barleycorn*, whose title is taken from a British folksong with roots that go back as far as the sixteenth century.

15. Telephone conversation with John Duffy, September 8, 2014. Italics indicate Duffy's spoken emphasis.

16. Ibid.

17. Email correspondence from the composer, September 4, 2015. Larsen has recorded with each of these conductors.

18. Personal interview with Philip Brunelle, September 12, 2014.

19. Larsen explained that she was uncomfortable using the photo in advertising for the symphony as it had nothing to do with the composition or the purpose of the event, so she had her image removed from the picture. Email correspondence from the composer, September 4, 2015.

20. Telephone conversation with Joel Revzen, September 4, 2014.

21. Ibid. See also Larsen, *Sonnets from the Portuguese.*

22. See Larsen, *Sonnets from the Portuguese.*

23. Ibid.

24. For Larsen's comments about her *String Symphony*, see *Libby Larsen: String Symphony* .

25. Telephone conversation with Joel Revzen, September 4, 2014. Italics indicate Revzen's emphasis in his speech.

26. Ibid.

27. See Jamison, *Exuberance*, for an extended discussion of this "abounding, ebullient, effervescent emotion." Jamison is a professor of psychiatry at the Johns Hopkins School of Medicine and a John D. and Catherine T. MacArthur Fellow. Larsen easily fits in the company of Teddy Roosevelt, John Muir, and Richard Feynman, "notable irrepressible types."

28. Personal interview with Philip Brunelle, September 12, 2014.

29. Ibid.

30. *Seven Ghosts* is a six-movement work for voices and a large and varied instrumental ensemble that sets texts from seven Americans whose lives Larsen believes "chang[ed] the heart of our culture." Among the texts she set is a letter that Lind wrote to Harriet Beecher Stowe. See Larsen, *Seven Ghosts.*

31. See Larsen, *Barnum's Bird.*

32. Ibid.

33. Personal interview with Philip Brunelle, September 12, 2014.

34. Ibid.

35. Ibid.

36. Ibid.

37. Ibid. Italics indicate Brunelle's spoken emphasis. Bracketed words are my best attempt to compress spoken comments.

38. Telephone interview with James Dunham, June 23, 2016. Italics indicate Dunham's spoken emphasis.

39. See http://jamesdunham.com/violist/biography/, accessed June 23, 2016. Dunham is also the violist in the Axelrod String Quartet, the quartet in residence

at the Smithsonian Institute in Washington, D.C. He is currently professor of viola and chamber music at the Shepherd School of Music at Rice University.

40. Telephone interview with James Dunham, June 23, 2016.

41. Ibid.

42. Ibid.

43. Ibid.

44. Ibid.

45. Telephone interview with Toni Lindgren, January 2, 2015.

46. "Kenwood Editions," named for the street on which Larsen lives, is published by LLP (Libby Larsen Publishing). Senchina joined Larsen in summer 2014, when Grace Edgar, a previous assistant, left to pursue a doctorate in musicology at Harvard. Edgar had worked with Larsen for three years, overlapping in her time with Toni Lindgren.

47. Telephone interview with Toni Lindgren, January 2, 2015.

48. Ibid.

49. Ibid.

50. Ibid.

51. Ibid.

52. Ibid.

53. Ibid.

54. See Goetzman et al., "Get Out of Town." The column was published once a year.

55. Ibid., 8. The six journalists are Keith Goetzman, David McKee, Adam Platt, Tad Simons, Bill Souder, and Glen Warchol. The reference to "bunny slopes" is an unfortunate use of cliché, given Larsen's formidable skiing skills.

56. See Gimbel, "Larsen: Symphony 4." Gimbel has also written on English composer Edward Elgar; see "Elgar's Prize Song."

57. Gimbel, "Larsen: Symphony 4."

58. Larsen, *Deep Summer Music.*

59. See Gimbel, "Larsen: Deep Summer Music." Gimbel has reviewed various Larsen CDs over the years and always negatively. Kalevi Ensio Aho (b. 1949) is a Finnish composer of both symphonic and chamber music.

60. Ibid.

61. Hertelendy, "Larsen: Every Man Jack."

62. See Catalano, "MIT Chamber Chorus."

63. See Lipman, "Backward & Downward with the Arts."

64. Ibid. Lipman is quoting from "An American Dialogue."

65. Ibid.

66. Ibid.

67. Ibid.

68. See Lipman, "Out of the Ghetto."

69. See Lipman, "Music and Musical Life."

70. Ibid., 25, 29–30. Lipman names the guilty avant-gardists: "Earle Brown, Charles Dodge, Morton Feldman, Dick Higgins, Lejaren Hiller, Alvin Lucier, Otto

Luening, Max Mathews, Pauline Oliveros, Morton Subotnick, and Vladimir Ussachevsky."

71. Ibid., 31.

72. Ibid., 31, 32.

73. Lipman backtracks on his assessment of Glass to acknowledge *Einstein on the Beach*. Ibid., 31.

74. Ibid.

75. Ibid.

76. Ibid., 32.

77. Ibid.

78. Ibid. In 1998 Larsen made the same argument against education as her primary goal for a composition in an address she delivered to the Society for American Music upon being named its Honorary Member. No one objected.

79. Ibid., 33. By 1985 the argument that music's sole purpose is to civilize and uplift listeners would be many decades out of date.

80. Ibid.

81. Ibid., 34.

82. Ibid.

83. Albany Records, founded in 1987, is one of a small number of labels that focuses on American classical music.

84. See Lipman, "Who's Killing Our Symphony Orchestras?"

85. Ibid. See paragraph 6 for this remark.

86. Ibid.

87. In 1968 Hiller took a position at the University of Buffalo and established its first computer music studio. He remained there until 1989.

88. The year after Brün's death, members of his circle formed the Herbert Brün Society to disseminate his work. See http://www.herbertbrun.net/about-us/, accessed May 31, 2015. The society is connected to the School for Designing a Society, founded by one of the original "Brünettes," Susan Parenti, and closely connected to Brün's ideas regarding social change.

89. See "Experimental Music Studios."

90. Now retired, Heidi Von Gunden declined to be interviewed for this project, but in a brief email dated October 23, 2014, she wished me luck with my "fascinating" work. I respect her decision but am sorry that readers will not have the opportunity to hear her reflections on Larsen's residency from the distance of a quarter century or her thoughts about being the only woman in a male-dominated profession and department for the length of her career.

91. I'm grateful to Elizabeth Hinkle-Turner for her lengthy, candid, and personally reflective telephone conversation with me April 15, 2015. Hinkle-Turner was a DMA composition student at Illinois from 1986 to 1991 and present at Larsen's forum. She was responsible for chauffeuring Larsen on various lengthy excursions during her residency, which gave the two women extended opportunities to talk. Her observations and insights were uniquely helpful in developing my understanding of the

environment in the University of Illinois School of Music during the time of her matriculation and especially of the dynamics of the composition program and faculty.

92. Repar earned her DMA from the University of Illinois in 1992 and is currently an associate professor of music at the University of New Mexico, where she founded the Arts-in-Medicine Program in 2002. She had studied with Herbert Brün for a year before completing her degree with Bill Brooks. Professor Repar has no memory of the particular events surrounding Larsen's residency.

93. Von Gunden described Larsen using these words in her own public Composers' Forum talk, which she gave on April 9, three weeks after Larsen's visit. Von Gunden explained that she provided the same warning to all forum guests who were unfamiliar with the particular ritual.

94. Telephone conversations with Hinkle-Turner, April 15, 2015.

95. See Larsen, *Overture: Parachute Dancing*, "Composer's Notes," for her complete notes on the piece.

96. Larsen's use of the word *generous* in her forum comments would be referenced in two later Composers Forums by different speakers. In a June 3, 2015, email, Larsen acknowledged that she didn't recall the precise context of her 1990 remark but explained as best she could what she likely meant at the time.

97. See "Best & Worst 1990."

98. Personal conversation with Bill Brooks, March 6, 2015, Sacramento, Calif. The + Series was Brooks's own concert series at the University of Illinois. This particular concert took place March 15, 1990.

99. I am grateful to Nolan Vallier for his work with the William Brooks Papers at the Sousa Music Archives at the University of Illinois on behalf of this project, and to Bill Brooks for sharing additional letters and emails that he had saved in his personal papers. In 1993 Brooks would participate in a panel discussion about women and composing at a Society of Composers Inc. Conference as the only male on the panel. As surviving correspondence from the time demonstrates, he and Larsen had developed a friendship in which each supported the other's creative efforts.

100. Telephone conversation with Elizabeth Hinkle-Turner, April 15, 2015.

101. Ibid.

102. Ibid.

103. Ibid.

104. Ibid.

105. Personal conversation with Bill Brooks, March 6, 2015, Sacramento, Calif.

106. Ibid.

107. Ibid.

108. Telephone conversation with Elizabeth Hinkle-Turner, April 15, 2015.

109. See Hinkle-Turner, *Women Composers and Music Technology in the United States*, 7. Of the ten professors who make up the Illinois composition faculty in 2015, one is a female, Assistant Professor Erin Gee. The program's Web page boasts a "diverse range of aesthetics and techniques" and a world-renowned faculty that "supports a lively, thoughtful, and intelligent culture that includes cooperative ex-

perimentation and enlightened, if sometimes controversial, approaches to music composition and research." Controversy appears to be a point of pride within the program. See "Composition—Theory."

110. Professor Sever Tipei declined to be interviewed for this project. In an email he explained that he doubted he'd be useful to my study given his recollections of the event as unflattering toward Ms. Larsen. I appreciate his response.

111. Telephone conversation with Elizabeth Hinkle-Turner, April 15, 2015.

112. Ibid. Today, of course, both situations could be cause for official reprimands at the least and potential legal action.

113. Telephone conversation with the composer, November 12, 2014.

114. Personal conversation with Bill Brooks, March 6, 2015. Brooks suggests that if the target were a male, it would probably be a racial or religious attack. "Racial or ethnic epithets go with the male; gendered epithets go with the women. People in power have to be attacked through the back door."

115. See Babbitt, "Who Cares If You Listen?," 40.

116. See "Computer Music Project." The Computer Music Studio was part of the EMS.

117. Personal conversation with Bill Brooks, March 6, 2015.

118. Letter from Libby Larsen to Lucinda Lawrence, March 16, 1990, box 12, folder 52, "Libby Larsen," William Brooks Papers, Sousa Music Archives, University of Illinois, Urbana-Champaign.

119. Letter from William (Bill) Brooks to Libby Larsen, September 14, 1990, box 12, folder 52, "Libby Larsen," William Brooks Papers.

120. Letter from William (Bill) Brooks to Libby Larsen, May 13, 1990, box 12, folder 52, "Libby Larsen," William Brooks Papers.

121. A copy of this proposal, finalized in 1995, can be read online; see Parenti, "Composing the Music School."

122. Ibid.

123. Ibid.

124. Telephone conversation with Elizabeth Hinkle-Turner, April 15, 2015.

125. Personal conversation with Wynne Reece, September 10, 2014. All quoted passages come from this conversation.

126. Wynne Reece finished law school in 2013 and in 2014 established Reece Law LLC in Minneapolis with her attorney father, James Reece. Reflecting, perhaps, a family inclination toward broad interests and involvements, in addition to her law practice Reece also has her own business as a wedding planner.

127. Personal conversation with Wynne Reece, September 10, 2014. Italics suggest Reece's spoken emphasis.

Conclusions: Reflections on a Life and the Process of Telling It

1. Edel, *Art of Biography*.
2. Personal interview with the composer, March 28, 2009.

3. See Larsen, *Birth Project*, 9.

4. Larsen uses the word *miracle* in her song number 7, "First Miracle."

5. Personal interview with the composer, September 3, 2014.

6. See Berg, "Listener's Gallery," 127. Berg's use of the word *crafts*man reflects the persistence of certain verbal habits, even while extolling the sensitive text setting of a female composer.

7. Larsen, *DDT*, unnumbered page.

8. Personal conversation with the composer, November 13, 2012.

9. Horowitz, "Flute."

10. See Sullivan, *Dancing Solo, Music of Libby Larsen*, liner notes.

11. Personal conversation with the composer, April 28, 2015.

12. Email correspondence from the composer, October 1, 2015.

13. Personal conversation with the composer, April 28, 2015.

14. Ibid. Italics indicate the composer's emphasis in her speech.

15. Ibid.

16. See American Composers Forum Fortieth Anniversary video at https://composersforum.org/, accessed July 7, 2015.

17. Ibid. See the video link.

18. The percentage of female composer faculty members is impossible to determine definitively given the variety of assignments, titles, and appointments used—full time, part time, adjunct, visiting, and split. I am grateful to McKenna Milici for compiling extensive data on this topic.

19. See Meah and Jackson, "Crowded Kitchens," for a recent study of the impact of increasingly shared household duties on this previously female domestic space.

20. In the course of my writing this biography, both Alice and Robert Larsen passed away.

21. Email correspondence from the composer, July 9, 2015.

22. Personal conversation with the composer, April 28, 2015. Italics indicate the composer's emphasis in her speech. The Dewey Decimal System is the creation of the American librarian Melvil Dewey and first appeared in 1876. Although not a thousand-year-old monastic tradition, the composer's point is well taken: classification systems in use at the time were gendered and made finding women composers a long and tedious task.

23. I have witnessed Larsen collaborating on multiple occasions and been struck by how much time she spends listening to and thinking about what others have said.

24. This work seems to no longer exist in its original form: at least Larsen can't locate it.

25. Personal conversation with the composer, April 28, 2015. Carl Stalling created scores for Looney Tunes and Merry Melodies cartoons, as well as some of the early animated Walt Disney shorts.

26. Ibid. Italics indicate emphasis in the composer's speech.

27. See Shain, *Myth of American Individualism*; Clark, *Communitarian Moment*; and Limerick, *Legacy of Conquest*, for three studies that complicate simple readings of American exceptionalism as rooted in individualism alone.

28. Jamison, *Exuberance*, 4.

29. Ibid., 24.

Bibliography

"2004 Fellows." *Music Teachers National Association*. Accessed June 10, 2015. https://www.mtna.org/fellow-program/fellow-listing/2004-fellows/.

"Action Painting." *MOMA*. Accessed January 5, 2015. https://www.moma.org/cef/abex/html/know_more12.html (Web page no longer available).

"Alan Freed Biography." *Rock & Roll Hall of Fame*. Accessed June 21, 2014. http://rockhall.com/inductees/alan-freed/bio/.

Anderson, Jack. "Diver Hints Mary Jo Might Have Been Saved." *St. Petersburg Times*, September 1, 1969.

Anthony, Michael. Review. *Minneapolis Tribune*, October 22, 1973.

Auden, W. H. "Yeats as an Example." *Kenyon Review* 10, no. 2 (Spring 1948): 187–95. Accessed December 16, 2014. http://www.jstor.org/stable/4332931.

Babbitt, Milton. "Who Cares If You Listen?" *High Fidelity*, February 1958, 38–40. Reprinted in *Source Readings in Music History: The Twentieth Century*, edited by Robert P. Morgan, 35–41. New York: W. W. Norton, 1998.

Baylor University. "OVRP Grant Supports Commission of a New Song Cycle on the Life of Mary Magdalene." *Research Tracks* 9, no. 2 (March 2012): 2. Accessed February 17, 2015. http://www.baylor.edu/content/services/document.php/170243.pdf.

Bellamann, Henry. "Charles Ives: The Man and His Music." *Musical Quarterly* 19, no. 1 (1933): 45–58.

Berg, Gregory. "The Listener's Gallery." *Journal of Singing* 64, no. 1 (September/October 2007): 123–29.

"Best & Worst 1990; Classical: Batons Hint at a Brave New World." *USA Today*, December 24, 1990, Life, 2D.

Biery, Marilyn Perkins. "New Music for Organ at the End of the Twentieth Century." *American Organist* 34, no. 7 (July 2000): 76–78.

Big Eyes. Directed by Tim Burton. Weinstein Company, 2014.

Bittleston, Misha. "The Truth about Mary of Magdala." Accessed February 19, 2015. http://www.bittleston.com/conceptual/magdalen/.

Blom, Jan Dirk. "Ulloa Circle." In *A Dictionary of Hallucinations*. New York: Springer-Verlag, 2010. Accessed September 30, 2014. http://hallucinations.enacademic.com/1935/Ulloa_circle.

Bly, Robert. *News of the Universe: Poems of Twofold Consciousness*. San Francisco: Sierra Club Books, 1995.

Bogdanov, Vladimir. *All Music Guide: The Definitive Guide to Popular Music*. San Francisco: Backbeat Books, 2001.

Brothers, H. J. "The Nature of Fractal Music." In *Benoit Mandelbrot: A Life in Many Dimensions*, edited by Michael Frame, 181–206. Hackensack, N.J.: World Scientific, 2015.

———. "Structural Scaling in Bach's Cello Suite No. 3." *Fractals* 15, no. 1 (2007): 89–95.

Broyles, Michael. *The Emergence and Evolution of Beethoven's Heroic Style*. New York: Excelsior Music, 1987.

———. *Mavericks and Other Traditions in American Music*. New Haven, Conn.: Yale University Press, 2004.

Bugliosi, Vincent. "Why Do I Doubt Both the Atheists and the Theists?" *Religious Tolerance*, 2011. Accessed February 12, 2015. http://www.religioustolerance.org/bugliosi01.htm.

Burkholder, J. Peter. *All Made of Tunes: Charles Ives and the Uses of Musical Borrowing*. New Haven, Conn.: Yale University Press, 1995.

Burr, Ty. "Bard of the Barn." *Boston Globe*, December 10, 2006. Accessed December 10, 2014. http://www.boston.com/ae/books/articles/2006/12/10/bard_of_the_barn/.

Cailliau, Robert. "A Little History of the World Wide Web." Posted 1995. Accessed July 8, 2015. http://www.w3.org/History.html.

Catalano, Peter. "MIT Chamber Chorus: Larsen, 'The Nothing That Is.'" *American Record Guide* 67, no. 4 (November/December 2004): 45–46.

Catechism of the Catholic Church. Accessed September 1, 2014. http://www.vatican.va/archive/ENG0015/__P3X.HTM.

"Christmas Rose." *Foliage and Flora*. Accessed August 29, 2014. http://www.novareinna.com/festive/rose.html.

Clark, Christopher. *The Communitarian Moment: The Radical Challenge of the Northampton Association*. Ithaca, N.Y.: Cornell University Press, 1995.

"Composition—Theory." *University of Illinois School of Music*. Accessed July 3, 2015. http://www.music.illinois.edu/divisions/9.

"Computer Music Project." *University of Illinois School of Music*. Accessed April 6, 2015. http://www.music.illinois.edu/about/facilities/music-building/computer-music-project.

Crall, Deborah B. "Context and Commission in Large-Scale Texted Works of Libby Larsen." PhD diss., Catholic University, 2013.

Daily Planet Staff. "Don't Trust Anyone over 30, unless It's Jack Weinberg." *Berkeley Daily Planet*, April 6, 2000. Accessed June 24, 2014. http://www.berkeleydailyplanet.com/issue/2000-04-06/article/759.

"The Doomsday Clock." *Southeast Missourian*, February 22, 1984.

"Doomsday Clock: Timeline." *Bulletin of the Atomic Scientists*. Accessed June 21, 2014. http://thebulletin.org/timeline.

Drohojowska-Philp, Hunter. *Rebels in Paradise: The Los Angeles Art Scene and the 1960s*. New York: Henry Holt, 2011.

"E. B. White Biography." *Biography*. Accessed November 17, 2014. http://www.biography.com/people/eb-white-9529308#synopsis.

"Earliest Music Instruments Found." *BBC News*, May 25, 2012. Accessed September 30, 2014. http://www.bbc.com/news/science-environment-18196349.

Ebony, David. "David Ebony's Top 10 New York Gallery Shows for September." *artnet news*, September 22, 2014. Accessed July 10, 2016. http://tinyurl.com/hcw4kwz.

Edel, Leon. "The Art of Biography: No. 1." Interview by Jeanne McCullough. *Paris Review* 98 (Winter 1985). Accessed June 21, 2015. http://tinyurl.com/zz6x8ab.

———. "The Figure under the Carpet." In *Telling Lives: The Biographer's Art*, edited by Marc Pachter, 16–35. Philadelphia: University of Pennsylvania Press, 1985.

———. *Literary Biography*. Bloomington: Indiana University Press, 1959.

Edgerly, Lois Stiles, ed. *Give Her This Day: A Daybook of Women's Words*. Gardiner, Maine: Tilbury House, 1990.

Emerson, Ralph Waldo. "The Snow-Storm." Accessed October 16, 2014. http://www.poetryfoundation.org/poems-and-poets/poems/detail/45872.

Eve, Debra. "Jenny Joseph's 'When I Am an Old Woman I Shall Wear Purple.'" *Later Bloomer*. Accessed February 12, 2015. http://www.laterbloomer.com/jenny-joseph/.

"Experimental Music Studios." *University of Illinois School of Music*. Accessed May 31, 2015. http://ems.music.illinois.edu/.

"Family Psychology." *American Psychological Association*. Accessed July 9, 2014. https://www.apa.org/ed/graduate/specialize/family.aspx.

Ferguson, John, ed. *A New Liturgical Year*. Minneapolis: Augsburg Fortress Press, 1997.

Fox, Richard K. *Bella Starr, the Bandit Queen, or, the Female Jesse James: A Full and Authentic History of the Dashing Female Highwayman*. New York: printed by author, 1889. Repr., Austin, Tex.: Steck , 1960.

Fuller, Margaret. *Woman in the Nineteenth Century*. New York: W. W. Norton, 1971.

Gabra, Gawdat, and Karen J. Torjesen , eds. "Claremont Coptic Encyclopedia." *Claremont Colleges Digital Library*. Accessed February 14, 2015. http://ccdl.libraries.claremont.edu/cdm/landingpage/collection/cce.

Gates, Henry Louis, Jr. "TV's Black World Turns—But Stays Unreal." *New York Times*, November 12, 1989. Accessed June 23, 2014. http://tinyurl.com/hqxabrc.

Gehman, Geoff. "Friendship Takes a Long Road Trip to LVCO Collaboration." *Morning Call*, April 1, 2001. Accessed October 21, 2014. http://tinyurl.com/zuascy4.

Gimbel, Allen. "Elgar's Prize Song: Quotation and Allusion in the Second Symphony." *19th-Century Music* 12, no. 3 (Spring, 1989): 231–40.

———. "Larsen: Deep Summer Music; Solo Symphony; Marimba Concerto." *American Record Guide* 64, no. 4 (July/August 2001): 142.

———. "Larsen: Symphony 4; Songs of Light & Love; Songs from Letters." *American Record Guide* 63, no. 6 (November/December 2000): 170–71.

Goetzman, Keith, David McKee, Adam Platt, Tad Simons, Bill Souder, and Glen Warchol. "Get Out of Town." *Twin Cities Reader*, January 1–7, 1992, 8.

Goode, Erich, and Nachman Ben-Yehuda. *Moral Panics: The Social Construction of Deviance*. 2nd ed. Chichester, UK: Wiley-Blackwell, 2009.

Granade, S. Andrew. *Harry Partch: Hobo Composer*. Rochester, N.Y.: University of Rochester Press, 2014.

Hampl, Patricia. *The Florist's Daughter: A Memoir*. Orlando, Fla.: Harcourt, 2007.

———. *A Romantic Education*. Boston: Houghton Mifflin, 1981.

———. *Virgin Time: In Search of the Contemplative Life*. New York: Farrar, Straus and Giroux, 1992.
Hanes, Elizabeth. "The End of Civilization?: 7 Moments in the History of the Doomsday Clock." *History*, June 19, 2012. Accessed August 27, 2014. http://tinyurl.com/zzjdd4z.
Haryana, Jasmine. "How to Write an Object Poem." *eHow*. Accessed October 23, 2014. http://www.ehow.com/how_5085351_write-object-poem.html.
Heilbrun, Carolyn G. *The Education of a Woman: The Life of Gloria Steinem*. New York: Dial Press, 1995.
———. *Writing a Woman's Life*. New York: W.W. Norton, 1988.
Hertelendy, Paul. "Larsen: Every Man Jack." *American Record Guide* 64, no. 4 (July/August 2001): 12.
Hinkle-Turner, Elizabeth. *Women Composers and Music Technology in the United States: Crossing the Line*. Burlington, Vt.: Ashgate, 2006.
"History." *Innova Recordings*. Accessed January 15, 2015. http://www.innova.mu/about/history-2.
"History." *Minnesota Opera*. Accessed July 10, 2016. http://www.mnopera.org/about/history/.
Holcombe, Alex O. "Seeing Slow and Seeing Fast: Two Limits on Perception." *Trends in Cognitive Sciences* 13, no. 5 (2009): 216–21. Accessed January 9, 2015. http://tinyurl.com/hb8jjr2.
Horowitz, Joseph. "Flute: Eugenia Zukerman Plays a Libby Larsen Work." *New York Times*, October 13, 1980, C16.
Howes, David. "The Expanding Field of Sensory Studies." *Sensory Studies*. Accessed February 24, 2015. http://tinyurl.com/hg4ngcf.
"In the Key of Now." *American Composers Forum*. Accessed July 7, 2015. https://composersforum.org/acf40.
"Is Neil Armstrong's Famous Moon-Landing Quote Really a Misquote?" *NDTV*, June 5, 2013. Accessed November 4, 2014. http://tinyurl.com/lfwwsq2.
Jamison, Kay Redfield. *Exuberance: The Passion for Life*. New York: Vintage Books, 2004.
Kearns, Doris. "Angles of Vision." In *Telling Lives: The Biographer's Art*, edited by Marc Pachter, 91–103. Philadelphia: University of Pennsylvania Press, 1985.
Kelly, Jennifer. *In Her Own Words: Conversations with Composers in the United States*. Urbana: University of Illinois Press, 2013.
Kennan, Kent. *The Technique of Orchestration*. Upper Saddle River, N.J.: Prentice-Hall, 1970.
"Kennedy Announces Blockade of Cuba during the Missile Crisis." *History*. Published 2009. Accessed July 1, 2014. http://tinyurl.com/z6uthr8.
Kerman, Joseph. *Opera as Drama*. New York: Alfred A. Knopf, 1956.
Kiernan, Denise. *The Girls of Atomic City: The Untold Story of the Women Who Helped Win World War II*. New York: Touchstone, 2013.
Kimber, Marian Wilson. *The Elocutionists: Women, Music and the Spoken Word*. Urbana: University of Illinois Press, 2017.

Krinsky, Charles. *The Ashgate Companion to Moral Panics*. Farnham, UK: Ashgate, 2013.

LaRue, Jan. *Guidelines for Style Analysis*. New York: W. W. Norton, 1970.

Lassila, Kathrin. "A Brief History of Groupthink: Why Two, Three, or Many Heads Aren't Always Better Than One." *Yale Alumni Magazine* 71, no. 3 (January/February 2008). Accessed June 2, 2015. https://yalealumnimagazine.com/articles/1947.

Lee, Hermione. "The Art of Life: Are Biographies Fiction?" Conversation with Katie Derham, Ray Monk, and Stephen Frears. Recorded January 23, 2014. Institute of Art and Ideas video, 25:24. Accessed June 14, 2014. http://iai.tv/video/the-art-of-life.

Limerick, Patricia Nelson. *The Legacy of Conquest: The Unbroken Past of the American West*. New York: W. W. Norton, 1987.

Lipman, Samuel. "Backward & Downward with the Arts." *Commentary Magazine*, May 1, 1990. Accessed May 26, 2015. http://tinyurl.com/j47el24.

———. "Music and Musical Life: The Road to Now." *New Criterion* 3 (August 1985): 23–37. Reprinted in *Arguing for Music, Arguing for Culture*, 19–43. Boston: David R. Godine, in association with the American Council for the Arts, 1990.

———. "Out of the Ghetto." *Commentary Magazine*, March 1, 1985. Accessed May 25, 2015. https://www.commentarymagazine.com/article/out-of-the-ghetto/.

———. "Who's Killing Our Symphony Orchestras?" *New Criterion* 12 (September 1993). Accessed April 8, 2015. http://tinyurl.com/jjjnkcn.

Lisle, Laurie. *Portrait of an Artist: A Biography of Georgia O'Keeffe*. New York: Seaview Books, 1980.

London, Jack. *John Barleycorn*. Radford, Va.: Wilder, 2011.

Longfellow, Henry Wadsworth. "Snow-Flakes." Accessed October 16, 2014. http://www.poetryfoundation.org/poems-and-poets/poems/detail/44649.

———. "There Was a Little Girl." Accessed July 13, 2015. http://www.poetryfoundation.org/poem/173916.

Lopez, Arthur. *Rodeo Reina del Cielo (Rodeo Queen of Heaven)*. 2007. Denver Art Museum. Accessed July 9, 2016. http://artlopezart.com/new-work/past-work/rodeo-queen-of-heaven.html.

"The MacDowell Colony." Sigma Alpha Iota. Accessed November 24, 2014. http://tinyurl.com/h7t7w56.

"Margaret Atwood's Orpheus and Eurydice Cycle." Accessed December 19, 2014. http://tinyurl.com/zakolmk.

"Marian Antiphons and Hymns." *Queen of Angels Foundation*. Accessed August 15, 2014. http://www.thequeenofangels.com/mary-the-queen/marian-antiphons/.

Marx, Leo. "The Idea of Nature in America." *Daedalus* 137, no. 2 (Spring 2008): 8–21.

"Mary of Magdala." *Future Church*. Accessed February 16, 2015. http://tinyurl.com/zef74dx.

"McCarthy-Welch Exchange." *American Rhetoric*. Accessed June 21, 2014. http://www.americanrhetoric.com/speeches/welch-mccarthy.html.

McClary, Susan. *Feminine Endings: Music, Gender, and Sexuality*. Minneapolis: University of Minnesota Press, 2002.

McCoy, Terrence. "Former Highest-Ranking U.S. Cardinal Blames 'Feminization' for the Catholic Church's Problems." *Washington Post*, January 13, 2015. Accessed January 13, 2015. http://wapo.st/1FPjZJd.

"McKnight Foundation Background." *McKnight Foundation*. Accessed January 16, 2015. https://www.mcknight.org/about-us/background.

Meah, Angela, and Peter Jackson. "Crowded Kitchens: The 'Democratisation' of Domesticity?" *Gender, Place and Culture* 20, no. 5 (2013), 578–96.

Merton, Thomas. *The Asian Journal of Thomas Merton*. San Francisco: New Directions Books, 1968.

Milford, Nancy. *Zelda: A Biography*. New York: Harper Perennial Modern Classics, 2011.

Mitchell, David. "The Essential Phases of Child Development." Accessed June 25, 2014. http://www.whywaldorfworks.org/02_W_Education/child_development.asp (Web page no longer available).

Mitternight, Andrea J. "An Original Work: 'Brothers and Sisters' and *Songs from Letters* by Libby Larsen." DMA diss., Louisiana State University, 2004.

"Morris Louis: Veils. September 10–October 18, 2014." *Mnuchin Gallery*. Accessed January 8, 2015. http://www.mnuchingallery.com/exhibitions/morris-louis-veils/desc.

Munro, Eleanor. *Originals: American Women Artists*. New York: Simon and Schuster, 1979.

Musil, Robert K. *Rachel Carson and Her Sisters: Extraordinary Women Who Have Shaped America's Environment*. New Brunswick, N.J.: Rutgers University Press, 2014.

"Nov. 15, 1969 Anti-Vietnam War Demonstration Held." The Learning Network, *New York Times*, November 15, 2011. Accessed November 4, 2014. http://tinyurl.com/jzf3ktv.

Novack, Saul. "The Significance of the Phrygian Mode in the History of Tonality." *Miscellanea Musicologica* 9 (1977): 82–177.

O'Keeffe, Georgia. *Georgia O'Keeffe*, New York: Viking Press, 1976.

Ong, Walter J. "The Shifting Sensorium." In *The Varieties of Sensory Experience*, edited by David Howes, 47–60. Toronto: University of Toronto Press, 1991.

Ostriker, Alicia. "Learning to Breathe under Water: Considering Muriel Rukeyser's Oceanic Work." Accessed February 7, 2015. http://www.poetryfoundation.org/article/246000.

Otten, Joseph. "Antiphon." In *The Catholic Encyclopedia*, vol. 1. New York: Robert Appleton, 1907. Accessed August 15, 2014. http://www.newadvent.org/cathen/01575b.htm.

Parenti, Susan. "Composing the Music School: Proposals for a Feminist Composition Curriculum." April 1995. Accessed March 10, 2015. http://ada.evergreen.edu/~arunc/texts/parenti/parenti.htm.

"Patricia Hampl: 'The Florist's Daughter.'" *The Diane Rehm Show*. NPR, November 27, 2007. Accessed August 24, 2014. http://tinyurl.com/j49p7kj.

Payne, Karen, ed. *Between Ourselves: Letters between Mothers and Daughters.* Boston: Houghton Mifflin, 1983.

"The Pope and the Sin of Environmental Degradation." *Living on Earth.* PRI, July 18, 2014. Accessed August 31, 2014. http://tinyurl.com/gqm8moh.

Powell, Susan, ed. *John Mirk's Festial.* Oxford: Oxford University Press, 2011.

Reese, Gustave. *Music in the Renaissance.* New York: W. W. Norton, 1954.

"Rev. James A. Duffy [obituary]." *Nebraska Register* 44, no. 8 (February 16, 1968). Accessed September 4, 2014. Reprinted at http://www.findagrave.com/cgi-bin/fg.cgi?page=gr&GRid=60579002.

Rone, Vincent E. "'A Voice Cries Out in the Wilderness': The French Organ School Responds to the Second Vatican Council of the Catholic Church." PhD diss., University of California, Santa Barbara, 2014.

Root, Marilyn. *Women at the Wheel: 42 Stories of Freedom, Fanbelts, and the Lure of the Open Road.* Naperville, Ill.: Sourcebooks, 1999.

Rosenberg, Matt. "Levittown." *Geography.* Accessed June 20, 2014. http://geography.about.com/od/urbaneconomicgeography/a/levittown.htm.

Ruether, Rosemary Radford. *New Woman, New Earth: Sexist Ideologies and Human Liberation.* Boston: Beacon Press, 1995. First published by Seabury Press, 1975.

Rukeyser, Muriel. *The Life of Poetry.* New York: A. A. Wynn/Current Books, 1949. Excerpts reprinted at http://www.english.illinois.edu/maps/poets/m_r/rukeyser/life.htm. Accessed February 7, 2015.

Runestad, Jake. "Giving Life to New Opera: The John Duffy Composers Institute." *New Music Box,* June 21, 2012. Accessed April 2, 2015. http://www.newmusicbox.org/articles/duffy-institute/.

Schaberg, Jane. *The Resurrection of Mary Magdalene: Legends, Apocrypha, and the Christian Testament.* New York: Continuum International, 2004.

Schafer, R. Murray. *The Soundscape: Our Sonic Environment and the Tuning of the World.* Rochester, Vt.: Destiny Books, 1994.

Schjeldahl, Peter. "When It Pours." *New Yorker,* September 22, 2014. Accessed July 10, 2016. http://www.newyorker.com/?post_type=article&p=2823459.

Schnittke, Alfred. "Polystylistic Tendencies in Modern Music (1971)." In *A Schnittke Reader,* edited by Aleksandr Ivashkin, translated by John Derek Goodliffe, 87–90. Bloomington: Indiana University Press, 2002.

Schwartz, Elliott, and Barney Childs, eds. *Contemporary Composers on Contemporary Music.* New York: Da Capo Press, 1978.

Shain, Barry Alan. *The Myth of American Individualism: The Protestant Origins of American Political Thought.* Princeton, N.J.: Princeton University Press, 1996.

Slayton, Michael K., ed. *Women of Influence in Contemporary Music: Nine American Composers.* New York: Scarecrow Press, 2010.

Smith, Catherine Parsons. "'A Distinguishing Virility': On Feminism and Modernism in American Art Music." In *Cecilia Reclaimed: Feminist Perspectives on Gender and Music,* edited by Susan Cook and Judy S. Tsou, 90–106. Urbana: University of Illinois Press, 1994.

Smith, Laura. "beautiful, sublime." *The University of Chicago, Theories of Media, Keywords Glossary*. Accessed January 10, 2015. http://csmt.uchicago.edu/glossary2004/beautifulsublime.htm.

Sokolski, Henry D., ed. *Getting MAD: Nuclear Mutual Assured Destruction, Its Origins and Practice*. Carlisle, Pa.: Strategic Studies Institute, 2004. Accessed July 9, 2016. http://www.strategicstudiesinstitute.army.mil/pdffiles/PUB585.pdf.

"Southern Baptist Convention Passes Resolution Opposing Women as Pastors." *New York Times*, June 15, 2000. Accessed February 19, 2015. http://tinyurl.com/zvfja73.

"The Southern Manifesto (text and signatories)." *Kdentify*. Accessed June 23, 2014. http://tinyurl.com/jadupzk.

"The Southern Manifesto." *Time* 67, no. 13 (March 26, 1956): 27. *Academic Search Complete*, EBSCO*host*. Accessed July 10, 2016.

Souvay, Charles. "Elias." In *The Catholic Encyclopedia*, vol. 5. New York: Robert Appleton, 1909. Accessed August 16, 2014. http://www.newadvent.org/cathen/05381b.htm.

Stanley, Liz. *The Auto/Biographical I: The Theory and Practice of Feminist Auto/Biography*. Manchester: Manchester University Press, 1992.

Stearns, David Patrick. "Contemporary Sounds in Indiana." *USA Today*, September 17, 1996, 7D.

Stevens, Wallace. "The Snow Man." Accessed October 20, 2014. http://www.poetryfoundation.org/poem/174502.

Stravinsky, Igor. *Poetics of Music: In the Form of Six Lessons*. Translated by Arthur Knodel and Ingolf Dahl. Cambridge, Mass.: Harvard University Press, 1947.

"Saint Teresa of Avila." *American Catholic*. Accessed August 20, 2014. http://www.americancatholic.org/features/saints/saint.aspx?id=1169.

Sullivan, Todd E. *Dancing Solo: Music of Libby Larsen*. Liner Notes. Minnesota Contemporary Ensemble, Innova 512 recording, 1997. Accessed December 4, 2014. http://www.innova.mu/sites/www.innova.mu/files/liner-notes/512.htm.

Thoreau, Henry David. *The Writings of Henry D. Thoreau: Walden*. Princeton, N.J.: Princeton University Press, 1971.

Tranströmer, Tomas. "Snow-Melting Time, '66." In *The Half-Finished Heaven: The Best Poems of Tomas Tranströmer*, translated by Robert Bly, 55. Minneapolis: Graywolf Press, 2001.

Tricker, R. A. R., *An Introduction to Meteorological Optics*. New York: Elsevier , 1970.

Ueland, Brenda. *Me: A Memoir*. Duluth, Minn. Holy Cow! Press, 1994.

Upright, Diane. "The Technique of Morris Louis." In *Morris Louis: The Complete Paintings*, 49–58. New York: Harry N. Abrams, 1985.

Vaughan, Peter. "We're Bullish on Libby." *Minneapolis Star*, reprinted in *Minnesota: The University of Minnesota Alumni Magazine* 80, no. 5 (March 1981): 40–41. Accessed December 10, 2014. http://tinyurl.com/zlfzzcy.

"Vietnam War: Allied Troop Levels 1960–73." *American War Library*. Accessed November 4, 2014. http://www.americanwarlibrary.com/vietnam/vwatl.htm.

Visser, Nick. "Hundreds of Thousands Turn Out for People's Climate March in New York City." *Huffington Post*, March 26, 2015. Accessed March 26, 2015. http://tinyurl.com/p6m7jqh.

Von Glahn, Denise. "Musical Actions, Political Sounds: Libby Larsen and Composerly Consciousness." In *Current Directions in Ecomusicology*, edited by Aaron S. Allen and Kevin Dawe, 258–72. New York: Routledge/Taylor and Francis, 2015.

———. *Music and the Skillful Listener: American Women Compose the Natural World.* Bloomington: Indiana University Press, 2013.

———. *The Sounds of Place: Music and the American Cultural Landscape.* Boston: Northeastern University Press, 2003.

Von Gunden, Heidi C. University of Illinois Faculty Profile. Accessed April 3, 2015. http://www.music.illinois.edu/faculty/heidi-c-von-gunden.

Wascoe, Rebecca. "Libby Larsen and the Song Cycle: A Discussion of 'My Ántonia.'" DMA diss., University of Illinois at Urbana-Champaign, 2008.

White, Lynn, Jr. "The Historical Roots of Our Ecologic Crisis." *Science* 155, no. 3767 (March 10, 1967): 1203–7.

Wilford, John Noble. "*Flutes Offer Clues to Stone-Age Music.*" *New York Times*, June 24, 2009. Accessed September 30, 2014. http://www.nytimes.com/2009/06/25/science/25flute.html.

Williams, Raymond. "Ideas of Nature." In *Problems in Materialism and Culture: Selected Essays*, 67–85. London: Verso, 1980.

Williston, Jay. "Thaddeus Cahill's Teleharmonium." *Synthmuseum*. Accessed February 24, 2015. http://www.synthmuseum.com/magazine/0102jw.html.

"With All Deliberate Speed." *American Treasures of the Library of Congress*. Accessed June 15, 2015. http://www.loc.gov/exhibits/treasures/trr007.html.

Xayhaothao, Doualy. "Fort Worth Opera Shelves World Premiere of 'A Wrinkle in Time.'" *Kera News*, Sunday, February 16, 2014. Accessed February 23, 2015. http://keranews.org/post/fort-worth-opera-shelves-world-premiere-wrinkle-time.

Yeats, William Butler. "Brown Penny." Accessed July 15, 2016. http://www.poemhunter.com/poem/brown-penny/.

———. "The Words upon the Windowpane." In *William Butler Yeats: Selected Poems and Four Plays*, edited and with an introduction by M. L. Rosenthal, 158–71. New York: Scribner Paperback Poetry, 1996.

Selected Works by Libby Larsen

Aubade. Accessed October 9, 2014. http://tinyurl.com/zhg6pz3.

Aubade. Unpublished score manuscript, 1982.

Barnum's Bird. "Composer's Notes." Accessed September 6, 2015. https://libbylarsen.com/index.php?contentID=235&resourceID=1378.

The Birth Project. Minneapolis: Libby Larsen, 2015.

Black Birds, Red Hills. "Composer's Note." Accessed July 10, 2016. https://libbylarsen.com/index.php?contentID=242&resourceID=1240.

Black Birds, Red Hills: A Portrait of Six Paintings of Georgia O'Keeffe. Oxford: Oxford University Press, 1996.

Bronze Veils. "Composer's Notes." Accessed December 20, 2014. https://libbylarsen.com/index.php?contentID=242&resourceID=1298.
Bronze Veils. ECS, 1984.
Circular Rondo. ECS, 1989.
Concerto: Cold, Silent Snow. "Composer's Note." Accessed October 13, 2014. https://libbylarsen.com/index.php?contentID=236&resourceID=1174.
DDT. Minneapolis: Libby Larsen, 2014.
Deep Summer Music, Solo Symphony, Marimba Concerto: After Hampton. Koch International Classics, 3-7520-2 111.
"Encounters with Minnesota Artists—Libby Larsen." Broadcast March 3, 1979. Twin Cities PBS video, 28:43. Accessed May 21, 2015. http://tinyurl.com/zdrgvff.
Eurydice. Unpublished score manuscript, 1978.
Fanfare for the Women. New York: Oxford University Press, 1996.
Frankenstein, or The Modern Prometheus. "Instrumentation." Accessed June 17, 2015. http://tinyurl.com/zavblhr.
Four on the Floor. New York: Oxford University Press. 1998.
Grand Larsen-Y: Vocal Music of Libby Larsen. Albany Records: Troy 634, 2004.
Hell's Belles. Minneapolis: Kenwood Editions, 2001.
Holy Roller. "Composer's Note." Accessed August 25, 2014. http://libbylarsen.com/index.php?contentID=242&profileID=1293.
In a Winter Garden. ECS, catalog no. 6504.
Libby Larsen: String Symphony, Songs of Light and Love, Songs from Letters, 2000 Koch International Classics 3-7481-2 HI.
Love after 1950. "Composer's Note." Accessed July 10, 2016. http://tinyurl.com/zeq7npm.
Love after 1950. New York: Oxford University Press, 2001.
The Magdalene. "Composer's Note." Accessed January 15, 2015. https://libbylarsen.com/index.php?contentID=241&resourceID=1643.
The Magdalene. Minneapolis: Kenwood Editions, 2012.
ME (Brenda Ueland). New York: Oxford University Press, 1998.
Missa Gaia: Mass for the Earth. ECS, 1992.
Missa Gaia: Mass for the Earth. Koch International Classics, 1995, 3-7279-2.
Notes Slipped under the Door. "Composer's Note." Accessed October 1, 2014. https://libbylarsen.com/index.php?contentID=241&resourceID=1218.
Now I Pull Silver. Minneapolis: Libby Larsen, 2008.
O Magnum Mysterium. Minneapolis: Libby Larsen, 2011.
Overture: Parachute Dancing. "Composer's Notes." Accessed May 29, 2015. http://tinyurl.com/zlaotna.
Rodeo Queen of Heaven. "Composer's Note." Accessed September 6, 2014. http://tinyurl.com/j9mtg8w.
Rodeo Queen of Heaven. Minneapolis: Libby Larsen, 2010.
"The Role of the Musician in the 21st Century: Rethinking the Core." Accessed March 11, 2015. https://libbylarsen.com/as_the-role-of-the-musician.

Saints without Tears. Minneapolis: Libby Larsen, 1976.
Seven Ghosts. Accessed September 6, 2015. http://tinyurl.com/zsmzyfy.
Slow Structures. "Composer's Note." Accessed October 14, 2014. https://libbylarsen.com/index.php?contentID=242&resourceID=1253.
Slow Structures for Flute, Violoncello and Piano. Minneapolis: Libby Larsen, 2005.
Songs from Letters. New York: Oxford University Press, 1989.
Sonnets from the Portuguese. "Composer's Note." Accessed April 8, 2015. http://tinyurl.com/hblpdyf.
String Quartet No. 4: Emergence. Minneapolis: Kenwood Editions, 2015.
Symphony: Water Music (Symphony No. 1). ECS, 1984.
Ulloa's Ring. ECS, 1987.
"While You Here Do Snoring Lie." Unpublished score manuscript, 1969.
The Womanly Song of God. "Composer's Note." Accessed January 10, 2015. http://www.singers.com/composers/Libby-Larsen/.

Index

academia, 3, 281n3; composers working outside, 244, 249, 258; male domination of, 100, 248, 257, 260, 283n62, 299n90
acoustic environment, 196, 204, 257. *See also* sounds
acoustics of music, course in, 110
action painting, 285n99
Adams, John, 240, 274n44
Advent, in *In a Winter Garden*, 47–49
Alabama, University of, 167
aliases, Larsen's, 283n50
Allan, Rebecca, 209
All around Sound, 194
Alsop, Marin, 226, 237
American Bandstand (TV show), 8
American Composers Forum, 260. *See also* Minnesota Composers Forum
American Composers Orchestra, 244
"American Dialogue, An" (Lipman), 239
American English, 229, 264; Larsen's sensitivity to, 40, 46, 153, 222, 256
American Guild of Organists, 230
American music, as Larsen's roots, 263
American Music Center, 146
Americanness, Larsen's, 264–65
American Symphony Orchestra League, 242
Ancia saxophone quartet, 98
Anderson, Irene, 21
Anderson, Laurie, 240
Anderson, Marion, 8
anger, Larsen's, 285n94
anthems, churches', 230
"Anything I Put My Mind To," in *Notes Slipped under the Door*, 164
"Arachne Gives Thanks to Athena" (Stallings), 198
Argento, Dominick, 109, 119, 125, 146–47, 286n11; influence on Larsen, 123, 258, 284n71
art, 137, 166, 231, 285n98; Cassatt's, 290n73; Larsen's glass, 285n95; O'Keeffe's, 167, 169, 289n66; O'Keeffe's techniques, 290n62, 290n69
"Art (Life Is Love . . .)," in *ME (Brenda Ueland)*, 152, 155–56, *159–60*
"art music," 116, 228, 254
Art of Arleen Auger, The, 228–29
arts, the, 238–39, 253, 264
ASCAP-Chorus America Award for Adventurous Programming, 230
Aspen Music Festival, 229
assassinations, Larsen's awareness of, 8–9
assistants, Larsen's, 233–35, 262, 269n15, 298n46
Atwood, Margaret, 133
Aubade, 77–78, *79–80*
audience, composers' choice about accessibility for, 244–45, 249, 283n47
Auger, Arleen, 228–29
Austin College, Larsen's residency at, 244
avant-garde, 285n98; Lipman's criticisms of, 240, 243, 298n70

Babbitt, Milton, 3, 249, 283n47

baby boom, 2
Baltimore Symphony Orchestra, 226
Bankhead, Tallulah, 178–79
Barnett, Carol, 260
Barnum, P. T., 231
Barnum's Bird, 231
Bartók, Béla, 19–20, 114
bassoons, in *Saints without Tears*, 40, 42, 44
Baxstresser, Suzanne, 101
Bay Area Women's Philharmonic, 226
Bayless, Anne Francis, 208–9
Baylor University, 191–92, 292n117
Beatae Mariae Virginis (mass), 37, 60
Beauchamp, James, 243
beauty: of art, 136–37; Larsen questioning standards of, 173–77, 180–82, 198; sublime vs., 285n102
bells: in *Hell's Belles*, 180; in *O Magnum Mysterium*, 203–4
Berg, Gregory, 256–57
Bernstein, Leonard, 8
Berry, Wendell, 56–58
"Beryl," in *Love after 1950*, 174
Between Ourselves (Payne), 163
Bible text, in *Missa Gaia: Mass for the Earth*, 56, 58
Biery, Marilyn Perkins, 36
Big Eyes (film), 269n11
"Big Sister Says, 1967: (a honky-tonk)," in *Love after 1950*, 173–76, *175–76*, 182, 198, 290n79
biography, 269nn4–5; effects of being subject of, 235, 255, 265–66; process of writing, 265–66
Birth Project, The, 256
Black Birds, Red Hills, 149, 167–72, *171*, 289n58, 289n66
"Black Bird Series (In the Patio IX)," in *Black Birds, Red Hills*, 169
"Black Bird with Snow-Covered Red Hills, A," in *Black Birds, Red Hills*, 169, 171
"Black Rock with Blue Sky and White Clouds," in *Black Birds, Red Hills*, 169–70, *171*
Black Water (Duffy), 224–25
"Blond Men (a torch song)," in *Love after 1950*, 173
blues, 46–47, 63
Bly, Robert, 82, 85, 92, 279n32
body, in Larsen's engagement with music, 173, 257
boogie-woogie: Larsen using, 46–47, 60, 173–74; mother's love of, 28, 274n30, 276n25
Borud, Russell, 263, 293n7, 294n34
"Boy's Lips (a blues)," in *Love after 1950*, 173
Bradshaw, Keith, 260
Brant, Henry, 196, 293n12
Brass Flight, 226
Bridges, Scott, 167
Bronze Veils, 135–44, *139–42*, 167, 169, 285n95, 289n61
Brooks, William "Bill," 243–44, 300n99; on Larsen's residency at University of Illinois, 245–47, 249–51
Browning, Elizabeth Barrett, 228
"Brown Penny" (Yeats), 123–24
Brün, Herbert, 243–44, 246, 299n87
Brunelle, Philip, 226–27, *227*, 230–32
Burke, Edmund, 285n102
Burke, Raymond, 145–46, 286n6
Button, Dick, 7

Cage, John, 8, 245, 263–64
Cahill, Thaddeus, 195
Calamity Jane, 162–64
Canticle of Mary, 150
car culture, 5, 26–29, 274n42, 281n16
Cardamone Jackson, Donna, 110, 147, 259, 282n43
Carlson, Bruce, 151
cars, Larsen's love for, 26–32, 182

Carson, Rachel, 2
Cassatt, Mary, 166, 172
Catalano, Peter, 238
Catholic Church, 126; changes in, 1, 18, 33, 36–37; as community of believers, 63–66; demotion of Virgin Mary in, 36–37, 295n42; importance of Mary Magdalene in, 182–83; influence on Larsen, 33, 48, 81, 99; Larsen leaving, 58, 68, 257; Larsen's education in, 17–18; Larsen's lack of reconciliation with, 63, 275n41; rituals of, 34–35, 63, 210; roles for women in, 68, 145–46, 183–84; systems of, 39, 145. *See also* religion; Vatican II
Celebration Mass, 46
cellos: in *Emergence*, 217, 296n62; in *Slow Structures*, 90, 93
Center Opera (now Minnesota Opera), 125
chamber music, 63
chamber orchestra, in *In a Winter Garden*, 47–52
chants: effects of, 103, 196; influence on Larsen, 81, 101, 126, 144; influence on Larsen's compositions, 60–63, 185–86, 204; in *The Magdalene*, 185–87. *See also* Gregorian chants
Charlotte's Web (White), 8, 107, 121–22
"Childhood," in *ME (Brenda Ueland)*, 152, *154–58*
childhood, Larsen's: family dinners in, 10–12; importance of school in, 15–16; sisters in, 14–15
children, 8, 12–14
Chinook Psalter text, in *Missa Gaia: Mass for the Earth*, 56, 58
choirs, 230; in *O Magnum Mysterium*, 203–4, 206–7
choral music, 102
chorus, high school, 101
Christianity, women's place in, 149–50, 191, 291n102. *See also* Catholic Church; religion
Christmas, Larsen's joy in, 202–3
"Christmas Rose Carol," in *In a Winter Garden*, 52, *53–55*, 276n39, 295n44
circles and connections, as composition theme, 57, 63, 72
circular breathing, 112
Circular Rondo, 112–14, *113*, 282n34
civil rights movement, 6–8, 272n19, 272n22
clarinets, in *Black Birds, Red Hills*, 167, 169
Clark, Dick, 8
Cleveland Quartet, 232
Cliburn, Van, 7–8, 241
Cold War, 1, 3–4, 48
Colette, Sister, 19–21, *34*, 112–13
Colgrass, Michael, 223
collaborations, Larsen's, 82, 120, 162, 191, 203, 223, 265; with Brunelle, 230–31; with conductors, 226–28; with Dunham, 232–33; efforts put into, 259, 261; with engineers and electroacoustic composers, 194, 262–63; with Fry Street Quartet, 207, 209, 211–12; with Hampl, 47–52; relations with assistants as, 233–35; strengths in, 222, 226, 231, 254, 266, 302n23; with Sutton, 111–12
Collected Poems (Rukeyser), 177
color: Louis's use of, 170, 172; O'Keeffe's use of, 167, 169–72, 290n69
color-field painting, 135–36
Columbia-Princeton Electronic Music Center, 8
Coming Forth into Day (Symphony No. 2), 227, 230–31
Commentary (magazine), 238
commodity, art as, 231
communication: by Larsen's parents, 11–12, 108; music as, 38, 249

communications class, 108–9
community, Larsen's engagement in, 264–65, 267
composer, Larsen as, 127, 252; assets in, 101, 106–7, 114; career of, 102, 106; encouragement for, 106–7, 111; not fitting stereotype of, 111, 222; recognition of self as, 109, 267; self-image as, 104, 143, 251; strengths as, 229–30, 233; wanting to be remembered as, 231–32
composer-in-residence, Larsen as, 69, 146, 209, 245
composers, 108, 230, 264; of "art music," 116; choice about accessibility for audience, 244–45, 249, 283n47; of electroacoustic music, 262–63; of electronic and computer music, 194, 243; influences on Larsen, 254, 263–64; Lipman's criticism of, 240–42; opera, 223–24; scarcity of women among, 243, 247, 260, 282n30, 302n118; stereotypes of, 111, 222, 251, 258; support for, 117–18, 231, 260; women (*see* women composers); working outside academia, 244, 249, 258
Composers Commissioning Program, of the Minnesota Composers Forum, 77–78
Composers Forums, at University of Illinois, 247–48, 300n93, 300n96
composing process, Larsen's, 110, 168, 211; research in, 225–26, 259; with vocal texts, 113, 162–63
"Composing the Music School" (Parenti), 250–51
composition programs. *See* music and composition programs
compositions, Larsen's, 21, 104, 115, 149, 191, 256; challenging expectations, 88, 92, 144; criticisms of, 236, 257–58; first, 19; heading toward quiet, 202, 294n30; number of, 236, 266; parents' reactions to, 19, 28, 274n43; religious/spiritual, 46, 256; resisting compartmentalization, 52–56, 152, 199–200, 257–58; revelations of self in, 151, 165–66, 178; soft pieces vs. display pieces, 201–2, 279n28; as theater pieces, 191, 238; themes of, 57, 63; titles as integral to, 84. *See also* goals of Larsen's compositions; influences on Larsen's compositions; inspirations for Larsen's compositions; music, Larsen's
concert halls, 196, 221, 293n12
"Concert Hall That Fell Asleep and Woke Up a Car Radio, The" (speech), 221
Concerto: Cold, Silent Snow, 70, 81–83
conductors, 226–28, 230
Cone, Edward T., 3
"Conversation in Avila," in *Saints without Tears*, 42–44
Copland, Aaron, 108
Coptic, in *The Magdalene*, 185, 291n100, 292n111
copyright issues, 121–22, 167
Corigliano, John, 240
country music, 111–12
Cowboy Songs, in *Silver Fox*, 126
Crane, Jeff, 262
creativity, 256; Larsen's, 123, 146, 234; love and, 158, 161
Crossroads Project, Fry Street Quartet's, 208, 210
Crouan, David, 35
Crumb, George, 40, 240, 246, 249
Cuban missile crisis, 1, 4
cultures, blended in *Missa Gaia: Mass for the Earth*, 56
"Current Trends in Contemporary Women Composers" (conference), 147

Dahle, Oscar B., 101–2

dance, 101, 210
Dancing Solo: Music of Libby Larsen, 167
Daniels, Kathryn, 173–75, 290n79
Davies, Robert, 208–9, 211
dawn greetings, *Aubade* in tradition of, 78
DDT, 2, 257
Dean, M. K., 56, 283n50
"Dear Mommy," in *Notes Slipped under the Door*, 165
Deep Summer Music, 32, 279n22
Del Tredici, David, 240
Déserts (Varèse), 197
Diaghilev, Sergei, 210
"Dies Irae," Larsen's references to, 46, 60
dissonance, 40; in *Emergence*, 212–13, 217, 219; in *Eurydice*, 130–31
Dixieland, 22
Doolittle, 284n90, 285n91
Doolittle, Hilda, 126–27, 131, 151, 284n90
"Doomsday Clock," 4, 48, 270n8, 271n10
Double Joy, 230
double string orchestra, in *Four on the Floor*, 226
Dove, Rita, 173
Downwind of Roses in Maine, 32, 67, 70, 82
draft lottery, 1, 100
Duffy, James (granduncle), 39
Duffy, John, 222–23, 225–26
Duncan, Isadora, 177
Dunham, James, 232–33, 297n39
Dwight, John Sullivan, 277n1
dynamaphone, 195

Earth (Holst Trope), 226
Earth Day, 144
ear training, Larsen teaching, 123
Eastern Bloc, defectors from, 7, 272n20
Eckhart, Meister, 56, 58
ecology, 210–11, 257. *See also* environment
economics, Larsen's talent in, 102–4
economy, postwar, 5
Edel, Leon, 255, 269n5
Edgar, Grace, 263, 269n15, 298n46
education, 2, 302n118; music's purpose and, 210, 241, 299n78; postsecondary (*see* academia). *See also* music and composition programs
education, Larsen's, 12; in Catholic school, 36–37; importance of, 15–16; music in, 17–18. *See also* University of Minnesota
egalitarianism, criticisms of, 239
Eisenhower, Dwight, 5, 7
electronic and computer music, 243, 262, 293n6
electronic music, musicians asked to honor, 194
Emergence: String Quartet No. 4, 198, 211–12, 296n62; commissioned by Fry Street Quartet, 207, 294n21; hopefulness in, 215–20
Emerson, Ralph Waldo, 85
Encounters with Minnesota Artists, 222
energy, Larsen's, 14–16, 229–30, 235, 265; attractiveness of, 146, 223; in compositions, 74–77, 114; learning to focus, 16, 21, 106; outlets for, 22–23, 69
Engelson, Thea, 167
engineers, collaborations with, 262–63
enhakē, 60, 277n55
Ensemble Singers, 230
entertainment, 231, 241
environment: acoustic, 196, 204, 257; Fry Street Quartet's efforts to increase consciousness of, 208–10; Larsen's awareness of, 68, 80–81; Larsen's compositions inspired by, 80–81, 97–98, 149; Larsen's concern for, 149, 209; of the Southwest, 168–69

environment, Larsen's, 69–70, 80–81. *See also* Midwest; Minneapolis
environmental crisis, 2, 220, 257, 276n42; *Emergence* reflecting, 213–17, 219; influence on Larsen, 70, 144
Erickson, Robert, 240, 243–44
"Eurydice" (Doolittle), 126–27
Eurydice, rage of, 127–29, 131
Eurydice: Through the Looking Glass (originally *Eurydice: Looking Back*), 126–33, *128–30*, *132–34*, 284n90, 285n94
"Evergreens, The," in *In a Winter Garden*, 49, *50–51*
Evers, Medgar, 8, 272n22
Every Man Jack, 225–26, 237–38, 296n14
Experimental Music Studios, 243
exuberance, 266, 297n27

faith, struggles with, 48–49
Falletta, JoAnn, 226
families, ideal, 5–6
family, Larsen's, 161, 255, 261; adult, 252–53, 255; childhood, 10–12, 14–15, 23–26; public vs. private personality and, 233–35
Fanfare for the Women, 196, 289n58
Farrar, John, 224
Faubus, Orval, 7
Feminine Endings (McClary), 251
feminism, 236, 276n42
Ferrand, Katherine, 198
Festival de Música Contemporánea de La Habana, 260
Fetler, Paul, 109, 146, 258, 286n11
fiddles, in *Rodeo Queen of Heaven*, 60, 63
fifths, spiral/circle of, 103
Fitzgerald, Scott and Zelda, 2, 269n11
Florida State University, 270n1
flowers, in Larsen's gardens, 261
flutes, 198; in *Aubade*, 78; in Larsen's compositions on nature, 70–71; in *Notes Slipped under the Door*, 164–65; in *Now I Pull Silver*, 198–200; in *Saints without Tears*, 40–44; in *Slow Structures*, 90–91, 93; in *Ulloa's Ring*, 73–76, 279nn20–21
food chemist, Larsen's father as, 13–14
"Footlight Wisdom," in *Hell's Belles*, 180, *181*, 182
Fort Worth Opera, 193
Four on the Floor, *29–31*, 46, 226, 245, 274n43, 275n48; speed of, 28–29
Francis, Pope, 56–57, 276n42, 286n6
Frankenstein; or, The Modern Prometheus, 194, 245
Frankenthaler, Helen, 135–36
Franklin, John Hope, 221
Frauenliebe und Leben (Schumann), 172, 228
Freed, Alan, 5
"Fresh Breeze," in *Symphony: Water Music*, 69
Frey, Matt, 223
"From Hell," in *Eurydice*, 131, *132–33*
"Frozen Fountain Carol," in *In a Winter Garden*, 54, 81, 85
Fry Street String Quartet: efforts to increase environmental consciousness, 208–10; *Emergence* commissioned by, 97, 207, 211–12, 294n21; playing *Emergence*, 212–19
Fuller, Buckminster, 7
Fuller, Margaret, 25
"Futurist's Orchestra" (Russolo), 195

Gaia theory, 73
Gehman, Geoff, 166
gender, 82, 145, 167, 262; continuing influence on Larsen, 149, 198, 220, 260–61; Larsen challenging assumptions of, 231, 247; Larsen's preference for female voices, 46, 126; male dom-

ination in academia, 100, 248, 257, 260, 283n62, 299n90; male domination in music world, 100, 111, 146–47, 257, 283n62, 299n90; nature and, 71, 278n5, 279n32; religion and, 36–37, 68, 145–46, 149–50, 184; women attacked on, 236, 248–50, 301n112
gender differences, in opportunities, 3, 68, 101, 103
gender relations, changing, 290n74
generation gap, 5, 100, 271n14
Genesis II (Vandervelde), 287n15, 287n19
George, Molly Larsen (sister), 14, *16*, *24*, *34*, 107
George W. Truett Theological Seminary, 191
German Romantics, 95
Gesamtkunstwerk (concept), 210, 295n57
Gideon, Miriam, 254
Gimbel, Allen, 236–37
"Ginny" doll, as bribe, 10–11
Girl Scouts, 26
"Giveaway, The," in *Saints without Tears*, 41–42
Glass, Philip, 240, 299n73
glass harmonica (crystallophone), 286n111
Gnostics, 184, 287n25
goals of Larsen's compositions, 82, 152, 231, 241; deliver hopeful message, 211; having listeners "be" the subject, 32, 167–68; inciting action, 224–25; not solely education, 210, 299n78
Grahams, Mrs., 18
Grammy, for *The Art of Arleen Auger*, 228–29
Greenberg, Clement, 135–36
Greene, Ethan, 224
"Greenwich Village," in *ME (Brenda Ueland)*, 152
Gregorian chants, 18–19; influence of, 20, 38; loss of, 35, 273n19
Gregory, Pope, 183
Gross, Dorothy, 257
Guang, Lu, 209
guitars, 113–14, 199

Hampl, Patricia, 47–52, 71, 81, 276n32, 288n28
handbell choir, in *Hell's Belles*, 180
Harissios Papamarkou Chair in Education and Technology, 221
Harjo, Joy, 56–58
Harriet, the Woman Called Moses (Musgrave), 240
Harrison, Lou, 196
Havana Contemporary Music Festival, 260
H.D. *See* Doolittle, Hilda
health, Larsen's, 235
Helen Marie, Sister, 18
Hell's Belles, 151, 166, 178–82, *181*, 291n95
"He Never Misses (1880)," in *Songs from Letters*, 163
Hertelendy, Paul, 237–38
Hiller, Lajaren, 240, 243, 299n87
Hinkle-Turner, Elizabeth, 244–49, 251, 287n26, 299n91, 300n109
Hitchcock, H. Wiley, 3
Ho, Fred, 223
Hoeschler, Linda, 260
Hoffman, Joel, 108
Holy Roller, 46–47
homes, Larsen's, 14, 142, 261, 285n95
Hopkins, Gerard Manley, 56, 58
Horowitz, Joseph, 257, 279n21
"Hot House: Meditation," in *In a Winter Garden*, 54
hula, Miss Yamamoto teaching, 17, 102
humor, in *Saints without Tears*, 40–46
Humphries, Aldine, 283n50
hymns. *See* music: sacred

Illinois, University of. *See* University of Illinois
Illinois Computer Music Program, 249
Illinois Experimental Music Studio (EMS), 249
"I Make My Magic," in *Love after 1950*, 177–78, *179*, 182
In a Winter Garden (Larsen and Hampl), 47–55, *50–51*, *53*, 81, 149, 206, 230
In Festis Beatae Mariae Virginis (mass), 37, 60
influences on Larsen's compositions, 20, 26, 28, 32, 166, 256, 284n71, 288n39; broad range of, 143, 148, 152; confluence of religion, nature, and gender, 149, 198, 220; hearing music in poems and paintings, 81, 84, 135, 166, 173, 288n30; Midwest environment, 257–58, 279n22; motherhood, 161–62, 255–56; nature, 67, 70–71, 97–98, 131–33, 149, 198, 209, 220, 257; religion, 38, 60, 202, 256; technology, 220–21
Innova Recordings, of Minnesota Composers Forum, 146, 259
inspirations for Larsen's compositions: environment, 80–81, 97–98, 149; poetry, 81, 288n30; women, 166, 172–73, 178–80, 289n58, 291n95
instrumental, *Black Birds, Red Hills* as purely, 167
instrumentation: in *Bronze Veils*, 136, 138; for *Frankenstein*, 194
insurance company, 109
Internet, Larsen embacing, 262
investment banker, as possible career, 102
Ives, Charles, 40, 60, 195–96, 254, 276n29, 282n39, 295n38; influence on Larsen, 47, 263–64, 288n39

Jamison, Kay Redfield, 266, 297n27
jazz, 60, 63, 113
John Duffy Composers Institute, 223–24
John Mirk's Festial, 13, 273n7
Joseph, Jenny, 180–82, 291n97
Juana Inés de la Cruz, 150
Juilliard, Larsen's audition for, 105
Julian of Norwich, 149–50

kalimba, 199, 202
Kaminsky, Laura, 209–10
Kane, Julie, 173
Keane, Margaret and Walter, 269n11
Keillor, Garrison, *112*
Keller, Armor, 182
Kennan, Kent, 3
Kennedy, Edward, 224–25
Kennedy, John F., 1, 8–9, 272n22
Kennedy, Robert F., 8, 272n22
Kenny, Maurice, 56, 58
Khrushchev, Nikita, 1
Kim, Jayoung, 277n55
Kim, Wonkak, 277n55
King, Billie Jean, 178–79
King, Martin Luther, Jr., 8, 272n22
Kirchoff, Leanna, 224
"Kiss, That's All, A," in *Notes Slipped under the Door*, 164
Koch (record label), 229, 237
Kolb, Barbara, 108
Kopechne, Mary Jo, 224–25
Korean War, 3
Kramer, Hilton, 238

La Barbara, Joan, 147
Lake Harriet: Larsen family's activities on, 23–26; in *ME (Brenda Ueland)*, 159–61; Ueland and Larsen sharing love of, 151, 153
Lake Harriet Concert Shell, *23*, 274n32
Landmark Center (Saint Paul), 119
Lane, Louis, 21
Lane, Miss, 18
Langsdorf, Martyl, 270n8

language, Larsen's sensitivity to, 229. *See also* American English
Lanz, Garth, 209
Larsen, Alice Brown (mother), *16*, 19, 22, 261, 274n42, 275n18; death of, 235; helping write letter for MacDowell Colony job, 107–8; love of boogie-woogie, 28, 274n30, 276n25; parenting by, 14–15, 26
Larsen, Duffy (sister), 15, *16*, 255, 274n28, 281n24
Larsen, Libby: First Communion, *34*; in Lake Harriet Concert Shell, *23*; at piano competition, *20*; on Prairie Home Companion, *112*; riding camel, *227*
Larsen, LuAnne (sister), 14, *16*, *34*, 107
Larsen, Maggie (sister), 15, *16*
Larsen, Molly. *See* George, Molly Larsen (sister)
Larsen, Robert (father), *16*, 22, 25–26; careers of, 13–14, 103, 273n11; family and, 10–12, 106, 166; taking Libby for auditions, 105, 281n25
Larsen family, 110, 274n41; activities on Lake Harriet, 23–26; Libby grounded by, 99, 255; Libby silenced in, 11, 191, 273n8; love of car culture, 26–28; music in, 22, 28, 102, 274n30, 276n25
Leo Irene, Sister, 18, 276n31
Leon, Tania, 223
Levittown, 2, 270n6
Lewis, Jerry Lee, 29
Library of Congress, Larsen at, 221
Life of Poetry, The (Rukeyser), 178
light, 72, 96; Larsen referencing in compositions, 67, 70, 79, 83–84; and water, 69, 73–74, 76, 83–84
lighting, in *The Magdalene*, 184–85
Lind, Jenny, 231
Lindgren, Toni, 151, 233–35, 269n15, 298n46
Lipman, Samuel, 238–43, 298n70, 299n73
listening, 123, 202, 235, 237
Lochhead, Liz, 173
Logan, Olive, 180
Lombardo, Robert, 108
London, Jack, *Every Man Jack* based on, 225–26, 237–38, 296n14
London Symphony Orchestra, 229
Longfellow, Henry Wadsworth, 85
Lopez, Arthur, 59–60, 63
Louis, Morris, 135, 138; techniques of, 136–37; use of color, 170, 172; "Veils" series by, 285n95, 289n61
love: creativity and, 158, 161; in *Love after 1950*, 173, 176
Love after 1950, 151, 166, 172–73, *175–76*, 176, *179*, 182, 290n74
Lovers, 282n37
Low, John, 110, 116
Lydell, William, 103
Lyric, 229
lyricism, Larsen's innate, 40

MacDowell Colony, 107–8, 282nn28–29
"Mad Wind's Night Work, The," in *Slow Structures*, 85–88, *86–87*
Magdalene, Mary, 150, 166–67, 182–92, 291nn101–2, 292n123
Magdalene, The, 166, 183–90, *185–90*, 287n25; chants in, 185–87; Coptic in, 291n100, 292n111; funding for, 187, 191; performances of, 191–92, 292n108; *Pistis Sophia* in, 150, 167, 182, 189, 292n109
"Magic City Golden Transit, The," in *Hell's Belles*, 182
Malcolm X, 8, 272n22
"Man Can Love Two Women (1880), A," in *Songs from Letters*, 163
Mannes, Larsen's audition for, 105, 143
Marathon, Vincent, 111–12
Marilyn, Sister, 276n31
Marimba Concerto: After Hampton, 210, 237, 280n60

marriage, Larsen's, 44, 133, 252–53, 255; in nonsanctified space, 39, 68, 275n18
Marriner, Neville, 223, 226
Martino, Donald, 196
Martirano, Salvatore, 243, 246
Mary Cassatt, 172, 290n73
Masque of Angels (Argento), 125
mass, as multisensory theatrical experience, 210
Mass of the Blessed Virgin Mary, influence on *Rodeo Queen of Heaven*, 63
math, Larsen's talent in, 102–3
McCarthy, Joseph, 4, 271n11
McClary, Susan, 147–48, 251, 287n15
McCoy, Terrence, 145
McFaul, Rebecca, 146, 207, 211
McGinley, Phyllis, 39–47
McGlaughlin, William, 142, 226
McKay, Florine (Larsen's alias), 111–12
Me: A Memoir (Ueland), 151–52
ME (Brenda Ueland), 151–61, *154–58*, *159–60*, 256, 288n29, 288n33
media, 118, 261–62, 272n19
Meet the Composers, 146, 222–23, 244
membranophones, 136
Menin, Peter, 3
Mentzer, Susanne, 172, 233
Meredith, James, 291n95
Merton, Thomas, 280n54
Messiaen, Olivier, 196
metallophones, 136
Micka, Mary Virginia, 150
Midwest environment, 151, 237; cultural, 125–26; influence of, 98, 257–58, 270n17; Larsen's attachment to, 82–83, 99, 143–44, 264; sunrise in, 78–80
Milford, Nancy, 269n2
military, 2–3, 13–14
Minneapolis–Saint Paul, 6, 151, 230, 236; car culture in, 26–27; cultural scene in, 125–26, 144, 288n28; environment of upper Midwest and, 69–70; influence on Larsen, 80–83; Larsen identified with, 14, 98; Larsen's attachment to, 82–83; *Some Pig* performed in, 120–21; weather's influence in, 48–50
Minnesota, 98, 237, 279n22
Minnesota, University of. *See* University of Minnesota
Minnesota Arts Ensemble, 28
Minnesota Composers Forum (MCF), 28, 230; *Aubade* commissioned by, 77–78; concerts produced by, 118–19; effects of, 146–47, 231; evolution of, 151, 260; incorporation of, 116–18, *117*, 283n54; Innova Recordings of, 146; Larsen administering, 119–20, 146, 151; Larsen and Paulus founding, 101, 114–16, 143, 147, 259, 265; lessons learned from, 261–62; program for, *118*; reasons for success of, 117–18
Minnesota State Arts Board, 146
Minnesota Symphony Orchestra, 223, 229; Larsen as composer-in-residence for, 69, 146, 209, 259
Missa Gaia: Mass for the Earth, 56–58, 67, 149, 210–11, 276n42
Mississippi State University, 191
Mitternight, Andrea J., 162
Monarch Brass, 226
mood, in *The Magdalene*, 184–85
Moody, Dwight, 123
Morse code: in *DDT*, 2, 97, 257; in *Marimba Concerto: After Hampton*, 220, 280n60
mother-daughter relationships, 161–66, 252, 256
motherhood, 151, 165; influence on compositions, 161–62, 255–56; Larsen balancing profession with, 252, 255, 282n32
Mudge, Tom, 262, 293n7

multiculturalism, criticisms of, 238–39, 242
multimedia productions, 210; *Black Birds, Red Hills* planned as, 167; *Emergence* as, 211; Fry Street Quartet's, 208–9; Larsen's multisensibility and, 197–98, 203; *The Magdalene* planned as, 184; *Mary Cassatt* as, 290n73; *O Magnum Mysterium* as, 203, 207; technology of, 197, 262–63
Musgrave, Thea, 240, 254, 282n32
music, 137, 249, 294n33; achievements of the 1960s, 7–8; Catholic Church and, 18–19, 35–37, 67, 126; at Christ the King school, 18–19, 38, 60; inward and outward, 201–2; Larsen family and, 21–22, 28, 102, 274n30, 276n25; in Larsen's early education, 17–19; Larsen's relationship with, 46, 173, 232; Larsen's respect for, 102, 217–19; nature and, 67, 72; power of, 210, 220; purposes of, 241, 258, 299n79; relation to poetry, 178; sacred, 35–37, 47, 60; as sacred, 275n41, 277n1; as social act, 224–25, 232, 244, 267; technology and, 194–95; Twin Cities Institute for Talented Youth program in, 103, 110. *See also specific genres*
music, Larsen's, 17, 38, 101–2; communication through, 38, 83–84, 226; family interwoven with, 261; visuals and, 152, 167–68. *See also* compositions, Larsen's
musical atmosphere: of *Circular Rondo*, 114; in *Ulloa's Ring*, 73–74
musicals, Larsen's love for, 111–12
musical styles, 19–22, 232, 263; Larsen blending, 44, 60–63, 104, 123; Larsen criticized for mixing, 236–37, 257–58; Larsen's range of, 52–55, 152, 244–46, 254; in *Love after 1950*, 173–74, 176
music and composition field: improving conditions for women composers in, 146–47; Larsen's achievements in, 182; male domination of, 100, 243, 248–51
music and composition programs, 2–3, 111, 122, 146–47, 258, 262; improving conditions for women composers in, 146–47; lack of opportunity in, 120, 302n118; Larsen choosing to work outside, 244, 257–58; Larsen's lessons from, 258–59; male domination of, 243, 260, 283n62, 299n90
"Music and Musical Life" (Lipman), 239–40
music culture, 222, 238–43, 251
musicians, Lipman's criticism of, 241–42
music library, Larsen working in, 110
musicology, Larsen's assistantship in, 110
music teachers, Larsen's, 274nn25–26
music theory, Larsen's exposure to, 103–4
music traditions: criticisms of Larsen's rejection of, 238–39; Larsen resisting compartmentalization, 52–56, 152, 199–200, 204, 257–58; Larsen's nods to, 113–14, 213
My Lord, What a Morning (Anderson), 8
mysterious, in nature, 279n32
mystery, religious, 35, 68
mysticism, 95–96, 206, 256
"My Throat Hurts," in *Notes Slipped under the Door*, 164

Naomi, Sister, 18, 33
National Association for the Advancement of Colored People (NAACP), 6
National Association of Schools of Music (NASM), 193–94, 202, 263

National Council of the Arts, 238–39
National Endowment for the Arts, New Music Panel of, 146
natural overtone series, 57, 277n47
nature, 72, 82, 279n32; gender and, 71, 278n5, 279n32; influence on Larsen, 149, 198, 209, 220; in Larsen's compositions, 70–71, 97–98, 131–33, 220; Larsen's love for, 73, 144, 168; Larsen wanting to be in, 68, 70, 82; O'Keeffe and, 149, 168; religion intertwined with, 56–57, 67, 68, 277n1; sounds of, 49, 69; spirituality and, 33, 36, 95–97, 257. *See also* outdoors
New Criterion (magazine), 238–39, 242
"New Music for Organ at the End of the Twentieth Century" (Biery), 36
News of the Universe (Bly), 82
New York City, Larsen's auditions in, 105, 143, 281n25
Nexus (ensemble), 2, 97
Northern Lights over the Twin Cities (Brant), 293n12
Notes Slipped under the Door, 161–62, 164–66
Nothing That Is, The, as theater piece, 238
Novo, Celia, 228
Now I Pull Silver, 198–202, *199*, *200*, 262
nuclear holocaust, influence on *In a Winter Garden*, 48–49, 52
Nuechterlein, John, 260

Oberlin, Larsen's audition for, 105–6
oboes, 112–14, 283n53
Odyssey Commissioning Program, of Plymouth Music Series, 231
O'Keeffe, Georgia, 166, 289n62; *Black Birds, Red Hills* as homage to, 149, 167–72; techniques of, 169–72, 290n62
Oliveros, Pauline, 240, 243, 247, 254, 269n12, 282n32
O Magnum Mysterium, 198, 202–7, *205*, *207–8*, 284n71, 295n42
Ong, Walter, 294n20
operas, 125, 126; Larsen and, 106, 110, 224; violence against women in, 224–25; young composers of, 223–24
operas, Larsen's, 109, 231, 238, 294n31; composed as graduate projects, 123, 125–26, 282n37
oratorio, *In a Winter Garden* as, 47–52
orchestras, treatment of women composers by, 147–48
orchestration, 123, 229, 258
Orpheus, *Eurydice* not taking viewpoint of, 127, 131
Orpheus and Eurydice Cycle (Atwood), 133
Ostriker, Alicia, 177–78
Oswald, Lee Harvey, 9
Oteri, Frank J., 223
Ottesen, Bradley, 208–9
outdoors, 26, 257; Larsen's activity in, 23, 26, 69. *See also* nature
Overture: Parachute Dancing, 229, 244, 247

Parenti, Susan, 250, 299n87
Park, Eun-hee, 277n55
Partch, Harry, 195, 197, 246, 293n18
"Paterfamilias," in *Saints without Tears*, 44, *45*, 60
Paulus, Stephen, 223, 283n62, 286n11; cofounding Minnesota Composers Forum, 101, 114–16, 120, 143, 147, 231, 259, 265
Paul VI, Pope, 183
Payne, Karen, 163
"Pedernal and Red Hills," in *Black Birds, Red Hills*, 169, 289n66
Penderecki, Krzysztof, 215–17, 296n61
Peppard, Christiana, 56–57
percussion: in *Bronze Veils*, 138, 141; in *DDT*, 257; in *Marimba Concerto*, 237,

280n60; in *Missa Gaia: Mass for the Earth*, 56
Perle, George, 3
Perlis, Vivian, 12, 101, 115, 117–18, 275n41
Perlman, Itzhak, 241–42
permeability, of art and music, 137
permissions, 121–22, 124
personality, Larsen's, 254; ambition, 235, 256; Americanness of, 264–65; collaborators on, 222, 226; courage, 12, 24–25; curiosity, 104, 222, 225–26; directness, 235; Duffy on, 225–26; exuberance, 12, 266; flexibility/multitasking, 261; generosity, 38, 266–67; hopefulness, 49; humanity and caring, 231, 253; humility, 234; humor, 38–39, 46, 107; increasing introspection, 234–35; not fitting stereotype of composers', 111; openness, 38, 232, 234, 256; passion to engage, 232, 253; public vs. private, 233–35, 252–53, 265; resoluteness, 222; sense of wonder, 234; service, 256; Sisters' influence on, 38, 99, 256, 266–67; thoughtfulness, 232; unboundedness, 203; work ethic, 253, 256
Peterson, Jeffrey, 187, 189, 191–92, 292n108
Phoenix, Paul, 203
physics department, acoustics of music course in, 110
piano competitions, Larsen's, *20*, 21
piano lessons, 19–21, 32
pianos, 22, 101; in *The Birth Project*, 256; in *Black Birds, Red Hills*, 167, 169; in *Four on the Floor*, 226; Larsen's, 109–10; in *Love after 1950*, 174, 178, 290n84; in *The Magdalene*, 185, 292n108; in *ME (Brenda Ueland)*, 161; in *Slow Structures*, 85, 90, 93; in *Ulloa's Ring*, 75–76
Pi Beta Phi, Larsen's rejection of rules of, 107
Pierrot lunaire (Schoenberg), 199–200
Pinions, 245
Pistis Sophia, 292n109; in *The Magdalene*, 150, 167, 184; *The Magdalene* based on, 182, 189
Plymouth Music Series, 230–31
Poème électronique (Varèse), 8, 197
poetry, 177–78, 256; compositions inspired by, 81, 288n30; used in Larsen's compositions, 84, 85, 172–73, 228
polystylism, 40
popular music, Larsen using, 46
Porpora, Nicola, 111
Postcard from Morocco (Argento), 284n71
Potsdam, Germany, 83
Prairie Home Companion, Sutton and Larsen on, 112
Presley, Elvis, 8
produced sounds, Larsen's use of, 194, 293n6
Psyche and the Pskyscraper, 282n37
publishing company, Larsen's, 234, 298n46

questioning, encouraged at school, 12
quiet, 278n19; compositions heading toward, 202, 294n30; stillness and, 84, 90, 291n89

race, 242, 271n15. *See also* civil rights movement
racism, 271n18, 272n19
Rausch, Robin, 282n29
reading, Larsen's broad range of, 104
recordings: of *The Art of Arleen Auger*, 228–29; changing technology of, 271n13, 293n16; in *Now I Pull Silver*, 200; in *O Magnum Mysterium*, 198, 203–4
"Red and Orange Hills," in *Black Birds, Red Hills*, 169–70
"Red Hills and Sky," in *Black Birds, Red Hills*, 169–70

"Red Scare," 4
Reece, James (husband), 39, 116, 252–53, 260, 301n126
Reece, Richard (brother-in-law), 120
Reece, Wynne (daughter), 165, 251–54, 301n126; effects of birth of, 148–49; on mother, 228, 256. *See also* motherhood
Reich, Steve, 240, 276n29
religion: influence in society, 13, 58, 149–50, 184, 273n8; influence on Larsen, 126, 149, 198, 262; influence on Larsen's compositions, 38, 46–47, 58, 185, 220, 256; Larsen's disappointment in, 36, 184; in *Missa Gaia: Mass for the Earth*, 56–58, 149; nature and, 56–57, 67–68, 277n1; rituals of, 34–35. *See also* Catholic Church
Repar, Patricia, 244, 300n92
Reskin, Barbara, 248
reviews, 162; criticisms, 235–43; on eclecticism, 257–58; of *Every Man Jack*, 237–38; of *ME (Brenda Ueland)*, 256; of *Notes Slipped under the Door*, 166; of *The Nothing That Is*, 238; of *String Symphony (Symphony No. 4)*, 236–37; of *Symphony: Water Music*, 239–41; of *Ulloa's Ring*, 257–58, 279n21
Revzen, Joel, 226–30
rhythm, 170; of American English, 107, 153, 222; in Circular Rondo, 114; in *Emergence*, 212, 219–20; in *Four on the Floor*, 29–30; in *Hell's Belles*, 180, 182; in *In a Winter Garden*, 49, 53; Larsen's attunement to, 131, 198, 222, 229, 257; Larsen's exposure to, 20, 38, 47, 112–13, 144; in *Love after 1950*, 178; in *ME*, 161, 165; of nature, 69, 83–84, 133; in *Saints without Tears*, 40, 44, 46; in *Slow Structures*, 90, 93; in *Ulloa's Ring*, 74; in words, 152, 173, 176, 178
Riedel, Johannes, 110, 195–96, 264, 282n39
Rimsky-Korsakov, Nikolai, 254, 281n13
Ring of Fire, 229
Rising Tide (Kaminsky), 210
ritual, Larsen drawn to, 123
Rochberg, George, 3
rock 'n' roll, 5
"Rock We Used to Sit On, The," in *Notes Slipped under the Door*, 164–66
Rodeo Queen of Heaven, *61–62*, *64–66*, 150, 277n55; chants in, 185–87; as homage to Virgin Mary, 37, 59–66
role models, Larsen's: composers as, 254, 282n32; search for, 150, 247; women as, 172, 259, 282n32
"Role of the Musician in the 21st Century, The" (speech), 193–94
Rone, Vincent E., 35, 59
Rosanne, Sister, 21, 274n26
Rosenberg, Harold, 285n99
Rosenthal, M. L., 124
Rukeyser, Muriel, 173, 177–78
rules, Larsen's appreciation for, 25
Runestad, Jake, 223–24
running, Larsen's, 73, 149, 235; love of, 17, 26; organizing cross-country team for, 101, 265
Russell Davies, Dennis, 116
Russolo, Luigi, 195
Rutenberg, Craig, 233

Sabin, Albert, 7
Sadat, Jehan, 227
sailing, 23–25, *24*, 274n28; Larsen's father judging, 25–26
Saint Paul Chamber Orchestra, 116, 229
saints, in McGinley's poems, 39–40
Saints without Tears, 38–47, 60, 113, 150–51
Salk, Jonas, 7

Sankey, Ira, 123
Sarton, May, 126, 288n30
saxophone, in *Holy Roller*, 46–47
Schaberg, Jane, 183
Schafer, R. Murray, 278n17
Scheherazade (Rimsky-Korsakov), 229, 254, 281n13
Schjeldahl, Peter, 135
Schnek, Christine, 183
Schnittke, Alfred, 40
Schoenberg, Arnold, 199–200, 284n81
"Schoenberg, Schenker, Schillinger," 232
Schubert Club of Saint Paul, 71, 151, 278n12
Schultz, Steve, 116
Schuman, William, 108
Schumann, Robert, 172
Science Museum of Minnesota, "Science of Sound" project at, 194
Scottish Chamber Orchestra, 229
Second Viennese School, 127–28
self-discipline, Larsen's appreciation for, 25
Senchina, Jason, 234, 298n46
senses, Larsen's use of all, 197–98, 203
sensorium, 197–98, 257, 294n20
Sequoia Quartet, 232
Seven Ghosts, 231, 297n30
sexual harassment, 248–50, 301n112
"Short Ride in a Fast Machine" (Adams), 274n44
Sifting through the Ruins, 233
Sigma Alpha Iota, 107, 191
silencing, 145; in Larsen family, 13–14, 191, 273n8
Silent Spring (Carson), 2, 257
"Silent Syllables," in *Slow Structures*, 85, 90, *91*
Silver Fox, 126
singer, Larsen's self-image as, 104
singing, Larsen's, 36, 106, 113. *See also* vocals
Sisters of Saint Joseph of Carondelet, 17–18, 36, 71, 273n16; influence on Larsen, 38, 49, 99, 256, 266–67, 274n26
sitars, 295n40; in *O Magnum Mysterium*, 203–4, 206
Slow Structures, 70, 81–83, 85, *86–87*, 88, *89*, 280n49
"Slow Structures," in *Slow Structures*, 85, 88–90, *89*
snow. *See* winter/snow/cold
"Snow-Flakes" (Longfellow), 85
"Snow Man, The" (Stevens), 81
"Snow-Melting Time," in *Slow Structures*, 85, 92–93, *94–97*
"Snow-Melting Time, '66" (Tranströmer), 85, 92–93, 280n47
"Snow-Storm, The" (Emerson), 85, 280n49
social act, music as, 224–25, 232, 244, 267
Soft Pieces, 201
"So Like Your Father's (1880)," in *Songs from Letters*, 163
Solo Symphony, 237
Some Pig (Larsen's opera out of *Charlotte's Web*), 8, 107, 120–22
Songs from Letters, 161–64, 229, 237, 289n46
Songs of Light and Love, 229, 237, 288n30
"Sonnet from Assisi," in *Saints without Tears*, 42, *43*
Sonnets from the Portuguese (Browning), 228
sound ecology, 196
soundmark, 278n17
sound projection, 195–97, 207
sounds: acoustic, 194, 206, 263; acoustics of music, 110; Larsen's sensitivity to, 68, 114, 141; of nature, 49, 69; produced, 194, 262, 293n6; spatial dimensions of, 195–96

Soviet Union, 4, 7. *See also* Cold War
space, sound in, 196
space race, 4–5
spiral of fifths, 103
spirituality: Larsen's, 36, 58, 202; in Larsen's compositions, 38, 256; nature and, 33, 36, 56–57, 95–97, 257
Spohnholz, Conrad S., 108, 282n29
sports, 7, 101, 272n20; Larsen's participation in, 23, 26, 228, 235; Ueland and Larsen sharing love of, 152–53
Stalling, Carl, 263
Stallings, A. E., 198
Starr, Belle, 126, 284n85
Stein, Gertrude, 178–79, 291n93
Stevens, Wallace, 81
Stiles, Tim, 194, 262–63
stillness. *See under* quiet
Stockhausen, Karlheinz, 246
Stokes, Eric, 109, 116, 119, 147, 259, 287n13
string quintet, in *Eurydice*, 133
String Symphony, 229–30
Subotnik, Morton, 194
suburbs, growth of, 2, 270n6
Sullivan, Todd E., 167, 258
"Susanna Does the Elders" (McClary), 287n15
Sutton, Vern, 106, *112*, 123, 127, 259; Larsen's collaborations with, 111–12; Larsen's support from, 111, 119, 125
Swift, Jonathan, 124
symphony, Larsen's "coming out," 54–55
Symphony: Water Music, 54, 67, 69, 291n89; Lipman's criticism of, 239–41; performances of, 229, 278n6
systems: family, 145, 273n8; Larsen and, 37–38, 107, 122, 184; Larsen's suspicion of, 2, 19, 33, 36, 100, 144, 212

teaching, as outlet for Larsen's creativity, 123
technology, 7, 197, 202; constraining Larsen's multimedia productions, 193–95, 197; Larsen embracing, 221, 261–63; Larsen's use of, 125, 203–7, 211, 220–21, 262–63; music and, 194–95; of recordings, 271n13, 293n16
teenage culture, 5
television, 5–6, 8–9, 271n15
telharmonium, 195
Tempest, The (Shakespeare), 104, 281n19
"Temptations of Saint Anthony, The," in *Saints without Tears*, 40, *41*
texts, 210; *The Birth Project*, 256; composing process with, 162–63; *Emergence* and, 198, 211–12; in *Missa Gaia: Mass for the Earth*, 56, 58; in *Now I Pull Silver*, 198–99, 201
theater of the mind, 153; in *Love after 1950*, 172; in *Notes Slipped under the Door*, 165, 172; *Now I Pull Silver* as, 200–201
theater pieces, 191, 238. *See also* multimedia productions
Theremin, Léon, 195
"There Was a Little Girl," in *Hell's Belles*, 178–79, 291n91
Thorne, Nicholas, 240
Three Pieces for Treble Wind and Guitar, 113
Threnody to the Victims of Hiroshima (Penderecki), 215–17, 296n61
time, 196, 280n52; flow of, 82–83, 167, 170–71; Larsen's changing relationship with, 148–49, 261; in *Slow Structures*, 88–90
timing, in *Bronze Veils*, 137–38, 141
Tipei, Sever, 243, 248, 301n110
titles, as integral to Larsen's works, 84
Torevell, David, 35
"To the Earth, Yearning," in *Eurydice: Through the Looking Glass*, 131–33, *134*
Tower, Joan, 147

Trahndorff, Karl Friedrich Eusebius, 295n57
Trakas, Irene, 290n62, 290n69
Transcendentalists, 95, 277n1
transportation, 15, 221
Tranströmer, Tomas, 85, 92–93, 280n47
trombones, in *Bronze Veils*, 136, 138, 141–42
Truman, Harry, 3
trumpet, in *Fanfare for the Women*, 196
Twin Cities Institute for Talented Youth program, 103, 110
Twin Cities Reader, 236

Ueland, Brenda: Larsen's similarities with, 151–53; memoir of, 151–61, 288n28, 288n33
Ulloa's Ring (composition), 70–72, *72*, *74–75*, *77*; energy in, 74–77; flute in, 73–76; piano in, 75–76; reviews of, 257, 279n21
Ulloa's ring (phenomenon), *71*, 71–72
Unanswered Question, The (Ives), 196, 295n38
universities. *See* academia
University of Alabama, 167
University of Illinois: Larsen's short-term residency at, 243–49, 258, 299nn90–91; music department of, 243, 250, 300n109
University of Minnesota: Composers Forum and, 114–16, 119; improving conditions for women composers, 146–47; Larsen as undergraduate at, 99, 104; Larsen daughters attending, 106, 281nn24–25; Larsen's degrees from, 109, 143; Larsen's highs and lows at, 111, 120–22, 133; Larsen's lessons from faculty at, 258–59; Larsen wanting assistantship in, 110, 122; turmoil during Larsen's years at, 99–100
University of Minnesota, Larsen's graduate programs at, 127, 282n39; composing operas for, 120, 125–26; doctoral program at, 122–23; in theory and composition department, 109–10, 112, 122–23; triumphs and traumas in, 133
University Opera Theater, 123
Up, Where the Air Gets Thin, 70
"Upon Orpheus," in *Eurydice*, 127–28, *128–30*
Upright, Diane, 137
USA Today (newspaper), 162
Utah State University, 209–10

Valente, Benita, 151, 229, 288n30
Van, Jeffrey, 113
Vandervelde, Janika, 146–48, 286n10, 287n15, 287n17, 287n20
Van Gogh, Vincent, 158
Varèse, Edgard, 8, 195, 197, 263–64
Vatican II: effects of, 1, 21, 34–37, 276n31; reactions to, 33–35, 68, 184
Veils (Louis), 136
Veni, Creator Spiritus, 38, 67
vibraphones: in *Bronze Veils*, 138, 141; in *O Magnum Mysterium*, 203–4, 206
Vietnam War, 1, 3, 99–100, 144, 280n1
violas: in *Black Birds, Red Hills*, 169–70; in *Emergence*, 217; in *Sifting through the Ruins*, 233
violence, 272n22; in Larsen's compositions, 217, 224–25; racism and, 6–7, 271n18, 272n22
violins: in *Emergence*, 207, 217; in *Eurydice: Through the Looking Glass*, 131
Virginia Arts Festival, 223
Virginia Symphony Orchestra, 226
Virgin Mary: in *Canticle of Mary*, 150; *Rodeo Queen of Heaven* as homage to, 37, 59–66, 150; Vatican II reducing worship of, 36–37, 295n42

visuals, 209, 237; *Emergence* and, 198, 211–12, 220; Larsen's musical response to, 152, 167–68; Larsen's sensitivity to, 135, 184; in *Now I Pull Silver*, 198, 201
VocalEssence, 226–27, 230–31
vocals, 167; in *The Birth Project*, 256; composing process with, 162–63; in *Eurydice: Through the Looking Glass*, 129–31, 133; in *Hell's Belles*, 180; in *In a Winter Garden* oratorio, 47–52; in Larsen's compositions, 256, 282n43, 285n94; in *Love after 1950*, 174; in *The Magdalene*, 184, 187; in *ME (Brenda Ueland)*, 152, 154, 256; in *Notes Slipped under the Door*, 164–65; in *O Magnum Mysterium*, 203–4; in *Sifting through the Ruins*, 233
voice, as Larsen's college major, 106
Von Gunden, Heidi, 243–44, 247–48, 299n90, 300n93
von Stade, Frederica, 178, 291n95

Wagner, Richard, 210
Walker Art Center, 125; Minnesota Composers Forum and, 116, 118–19; Morris Louis exhibit at, 135–36
"Warning" (Joseph), 180–82
Wascoe, Rebecca, 187–89, 191–92, 292n113
water: Larsen referencing in compositions, 67, 69, 73, 83–85, 185, 211; Larsen's compositions on, 97–98, 278n6; Larsen's love of, 69, 97; light and, 72, 74, 76, 84; sounds of, 69, 92–93
"Water Is Wide, The," in *Emergence*, 217, 219
Waters, Robert, 208–9
"Weaver's Song and Jig," 112
Weil, Suzanne, 116, 135
Weinberg, Jack, 5, 271n14
Western Women, 262
Wetherbee (Rosewall), Ellen, 126–27
"What Could Possibly Happen," in *Notes Slipped under the Door*, 164
"What Is New Music?" (Hinkle-Turner), 246
"When I Am an Old Woman," in *Hell's Belles*, 180–82, 291n97
"While You Here Do Snoring Lie," *105*
Whitaker, Lyman, 209
White, E. B. (Elwyn Brooks), 121–22, 283n66
"Who Cares If You Listen?" (Babbitt), 249, 283n47
Williams, Brent, 277n55
wind, in Larsen compositions, 85
winter/snow/cold, 81; Larsen's vocabulary of, 82–85; in *Slow Structures*, 88–91, 280n49
Wittich, Lois Ann, 104–5
Wolpe, Stephan, 108
women, 191, 291n101; attitudes toward, 13, 172, 236; Larsen as, 161, 231; Larsen questioning beauty standards for, 173–77, 180–82, 198; Larsen's compositions inspired by, 166, 172–73, 178–80, 289n58, 291n95; Larsen's homages to, 149–50; Larsen's relationships with, 71, 164, 166; Lipman's criticism of, 240–41; relationships among, 150, 173, 176; as role models, 150, 172, 259; roles available to, 2, 183–84, 251, 292n104; silencing of, 13–14, 183; violence against, 224–25
women composers, 251, 282n32; attacks on, 249–50; Larsen as, 146, 231; marginalization of, 147–48, 262, 286n7, 302n22; scarcity of, 243–44, 247, 260, 282n30, 302n118
Women Composers and Music Technology (Hinkle-Turner), 247, 300n109
Woods, Darren K., 193

Woods, William, 108
Words upon the Windowpane, The, 123–25, 195, 284n75
World War II, 2, 5, 13
Wrinkle in Time, A, 193, 195, 197, 261
Wuorinen, Charles, 246, 249
Wyatt, Scott, 243

Yamamoto, Miss, 17
Yeats, William Butler, 123, 284n75

Zelda (Milford), 269n2
Zelle, Peter, 285n95
Zukerman, Arianna, 162, 164–66
Zukerman, Eugenia (Genie), 102, 116; *Aubade* written for, 78–79; Larsen's relationship with, 73, 162, 166, 278n11; *Notes Slipped under the Door*, 164–66; *Ulloa's Ring* written for, 71–72
Zukerman, Pinchas, 116, 226

DENISE VON GLAHN is the Curtis Mayes Orpheus Professor of Musicology at Florida State University, where she is also the coordinator of the Musicology Area and director of the Center for Music of the Americas. She has written three previous books: *The Sounds of Place: Music and the American Cultural Landscape*, which won an ASCAP-Deems Taylor Award in 2004; *Leo Ornstein: Modernist Dilemmas, Personal Choices*, coauthored with Michael Broyles, which won the Irving S. Lowens Award in 2009; and *Music and the Skillful Listener: American Women Compose the Natural World*, which won the Pauline Alderman Award in 2015.

MUSIC IN AMERICAN LIFE

Only a Miner: Studies in Recorded Coal-Mining Songs *Archie Green*
Great Day Coming: Folk Music and the American Left *R. Serge Denisoff*
John Philip Sousa: A Descriptive Catalog of His Works *Paul E. Bierley*
The Hell-Bound Train: A Cowboy Songbook *Glenn Ohrlin*
Oh, Didn't He Ramble: The Life Story of Lee Collins, as Told to Mary Collins *Edited by Frank J. Gillis and John W. Miner*
American Labor Songs of the Nineteenth Century *Philip S. Foner*
Stars of Country Music: Uncle Dave Macon to Johnny Rodriguez *Edited by Bill C. Malone and Judith McCulloh*
Git Along, Little Dogies: Songs and Songmakers of the American West *John I. White*
A Texas-Mexican *Cancionero*: Folksongs of the Lower Border *Américo Paredes*
San Antonio Rose: The Life and Music of Bob Wills *Charles R. Townsend*
Early Downhome Blues: A Musical and Cultural Analysis *Jeff Todd Titon*
An Ives Celebration: Papers and Panels of the Charles Ives Centennial Festival-Conference *Edited by H. Wiley Hitchcock and Vivian Perlis*
Sinful Tunes and Spirituals: Black Folk Music to the Civil War *Dena J. Epstein*
Joe Scott, the Woodsman-Songmaker *Edward D. Ives*
Jimmie Rodgers: The Life and Times of America's Blue Yodeler *Nolan Porterfield*
Early American Music Engraving and Printing: A History of Music Publishing in America from 1787 to 1825, with Commentary on Earlier and Later Practices *Richard J. Wolfe*
Sing a Sad Song: The Life of Hank Williams *Roger M. Williams*
Long Steel Rail: The Railroad in American Folksong *Norm Cohen*
Resources of American Music History: A Directory of Source Materials from Colonial Times to World War II *D. W. Krummel, Jean Geil, Doris J. Dyen, and Deane L. Root*
Tenement Songs: The Popular Music of the Jewish Immigrants *Mark Slobin*
Ozark Folksongs *Vance Randolph; edited and abridged by Norm Cohen*
Oscar Sonneck and American Music *Edited by William Lichtenwanger*
Bluegrass Breakdown: The Making of the Old Southern Sound *Robert Cantwell*
Bluegrass: A History *Neil V. Rosenberg*
Music at the White House: A History of the American Spirit *Elise K. Kirk*
Red River Blues: The Blues Tradition in the Southeast *Bruce Bastin*
Good Friends and Bad Enemies: Robert Winslow Gordon and the Study of American Folksong *Debora Kodish*
Fiddlin' Georgia Crazy: Fiddlin' John Carson, His Real World, and the World of His Songs *Gene Wiggins*
America's Music: From the Pilgrims to the Present (rev. 3d ed.) *Gilbert Chase*
Secular Music in Colonial Annapolis: The Tuesday Club, 1745–56 *John Barry Talley*

Bibliographical Handbook of American Music *D. W. Krummel*
Goin' to Kansas City *Nathan W. Pearson Jr.*
"Susanna," "Jeanie," and "The Old Folks at Home": The Songs of Stephen C. Foster from His Time to Ours (2d ed.) *William W. Austin*
Songprints: The Musical Experience of Five Shoshone Women *Judith Vander*
"Happy in the Service of the Lord": Afro-American Gospel Quartets in Memphis *Kip Lornell*
Paul Hindemith in the United States *Luther Noss*
"My Song Is My Weapon": People's Songs, American Communism, and the Politics of Culture, 1930–50 *Robbie Lieberman*
Chosen Voices: The Story of the American Cantorate *Mark Slobin*
Theodore Thomas: America's Conductor and Builder of Orchestras, 1835–1905 *Ezra Schabas*
"The Whorehouse Bells Were Ringing" and Other Songs Cowboys Sing *Collected and Edited by Guy Logsdon*
Crazeology: The Autobiography of a Chicago Jazzman *Bud Freeman, as Told to Robert Wolf*
Discoursing Sweet Music: Brass Bands and Community Life in Turn-of-the-Century Pennsylvania *Kenneth Kreitner*
Mormonism and Music: A History *Michael Hicks*
Voices of the Jazz Age: Profiles of Eight Vintage Jazzmen *Chip Deffaa*
Pickin' on Peachtree: A History of Country Music in Atlanta, Georgia *Wayne W. Daniel*
Bitter Music: Collected Journals, Essays, Introductions, and Librettos *Harry Partch; edited by Thomas McGeary*
Ethnic Music on Records: A Discography of Ethnic Recordings Produced in the United States, 1893 to 1942 *Richard K. Spottswood*
Downhome Blues Lyrics: An Anthology from the Post–World War II Era *Jeff Todd Titon*
Ellington: The Early Years *Mark Tucker*
Chicago Soul *Robert Pruter*
That Half-Barbaric Twang: The Banjo in American Popular Culture *Karen Linn*
Hot Man: The Life of Art Hodes *Art Hodes and Chadwick Hansen*
The Erotic Muse: American Bawdy Songs (2d ed.) *Ed Cray*
Barrio Rhythm: Mexican American Music in Los Angeles *Steven Loza*
The Creation of Jazz: Music, Race, and Culture in Urban America *Burton W. Peretti*
Charles Martin Loeffler: A Life Apart in Music *Ellen Knight*
Club Date Musicians: Playing the New York Party Circuit *Bruce A. MacLeod*
Opera on the Road: Traveling Opera Troupes in the United States, 1825–60 *Katherine K. Preston*
The Stonemans: An Appalachian Family and the Music That Shaped Their Lives *Ivan M. Tribe*

Transforming Tradition: Folk Music Revivals Examined *Edited by Neil V. Rosenberg*

The Crooked Stovepipe: Athapaskan Fiddle Music and Square Dancing in Northeast Alaska and Northwest Canada *Craig Mishler*

Traveling the High Way Home: Ralph Stanley and the World of Traditional Bluegrass Music *John Wright*

Carl Ruggles: Composer, Painter, and Storyteller *Marilyn Ziffrin*

Never without a Song: The Years and Songs of Jennie Devlin, 1865–1952 *Katharine D. Newman*

The Hank Snow Story *Hank Snow, with Jack Ownbey and Bob Burris*

Milton Brown and the Founding of Western Swing *Cary Ginell, with special assistance from Roy Lee Brown*

Santiago de Murcia's "Códice Saldívar No. 4": A Treasury of Secular Guitar Music from Baroque Mexico *Craig H. Russell*

The Sound of the Dove: Singing in Appalachian Primitive Baptist Churches *Beverly Bush Patterson*

Heartland Excursions: Ethnomusicological Reflections on Schools of Music *Bruno Nettl*

Doowop: The Chicago Scene *Robert Pruter*

Blue Rhythms: Six Lives in Rhythm and Blues *Chip Deffaa*

Shoshone Ghost Dance Religion: Poetry Songs and Great Basin Context *Judith Vander*

Go Cat Go! Rockabilly Music and Its Makers *Craig Morrison*

'Twas Only an Irishman's Dream: The Image of Ireland and the Irish in American Popular Song Lyrics, 1800–1920 *William H. A. Williams*

Democracy at the Opera: Music, Theater, and Culture in New York City, 1815–60 *Karen Ahlquist*

Fred Waring and the Pennsylvanians *Virginia Waring*

Woody, Cisco, and Me: Seamen Three in the Merchant Marine *Jim Longhi*

Behind the Burnt Cork Mask: Early Blackface Minstrelsy and Antebellum American Popular Culture *William J. Mahar*

Going to Cincinnati: A History of the Blues in the Queen City *Steven C. Tracy*

Pistol Packin' Mama: Aunt Molly Jackson and the Politics of Folksong *Shelly Romalis*

Sixties Rock: Garage, Psychedelic, and Other Satisfactions *Michael Hicks*

The Late Great Johnny Ace and the Transition from R&B to Rock 'n' Roll *James M. Salem*

Tito Puente and the Making of Latin Music *Steven Loza*

Juilliard: A History *Andrea Olmstead*

Understanding Charles Seeger, Pioneer in American Musicology *Edited by Bell Yung and Helen Rees*

Mountains of Music: West Virginia Traditional Music from *Goldenseal* *Edited by John Lilly*

Alice Tully: An Intimate Portrait *Albert Fuller*

A Blues Life *Henry Townsend, as told to Bill Greensmith*
Long Steel Rail: The Railroad in American Folksong (2d ed.) *Norm Cohen*
The Golden Age of Gospel *Text by Horace Clarence Boyer; photography by Lloyd Yearwood*
Aaron Copland: The Life and Work of an Uncommon Man *Howard Pollack*
Louis Moreau Gottschalk *S. Frederick Starr*
Race, Rock, and Elvis *Michael T. Bertrand*
Theremin: Ether Music and Espionage *Albert Glinsky*
Poetry and Violence: The Ballad Tradition of Mexico's Costa Chica *John H. McDowell*
The Bill Monroe Reader *Edited by Tom Ewing*
Music in Lubavitcher Life *Ellen Koskoff*
Zarzuela: Spanish Operetta, American Stage *Janet L. Sturman*
Bluegrass Odyssey: A Documentary in Pictures and Words, 1966–86 *Carl Fleischhauer and Neil V. Rosenberg*
That Old-Time Rock & Roll: A Chronicle of an Era, 1954–63 *Richard Aquila*
Labor's Troubadour *Joe Glazer*
American Opera *Elise K. Kirk*
Don't Get above Your Raisin': Country Music and the Southern Working Class *Bill C. Malone*
John Alden Carpenter: A Chicago Composer *Howard Pollack*
Heartbeat of the People: Music and Dance of the Northern Pow-wow *Tara Browner*
My Lord, What a Morning: An Autobiography *Marian Anderson*
Marian Anderson: A Singer's Journey *Allan Keiler*
Charles Ives Remembered: An Oral History *Vivian Perlis*
Henry Cowell, Bohemian *Michael Hicks*
Rap Music and Street Consciousness *Cheryl L. Keyes*
Louis Prima *Garry Boulard*
Marian McPartland's Jazz World: All in Good Time *Marian McPartland*
Robert Johnson: Lost and Found *Barry Lee Pearson and Bill McCulloch*
Bound for America: Three British Composers *Nicholas Temperley*
Lost Sounds: Blacks and the Birth of the Recording Industry, 1890–1919 *Tim Brooks*
Burn, Baby! BURN! The Autobiography of Magnificent Montague *Magnificent Montague with Bob Baker*
Way Up North in Dixie: A Black Family's Claim to the Confederate Anthem *Howard L. Sacks and Judith Rose Sacks*
The Bluegrass Reader *Edited by Thomas Goldsmith*
Colin McPhee: Composer in Two Worlds *Carol J. Oja*
Robert Johnson, Mythmaking, and Contemporary American Culture *Patricia R. Schroeder*
Composing a World: Lou Harrison, Musical Wayfarer *Leta E. Miller and Fredric Lieberman*

Fritz Reiner, Maestro and Martinet *Kenneth Morgan*
That Toddlin' Town: Chicago's White Dance Bands and Orchestras, 1900–1950 *Charles A. Sengstock Jr.*
Dewey and Elvis: The Life and Times of a Rock 'n' Roll Deejay *Louis Cantor*
Come Hither to Go Yonder: Playing Bluegrass with Bill Monroe *Bob Black*
Chicago Blues: Portraits and Stories *David Whiteis*
The Incredible Band of John Philip Sousa *Paul E. Bierley*
"Maximum Clarity" and Other Writings on Music *Ben Johnston, edited by Bob Gilmore*
Staging Tradition: John Lair and Sarah Gertrude Knott *Michael Ann Williams*
Homegrown Music: Discovering Bluegrass *Stephanie P. Ledgin*
Tales of a Theatrical Guru *Danny Newman*
The Music of Bill Monroe *Neil V. Rosenberg and Charles K. Wolfe*
Pressing On: The Roni Stoneman Story *Roni Stoneman, as told to Ellen Wright*
Together Let Us Sweetly Live *Jonathan C. David, with photographs by Richard Holloway*
Live Fast, Love Hard: The Faron Young Story *Diane Diekman*
Air Castle of the South: WSM Radio and the Making of Music City *Craig P. Havighurst*
Traveling Home: Sacred Harp Singing and American Pluralism *Kiri Miller*
Where Did Our Love Go? The Rise and Fall of the Motown Sound *Nelson George*
Lonesome Cowgirls and Honky-Tonk Angels: The Women of Barn Dance Radio *Kristine M. McCusker*
California Polyphony: Ethnic Voices, Musical Crossroads *Mina Yang*
The Never-Ending Revival: Rounder Records and the Folk Alliance *Michael F. Scully*
Sing It Pretty: A Memoir *Bess Lomax Hawes*
Working Girl Blues: The Life and Music of Hazel Dickens *Hazel Dickens and Bill C. Malone*
Charles Ives Reconsidered *Gayle Sherwood Magee*
The Hayloft Gang: The Story of the National Barn Dance *Edited by Chad Berry*
Country Music Humorists and Comedians *Loyal Jones*
Record Makers and Breakers: Voices of the Independent Rock 'n' Roll Pioneers *John Broven*
Music of the First Nations: Tradition and Innovation in Native North America *Edited by Tara Browner*
Cafe Society: The Wrong Place for the Right People *Barney Josephson, with Terry Trilling-Josephson*
George Gershwin: An Intimate Portrait *Walter Rimler*
Life Flows On in Endless Song: Folk Songs and American History *Robert V. Wells*
I Feel a Song Coming On: The Life of Jimmy McHugh *Alyn Shipton*

King of the Queen City: The Story of King Records *Jon Hartley Fox*
Long Lost Blues: Popular Blues in America, 1850–1920 *Peter C. Muir*
Hard Luck Blues: Roots Music Photographs from the Great Depression *Rich Remsberg*
Restless Giant: The Life and Times of Jean Aberbach and Hill and Range Songs *Bar Biszick-Lockwood*
Champagne Charlie and Pretty Jemima: Variety Theater in the Nineteenth Century *Gillian M. Rodger*
Sacred Steel: Inside an African American Steel Guitar Tradition *Robert L. Stone*
Gone to the Country: The New Lost City Ramblers and the Folk Music Revival *Ray Allen*
The Makers of the Sacred Harp *David Warren Steel with Richard H. Hulan*
Woody Guthrie, American Radical *Will Kaufman*
George Szell: A Life of Music *Michael Charry*
Bean Blossom: The Brown County Jamboree and Bill Monroe's Bluegrass Festivals *Thomas A. Adler*
Crowe on the Banjo: The Music Life of J. D. Crowe *Marty Godbey*
Twentieth Century Drifter: The Life of Marty Robbins *Diane Diekman*
Henry Mancini: Reinventing Film Music *John Caps*
The Beautiful Music All Around Us: Field Recordings and the American Experience *Stephen Wade*
Then Sings My Soul: The Culture of Southern Gospel Music *Douglas Harrison*
The Accordion in the Americas: Klezmer, Polka, Tango, Zydeco, and More! *Edited by Helena Simonett*
Bluegrass Bluesman: A Memoir *Josh Graves, edited by Fred Bartenstein*
One Woman in a Hundred: Edna Phillips and the Philadelphia Orchestra *Mary Sue Welsh*
The Great Orchestrator: Arthur Judson and American Arts Management *James M. Doering*
Charles Ives in the Mirror: American Histories of an Iconic Composer *David C. Paul*
Southern Soul-Blues *David Whiteis*
Sweet Air: Modernism, Regionalism, and American Popular Song *Edward P. Comentale*
Pretty Good for a Girl: Women in Bluegrass *Murphy Hicks Henry*
Sweet Dreams: The World of Patsy Cline *Warren R. Hofstra*
William Sidney Mount and the Creolization of American Culture *Christopher J. Smith*
Bird: The Life and Music of Charlie Parker *Chuck Haddix*
Making the March King: John Philip Sousa's Washington Years, 1854–1893 *Patrick Warfield*
In It for the Long Run *Jim Rooney*
Pioneers of the Blues Revival *Steve Cushing*

Roots of the Revival: American and British Folk Music in the 1950s *Ronald D. Cohen and Rachel Clare Donaldson*
Blues All Day Long: The Jimmy Rogers Story *Wayne Everett Goins*
Yankee Twang: Country and Western Music in New England *Clifford R. Murphy*
The Music of the Stanley Brothers *Gary B. Reid*
Hawaiian Music in Motion: Mariners, Missionaries, and Minstrels *James Revell Carr*
Sounds of the New Deal: The Federal Music Project in the West *Peter Gough*
The Mormon Tabernacle Choir: A Biography *Michael Hicks*
The Man That Got Away: The Life and Songs of Harold Arlen *Walter Rimler*
A City Called Heaven: Chicago and the Birth of Gospel Music *Robert M. Marovich*
Blues Unlimited: Essential Interviews from the Original Blues Magazine *Edited by Bill Greensmith, Mike Rowe, and Mark Camarigg*
Hoedowns, Reels, and Frolics: Roots and Branches of Southern Appalachian Dance *Phil Jamison*
Fannie Bloomfield-Zeisler: The Life and Times of a Piano Virtuoso *Beth Abelson Macleod*
Cybersonic Arts: Adventures in American New Music *Gordon Mumma, edited with commentary by Michelle Fillion*
The Magic of Beverly Sills *Nancy Guy*
Waiting for Buddy Guy *Alan Harper*
Harry T. Burleigh: From the Spiritual to the Harlem Renaissance *Jean E. Snyder*
Music in the Age of Anxiety: American Music in the Fifties *James Wierzbicki*
Jazzing: New York City's Unseen Scene *Thomas H. Greenland*
A Cole Porter Companion *Edited by Don M. Randel, Matthew Shaftel, and Susan Forscher Weiss*
Foggy Mountain Troubadour: The Life and Music of Curly Seckler *Penny Parsons*
Blue Rhythm Fantasy: Big Band Jazz Arranging in the Swing Era *John Wriggle*
Bill Clifton: America's Bluegrass Ambassador to the World *Bill C. Malone*
Chinatown Opera Theater in North America *Nancy Yunhwa Rao*
The Elocutionists: Women, Music, and the Spoken Word *Marian Wilson Kimber*
May Irwin: Singing, Shouting, and the Shadow of Minstrelsy *Sharon Ammen*
Peggy Seeger: A Life of Music, Love, and Politics *Jean R. Freedman*
Charles Ives's *Concord*: Essays after a Sonata *Kyle Gann*
Don't Give Your Heart to a Rambler: My Life with Jimmy Martin, the King of Bluegrass *Barbara Martin Stephens*
Libby Larsen: Composing an American Life *Denise Von Glahn*

The University of Illinois Press
is a founding member of the
Association of American University Presses.

Composed in 10.25/13.25 Adobe Minion Pro
by Lisa Connery
at the University of Illinois Press
Cover designed by Dustin J. Hubbart
Cover illustration: Courtesy of Libby Larsen
Manufactured by Cushing Malloy, Inc.

University of Illinois Press
1325 South Oak Street
Champaign, IL 61820-6903
www.press.uillinois.edu